NATIONAL POLICE LIBRARY

20020912

Muslims in the West

DISCARDED
NATIONAL POLICE LIBRARY

Muslims in the West

From Sojourners to Citizens

Edited by
YVONNE YAZBECK HADDAD

NATIONAL
POLICE
LIBRARY
X

OXFORD
UNIVERSITY PRESS
2002

OXFORD

UNIVERSITY PRESS

Oxford   New York
Auckland   Bangkok   Buenos Aires   Cape Town   Chennai
Dar es Salaam   Delhi   Hong Kong   Istanbul   Karachi   Kolkata
Kuala Lumpur   Madrid   Melbourne   Mexico City   Mumbai   Nairobi
São Paulo   Shanghai   Singapore   Taipei   Tokyo   Toronto

and an associated company in Berlin

Copyright © 2002 by Oxford University Press, Inc.

Published by Oxford University Press, Inc.
198 Madison Avenue, New York, New York 10016

www.oup.com

Oxford is a registered trademark of Oxford University Press

All rights reserved. No part of this publication may be reproduced,
stored in a retrieval system, or transmitted, in any form or by any means,
electronic, mechanical, photocopying, recording, or otherwise,
without the prior permission of Oxford University Press.

Library of Congress Cataloging-in-Publication Data

Muslims in the West : from sojourners to citizens /
edited by Yvonne Yazbeck Haddad.
p. cm.
Includes bibliographical references and index.
ISBN 0-19-514805-3; ISBN 0-19-514806-1 (pbk.)
1. Muslims–Non-Muslim countries–Social conditions–20th century.
I. Haddad, Yvonne Yazbeck, 1935–
BP52.5 .M885   2001
305.6'971–dc21   2001021780

Acc. no.   20020912

Classmark   305.697

HAD

1 3 5 7 9 8 6 4 2

Printed in the United States of America
on acid-free paper

To
Joseph Allyn and
Katherine Anne MacPhail

Foreword

For some time, when speaking of Islam, the second largest of the world's religions, experts and the media alike talked about Islam versus the West, often employing the language of conflict and confrontation. Islam was seen as a foreign religion, usually grouped with Buddhism and Hinduism in contradistinction to the Judeo-Christian tradition. It is only in recent years that we have begun to realize that, within a span of a few short decades, Islam, once invisible or marginal, has emerged as the second-largest religion in much of Europe and North America. Awareness and appreciation of this changed reality has come slowly. Adjustment to the fact that it is no longer viable to think of Islam and Muslims as "foreign" has not been easy, either for Muslims or for non-Muslims in the West. The long-regarded "other" must now be appreciated as part of the fabric of western societies, a neighbor and a fellow citizen. Of equal importance, as one of the children of Abraham, Muslims have a rightful place as part of the Judeo-Christian-Islamic tradition.

Like many immigrant religious and ethnic minority communities before them, Muslims have been challenged to define and determine their place in society. They struggle with issues of identity, intermarriage, gender relations, worship, and education, as well as civil rights and responsibilities. Some are torn between the land of their birth and their newly adopted homeland. If some integrate easily, others, as one young Muslim friend frustratingly described his parents, "live in denial. Live in denial of the fact they have been in America for years and are going to die here not back in Pakistan." Despite the commonalities of experience, there are also distinctive differences among Muslims who live in western Europe and in North America, as well as among Muslims within specific countries. In many European countries, the bulk of the Muslim populations has consisted of laborers whose integration into society and whose attainment of equal rights have often been more difficult than in the United States where, despite some social difficulties, the Muslim community has found it easier to win acceptance, partly because it includes a significant number of professionals. A distinctive characteristic of Islam in America is the interface between immigrant communities and an indigenous and vibrant African American Muslim community.

Muslims in the West: From Sojourners to Citizens is an excellent guide to the changing demographic and faith landscape of Islam in the West. The editor of the volume, Yvonne

Haddad, is among the most knowledgeable and prolific experts. She has assembled a group of authors from North America and Europe—historians, social scientists, and scholars of religion and culture—who speak from knowledge and from firsthand experience. The series of case studies presented here provides an excellent introduction to the history and experiences of Muslims in the West and the diverse responses of their newly adopted countries.

As we enter the twenty-first century, emigration and globalization are transforming the religious and cultural landscape of our world. There are more Muslims living in diaspora communities than at any time in history. Muslim minority communities have faced many hurdles in making the transition; other hurdles continue to exist. Muslims and non-Muslim citizens and communities alike face the challenges of living in a pluralistic society. Can the majority of Muslims retain both their faith and their identities and do so in a manner that enables them to also accept and function within the secular, pluralistic traditions of Europe and America? The pluralism of countries in the West is likewise being tested. Is Western pluralism a limited form of pluralism? Is it inclusive or exclusive, primarily secular or Judeo-Christian? Can Muslims (as well as Hindus, Sikhs, Buddhists, and others) come to be accepted as no longer sojourners, not simply worshippers of foreign religions, but truly and fully as fellow citizens with equal religious and political rights?

We live at a religiously momentous time, during which we are witnessing a global religious resurgence of all major faiths, as well as a geographical globalization of many due to migration and emigration. Demographically, Islam is among the fastest growing of the world's religions, both globally and in the West. If Muslims were relatively invisible in the West only a few decades ago, today the religious landscapes of many cities and towns include mosques and Islamic centers alongside churches and synagogues. Increasingly, many will come to realize that the major Muslim communities and cities of the world of Islam include not only Cairo, Damascus, Islamabad, Kuala Lumpur, and Khartoum but also London, Bradford, Paris, Marseilles, New York, Detroit, and Los Angeles. *Muslims in the West: From Sojourners to Citizens* is an excellent place to obtain a perspective on the origins and development of Muslim communities in the West and on their future prospects, as well as to appreciate the continued vitality and dynamism of Islam and Muslims in adapting to new environments and cultures.

Washington, D.C.   John L. Esposito
July 2000   University Professor and Director
                                   Center for Muslim-Christian Understanding
                                                        Georgetown University

Acknowledgments

This book brings together studies on the development of Muslim communities in Europe and North America and the challenges they face in integrating into their adopted countries of residence. It also looks at the policies that these states have implemented in an effort to incorporate Muslims as citizens. The articles by Barbara Stowasser, Kathleen Moore, and Mamoun Fandy were prepared for a conference on "Muslim Diasporas in the West: From Immigrants to Minorities," sponsored by the Center for Muslim-Christian Understanding, Edmund A. Walsh School of Foreign Service, Georgetown University, on April 17, 1998. Special thanks are due to Patricia Gordon and Faeda Totah, who oversaw all local arrangements for the conference; to Thea Ewing, who maintained general organizational oversight of the manuscript; and to Kim Harrington, who helped to compile the bibliography.

Contents

Contributors

JOCELYNE CESARI is senior research fellow with special interest in Muslim minorities in France and Europe at the National Center for Scientific Research (CNRS) in Paris and visiting professor at Columbia University in New York. She is the author of several books and articles, including *Les anonymes de la mondialisation, Cultures, conflits, et la France, Géopolitique des islams, Faut-il avoir peur de l'islam?, Etre musulman en France aujourd'hui, L'Islam en Europe,* and *Etre musulman en France: Mosquées, militants et associations.*

JOHN L. ESPOSITO is University Professor and director of the Center for Muslim-Christian Understanding in the School of Foreign Service at Georgetown University. He has served as president of the Middle East Studies Association of North America and of the American Council for the Study of Islamic Societies and is vice chair of the Center for the Study of Islam and Democracy. He is editor in chief of the four-volume *Oxford Encyclopedia of the Modern Islamic World* and *The Oxford History of Islam.* His publications include *The Islamic Threat: Myth or Reality?; Islam and Democracy* and *Makers of Contemporary Islam* (with John Voll); *Islam and Politics; Islam: The Straight Path; Political Islam: Revolution, Radicalism or Reform?; Religion and Global Order* (with M. Watson); *Islam and Secularism in the Middle East* (with Azzam Tamimi); *The Iranian Revolution: Its Global Impact; Islam, Gender, and Social Change* and *Muslims on the Americanization Path* (with Yvonne Haddad); *Women in Muslim Family Law; Voices of Resurgent Islam; Islam in Transition: Muslim Perspectives* (with John Donohue); *Islam in Asia: Religion, Politics, and Society;* and *Islam and Development.*

MAMOUN FANDY is research professor of politics at Georgetown University's Center for Contemporary Arab Studies. His research focus is the politics of North Africa and the Arabian Gulf. His articles have appeared in the *Middle East Journal, Comparative Studies in Society and History, Middle East Policy,* the *New York Times,* the *Los Angeles Times,* and more regularly in the *Christian Science Monitor.* He is author of *Saudi Arabia and the Politics of Dissent.* He has two forthcoming books, *Kuwait and a New Concept of International Politics* and *Egypt: An Old Society and a New Modern State.* He is also the executive director of the Council on Egyptian-American Relations.

YVONNE HADDAD is professor of history of Islam and Christian-Muslim Relations at the Center for Muslim-Christian Understanding, Edmund B. Walsh School of Foreign Service, at Georgetown University. She is past president of the Middle East Studies Association and a former editor of *Muslim World*. Her published works include *Contemporary Islam and the Challenge of History*, *Islam, Gender and Social Change*, *Islamic Values in the United States* (with A. Lummis), *The Contemporary Islamic Revival* (with J. Voll and J. Esposito), *The Islamic Understanding of Death and Resurrection* (with J. Smith), *The Muslims of America, Mission to America* (with J. Smith), *Muslim Communities in North America* (with J. Smith), and *Christian-Muslim Encounters* (with W. Haddad). She is an associate editor of the *Oxford Encyclopedia of the Modern Islamic World*.

KARIM H. KARIM is assistant professor at Carleton University's School of Journalism and Communication. He previously worked as senior policy analyst in the Multiculturalism Program of the Canadian federal government. He holds degrees in Islamic and communication studies from Columbia and McGill universities. His most recent publication is *The Islamic Peril: Media and Global Violence*. He has also published chapters in edited collections and articles in international journals on Muslim uses of the Internet, diasporic communication, ethnic media and the public sphere, cultural policy, technology and society, and culture and human rights, including *From Ethnic Media to Global Media: Transnational Communication Networks among Diasporic Communities* and *Images des arabes et des musulmans: Recension de la recherche*.

MIRA VAN KUIJEREN is attending the faculty of history and art at the University of Rotterdam. She specialized in contemporary history and French language at the State University of Groningen and at the Sorbonne in Paris. She wrote a master's thesis on French-Algerian relations since 1989. Currently a Ph.D. student at the University of Rotterdam, she is engaged in research on French and Dutch headscarf affairs.

KAREN LEONARD is professor of anthropology at the University of California, Irvine, where she specializes in the history of India. She has published on the social history and anthropology of India and on Punjabi Mexican Americans and Asian Americans in California. She is currently studying the construction of identity in the diaspora among emigrants from Hyderabad, India, who are settling in Pakistan, Britain, Canada, the United States, Australia, and the Gulf states of the Middle East. She has numerous publications, including *Making Ethnic Choices: California's Punjabi Mexican Americans*.

HANS MAHNIG was a political scientist working at the Swiss Forum for Migration Studies in Neuchâtel. He was a Ph.D. student at the Institut d'Etudes Politiques in Paris in the policies against social and ethnic segregation in European cities, interested in comparative research on immigration and immigrant policy as well as in the politics of religion and culture. His recent publications include *Between Economic Demands and Popular Xenophobia: The Swiss System of Immigration Regulation; Regulation of Migration: International Experiences; La question de l'intégration ou comment les immigrés deviennent un enjeu politique—une comparaison entre la France, l'Allemagne, les Pays-Bas et la Suisse;* and *Country Specific or Convergent? A Typology of Immigrant Policies in Western Europe* (with Andreas Wimmer).

KATHLEEN M. MOORE is associate professor of political science at the University of Connecticut. She is author of *Al-Mughtaribun: American Law and the Transformation of Muslim Life in the United States* and is currently studying the intersection of the processes of globalization with local practices of Islamic legal interpretation in British and American settings. She has published articles on topics ranging from questions of legal Orientalism in American courts, to the legal mobilization of Muslim advocacy groups to defend the right of women to wear Islamic headscarves in the workplace, to British Muslims' rights-conscious demands on legal structures after the Rushdie affair.

MOHAMED NIMER is the director of research at the Council on American-Islamic Relations. He writes reports and conducts surveys on issues related to the American Muslim community. His recent writings include *Religious Accommodation Policy in American School Districts*. His popular writings include "Will Muslims Find Room in the Republicans' Big Tent?," published in the *Orlando Sentinel*, 8 July 1999. In 1998, he testified before the U.S. Commission on Civil Rights on the religious accommodation of Muslim students in public schools. Nimer earned his doctorate in political science in 1995 from the University of Utah. He was president of the Islamic Society of Salt Lake City from 1984 to 1987, when he founded the first mosque in the capital of Utah. He has also published *Backtracking on Democratization in Egypt: Implications for U.S. Policy in Urban Terrorism*.

SULAYMAN S. NYANG is professor of African studies at Howard University. Until the end of 1999, he served as the lead developer of the African Voices Project of the Museum of Natural History of the Smithsonian Institution in Washington, D.C. He is now a co-director of the Muslims in American Public Square Project at the Center for Muslim-Christian Understanding at Georgetown University. His best-known works are *Islam, Christianity and African Identity*, *Religious Plurality in Africa* (with Jacob Olupona), *Islam in the United States of America*, and *A Line in the Sand: Saudi Arabia's Role in the Gulf War*.

TARIQ RAMADAN teaches philosophy at the College of Geneva and Islamic Studies at Fribourg University. He is actively engaged as an expert on Islamic revival and the identity and challenges of Muslims living as a minority. Among his books are *Les musulmans dans la laïcité: Responsabilités et droits des musulmans dans les societés occidentales*, *Islam, le face à face des civilisations: Quelle projet pour quelle modernité*, *De la souffrance: Etudes Nietzscheene et islamique*, *Muslims in France: The Way towards Coexistence*, and *Peut-on vivre avec l'islam* (with Jacques Neirynck).

ANNE SOFIE ROALD was previously lecturer and researcher at Lund University in the South of Sweden. She is associate professor in International Migration and Ethnic Relations (IMER) at Malmö University. Her publications include *Tarbiya: Education and Politics in Islamic Movements in Jordan and Malaysia* and *Islamic Images of Women: The Cultural Encounter between "Islam" and "the West."* She has published articles on gender relations in Islam and is researching the Muslim Gulf and converts to Islam.

MARIA ADELE ROGGERO, a graduate in religious sciences of the Theological Faculty of Turin, is working in the field of intercultural immigration and interreligious dialogue.

She is a member of the Catholic Commission for ecumenism and interreligious dialogue in Turin and the president of M.E.I.C. (Movimento Ecclesiale di Impegno Culturale) Laboratory for Christian-Islamic Dialogue. Her publications include *Cristianesimo e religioni nel dibattito teologico contemporaneo*, *Religiosità e cultura*, *dal progetto positivistico al dialogo interreligioso*, *I matrimoni islamo-cristiani*, and *Famiglia islamica e scuola a Torino*, in I. Siggillino, *I luoghi del dialogo*.

JØRGEN BÆK SIMONSEN is professor at the Carsten Niebuhr Institute for Near Eastern Studies, University of Copenhagen. Since the late 1980s, he has conducted research on Islam and Muslims in Denmark and written extensively on the subject. He is a member of the board at the Center for Middle East Studies, University of Odense, and at the Center for Dialogue between Muslims and Christians in Denmark and served as director for the Carsten Niebuhr Institute from 1996 to 2000. His publications include *Islam in Denmark*, *Genesis and Early Development of the Caliphal Taxation System*, *Islam in a Changing World*, *Europe and the Middle East*, and *Visions for Freedom of Religion, Democracy and Ethnic Equality*.

JANE I. SMITH is professor of Islamic studies and co-director of the Macdonald Center for Christian-Muslim Relations at Hartford Seminary. She has done extensive work on Muslim communities in America, Christian theology in relation to Islam, historical relations between Christians and Muslims, Islamic conceptions of death and the afterlife, and the role and status of women in Islam. She also is co-editor of the *Muslim World*, editor of the *Encyclopedia of Women in Islamic Cultures*, convener of the North American Regional Research Team for the Pew Program "Christian Theological Education in Muslim Contexts," and associate editor of the *Encyclopedia of Women and Religion in North America*. Her publications include *Islam in America*; *Muslim Communities in North America* (with Yvonne Haddad); and *Mission to America: Five Islamic Sectarian Communities in the United States* (with Yvonne Haddad).

BARBARA FREYER STOWASSER is professor of Arabic in the Department of Arabic, College of Arts and Sciences, Georgetown University. She is the director of the Center for Contemporary Arab Studies. She served as the thirty-fourth president of the Middle East Studies Association (1998–1999). Her publications include *Women in the Qur'an: Traditions and Interpretation*, *The Islamic Impulse*, *Religion and Political Development: Some Comparative Ideas on Ibn Khladun and Machiavelli*, articles published in American, German, Arabic, and Turkish journals and periodicals, and book chapters in collected volumes.

THIJL SUNIER is on the faculty of history and art at the University of Rotterdam. He specialized in cultural anthropology at the universities of Utrecht and Amsterdam, where he completed his Ph.D. thesis, which was published as *Islam in Beweging: Turkse jongeren en islamitische organisaties* (1996). He participated in research on interethnic relations in a postwar neighborhood of the city of Haarlem, conducted research among Turkish youth and Turkish Islamic organizations in the Netherlands, and did comparative research among Turkish youth in France, Germany, Great Britain, and the Netherlands. Presently he is engaged in international comparative historical research on nation building and multiculturalism in France and the Netherlands. His publications include articles and books on migrants and Muslims in Europe and Islam and politics in Turkey and Central Asia, including *Turkije: mensen, politiek, economie, cultuur*.

LIYAKAT TAKIM is currently a visiting assistant professor in the Department of Religious Studies at the University of Miami in Coral Gables, Florida. He has translated numerous books including *Questions of Jurisprudence*. He has also authored articles on Islam in America and Islamic biographical dictionaries. He has traveled extensively in the Muslim world and is currently conducting research on the Muslim communities in America and the companions of the Shi'i imams.

THERESA ALFARO VELCAMP is a Ph.D. candidate and university fellow in Latin American history at Georgetown University. Her dissertation examines the Arab diaspora in Mexico in the late nineteenth and early twentieth centuries. Velcamp has published a review article on the historiography of Arab immigration in Argentina in *Arab and Jewish Immigrants in Latin America. Images and Realities* and *Immigrants and Minorities*. She received an M.A. in Latin American studies from Georgetown University and an M.Sc. in comparative politics from the London School of Economics and Political Science in England.

STEVEN VERTOVEC is research reader in social anthropology at the University of Oxford and director of the British Economic and Social Research Council's Research Programme on Transnational Communities. His research interests include globalization and transnationalism, ethnicity, Hinduism and Islam, religious minorities, and multiculturalism. He is the author of *Hindu Trinidad: Religion, Ethnicity and Socio-Economic Change*; editor of *The Hindu Diaspora: Comparative Patterns*; and co-editor of *Migration and Social Cohesion, South Asians Oveseas: Migration and Ethnicity, The Urban Context: Ethnicity, Social Networks and Situational Analysis, Islam in Europe: The Politics of Religion and Community, Muslim European Youth: Reproducing Religion, Ethnicity and Culture*, and *Migration, Diasporas and Transnationalism*.

KARI VOGT, associate professor at the Department of Cultural Studies, University of Oslo, Norway, has written widely on Christian and Islamic issues. Her most recent book, *Moskeer og islamske organisasjoner i Norge*, discusses Islam in Norway. Her other publications include *Islam hus: verdensreligion på frammarsj, Between Desert and City. The Coptic Orthodox Church Today, Kommet for å bli: Islam i Vest-Europa*, and *Den Islamike bolge: myte eller realitet?*

Muslims in the West

Introduction

Jane I. Smith

The current encounter of Muslims with the West is tapping into a long and rich history of conquest, cooperation, fears, and misconceptions. From the earliest days of Islam as a religious and cultural force, Muslims have knocked at the gates of Europe, and some scholars claim that Muslims were among the earliest explorers of the Americas. During the first Islamic century, inhabitants of what is now western Europe watched with mounting alarm as Muslim forces swept across North Africa, into Spain, and briefly to central France. The mobilization of forces by Pope Urban II in the crusading effort to regain "Christian" Jerusalem laid the foundation for the kind of "Crusader- and anti-Crusader" mentality that has influenced attitudes of the Christian West and the Islamic East toward each other for centuries.

Western Christians freely borrowed from Islamic sciences, philosophy, medicine, and the arts developed during the tenth through the fifteenth centuries in Spain. Nonetheless, the Spanish inquisition at the time of the Christian monarchs Ferdinand and Isabella saw Muslims expelled almost entirely from the West. In the coming centuries, Muslims again moved westward, with the Turks capturing Constantinople and twice knocking on the doors of Vienna. In the process of these advances considerable numbers of East Europeans adopted Islam. The nineteenth and early twentieth centuries once more brought the incursion of western forces and influences in the Middle East with the political dissection of Islamic lands by colonialist powers. The legacy of colonialism continues as a powerful force affecting the relationship between Muslims and citizens of Europe and America.

The twentieth century also saw a different kind of Islamic movement westward, one in which citizens of Muslim lands came in increasing numbers seeking employment, refuge, acceptance, and, in some cases, religious freedom. Motivations have changed from conquest to settlement for economic and political reasons, although the lands of Europe and America until recently have absorbed their new residents with little sense of disruption of the continuity of their basically Christian heritage. The reality that Islam is now second in number of adherents only to Christianity in almost every western country presents a very new set of challenges, both to the Muslims who have chosen to make this move and to the host cultures that are increasingly feeling the pressure to accommodate their new citizens.

While the picture of Islam in the United States seems somewhat different from that in other western countries because of the very sizeable number of adherents who are African American, a closer look at the experiences of immigrant Muslims in North

America reveals that there are clear similarities between those experiences and those of Muslims in western Europe. The earliest American immigrants generally came for purposes of employment, as was the case in some European states. In the United States, Canada, and Mexico, immigrants were primarily from the Middle East and began arriving in the second half of the nineteenth century. For the most part, significant Muslim emigration to Europe came somewhat later, encouraged by many European countries to meet their particular labor needs, especially after the Second World War. What the immigrants shared was the understanding that their reasons for entry into a new country were primarily if not exclusively economic and that soon they would be returning to their home countries. Both the "guest workers" and those who contracted with them believed that their stay in the West would be brief. Europeans did not expect a permanent intrusion of Islam into their respective cultures. Islam was seen as a kind of transient "cultural baggage," as Thijl Sunier and Mira van Kuijeren report in their chapter on the Netherlands, brought by immigrants who would soon be going home.

In most countries, however, the situation changed. The specifics of the history and system of government of individual states provide important differentiating factors, of course, but in general it can be said that many Muslims who expected to repatriate to their home countries increasingly found themselves contemplating permanent residence in the West. Their children were becoming fluent in the language of the land and were receiving a good education, economic opportunities were better in Europe or America than in the home country, and in some cases political circumstances mitigated against return.

As labor needs changed and as countries became more aware of the presence of new populations, new immigration laws were passed in many countries, making it more difficult for new waves of migrant workers to come. At the same time, many governments realized that immigrant male workers, who were usually single, needed to be joined by members of their families, so opportunities for reuniting and moving family members to the new country were created. To these populations of initial workers, and then their families, new waves of immigrants were added throughout the 1980s and 1990s, namely those who were seeking political asylum because of revolutions, wars, and civil unrest in a variety of Muslim countries. In general, Europe and America provided open doors to refugees and asylum seekers, although their arrival further complicated the process of mutual accommodation between Islam and western societies.

Countries such as the Netherlands, England, and France expected their former colonies to become economically independent. When that did not happen, members of those societies often looked to their former colonizers to be their new economic hosts. Thus, in many western European countries the majority of immigrant Muslims represent areas of former colonial presence, such as North Africans in France or South Asians in England. In Germany most Muslim workers are Turkish; in Switzerland, most are North African among French speakers and Turks and former Yugoslavs among German speakers. Citizens of the former Yugoslavia also have come to many other European societies, as well as to North America. In the United States and Canada, as in European countries, recent immigrants are much more likely to be well educated than their forebears. This is especially the case in the United States after the mid-1960s, with the repeal of the Asia Exclusion Act. In part this change reflects the preference of western governments, such as Canada, for applications from immigrants with high levels of education.

There have been many other reasons, of course, why Muslim individuals have made their homes in western countries. Since the nineteenth century, Muslim students have been visible in European and American universities and have been key players in the establishments of such organizations as the Muslim Student Association of North America. Many have returned to their home countries to use their western education for the economic and social betterment of those societies, as well as to influence the development of Islamic thought and movements. But many others, representing a variety of national backgrounds, have opted to stay and to make the West their home. While this has been most apparent in the United States and Canada during the late twentieth century, it is also a significant phenomenon in western Europe. Today, as Tariq Ramadan illustrates, students and other young Muslims are working creatively for the establishment of a genuinely European Islam.

With the "guest workers," political asylum seekers, students, and others, then, a new religion has become visible, established, and vocal in the West. Europeans and Americans are just beginning to think about the ramifications for western society of the growing numbers of Muslims. Many new social, educational, and legal issues have come to the fore as a result of the presence of Islam and of Muslim efforts to practice their faith. Western societies are still in the early stages of considering what kinds of accommodation need to be made and what the implications are for enacting appropriate legislation to protect the rights of Muslims. In many countries, the situation is complicated by the presence of immigrants who lack the required documentation, so some have suggested that there are really three categories of Muslim immigrants: citizens, legal residents who are not (yet) citizens, and illegal or undocumented persons.

Western Perceptions of Islam

One of the most significant concerns both for immigrant Muslims and for the societies in which they have settled is the reality of western perceptions, and often fears, of Islam. The way that the West sees Islam is, naturally, conditioned to a large extent by the historical legacy initiated in the Middle Ages by the Crusades, as well as by current perceptions of an "essentialized," violent, and changeless religion, as Jocelyne Cesari underscores in her treatment of Islam in France. Such responses are reinforced by the constant barrage of media reports about Muslim extremist activity in other parts of the world. Cesari observes, however, that French attitudes toward Islam are softening because the Muslim community has been visible in the country long enough for citizens to see that it is generally peaceable; concerns over possible extremism on French soil have led to creative political efforts to improve relations with Islam. In countries in which Muslim presence is more recent, these kinds of efforts are not yet under way. Hans Mahnig says in his chapter on Switzerland that it was at just about the time that Muslims started to become more vocal about their needs and desires in Swiss society that international events highlighting extremism raised levels of Swiss fear and made the task more complicated. What has been called "Islamophobia" in Britain, as detailed by Steven Vertovec, could be said to have a range of manifestations in various western countries.

Sometimes it is Arabs who are the particular objects of discrimination, again because of reports of extremist activities in the Arab world, while other Muslims are seen as less culpable. Karen Leonard notes, for example, that one of the reasons South Asians have been able to assume leadership positions in American Islam is that they are not linked to international politics in the way that Arabs are. Anti-Arab prejudice as an influence on and as fostered by U.S. foreign policy is underscored in Mamoun Fandy's chapter on the American government and the "Islamists." Mohamed Nimer takes the reader through a series of ways in which Muslim organizations in the United States are high-lighting and combating specific instances of anti-Muslim prejudice in general and anti-Arab prejudice in particular. Stereotypical images of Muslims, particularly but not exclusively Arabs, are prevalent in most western societies. Theresa Alfaro Velcamp, for example, talks about the "*turco*" stereotype of tricky traders, swindlers, and crafty, mustachioed Arabs. Combating these kinds of pervasive portrayals is a major part of the task Muslims face as they work to project an image of Islam as peaceable and workable in western societies.

America has long been a country of vastly differing cultural heritages, "built on the backs of immigrants," as the phrase is often turned. Despite the claim of many of its immigrant and native peoples that the ideal of a society of equals, despite its heterogeneity, has never been achieved, it remains a country used to the presence of a wide diversity of cultures and races. While it is probably not true that Muslims are more welcome in the United States than in Canada or Europe simply because of that history of diversity, it is certainly the case that, for many Europeans and Canadians, concerns for the stability of their (mainly) homogeneous societies rise with the increasing presence of a Muslim population. Scandinavian countries, for example, are particularly conscious of such concerns. The presence of Muslims in Denmark, says Jorgen Bæk Simonsen, is clearly seen as a threat to the homogeneity of Danish society, just as the presence of guest workers endangers the livelihoods of Danish workers at a time of high unemployment. Danes fear that they will become a minority in their own society, and Muslims are clearly described as "the problem." One result, he says, is a growing sense of "us" and "them," as a previously homogeneous society changes into one that is multicultural, multilingual, and multireligious. Italians, even more than other Europeans, argues Maria Adele Roggero, have always thought of themselves as a society with a single culture and a single religion. The fairly recent arrival in Italy of Muslims with a wide variety of national and cultural backgrounds has brought uncertainty and fear, often exacerbated by the polemics of the media and of local politicians. Those who oppose the growing presence of Muslims in Canada, reports Karim H. Karim, argue that the integrity of Canadian society is in the process of being destroyed. Some base their discourse openly on the assumption that Canada is a white, Christian country and should remain so and are vocal about their fear of being overwhelmed by the followers of an alien religion. It is not surprising to note that in many western countries means have been devised to segregate Muslims from the rest of society, an effort that often has been subtly reinforced by those Muslims who themselves fear the consequences of integration into a western secular culture.

Freedom of Religion

The separation of church and state has been integral to the structure of American society from its inception and has come to characterize most European countries since the early or middle part of the twentieth century. In France and Switzerland, such separation is known as *laïcité*, or the functional relegation of religion to the private sphere. Swedish society, says Anne Sofie Roald, has been constituted on a basically secular world view since freedom of religion was introduced in 1951. Religion has no part in official or public life and is to be observed in the home or other private institution. The constitutions of a number of countries specifically state that all religious denominations and groups are to be given equal opportunity. This separation has worked quite successfully in most western states, at least insofar as it has pertained to different Christian denominations or to Jews. With the presence of Muslims who are increasingly verbal in their requests to practice their faith publicly, the situation is changing. As Hans Mahnig notes for Switzerland, in many places the principle of neutrality, with the resulting separation of religion and state, is as much a problem for Muslims as it is an opportunity. Their demands to display religious symbols publicly, including the wearing of Islamic dress and other forms of outward affirmation of Islamic identity, are leading both to discomfort on the part of other citizens and occasionally to legal wrangling over such public practice. Kathleen Moore details a number of cases in the American context in which the claims of Muslims to their fundamental "rights" challenge and are challenged by U.S. laws.

The right to practice one's faith and the official recognition of that faith are not always synonymous. In Italy, for example, the constitution guarantees freedom of religion, but the government has not yet accorded official recognition to the religion of Islam. The same is true in Switzerland. Muslims are pressing hard for this recognition, not least because in some cases it would bring needed public financing. In some countries, such financial support is offered according to the number of adherents, as in Norway, where, according to Kari Vogt, monies are paid directly to mosques and congregations, rather than to umbrella organizations. Therefore, it is of great importance for the mosques that those who attend be officially registered. In other cases, such as Sweden, state financial support is granted to the three major Muslim confederations recognized by the government. These groupings are led primarily by Turks and Arabs, which puts Muslims with other kinds of cultural identification at a distinct disadvantage. Religious organizations in the Netherlands can apply for government subsidies so long as they demonstrate their intention to work toward the goal of integration into Dutch society. This has led to some tensions in the Muslim community, given the uncertainty of many Muslims about whether they really want to integrate. In the United States, the funding issues take on somewhat different dimensions, particularly when overseas organizations offer financial incentives to encourage American Muslims to adopt particular ideological perspectives and strategies. Liyakat Takim, in his presentation of Shi'i Islam in America, describes competition and conflict among different mosques as they look primarily to foreign sources of funding, often administered through foundations established in the United States.

The Public Practice of Islam

Not all Muslims now living in the West wish to practice their faith publicly, and many do not actively practice it at all. For a significant number, however, visibility, recognition, and access are of great importance. The insistence on a public presence, as well as recognition of Islam and the Muslim community, involves a number of clear requests that Muslims are making of their host societies. Most important is acknowledgment of their presence and recognition of their status as the second largest religion in virtually every western country. This involves both general awareness and acceptance on the part of the citizenry and the more official recognition that still has not been granted in a number of places. It also focuses on a number of very specific requests that involve the public practice of the faith. Among them are the following:

1. *The building of mosques.* For many Muslims, one of the greatest practical challenges is finding proper spaces for meeting and worship. Many have met in private homes or other spaces, but now these are often too small to accommodate growing numbers of Muslim worshipers. Mosques have been part of the landscape in some countries for many decades, but the past ten years or more have seen a great increase in the number of mosques built for that specific purpose, as well as the conversion of other buildings for worship. Some non-Muslims have objected to new construction on the basis that the architecture is "foreign," that the call to prayer is "intrusive," that there is too much traffic at the times of prayer, and so on. Others are recognizing that mosque communities are not a threat to the social order and should enjoy the same rights and privileges as Christians or other religious groups.

2. *Cemeteries.* Muslims in most western nations are now increasingly vocal about the need to have either plots of land that are specifically designated as Muslim cemeteries or sections of existing burial grounds where they can lay the dead to rest according to Islamic custom. In many countries, these demands are being heard and addressed.

3. *Islamically acceptable food.* Vigilant efforts have been made in the United States for decades, and now also in many European countries, to insist that *halal* (Islamically acceptable) food is available in public institutions such as schools and hospitals. They are also providing *halal* meat from appropriately slaughtered animals in their own butcher shops, after having relied for many years on Jewish shops that sell *kosher* meat.

4. *Employment.* While many Muslims were brought to European countries specifically to meet demands for certain kinds of labor, often unskilled, the fact remains that in a number of places unemployment among Muslims is high and that the jobs they are able to get are not commensurate with their skills or educational levels. Barbara Freyer Stowasser, in her chapter on Turks in Germany, reports that the first jobs for Muslims were physically very demanding and potentially dangerous. Since the early 1980s, Muslims have been faced with growing unemployment and today have the highest percentage of unemployed workers of any immigrant group in Germany. A number of issues are just beginning to be raised concerning immigrants and employment, such as the relationship of job opportunities to racial and religious discrimination, the obvious and growing movement of people from poorer to richer countries, the necessity of finding younger laborers in western societies in which the proportion of elderly (who need retirement income) in the population is growing steadily, and the willingness of many immigrants to do the kinds of labor that westerners disdain.

5. *Facilities.* Many places of employment and public institutions, such as schools, are recognizing that greater attention must be paid to accommodating those Muslims who wish to observe the appropriate practice of Islam. This includes such requests as facilities for washing and preparation for the prayer, a clean and (if possible) private place for the prayer itself, consideration of time off for the observance of Islamic reli-

gious holidays or participation in the pilgrimage to Mecca, and special consideration of Muslims who are fasting during the month of Ramadan. In some cases, such facilities are being provided, but these demands again bring to the fore issues of the separation of church and state, of parity with Jewish and Christian communities, and of whether Islam should or can be confined to the private sphere.

6. *Appropriate appearance and dress.* Most conspicuous in this category is the wearing of the headscarf, which some Muslim women insist must be their prerogative in public. "Headscarf affairs" have been part of the landscape of most European countries, and almost everywhere (with the exception of Italy, according to Roggero) there are reports of women who have been discriminated against, including being fired from their jobs for wearing the *hijab*, or head covering. Appropriate appearance for men may also mean wearing a beard or small cap, which many believe is necessary in order to follow the practice of the Prophet. Both Moore and Nimer cite a number of cases brought before the American courts that deal with requests from Muslims to wear head coverings or beards.

7. *Islamic banks.* As Muslims become increasingly organized, more literature is being developed about what is considered by various schools of interpretation to be Islamic and non-Islamic ways of conducting business. Muslim journals publish frequent articles about what does or does not constitute usury, which is forbidden in Islam, and how to appropriately invest one's money. Part of this effort has been the establishment of Islamic banks or alternatives for Muslims who want to be financially successful and also to "follow the rules."

8. *Religious rights in the public schools.* Because they are concerned about the imposition of western secular values on their children in the public schools, some Muslim parents choose to put their children in private Muslim schools, and some choose to educate them at home. This is not always possible, however, for financial and other reasons, with the result that most Muslim children do attend public schools and are subject to the rules and regulations of those schools. Many Muslims are now requesting that recognition be given to some of the special requirements for their children, such as the need for girls to wear appropriate dress for physical education, the need to avoid unnecessary mixing of girls and boys and single-sex sports, and the creation of opportunities for Muslim children to celebrate and tell their classmates about their religious holidays.

Schooling

The matter of schooling for children has raised a number of serious issues for Muslim immigrants. While many Muslims are members of the well-educated professional class, others who have come as laborers, asylum seekers, and refugees may lack proficiency in the language of the host country. Children of such immigrants may be at a liability if their parents are not able to provide the kind of assistance with their children's homework that is required. Often conditions at home are so crowded, as Stowasser observes, that children do not have appropriate places to study. In Germany, as in many other states in Europe and Canada where the government provides the budget to support alternative religiously based schools, Islam has not been officially recognized in the way that Roman Catholicism, Protestantism, and Judaism have. In addition, Islamic religious instruction is not part of the regular school curriculum, with the result that Muslim children can learn about other religions but not their own. Thus, Islamic instruction, a high priority for many parents, is not always easy to come by and must be offered in the mosque or privately at home. Many Muslims are struggling to be able to provide contemporary religious material that will be as attractive and appealing to students as that provided for other religions. Vogt notes that finding pedagogically acceptable and modern Qur'an education is a high priority for Norwegian Muslims.

The presence of Muslims is challenging educational policies as governments grapple with such issues as whether to immerse the children of temporary guest workers in the national system or prepare them for their eventual return to their homelands, whether it is the responsibility of the state to provide religious instruction, and who is qualified to administer such education. The expectation on the part of Muslim immigrants and host societies alike that Muslims would not be permanent residents of western countries, the so-called myth of return, for a long time served to reinforce the lack of integration into the host society. A clear exception, however, as Simonsen cites in relation to Denmark, has been the insistence of the government that children go to public schools. This, he says, resulted in profound consequences for guests and hosts, which are still being played out. The Netherlands, which promotes religious freedom, nonetheless has long been subject to what Sunier and van Kuijeren call "pillarization," the differentiation of the religious education of Protestants and Catholics. Officially it ended in the 1960s, but the practice is still evident in the lower grades of public education. The desire of some Muslims for separate Islamic schools is seen by many as another instance of pillarization. In some cases, cultural practices particular to certain Muslim societies become translated into the school environment with problematic results. This raises the issues of how to prepare teachers to be sensitive to cultural differences and the degree to which such differences should (or should not) be accommodated. Roald notes the observation of some Swedish school officials, for example, that boys from certain immigrant families do not show as much respect to girls or to female teachers as they should, that there is sometimes a lack of mutual respect between teachers and students, that Swedes look on Muslim families as indulging their children (especially boys), and that Muslims look on Swedish society as having no respect for families or for elders.

American Muslim students, aided by the efforts of organizations like the Council for American Islamic Relations (CAIR), have made considerable strides in gaining access to facilities and opportunities. They still struggle in some cases with questions of dress or participation in activities that offer too free mixing of boys and girls, but from the Muslim perspective progress is evident. The question of whether or not to educate children in the public schools is the subject of a great deal of conversation in the United States, with some arguing that such exposure is crucial for the survival of the Muslim when he or she reaches adulthood and has to enter American society and others wanting to protect and to educate children Islamically as long as possible. Finances are always an issue, and many choose public schooling simply because the resources are not available to hire well-trained teachers for Islamic schools. Takim observes that a particular problem for Shi'i students in America is the effort to structure Islamic schools and curricula on the hermeneutic model of Shi'i Imams who live in Iran or Iraq when such models may not be appropriate and functional in American culture.

Changing Roles for Women

It is clear that for Muslims in both Europe and America, one of the major items on the agenda of the new century is continued conversation and exploration of new roles and opportunities for women. First-generation immigrants coming from rural or traditional Muslim countries often find it difficult to reconcile their assumption that women should not be too visible in the public arena with western women's active participation in all spheres. New interpretations of Islam, however, are providing for increasing opportunities (sometimes with the insistence that women take advantage of those opportunities) for women. The debate within the Muslim community itself centers on the challenge of whether or not to replicate the kind of modernization that has taken place in Turkey, North Africa, the Arab world, and South and Southeast Asia. Such modernization is being challenged by Muslims of a more conservative orientation, including many who are well educated, as well as members of the middle and/or working classes.

Economic factors sometimes play a role in the public participation of women as the need for a double income for the family forces a rethinking of traditional roles for women. Other professionally trained women want to be part of the workforce because of personal desire and not necessarily because of financial need. One of the justifications for the activity of women in public, of course, is that if they so choose they can have the protection afforded them by wearing conservative Islamic dress. Such outward symbolism is often difficult for other Europeans and Americans to understand or appreciate, particularly since it seems to them to signal what they believe to be the oppression of women in Islam and the opposite of the ideal of gender equality.

In both Europe and America, women have become more active in mosques and Islamic organizations. There is a noticeable growth in the number of women's organizations, both informal and those structured for social action. State-supported social programs in some European countries serve as agents of support for women who are looking for ways to move from the private domain of the family into more public arenas. Female education is now being more actively encouraged by a growing number of Muslims living in the West, with the result that more women are assuming organizational leadership positions. Sulayman Nyang notes the increase in the number of African women who have come to the United States for higher education after their countries have achieved independence, many of whom have later chosen not to return home and to become increasingly active in public institutions and organizations. As Muslims consciously try to avoid what they see as the excesses of western feminism, however, they are cautious about their definitions of appropriate opportunities for women. Public involvement is often challenged by the arrival of new and conservative immigrants and of Imams and leaders who are not accustomed to having women play prominent roles in mosques or Islamic organizations, as Karim observes in Canada.

Leadership

The issue of leadership of European and American Islam is of extreme importance as Muslims try to understand questions of faith, practice, and identity in a new culture. Imams who have been trained in traditional Islamic cultures and institutions and arrive in the West to assume leadership positions in mosques and Islamic organizations often know little of the societies into which they are suddenly thrown. This can lead to tensions within Islamic communities, especially when those communities are now composed of second and third generations who are themselves well acclimated to living in the West. Many Muslim youth are especially restless with the leadership of men whom they see as programmed to try to replicate a traditional Islam that is not relevant to Muslim life in the West, or a version of the faith that is so culturally bound that it reflects life in a "foreign" country, rather than in Europe or America.

In general, Imams who function in the West suffer not only from a lack of understanding of the new culture but also from not being well trained in the language of the country in which they find themselves. Imams increasingly are being called on to play roles parallel in function to those of priests or pastors, for which they are not prepared. Appropriate training of Imams and Muslim leaders, including knowledge both of the traditional Islamic sciences and of western society and culture, is high on the agenda of matters to be addressed in the immediate future. In the United States over the past decade, there have been conscious efforts to locate Islamically trained chaplains for the military, prisons, hospitals, and college campuses and to find ways to provide for that training in the western context. Such movements are also beginning in some European countries.

Given the general lack of appropriately prepared leadership, the question "Who has the authority to interpret Islam in a western Muslim community?" increasingly is being formulated. Mosques have very different policies as to how to select an Imam, what credentials are necessary, what his functions should be, and how much authority he has over the lives and practices of those attending his mosque. In many places, the influence of leaders and organizations in overseas countries is still very strong. Movements such as the Jama'ti Islami in Pakistan and India, the Ikhwan al-Muslimun in Egypt, Syria, and Jordan, Ghannouchi's Islamic Movement of Tunisia (MTI), and the FIS in Algeria, as well as Shi'i leaders in Iran and Iraq, continue to influence western Muslims, often insisting that the membership maintain allegiance to their interpretation of Islam. In other cases, foreign influence is connected to financial support. The Rabitat al-Alam al-Islami of Saudi Arabia has directly influenced the development of Islam in Europe and North America by providing funding for mosque construction and the salaries of Imams.

For some Muslims, this kind of external authority may no longer feel relevant for their changing circumstances. They are seeking new kinds of leadership training and new sources of authority located within, and knowledgeable about, western culture and civilization. When possible, members of Muslim communities in Europe and America coordinate their activities and interpretations in ways that allow them to honor traditional understandings but adapt to new situations. In some countries, as Roggero notes is the case in Italy, new converts to Islam are playing especially important leadership roles. Because of their knowledge of the language and the culture, their generally high levels of education, and their enthusiasm for the new religion of choice, they are active in helping Muslim communities adapt to life in the West and reinterpret Islam to be relevant for the time and place. They also serve as intermediaries between government agencies and Muslim communities.

Islamic Organizations

The organizing of Muslims in the diaspora has been promoted by various interests. On one level, European governments were eager to identify leadership that could serve as interlocutors to the emergent community. At the same time, self-appointed elders of the community in search of recognition and parity with citizens of other faiths tried to replicate the institutions and associations of particular nation states. Where subsidies for particular forms of organizations existed, they formulated and reformulated themselves in order to take advantage of the funds. When laws favored one form of governance over another, they chose the option that maintained their control. Thus, organizations proliferated.

In the United States, the earliest serious efforts at Muslim organization began in the middle of the twentieth century and have grown in number and focus throughout the succeeding years. These organizations represent Muslims at the national and local levels and reflect political and legal concerns, professional identities, ideological leanings, national origins, and a range of other issues. As Nimer stresses in his chapter on Muslims in public life in America, many organizations are devoted specifically to the cause of identifying and fighting discrimination and giving Muslims public voice. While there is considerable debate in America, as in other countries, about the extent to which it is appropriate for Muslims to be involved in politics, many organizations are now devoted specifically to encouraging such involvement, identifying Muslim candidates and those whose voting record would appeal to Muslims, and to getting out the Islamic vote. Basic to the activities of many of these organizations is empowerment within western society.

Tariq Ramadan, in his chapter on Islam and Muslims throughout Europe, identifies some of the new associations that are growing up to address appropriate modes of Muslim participation in European life and culture. Leaders of many of these organizations, he says, are initiating conversations between Muslims and other Europeans, as well as between European Muslims and those from traditional cultures, in the effort to develop better understanding and a set of laws that are both Islamic and adaptable to European life. Challenged by the plurality of voices representing different international allegiances and the need to achieve national recognition, Muslims in Europe are struggling to identify their common goals. As Mahnig observes in relation to Switzerland, immigrants and refugees come from countries that not only are different in perspective but also currently may be engaged in political strife, making it more difficult for Swiss Muslims to focus on their commonalities, rather than their differences. The heterogeneity of the Muslim population has made it hard for it to adopt a common strategy. The same is true in Canada, where the proliferation of Muslim associations effectively means that there is no voice that is capable of speaking for the interests of all Canadian Muslims.

Somewhat different kinds of organization are represented in the Sufi movements that are visible in many parts of Europe and America. In the United States for most of the twentieth century, Sufism resembled more a freelance New Age movement than the kind of teaching and training represented by the more traditional Sufi orders of other parts of the Islamic world. In recent years, however, the immigrant populations have included persons trained in the classical disciplines of Sufism who are stressing association with the traditional orders and organizations, some of it imported and "legitimized" by the leadership of trained *shaykhs* and *pirs* from abroad. Despite efforts of modernists and Islamists to label Sufism a heresy, it appears to be thriving in pockets of the West.

In general, Sufi organizations focus on spiritual training and development and do not involve themselves in the kinds of social and political issues that appeal to other Muslim groups. They tend to treat religion on the strictly personal level, often as a way of relieving stress and even illness, without crystallizing into organizational forms. Many of the more recent Sufi movements in America are influenced by traditional orders in Africa and are of particular appeal to African immigrants, as well as to African American Muslims. Velcamp reports that there is some Sufi activity in Mexico today, while both Vogt and Roggero, in writing about Norway and Italy, respectively, stress the importance of Sufi brotherhoods in the lives of many European Muslims.

Immigrant Muslim Identity

Nearly all of the chapters in this volume deal with some aspect of the crucial matter of Muslim identity in the new western context. The question is whether it is better for Muslims to try to maintain a separate identity, unassimilated into and as uninvolved as possible with western culture, or to strive for ways in which to integrate fully at the same time that they affirm the importance of their Islam. What does it mean to be Muslim and Swedish, or German, or Dutch, or American? Tariq Ramadan devotes virtually all of chapter 10 to a consideration of this important question in relation to European Islam and argues forcefully that participation in European culture need not mean secularization or assimilation or the losing of one's Islamic identity. The protection of European laws, he maintains, does allow Muslims to practice their Islam to the fullest extent.

The initial inclination of early immigrant Muslims to define themselves as Muslim or by their nationality, rather than by their adopted country, has contributed to their stigmatization. In Sweden, for example, this is exacerbated by the fact that Swedes view immigrants as temporary, and always "the other." In part, this reflects the "intermediate state" of those workers who expected not to remain in the West. Many of them still find Swedish culture relatively inaccessible, because of a number of factors such as problems learning the language, the tightness of the Swedish social structure, and their own lack of education. Is it possible for Muslims in this context to find their own identity as Swedes who are also Muslim? The experience of Muslims in Sweden is similar to that of Muslim immigrants in Germany. There, as Stowasser notes, the second- and third-generation Turks have acquired a good command of the language and have been able to form a Turkish middle class, which helps give them a firmer sense of identity. Still, many feel excluded from German culture and continue to wonder whether becoming truly German means that one must forsake being a Turk. In the Netherlands, basic rights to live according to specific cultural backgrounds are granted by the government with the understanding that practitioners are also expected to integrate. Such integration, Muslims perceive, is generally understood to come at the price of their becoming less Muslim. To some extent, as is the case in Norway, Germany, Switzerland, France, and the Netherlands, the proliferation of Muslim organizations with ties to the home countries tends to foster solidarity with that home country, rather than with the new place of residence. This has led the younger generation to want to follow a separate course, assured of the knowledge that they are European. They are supported by the development of other organizations, as Ramadan points out, that are working to help Muslims understand themselves as citizens of Europe who affirm their Islamic identity.

In America, the question of identity is perceived by the Muslim leadership as paramount to the well-being of the community. As citizens, Muslims strive to carve a place in American society without compromising what they understand to be the essentials of the faith and without transgressing its boundaries. "Americanization" has been the inevitable result of the immigrant experience, says Leonard, regardless of the efforts of immigrants to avoid it. These efforts are not restricted to the Sunni population but are quite as evident among Shi'i Muslims in America, who may find identity issues even harder because of the strong ties with and reliance on leadership from countries abroad. Shi'i public discourse is much more limited, and Shi'i Muslims have generally tended to look inward rather than outward for their identity. Gradually, members of the Shi'i community are becoming more involved in local activities, sometimes together with Sunnis, and are seemingly beginning to acknowledge their role as American citizens, as well as representatives of a particular branch of Islam.

The struggle for identity is not only about religion but also about national and ethnic association. Nyang notes that African immigrants are juggling multiple identities, affirming one and then another depending on the context in which they are operating. They see themselves as Muslims, as representing particular African nations (although there is often ambivalence depending on political conditions in the home country), as Americans, and as black members of an American society that has not yet succeeded in freeing itself of racism. This quandary is also evident among the second-generation Muslims in Mexico. They are seen to be in a transition from Arab to Mexican identity, in the process of which they are negotiating a space in Mexican society in which they can both practice their faith and accommodate to Mexican culture. Karim's description of the Canadian Muslim experience may well apply to many Muslims who are attempting to define themselves in a new context: "Debates on hyphenated Canadianism do not even begin to scratch the surface of the multiple identifications that individuals carry in their minds and souls."

A New Islamic "Home" in the West

While the concerns of hyphenated, multiple, or overlapping identities are real for all immigrant Muslims, whether or not they are consciously addressed, they are of particular interest to the younger generation dedicated to the creation of a genuinely European, or American, Islamic community. As Ramadan argues, isolationism and "ghettoization" have been proven not to work, either for Muslims themselves or for the countries to which they have come. It is the youth of the communities, members of the second and third generations, who are the vanguard in helping think through the positive relation of Islam to the adopted country, and of discovering ways to create a new European Islamic culture different from but integral to that of the prevailing cultures. Cesari provides examples of the intergenerational tensions that frequently exist when she describes the struggles that first-generation Muslims have faced as their young people learn to deal with the forces of secularization and modernization. While parents and grandparents may attempt to inculcate the culture of the home country in their youth, many young Muslims are choosing for themselves what parts of Islam they want to maintain and what they wish to leave behind. Traditional locations for Islamic activity, such as mosques, are often less important to French Muslim young people than neighborhood meeting centers where they work with children to provide instruction and support. In the Netherlands, the youth are now getting organized to address particular issues, such as that of the headscarf, debating appropriate legislation and working to show how Islam and modernity are not antithetical.

Clear generational differences are emerging in America, too. Leonard observes that, as young Muslims grow up fluent in English from birth, not knowing another culture firsthand, and probably learning a more "orthodox" or standard Islam than one particularized by one society or another, they are becoming more interested in stressing similarities over differences. They are also creating a range of new ways in which to pass the Islamic message along to others, such as rap music, Sufi dancing and singing, and even a kind of Islamic American English. The growth of national as well as local youth organizations, Muslim summer camps, apprenticeships for young people, and time devoted to the concerns of the younger generation at meetings of national organizations such as the Islamic Society of North America (ISNA) and the Islamic Circle of North America (ICNA) contribute to giving young people confidence in their opinions and their hopes for an Islam that is fully at home in American society.

Classical Islamic definitions of the world have generally portrayed it as divided between the abode of war (*dar al-harb*), where Islam is not practiced, and the abode of Islam or peace (*dar al-islam*) when Islamic law is the rule for society. Although those divisions have not been functional for many centuries, the idea that Islam cannot be truly practiced in a foreign environment, or even that Muslims in the strict sense should not try to live permanently in non-Muslim societies, has been powerful. What clearly is happening in both Europe and America is that western countries are being understood not simply as appropriate, though non-Islamic, places for Muslims to live, but that the very environment is being reinterpreted specifically to be an "abode of Islam." Sometimes the discussion is put in the context of North America, including Mexico, being *dar al-da'wa*, a place in which it is appropriate to express one's Islamic faith in the public arena in a great variety of ways. There is even literature to suggest that as Prophet Muhammad undertook the emigration (*hijra*) to Medina and made the new locale a home for Islam, so Muslims who emigrate to Europe and America are undertaking a kind of *hijra* and will both find and help create in the new locale an appropriate place in which they can engage the practice of Islam. For this goal truly to be realized will take serious efforts on the part of immigrant Muslims in developing a new *fiqh* (jurisprudence) appropriate to the new situation. It will also require concerted attempts on the part of host cultures to rethink current legislation in ways that respond to Islam not as a monolith but as a representation of a range of different practices and interpretations. If western countries are able to make these kinds of accommodations, it will go a long way toward helping us, as Kathleen Moore says, "to reform the dichotomous structure of how we view Muslims' place in the new world order."

Part I

Carving up Muslim Space
in Western Europe

1

Islamophobia and Muslim Recognition in Britain

Steven Vertovec

Over the past decade, Muslims in Britain have been the focus of increasing public attention. One widespread form of such attention has been highly negative: Muslims have been portrayed in all kinds of media in very derogatory and vilifying ways. Among the effects of such depiction, which has contributed to what is now widely referred to as "Islamophobia," Muslims in Britain have been subject to considerable discrimination and even violence. At the same time, however, another form of public attention has been much more positive. Muslims have made very significant strides in achieving multiple forms of recognition and accommodation in a variety of public spheres and institutions in Britain, right up to representation in the House of Lords. How are these two simultaneous yet opposite trends to be understood?

Background

For more than two hundred years, a variety of South Asian religious traditions were present in Britain, mainly through the presence of small numbers of sailors, students, and emissaries. However, such presence did not have much public profile or social impact. Prior to the Second World War, small pockets of Muslim men, particularly Yemeni and Bengali sailors, were found in port cities such as London, Cardiff, and Glasgow. Islamic practices were maintained in a more or less formal manner, but for the most part the Muslim presence in Britain was inconspicuous. It was only during the years following the war that a large, permanent, visible, predominantly South Asian, and—eventually—politically active Muslim population grew in Britain.[1]

The growth in the numbers of settled and largely South Asian Muslims began with the rebuilding of the British economy following the Second World War. This restructuring called for an infusion of unskilled and semiskilled labor in industrial sectors that were poorly paid and otherwise deemed undesirable by many indigenous Britons. Such was the case in many kinds of factories surrounding London and in the Midlands, and especially in the textile towns of the north (such as Bradford, Leeds, and Manchester) where new machinery necessitated round-the-clock shift work.

In many areas of the (at that time recently decolonized) South Asian subcontinent, a variety of men had forged links with Britain by way of colonial administration, military service, merchant seamanship, or even trips as itinerant peddlers within Britain itself. These individuals acted as bridgeheads for "chain" migration flows to follow, while some

British companies advertised directly in India and Pakistan for workers to come to Britain and gain employment. Throughout the 1950s, citizens of the British Commonwealth had almost unrestricted right of entry into Britain.

Chain migration—by which individuals migrated and subsequently brought over relatives and friends, who, in turn, brought over their own relatives and friends—characterized the influx of South Asians through the late 1950s into the 1960s (that is, until well after various kinds of legislation were introduced to limit immigration). The first, "pioneer" immigrants found jobs and accommodation in some industrial towns, with subsequent immigrants called over to join them. In this way, settlements of persons from the same family, village, or district became established in a single neighborhood of a British city. Concentrations of immigrants from specific parts of South Asia thus grew in specific parts of Britain. With respect to the Muslim population, the north of Britain is largely settled by Pakistanis, especially from the Mirpur district of Azad Kashmir. Bangladeshis from the area of Sylhet are most numerous in East London, Gujarati Indians live in large numbers across the Midlands, and all groups are dispersed throughout north and west greater London.

Throughout the 1950s and 1960s, the bulk of the South Asian population of Britain was composed of men. These workers had left their wives and families behind with the goal of working and saving money in Britain for a number of years before returning home to contribute to the material well-being of their immediate families and to help enhance the general prestige of their overall extended families. Islamic practice among the immigrants in these years was limited to individual daily prayers, often performed alongside factory machinery. Eventually, some collective prayer was held in makeshift prayer rooms or in houses roughly converted into mosques. No large formal religious undertakings, purpose-built mosques, organized religious education, or sermons by Imams were part of the scene for most Muslims in Britain at this time.

By the late 1960s and early 1970s, successive immigration laws basically ended the primary flow of South Asians to Britain. However, by this time, many had decided to settle in Britain on a permanent, or at least a longer-term, basis; this, therefore, entailed the reunification of South Asian wives and children with their men in Britain. Coincidentally, in the same period, the "Africanization" policies in some East African countries drove out the once well established Indian (mainly Gujarati) communities. Tens of thousands, including substantial numbers of Indian Muslims, therefore arrived as refugees in complete family units. The new and growing presence of complete South Asian Muslim families, together with their intention of remaining in Britain, dramatically transformed both the extent and the nature of the Islamic presence throughout the country.

The rapid development of Muslim organizations in Britain can be observed in the proliferation of mosques, *madrasas* (religious supplementary schools), and Muslim associations. Like the general size of the Muslim population, the number of such institutions rose rapidly in the 1970s. This growth doubtless is linked to the reunion of families (and the arrival of other families from East Africa) during this period. The increasing presence of families stimulated thoughts of permanent settlement for the immigrants and refugees. This, in turn, raised awareness of the need for a variety of forms of communal religious expression: mosques for collective prayer, *madrasas* and Qur'anic schools for religious education of the young, formal associations for local and national coordination with regard to funding, and liaision with government authorities to lobby for religious accommodations and safeguard collective rights. The growth of such institutions also reflects the fact that by the early 1970s, immigrants had gained greater familiarity with local British administrative structures relating to, among other things, planning permission, charitable status, and allocation of public resources.

Although the first known mosque in Britain was established in Woking in 1889, the religious landscape of Britain really began to change only after the beginning of postwar migration. In 1963 a total of 13 mosques were registered in Britain; this number increased to 49 mosques in 1970, 99 in 1975, 203 in 1980, and 338 by 1985.[2] These figures, however, represent only those mosques officially registered. Many more have been established by Muslims in Britain, particularly very small ones based in converted houses (often unapproved by local government). One recent survey suggests that there are at least 849 mosques in Britain, registered and unregistered, and an additional 950 British Muslim organizations.[3] These mosques and organizations now serve a sizeable Muslim population.

According to the 1991 census, of a British population of 55 million, South Asians constitute 1,479,645; of those, 840,255 are Indians, 476,555 are Pakistanis, and 162,385 are Bangladeshis.[4] It is estimated that of this total South Asian population, perhaps 44 percent are Muslim, two-thirds of whom are Pakistanis.[5] A sizeable proportion of each of these groups, it should be noted, is made up of "East African Asians" (and smaller numbers of Indians from Mauritius, Fiji, and the Caribbean) whose social, cultural, and economic patterns may differ from those of their counterparts who came directly from the subcontinent. Estimates of "community" numbers vary widely. While Muslim groups themselves estimate that there are about two to three million Muslims in Britain, academic guesses range from one to one and a half million.[6] In any case, Muslims are the largest religious minority group in Britain. Religious affiliation is especially difficult to derive, however, since official sources such as the census have not included a religion question.

Many estimates of the number of Muslims in Britain are made by counting persons who were born in largely Muslim countries or who belong to households headed by such.[7] For persons originating from countries that are not wholly Muslim, such as India, the proportion of Muslims in the country of origin is taken into account with regard to the population from that country now resident in Britain. However, such a method of counting may be quite misleading, given different regional origins, migration strategies, and settlement histories among persons of different social-religious backgrounds. This method of estimating the number of Muslims by country of origin is also unsatisfactory because it considers only persons of a general Muslim heritage. It counts as Muslims those who may not consider themselves practicing (many Iranians, for instance, left Iran after the Islamic revolution specifically because they were not religiously inclined) and does not count a large number who do (including British converts or Muslims coming from countries often not considered to have much of a Muslim presence, such as Indian Muslims from Fiji, Mauritius, Trinidad, and Guyana). Therefore some observers make a distinction between "active" membership (which is almost impossible to enumerate) and "community" membership (which is based on gross counts based on place of origin).[8]

The differing regional and linguistic origins of each religious community within the British South Asian population account for ongoing social and cultural complexity.

Certain beliefs and practices (including specific rites, roles, texts, lore, calendars, and patterns of worship) characteristic of local contexts in the subcontinent have been reproduced in Britain, especially where large numbers of persons from these contexts have settled. These include Sufi-derived practices and collectivities centered on specific *pirs* (saints or holy men) among Mirpuri Muslims. Further, several sects or schools of thought and teaching within Islam are now found in Britain, including Barelwi, Deobandi, and Ahl-i-Hadith traditions.[9]

In the 1950s and early 1960s, the British South Asian population consisted mainly of pockets of men whose day-to-day existence was centered solely on working and saving money. Religious life was little organized, mostly individualistic, and often drew believers from a range of differing regional, linguistic, or other backgrounds. With the settlement of family groups in the late 1960s and early 1970s, a variety of Muslim organizations rapidly proliferated. Each South Asian religious group in Britain has now organized itself (including considerable efforts at fund-raising) and has negotiated with local government bodies for specific forms of accommodation. Finding appropriate places of worship usually has been the first item on the agenda. Catering to the needs of specific ("sectarian," linguistic, even extended-family-based) local Muslim communities, the proliferation of organizations has created a context in which mobilization of Muslims into a unitary movement have been extremely difficult to achieve. Lack of unity among Muslim groups and associations has significantly hampered the processes of public recognition and accommodation, both locally and nationally, for many years.[10]

Arguably the most successful effort at Muslim unification in Britain came in November 1997 with the inauguration of the Muslim Council of Britain (MCB). MCB is an umbrella organization of some 250 local, regional, and national Muslim institutions. It came as the culmination of various steps taken during the 1990s by the United Kingdom Action Committee on Islamic Affairs. (UKACIA was set up by British Muslim professionals to present a moderate Muslim public image, while lobbying for the recognition of various minority rights, in the wake of the Rushdie Affair of the late 1980s.) It became clear that such an umbrella organization was needed when in 1994 the then (Conservative) Home Office secretary demanded that Muslims form a single representative body or he would not even speak with them.

The aims of MCB include promoting consensus and cooperation in the community, giving voice to issues of common concern, removing disadvantages and discrimination faced by Muslims, fostering a better appreciation of Islam and Muslim culture, and working for the good of society as a whole. With a view to representing all British Muslims, MCB lobbies government departments (especially the Home Office), organizes public events attended by key figures (including the prime minister), holds consultations with public bodies such as the Metropolitan Police and with newspaper editors and journalists, issues press statements on a variety of contemporary issues, publishes a regular newsletter, and maintains a multilevel website (www.mcb.org.uk). Its primary aims are to change negative public images and attitudes toward Muslims and to campaign for an end to the myriad forms of religious discrimination that characterize the notion of Islamophobia.

To what does Islamophobia in Britain refer, then, and how do various organizations such as MCB propose to combat it?

Islamophobia

In the mid-1980s, certain confrontational statements about the accommodation of minorities in British state schools were made in a right-wing journal by Ray Honeyford, headteacher of a Bradford school. This stimulated much public debate over the place of minorities in British society, strategies of assimilation or cultural pluralism, and whether an apparently racist headteacher should be in charge of a largely Asian/Muslim school.[11] Throughout the debate, Bradford Muslims held demonstrations calling for his removal. The case was important insofar as it raised consciousness and the will to voice concerns among Muslims in Britain (and particularly in Bradford[12]) about issues of stereotyping, discrimination, and treatment of Muslim needs within public institutions.

"The Honeyford affair" was soon surpassed in terms of public attention by "the Rushdie Affair."[13] Although it broke some time after the book was actually published, the "Affair" rapidly broadened and in a way eventually concretized the place of Muslims in the public sphere. The nature of media coverage surrounding the Rushdie Affair transformed the dominant view toward Muslims in Britain.[14] The book burning in Bradford on January 14, 1989 (orchestrated by Muslim groups as a media event, yet without much forethought as to its 1930s' Nazi allusion), was seized on by the press as evidence of an "uncivilized" and "intolerant" Muslim nature. The February 1989 *fatwa* of Ayatollah Khomeini, calling for the death of Salman Rushdie, was taken as further evidence of this intolerance, which was portrayed as a worldwide Muslim threat that had infested the body Britain. Little attention was ever given to the Muslims' own perceptions and feelings of offense and hurt beyond the public demonstrations. Media treatment of the Rushdie Affair, which did include some irresponsible and inflammatory statements by alleged "Muslim leaders," created or bolstered an image of a Muslim population that was homogeneous in its antimodern values and dangerous in its passions, posing a challenge both to nationalist ideologies of "Britishness"[15] and to liberal notions about freedom and human rights.[16]

Not long after the Rushdie Affair died down, the Gulf War again focused public attention on the British Muslim population. Because British Muslims were portrayed generally as somehow linked to a worldwide antiwestern, Islamic fundamentalist movement, their loyalty to the allied cause against Iraq was questioned.[17] Since then, newspapers have given considerable attention to a great variety of Muslim-related matters. These include education, and especially the battle for government funding of the Islamic school in Brent; various mosque disputes; and almost anything to do with the so-called Muslim Parliament, which was an unsuccessful attempt under the controversial leadership of Kalim Siddiqi in the mid-1990s to unite British Muslims after the Rushdie Affair.

The late 1980s and 1990s have also been characterized by public concerns, on an international scale, with an undefined global movement called "Islamic fundamentalism" characterized by terrorist methods, antiwestern rhetoric, and antimodern, antiliberal sentiments.[18] Essentialist notions of culture—by which all persons of a particular descent are considered to have the same social relationships, behaviors, and values—foster the view that there is such a thing as "the Muslim community." Further, this community must in essence be of the same nature as those "fundamentalists" seen in North Africa or the Middle East. So-called Muslim fundamentalists make political demands that pose a threat to western established social and philosophical order. Because British Muslims increasingly make political demands, "common sense" logic argues that they must pose a parallel, if not identical, fundamentalist threat. Yet, when one examines the kinds of demands made by British Muslim organizations and spokesmen, it is apparent that for the most part they are asking only for an exercise of liberal rights according to wholly British procedures and standards. But, because the demands are made by Muslims, tarred with the same brush as Middle East extremists, they are usually not seen that way.

Throughout the 1990s, this kind of logic has been fueled by national events like the Rushdie Affair, and international developments, including terrorist activities by political Islamicists such as the bombings of the U.S. embassies in Nairobi and Tanzania in 1998. There has been a noticeable increase in derogatory images of Islam, patterns of anti-Muslim discrimination in employment, institutional intolerance of Muslim values, and occasional acts of physical violence against Muslims in Britain. All this is cited both by the Muslim press and by left-leaning newspapers such as the *Guardian* as evidence of a growing "Islamophobia" in Britain.

In 1996 the Runnymede Trust, an independent charity concerned with research and social policy surrounding race and ethnicity, established the Commission on British Muslims and Islamophobia. The following year the Commission published its report, entitled *Islamophobia: A Challenge for Us All.*[19] The key functions of the Runnymede Commission, expressed in its report, were media analysis and extended interviews with a range of British Muslims regarding their experiences of discrimination. It justified the neologism Islamophobia on the grounds that "anti-Muslim prejudice has grown so considerably and so rapidly in recent years that a new item in the vocabulary is needed so that it can be identified and acted against." For the purposes of the Commission, "Islamophobia" refers to "unfounded hostility towards Islam," as well as to "the practical consequences of such hostility in unfair discrimination against Muslim individuals and communities, and to the exclusion of Muslims from mainstream political and social affairs."[20] The Runnymede report contains sixty recommendations that address numerous policy domains. It was launched in a public meeting with the Home Secretary, and 3,500 copies were distributed to metropolitan authorities, race equality councils, police forces, government departments, unions, professional associations, think tanks, and universities across Britain.

The Runnymede Commission describes various dimensions of anti-Muslim prejudice in Britain, relying especially on numerous statements and images that have appeared in recent years in the media. The Commission observes that certain "closed" views of Islam that generally support a "clash of civilizations" perspective pitting "us/the West" versus "them/Muslims" are widespread in Britain. These include false assumptions that Islam is monolithic and static, has little in common with values and practices of other (especially western) culture and thus is inferior to western culture, is violent, aggressive, undemocratic, and supportive of terrorism, and therefore represents an enemy. The report of the Runnymede Commission subsequently describes anti-Muslim prejudice in the media, aspects of Muslim exclusion in employment, politics, administration, and health, violence against Muslims in Britain, issues concerning Muslims and the education system, and the role and state of law concerning aspects of Islamophobia.

Among its sixty recommendations, the Commission proposes that various national and local institutions undertake the following: review equal opportunity policies and guidelines on good practice in employment, service delivery, and public consultation to ensure that these refer explicitly to religion, as well as to race and ethnicity; include religion in mechanisms of ethnic monitoring and ensure there is a question about religion in the 2001 census; review the procedures for the provision of state funding to religiously based schools; scrutinize measures and programs aimed at reducing poverty and inequality, with special reference to their impact on Muslim communities; urge all citizens to routinely report to the Press Complaints Commission when media coverage concerning Muslims is felt to be distorted; and urge the Press Complaints Commission itself to review its code of practice to strengthen statements about avoiding racial and religious discrimination.

By way of advocating greater recognition of British Muslims, the Runnymede Commission asks political parties to increase the likelihood that Muslim candidates will be selected for winnable seats and proposes the appointment of Muslims to the House of Lords. The key recommendation made by the Runnymede Commission, however, is for the introduction of some form of new legislation that recognizes violence and discrimination based on religion, alongside existing legislation that focuses on racial violence and discrimination. This reflects the campaigns of Muslims and others over many years for legislative remedies to Islamophobic discrimination and violence.

Among leading non-Muslim liberal intellectuals at the end of the 1980s and early 1990s, the main issue in the notorious Rushdie Affair was freedom of expression for authors, although this was often affirmed without reference to the responsibilities of the authors themselves. To British Muslims, the issue at stake was not freedom of expression but, really, blasphemy. They were concerned with the kinds of offenses that were included under the British law of blasphemy and, most important, which religions it covered and whether offenses to religious groups such as slander and incitement to hatred were similar to offenses relating to "race" and ethnicity. The rise of specifically anti-Muslim forms of racism has been particularly marked since the Rushdie Affair, which has led to calls for new or extended legislation.[21]

In Britain, Muslims-qua-Muslims are not protected from discrimination by law. An important ruling by the House of Lords in 1983 (*Mandla v. Dowell-Lee*, following a head teacher's refusal to allow a Sikh boy to wear a turban in school) established that Sikhs—and, by extension, Jews—are considered an ethnic group and therefore are protected by the 1976 Race Relations Act. However, the court in 1988 (*Nyazi v. Rymans Ltd.*, concerning the refusal of an employer to allow an employee time off to celebrate 'Eid al-Fitr) ruled that Muslims do not constitute such a group and therefore are not protected by the act, since their regional and linguistic origins are more diverse.

The implications of this 1988 ruling were evident in a 1991 case (*Commission for Racial Equality v. Precision Engineering Ltd.*) after an employer stated that he refused to employ Muslims because he considered them extremist. While his anti-Muslim sentiments were not brought into question by the court, the employer was found guilty of indirect discrimination against Asians since most British Muslims are of such descent. The same ruling was made in the 1996 case of *J. H. Walker Ltd. v. Hussain*, when an employer refused an employee leave of absence to celebrate a Muslim festival. There have also been unsuccessful claims by Muslim workers in Yorkshire mills, who have alleged that Muslims are treated worse than other employees in terms of assigned tasks, pay rate, and holiday benefits. Recently numerous incidents of discrimination have been highlighted by the Muslim press, which suggests that many employers (including, for instance, McDonald's) exhibit hostility toward Muslim women employees who refuse to remove their headscarves at work.

With the support of Muslim organizations and Muslim newspapers, the Commission for Racial Equality has advocated measures to redress the situation.[22] These include a call for legislators to consider enacting special laws (as in Northern Ireland) against religious discrimination and incitement to religious hatred, similar to existing laws that pertain to all of the United Kingdom with regard to racial discrimination and incitement to racial hatred. The CRE also sees the need for changes in law concerning blasphemy; at present, only Christianity is protected under such law. The CRE and others believe that either the blasphemy law should be extended to other faiths or that it should be abolished altogether. Many Muslims prefer the former option, since this, they say, would remove *The Satanic Verses* from British bookshops. In its Second Review of the Race Relations Act 1976, the Commission concluded that

> while the blasphemy law is concerned with certain forms of attacks on *religion* as such, a law of incitement to religious hatred is concerned with stirring up hatred against persons, identified by their religion. Arguments that freedom of speech should include the right to stir up hatred against persons inevitably seem limp, and the more so when this is done on grounds of religion, since the freedom to practise the religion of one's choice is itself recognised in international law. No country can be said to guarantee the freedom to practise the religion of one's choice if, at the same time, it permits others lawfully to stir up hatred against those doing just that.[23]

In July 1993, the United Kingdom Action Committee on Islamic Affairs (UKACIA) issued a memorandum entitled "Muslims and the Law in Multi-Faith Britain: Need for Reform," which it submitted to the secretary of state at the Home Office. The document called for legislation in three areas that affect Muslims. There is pressing need, it said, for laws concerning (a) vilification of religious beliefs and practices, as well as group defamation, (b) incitement to religious hatred, and (c) discrimination on religious grounds. Such legal frameworks would likely do much to protect Muslims from certain emergent forms of "anti-Islamic racism," although their effect on local, everyday spheres of social, economic, and political life would probably be minimal. In 1994 the then Conservative home secretary was unmoved by the submission, rejecting the call for extended legislation on grounds of "lack of hard evidence of discrimination against individuals on religious rather than racial grounds."

In 1994, the CRE, in an attempt to collect evidence of cases of religious discrimination, conducted a survey of 2,047 agencies such as Race Equality Councils, Law Centers, Citizens' Advice Bureaus, and individuals such as lawyers and academics. Response to the survey was low, and the CRE received specific information on only thirty-eight cases of alleged religious discrimination. It noted that this finding was unsurprising, given the lack of monitoring mechanisms regarding this topic.[24] In 1995 the CRE established a Project Group to develop work further in this area and eventually concluded that "the overwhelming majority of those who participated in the consultation believed there was a need for legislation outlawing religious discrimination."[25]

These issues have remained on the agenda of many concerned public bodies. Under the auspices of the Department of the Environment, Transport and Regions, in 1996 the Inner Cities' Religious Council published a statement, "Challenging Religious Discrimination: A Guide for Faith Communities and Their Advisors," which points to a number of policy areas surrounding religious discrimination and underlines relevant aspects of race relations legislation. In 1997, the CRE also issued a leaflet, *Religious Discrimination: Your Rights*, which calls to the attention of the public ways in which unfair treatment on the basis of religion can be redressed by way of existing legislation on grounds of indirect racial discrimination.

Once more in 1998, the extent of antidiscrimination law was probed. A High Court case involved a branch organizer of the British National Party who distributed "Rights for Whites" stickers and leaflets campaigning against Muslims and the conversion of an old dairy into a mosque. He was brought to court under section 23 of the Public Order Act and charged with possessing material that stirred racial hatred. The Queen's Council told the judge: "There has been a campaign in which offensive posters and stickers have been placed in and around the area of the mosque and in the civic centre. Muslims going to prayer at the mosque have been subject to verbal abuse and spat upon."[26] However, the Crown Prosecution Service concluded that, while the law was unclear, Muslims were a religious, rather than an ethnic, group and therefore not covered by the Race Relations Act or other race protection laws in the Public Order Act. One lawyer involved with the case concluded, "You're left with the absurd situation that you can be as rude as you wish against Muslims but you're not allowed to abuse Jews or Sikhs."

The change of government from Conservative to New Labor has been welcomed widely by campaign groups as a chance to increase awareness and action surrounding the plight of British Muslims. In 1998, a Religious Discrimination and Remedies bill was presented in Parliament that called for the outlawing of discrimination on grounds of religion and of incitement to religious hatred. John Austin, the Member of Parliament who introduced the bill, reiterated (1) that it is anomalous to have religious discrimination unlawful in one part of the United Kingdom (Northern Ireland) and not in another, (2) that employers are free to discriminate on grounds of religion but not race, and (3) that Jews and Sikhs are protected by law, but Hindus and Muslims are not.

In October 1999, however, despite arguments put forward by the new Muslim peers Lord Ahmed and Baroness Uddin, the call for an extension of the Race Relations Act to cover religious discrimination was rejected by Lord Bassam, Home Office minister in the House of Lords. Bassam, like the home secretary of the previous government, argued for yet more and clearer evidence that such anti-Muslim discrimination exists. He suggested that, when perpetrators attack Muslims, they do so not because of hostility to the tenets of Islam but for racist reasons. Bassam concluded that existing legislation is sufficient to protect Muslims and others from discrimination.

Despite this setback—or, rather, because of Bassam's reasoning—the Home Office has commissioned a research project at the University of Derby to survey the existing situation, look for evidence of religious discrimination, and suggest a range of possible policy responses. The Derby Project's Interim Report[27] first attempts to conceptually clarify a number of dimensions. Echoing the range of issues described in the report of the Runnymede Commission on Islamophobia, Derby's report includes distinctions between "religious prejudice" (stereotyping that leads to discriminatory behavior), "religious hatred" (attitudes that can result in intimidating and violent behavior), "religious disadvantage" (lack of access to a range of social institutions or lack of equal provision in public institutions), "direct religious discrimination" (deliberate exclusion from opportunities, employment, or services on grounds related to religious belief, identity, or practice), and "indirect religious discrimination" (exclusionary effects of decisions, structures, or patterns of behavior and organization that can unintentionally result in discrimination, such as nonrecognition of dietary requirements).

Reviewing the state of legal responses to questions of discrimination against Muslims and other religious minorities, the Derby Report suggests that court rulings of "indirect racial discrimination" are highly unsatisfactory, especially since they are made very inconsistently. Further, the Report points out that even where courts may uphold an aspect of religious identity or practice by way of reference to ethnicity, judges and tribunal panels may nonetheless be reluctant to proscribe legal protection if it is seen to inconvenience the majority. For example, the Report recounts:

> In *Ahmad v. Inner London Education Authority* the applicant, a teacher employed by the Authority, alleged that the Authority's refusal to allow him time off to pray amounted to constructive dismissal. In rejecting this on behalf of the Court of Appeal, Lord Denning argued that to give the Muslim community "preferential treatment over the great majority of the people" on the basis of a freedom to practice their religion would be counterproductive, provoking discontent "and even resentment" amongst Mr. Ahmad's colleagues.[28]

So, despite numerous campaigns and high-profile activities by prominent public bodies, there is considerable frustration among British Muslims (again, as described by organs such as *Muslim News* and *Q-News*) that most instances of everyday discrimination remain unchallenged. It would be highly misleading, however, to suggest that the Muslim presence in Britain has gone unrecognized and unsupported. Over the past ten years especially, quite the reverse has been the case.

Muslim Recognition

Well before the Rushdie Affair, Muslim communities in Britain had become increasingly organized and articulate in their calls (mainly on the local level) for the recognition of minority rights, fair treatment, and political representation in a variety of public arenas. Muslim mobilization has called for the broad acceptance and accommodation of practices, values, moralities, and legal systems quite different from long-standing British traditions. The struggle to achieve these accommodations has consolidated and galvanized many local Muslim groups, associations, and umbrella organizations.[29]

Over the years and in different cities, public accommodation of Muslim needs and concerns has included permission to establish facilities for ritual slaughtering of animals for food; to set aside areas of local cemeteries for Muslim use; to provide *halal* (permitted) meat in public institutions such as schools, hospitals, and prisons; to designate prayer facilities or time for prayer in the workplace and to allow time off for religious festivals; and to broadcast public *azan* or call to prayer from mosques over loudspeakers (though often at monitored decibel levels no louder than church bells).

Other accommodations also have been successfully campaigned for regarding Muslim concerns in the education system (issues described later). Now, particularly in cities with large Muslim populations, such matters are not only often permitted routinely, but Muslim organizations are regularly included in local government consultations about matters concerning community relations. In some cities, they have effectively linked to provide a common front in dealing with local and county authorities, for example the Bradford Council of Mosques and Leicester's Federation of Muslim Organizations.[30] It has been on this local level that Muslim political engagement has emerged most strongly. Nielsen observes that "the decade until 1988 had witnessed a major change in the way in which Muslim organizations took part in public life. They had previously been marginal and often timid; they had tended to implicitly present themselves as ethnic minorities as they sought to fit in through the community and race relations structures. By the end of the decade many had laid claim to participation in the public space; they had effectively integrated into the organizational politics of the local scene functioning like most other special interest groups, standing out only by the express Muslim identity."[31]

One reason for this shift is doubtless the greater familiarity with and confidence felt by Muslims in engaging with formal structures such as government agencies. Part of this familiarity and confidence came through the emergence of a younger generation of Muslim community activists and organizers who had been raised and educated in Britain. Another reason for the shift is likely linked to the changes in the late 1970s and early 1980s, with the expansion of local government funding of minority groups.[32]

The formal political route has been of increasing importance for British Muslims. Direct party political methods have not been successful. In 1991, for instance, the Islamic Party of Great Britain contested its first seat but did not receive much support. Although that situation has not changed much, Muslims do figure importantly in the strategies and concerns of mainstream political parties. Local politicians are always sure to meet with designated Muslim leaders who promise to deliver "the Muslim vote." It is the Labor Party that has traditionally received the bulk of Muslim support in Britain; this is particularly evident in the success of Muslim candidates for Labor in local government elections. In 1981 only three of Bradford's ninety councilors were Muslim; by 1992 there were eleven Muslim councilors, including the deputy leader of the ruling group. Bradford also boasted the country's first Asian, and Muslim, Lord Mayor in 1985–86. The city of Leicester has produced not only a number of Muslim councilors but also a Muslim chief executive, as well as a Muslim chief police superintendent. In June 1994, Waltham Forest produced the first Muslim woman to be elected mayor. Muslim representation in local government continued to expand considerably throughout the 1990s. At present there are some 150 Muslim councilors in local government across Britain.[33]

Nationally the Labor landslide in the election of 1997 brought with it the first Muslim Member of Parliament, Muhammad Sarwar, representing the seat of Glasgow Govan. Unfortunately, Sarwar was soon thereafter suspended, though eventually acquitted, following charges of electoral fraud. Soon after coming into government, Labor also appointed three Muslims as life peers in the House of Lords: Lord Ahmed, Baroness Uddin, and Lord Ally (although Ally is often not recognized by British Muslims as their representative because he is openly gay). This was represented in much of the press as evidence that the prime minister and his New Labor party were making significant public gestures to recognize Islam. Further, in February 1998 the prime minister gave a warm speech at the first annual function in the House of Commons for 'Id al-Fitr, an event also instituted to give more public recognition to the valued place of Muslims in Britain (although, demonstrating a still awkward relationship between official institutions and Muslims, ham sandwiches were served).

Ahmed, Uddin, and Ally joined an already existing Muslim hereditary peer, the eighth Earl of Yarborough, a Conservative who subsequently lost his right to sit in the House of Lords in a reorganization that meant the abolition of the right of most hereditary peers to sit and vote. The first British Muslim recently elected to the European Parliament comes from the Conservative Party. Other prominent public appointments of Muslims include a special police policy adviser on Muslim affairs and a Muslim deputy assistant commissioner of the Metropolitan Police. A new position of national Muslim prison adviser has also been created.

Public media have also developed a greater awareness of British Muslim concerns. During Ramadan, for instance, features regularly appear in the mainstream press such as the *Times* and the *Guardian* (the latter publishes a Ramadan timetable supplied by the Muslim Council of Britain) and in a special series of programs on BBC television. Realizing the media's potential for hardening Islamophobic attitudes, the BBC World Service has committed itself not to link the terms "extremist" or "terrorist" with Muslims or Islam. In 1999 the Broadcasting Standards Commission published a set of guidelines, "Religious Language and Imagery in a Multi-Cultural Society." Producers are urged to be aware how their words and representations might cause offense, especially to groups like Muslims, who are described as "inordinately sensitive at the way Islam is portrayed in English-speaking culture."

Media operated and controlled by Muslims have developed considerably in the past ten years. Key examples include monthly Muslim newspapers such as *Q-News* and *The Muslim News*. The latter often includes exclusive interviews with political figures, including the prime minister and ministers from the Home and Foreign Offices. Further, there are now at least fifteen "Ramadan radio" stations in places such as Birmingham, Bradford, Glasgow, Luton, and Manchester, granted licenses to broadcast for various periods of the day.

Schools and education have provided a focus of much Muslim mobilization over the past twenty years or so in Britain. Most concerns and actions have aimed to ensure that Muslim pupils need not act in ways, or participate in activities, contrary to their and their parents' religious beliefs and cultural traditions. Key areas of concern for Muslim parents include:

Preference for single-sex education, especially for girls

Modesty in dress and in physical education activities (such as swimming, showers, and changing rooms)—again, especially for girls. All schools in Britain have been sent guidelines by the Department for Education and Employment urging that schools be sensitive to making "arrangements for Muslim girls, who are required by their religion to dress modestly, providing they wear appropriate clothing in school colours." However, cases still regularly arise of schools at which Muslim girls are told to remove their *hijabs* (headscarves).

Prayer times and religious holidays in the school timetable and calendar

Halal food in school cafeterias

Sensitivity to the interests of parents in aspects of curriculum, including sex education, forms of art, dance and music, and religious education

Exemption from school fundraising activities involving lotteries and gambling

Recruitment of more staff members and governors of schools from minority/Muslim communities

Such concerns for establishing sensitivities, accommodations, and provisions concerning Islam in the educational systems have led Muslim organizations to call for state support for separate Islamic schools. In Britain there are already some 60 independently funded Muslim schools. Citing inequity, Muslim activists have pointed to long-standing state financial support for 30 Jewish schools, 28 Methodist schools, and 2,160 Roman Catholic schools. Over the past fifteen years or so, advocates have insisted that the state should demonstrate equal treatment for Muslims and their schools. The case of the Islamia School in Brent, west London, has provided the litmus test for this campaign. Islamia's well-publicized requests for state financial support, made especially by Yusuf Islam (formerly the pop singer Cat Stevens), were repeatedly refused by the Conservative government throughout the late 1980s and 1990s. Finally, in 1997, the Labor government approved state funding for Islamia and another Muslim school in Birmingham (along with two Sikh schools, a Seventh-Day Adventist school, and a Greek Orthodox school).

Many other areas of concern for recognition and public accommodation of specific practices, values, and traditional institutions have been voiced or defended following some form of public condemnation in Muslim communities in Britain. In recent years, cases have arisen in which these issues were debated in court, in Parliament, in local government, or in the media.[34] These cases have dealt with the following kinds of concerns:

Polygamy, practiced by some Muslim communities. Polygamous marriages are, on the whole, banned for persons domiciled in Britain.

Talaq, a form of Islamic divorce initiated by men. The call for acceptance of this in British law is still highly contested.

A wide range of forms of arranged marriage practiced by a variety of South Asian communities. These are generally accepted in the eyes of British authorities, unless considerable coercion (on occasion evidenced by kidnapping or deceit) is demonstrated.

Marriages within various degrees of relationship—for instance, among first cousins. This is widely practiced among Pakistani Muslim families in Britain.

Time off work for religious purposes (such as going to mosques for Friday prayer) or appropriate prayer facilities in the workplace. Some employers are addressing such demands; in factories with large numbers of Muslims, prayer facilities are often allocated. The CRE has been approached on several occasions where discrimination is suspected in cases of refusal of demands in this area.

Beards: since meetings with MCB representatives, the Ministry of Defense allows Muslim military personnel to wear trimmed beards.

Chaplaincy in prisons and hospitals. Following consultations with Muslim representatives, the Prison Service and the National Health Service have drawn up guidelines surrounding the provision of Imams in these institutions.

Provision of *halal* (sanctioned) food in public institutions such as prisons, hospitals, and schools.

Islamic ritual slaughter (*dhabh*), which is abhorred by many non-Muslims since it is often interpreted as prescribing that the animal remain conscious when its throat is slit. The most vocal opponents of *halal* food provisions and *dhabh* emerged as the unlikely pairing of animal rights activists, who were against the method of slaughter, and right-wing nationalists, who were against accommodating seemingly alien customs of minorities. According to the terms of the Slaughter of Poultry Act of 1967 and the Slaughterhouses Act of 1979, Jews and Muslims may slaughter poultry and animals in abattoirs according to their traditional methods. The right to engage in ritual slaughter in inspected abattoirs was maintained, largely through the political lobbying of Jewish, rather than Muslim, groups.

Matters surrounding burial, such as gaining designated areas of public cemeteries for specific religious communities, obtaining permission for burial in a cloth shroud instead of a coffin, and urging issuance of death certificates for burial within twenty-four hours (MCB has held consultations with the Coroner's Office and the Association of Local Authorities regarding these matters).

Taking oaths on scriptures. Under the Oaths Act of 1978, Muslims may swear on the Qur'an (although, when Lord Ahmed requested a Qur'an as he was sworn into the House of Lords in 1998, nobody could find one).

Altering work and school uniform codes to allow Muslim women to wear traditional forms of dress, especially headscarves (this is still one of the most contested issues among Muslims. Almost every issue of the monthly *Muslim News* highlights cases of discrimination, especially among employers, against Muslim women wearing *hijab*).

Beyond mere accommodation of practices, values, and traditional institutions, however, many members of Muslim communities have called for explicit legal measures to protect their rights and to help safeguard against discrimination. Each effort in mobilizing and lobbying—whether successful, unsuccessful, or still in process—has brought new experience and, thereby, new confidence in Muslim organizational efforts. In recent years, this, in turn, has encouraged activity concerning access to resources and social service provision. Examples of such activity can be seen in applications by Muslim women's groups seeking public funding for education and community activities, the rise of Muslim housing associations and employment advice centers, and calls by Muslims for special promotion of health awareness campaigns and programs and the provision of suitable hospital facilities.

In these ways, the local and national mobilization of British Muslims has developed by way of voicing a range of values and concerns. Many significant institutional accommodations and modes of public recognition have been achieved. Such successes in affecting a number of policy domains and gaining a hold in public space have come about over the past ten to twenty years—at the same time as the purported growth in Islamophobia.

Some observers argue that Islamophobia in Britain has not actually increased in the past decade but that, instead, we have merely witnessed a growing public scrutiny of it. This is akin to the argument that racist crimes have not actually increased over the years; rather, there has been simply more vigilant monitoring of them. There is likely some truth to this view, but it obscures other processes arguably under way.

It is possible to interpret the rise in Islamophobia in Britain alongside advances in Muslim recognition through a kind of linked or circular operation. In one process, as a result of the increased vilification of Islam in the media and discrimination against Muslims in everyday spheres (both fueled by assumed connections between British Muslims and international Islamic extremism), a variety of countermeasures—including changes to legislation, various institutional guidelines, and public policy adjustments— have been advocated by Muslim groups, Muslim media, and public bodies composed of Muslims and concerned others such as interfaith groups and antiracists.

In a kind of reactionary process, anti-Muslim sentiments have swelled as part of a greater xenophobia, as many white non-Muslims in Britain object to changes in "their" schools, public policies, and social services that have been made in order to accommo-date the perceived inferior ways of "outsiders." As Islamophobia further increases, so does the now well-mobilized call for even more far-reaching forms of recognition. As the public sphere shifts to provide a more prominent place for Muslims, Islamophobic tendencies may amplify.

While "recognition" carries varying informal and formal/legal meanings in different national contexts, it generally implies a provision of equal and positive public place for the unique identities, interests, and needs of specific groups.[35] In one sense, recogni-tion refers to the granting of certain freedoms or minority rights, including freedom to organize, to exercise certain religious practices, and to pursue education independently. It may also refer to the ability to gain access to public resources for associations, cultural centers, and places of worship. Recognition also refers to access to institutional mecha-nisms of direct representation, in the sense of empowering individuals to voice collec-tive interests with respect to different policy domains, including directly elected politi-cians, appointed members on sitting bodies, and participants in consultative forums.[36]

In yet another sense, following the seminal argument of Charles Taylor,[37] recogni-tion may mean redressing serious forms of discrimination and inequality that arise from prior *withholding* of recognition of certain minority groups. Further, their misrepresen-tation or false depiction can be a form of oppression. This certainly applies to British Muslims, for whom frequent maligning of image has contributed to forms of discrimi-nation and even violence directed against them. As a kind of corrective, Nancy Fraser proposes a different way to characterize recognition, namely as "upwardly revaluing disrespected identities and the cultural products of maligned groups" with the specific aim of "positively valorizing" them.[38]

Therefore, public recognition by way of (a) securing legitimate rights to be different, (b) giving representative status in decision-making institutions, and (c) promoting a readjusted public image can be seen as key ways of seeking at least to remedy past or ongoing patterns of injustice. The circular process involving the accommodation of Muslim interests and the rise of reactionary Islamophobic attitudes can and should be broken once Muslims and Islam have gained the public standing—in terms of rights, representation, and image—that is due any such group of citizens.

Notes

1. See, for example, Colin Clarke, Ceri Peach, and Steven Vertovec, eds., *South Asians Overseas: Migration and Ethnicity* (Cambridge: Cambridge University Press, 1990); Kim Knott, "Bound to Change? The Religions of South Asians in Britain," in *Aspects of the South Asian*

Diaspora, ed. Steven Vertovec (Delhi: Oxford University Press, 1991), 86–111; Gerald Parsons, ed., *The Growth of Religious Diversity: Britain from 1945*, 2 vols. (London: Routledge, 1993–1994); Steven Vertovec and Ceri Peach, "Introduction: Islam in Europe and the Politics of Religion and Community," in *Islam in Europe: The Politics of Religion and Community*, ed. Vertovec and Peach (Basingstoke: Macmillan, 1997), 1–29.

2. Jørgen S. Nielsen, *Muslims in Western Europe* (Edinburgh: Edinburgh University Press, 1992).

3. Paul Weller, ed., *Religions in the UK: A Multi-Faith Directory* (Derby: University of Derby, 1997).

4. Ceri Peach, ed., *Ethnicity in the 1991 Census, vol. 2: The Ethnic Minority Populations of Great Britain* (London: Office for National Statistics/HMSO, 1996).

5. Twenty-eight percent are Hindus, mainly Gujaritis, 21 percent Sikhs, and 6 percemt Christians.

6. Weller, ed., *Religions in the UK*; Ceri Peach, "The Cultural Landscape of South Asian Religion in English Cities" (seminar paper given at School of Geography, University of Oxford, 2000).

7. Ceri Peach, "The Muslim Population of Great Britain," in *Ethnic and Racial Studies* 13 (1990): 414–19; Nielsen, *Muslims in Western Europe*.

8. See Weller, ed., *Religions in the UK*.

9. Francis Robinson, "Varieties of South Asian Islam" (Coventry: Centre for Research in Ethnic Relations, University of Warwick, *Research Paper* No. 8); Nielsen, *Muslims in Western Europe*; Phillip Lewis, *Islamic Britain: Religion, Politics and Identity among British Muslims* (London: Taurus, 1994).

10. Jørgen S. Nielsen, "Muslims in Britain and Local Authority Responses," in *The New Islamic Presence in Western Europe*, ed. Thomas Gerholm and Yngve G. Lithman (London: Mansell, 1988), 53–77; Nielsen, *Muslims in Western Europe*; Jean Ellis, *Meeting Community Needs: A Study of Muslim Communities in Coventry* (Coventry: Centre for Research in Ethnic Relations, University of Warwick, Monographs in Ethnic Relations, No. 2); Lewis, *Islamic Britain*; Philip Lewis, "The Bradford Council of Mosques and the Search for Muslim Unity," in *Islam in Europe: The Politics of Religion and Community*, ed. Steven Vertovec and Ceri Peach (Basingstoke: Macmillan, 1997), 103–27.

11. Michael Halstead, *Education, Justice and Cultural Diversity: An Examination of the Honeyford Affair 1984–1985* (London: Falmer Press, 1988).

12. Lewis, *Islamic Britain*.

13. Lisa Appignanesi and Sara Maitland, *The Rushdie File* (London: Fourth Estate, 1989); Malise Ruthven, *A Satanic Affair: Salman Rushdie and the Wrath of Islam* (London: Hogarth Press, 1990); Lewis, *Islamic Britain* and "Bradford Council"; Vertovec and Peach, "Introduction."

14. Bhikhu Parekh, "The Rushdie Affair and the British Press: Some Salutary Lessons," in *Free Speech—Report of a Seminar* (London: CRE and the Policy Studies Institute, Discussion Papers 2 1990), 59–78.

15. Talal Asad, "Multiculturalism and British Identity in the Wake of the Rushdie Affair," *Politics and Society* 18 (1990): 455–80.

16. Tariq Modood, "British Asian Muslims and the Rushdie Affair," *Political Quarterly* 61 (1990): 143–60.

17. Saeedea Khanum, "War Talk," *New Statesman & Society* (1 Feb. 1991): 12–13.

18. John Esposito, *The Islamic Threat: Myth or Reality?* (Oxford: Oxford University Press, 1992); Fred Halliday, *Islam and the Myth of Confrontation: Religion and Politics in the Middle East* (London: Taurus, 1996).

19. Runnymede Trust Commission on British Muslims and Islamophobia, *Islamophobia: A Challenge for Us All* (London: Runnymede Trust, 1997).

20. Ibid., 1.

21. See Commission for Racial Equality (CRE), *Law, Blasphemy and the Multi-Faith Society–Report of a Seminar* (London: CRE and the Policy Studies Institute, Discussion Papers 1, 1989); CRE, *Britain: A Plural Society*, London: CRE and the Runnymede Trust, Discussion Papers 2, 1990a; CRE, *Free Speech–Report of a Seminar* (London: CRE and the Policy Studies Institute, Discussion Papers 2, 1990b).

22. Commission for Racial Equality, *Second Review of the Race Relations Act of 1976* (London: CRE, 1992).

23. Ibid., 60, emphasis in original.

24. University of Derby, Religious Resource and Research Centre (2000), *Research Project on Religious Discrimination: An Interim Report* (London: Home Office, 2000).

25. Ibid., 41.

26. *Guardian*, 28 Oct. 1998.

27. University of Derby, *Research Project on Religious Discrimination*.

28. Ibid., 21.

29. Nielsen, "Muslims in Britain and Local Authority Responses"; Steven Vertovec, "Multicultural, Multi-Asian, Multi-Muslim Leicester: Dimensions of Social Complexity, Ethnic Organisation and Local Government Interface," in *Innovation* 7, no. 3 (1994): 259–76; Steven Vertovec, "Muslims, the State and the Public Sphere in Britain," in *Muslim Communities in the New Europe*, ed. Gerd Nonneman, Tim Niblock, and Bogdan Sjazkowski (London: Ithaca Press), 167–86; Vertovec and Peach, "Introduction."

30. Lewis, *Islamic Britain*; Vertovec, "Multicultural, Multi-Asian, Multi-Muslim Leicester."

31. Nielsen, *Muslims in Western Europe*.

32. Iris Kalka, "Striking a Bargain: Political Radicalism in a Middle-Class London Borough," in *Black and Ethnic Leadership in Britain*, ed. P. Werbner and M. Anwar (London: Routledge), 203–25.

33. Muhammad Anwar, personal communication.

34. Raymond Charlton and Ronald Kaye, "The Politics of Religious Slaughter: An Ethno-Religious Case Study," *New Community* 12 (1985): 490–503; Nielsen, "Muslims in Britain and Local Authority Responses"; Bhikhu Parekh, "British Citizenship and Cultural Difference," in *Citizenship*, ed. G. Andrews (London: Lawrence & Wishart, 1991), 183–204; Bhikhu Parekh, "Equality, Fairness and Limits of Diversity," *Innovation* 7, no. 3 (1994): 289–308; David Pearl, "South Asian Communities and English Family Law, 1971–1987," *New Community* 14 (1987): 161–69; Sebastian Poulter, *Asian Tradition and the English Law* (London: Trentham Books, 1990); Vertovec and Peach, "Introduction."

35. See Jan Rath, Kees Groenendijk, and Rinus Pennix, "The Recognition and Institutionalization of Islam in Belgium, Great Britain and the Netherlands," *New Community* 18 (1991): 101–14; Parekh, "Equality, Fairness and Limits of Diversity"; Vertovec and Peach, "Introduction"; Steven Vertovec, "Introduction," in *Migration and Social Cohesion*, ed. Steven Vertovec (Cheltenham: Edward Elgar, 1999a), 1–44.

36. Steven Vertovec, "Minority Associations, Networks and Public Policies: Re-assessing Relationships," *Journal for Ethnic and Migration Studies* 25, no. 1 (1999b): 21–42.

37. Charles Taylor, *Multiculturalism and "The Politics of Recognition"* (Princeton: Princeton University Press, 1992).

38. Nancy Fraser, "From Redistribution to Recognition? Dilemmas of Justice in a 'Post-Socialist' Age," *New Left Review* 212 (1995): 68–93.

2

Islam in France: The Shaping of a Religious Minority

Jocelyne Cesari

Islam is now commonly considered to be the second largest religion in France behind Christianity. Accepting this demographic reality has never been easy for many French citizens. Too often discussions about Islam in France begin and end with a treatment of Muslims as a social problem. Too often the question is asked: Can Muslims fit into French society? That question presupposes that Islamic values are inherently incompatible with western ones and that Muslims constitute a "dangerous class."

The West has stereotyped Islam as a strange religion, completely different from Christianity or Judaism, even though it is now firmly established within most western countries. Western perceptions are still based upon "essentialized" images of a violent and changeless Islam, holdovers from the colonial past. Though inaccurate, they still provide the basis for western understandings of those situations that involve Muslims. Samuel Huntington, for example, still posits a static vision of Islamic civilization and a unique Muslim psyche that compels conformity to Islamic law in all places at all times—as though Muslims were a species unto themselves. His theoretical work *Clash of Civilizations*[1] illustrates how easily such misperception leads to visions of Islam as the new threat in a postcold war world. Thinking along the same lines that Huntington has articulated, westerners generally attribute to Muslims in their midst the same potential for violence that has occurred in areas of major Muslim unrest. Events like the Salman Rushdie Affair and the Gulf War, along with claims that Islam opposes modernity and secularism, serve only to reinforce distrust of Islam.

The French Version of the Clash of Civilizations

The widespread misconception of Islam has its own particular version in France, where fears of a growing Muslim visibility have, since the 1980s, unleashed French passions, especially in the form of racist murders in suburban housing projects. Currently there are approximately four million Muslims in France, half of whom are French citizens. Although they come in significant numbers from various Muslim countries like Turkey and Senegal, the vast majority have arrived from North Africa. These North Africans, although less culturally distinctive than some of their coreligionists, pose the greatest of challenges to the French tradition of assimilation. Their difficulties with their compatriots derive from troubled French memories of colonialism in North Africa, during which period Muslims were not deemed citizens unless they first renounced Islamic law, even though they had already been granted French nationality (Algeria was a French department). As a result, many French people, struggling with contradictory feelings of superiority and humiliation, anguish over the settlement of Muslims in France since the Algerian War of Independence. How ironic! History is repeating itself on the "upper" side of the Mediterranean with a twist: the same people who, as a ruling minority, once sought to constrain an Algerian majority on North African soil now finds itself, as a governing majority, trying to assimilate an Algerian minority on its own French ground.

Rancor toward Islam runs yet higher because its arrival inflames old passions that have long simmered beneath the surface of "*laïcité*." *Laïcité* refers to the uneasy compromise that French people have made between the letter of the law of separation of state and church and its peculiar implementation within French culture. Quite paradoxically, when passed in 1905, the law's primary intention was not to champion religious freedom per se in France. Rather, it was to weaken Catholic influence by putting Catholicism on an equal footing with religious minorities within the public domain. Practically speaking, conformity to the law meant confining religious belief to the private sphere. Ideally speaking, conformity meant and still means extirpating homage to religious values from all spheres: personal, familial, social, cultural, and political. Through the decades, major religious groups—Christian and Jewish—have made uneasy peace with *laïcité* by relegating religious expression to private domains. Muslim settlement in France has disrupted that peace. It has introduced new confusion over boundaries between public and private space and led to renewed controversy over religious freedom and political tolerance. The "Islamic headscarf" affair of 1989 is the example par excellence of such controversy. It entangled one Muslim girl who wore her *hijab* to school in a legal crusade that sought to liberalize interpretations of *laïcité* by asserting her right to display a religious symbol in public. Since 1989, that crusade has repeatedly gained from the Council of State reaffirmation that the public display of a religious symbol—*whatever it is*—does not break the law. Each reaffirmation has highlighted the shallowness of French religious tolerance and inflamed animosity toward those Muslim newcomers who would edify a people that prides itself on equality, fraternity, and liberty.

Misunderstanding of the display of religious symbols further increases French animosity toward Islam. The most conspicuous displays are blindly interpreted as evidence of renewed religious fervor. When, in the early 1980s, immigrants built mosques, opened *halal* butcher shops, and claimed land for Muslim sections in cemeteries, the majority of the French people, scholars included, feared for a "return of Islam." In actuality, the Muslims in question were not becoming more observant. Having resolved upon permanent residence in France, they were simply changing their attitude in favor of greater participation in French society. Indeed, their earlier migrations were considered temporary by both French and North African political authorities, as well as by the migrants themselves. They, the migrants, wanted only to save money to invest upon return home. They were never interested in becoming citizens of the nation that had colonized their country. Only after the early 1980s did they determine that return home was impossible; only then did they begin regarding themselves as a part of French society, carving out within it their niche.

Failing to recognize cultural and social differences among Muslims, many French people have been misled by the coincidence of local increases in Islamic visibility and the rise of political Islam within the Arab and Muslim world. In their confusion, they wrongly associate peaceful French Islam with the wider movement of Islamic fundamentalism. They overlook transformations in Islamic identity occurring among Muslims who are born and/or educated in France. These are "new Muslims" who relate to Islam in remarkably modern terms—who are secularizing Islam, much the way their Christian peers have secularized Christianity. For them, Islam constitutes a cultural or ethical frame of reference, fairly detached from ritualistic practice.

Whether disinterested academic researcher or concerned French citizen, once one sidesteps misconceptions about Islam, one faces a single basic question: When and on what terms should followers of Islam be definitively accepted as a legitimate religious minority within France? That question cannot be approached simplistically, as though Muslims constitute a single homogenous group. Muslims in France show extreme social and cultural heterogeneity. They identify differently with Islam according to their national origin, age, gender, and social background. Nor can change within Muslim groups be understood independent of changes occurring within France itself. Dramatic forces at work upon French society may, in some cases, actually influence the Muslim community more than its own internal dynamics. Muslims are not, for example, immune to legal and political allegations that they have disrupted the cultural status quo. Such charges force them to develop secular resources for an ideological battle in the courts, the schools, the press, and the streets that distract them from their own religious priorities. Hence, the rise of Islam in France and, more broadly speaking, within the democratic context, might be better understood as a consequence of Muslims' self-perception as a religious minority within a plural society, rather than as the outcome of international fundamentalist influences. To their newly perceived status as religious minority, Muslims have demonstrated three major responses that may be characterized as follows: ethnic, secularized, and fundamentalist.

When Islam Is Embedded in Ethnicity

For first-generation North African immigrants in France, religious identity and national identity have become one and the same. Algerians, for example, who have settled in France not only conceive of themselves as Muslims who practice according to Algerian custom. They also reaffirm whatever particular meaning Islam has accrued in the course of Algerian history. Thus, generally speaking, no first-generation North African immigrant can contemplate his religion without remembering a painful time when preservation of Islam played a crucial role in his nation's struggle against French domination. No wonder these North Africans were so slow to acknowledge the permanence of their resettlement in the land of their former oppressor. Instead, they postponed, in so many cases, reunion on French soil with family they had left.[2] For the same reason, they were reluctant to acquire French nationality, viewing that acquisition as a betrayal of their nation's prior struggle against colonialism. Even today, elder North African Muslims entertain hopes of returning permanently to their homelands, even though their rare attempts to do so have generally failed. Their ongoing adherence to Islam is still one of their primary bulwarks against assimilation. It is made all the easier by the thoroughness with which Islam pervades daily life, demanding continuous distinction between *haram* (forbidden) and *halal* (permitted), whether through, for example, dietary rules, separation between men and women in public spaces, or the establishment of mosques.

Because religious identity is so closely tied to national identity for North Africans, ethnic differences set Muslim communities apart from and at odds with one another. Thus, Muslim fragmentation along ethnic lines stands as the major obstacle to Muslims' unification into a single coherent religious minority in France.[3] Mosques, which should exclusively be emblematic sites of religious unity, function equally as ethnically oriented centers that provide social and financial assistance, education of children, and ethnic and national linkages back to countries of origin. As a result, separate mosques stand within the same neighborhood for North Africans and Turks, among others, even though neither ritualistic nor religious differences distinguish them. Once one recognizes the toll that fragmentation exacts upon the Islamic community, one must ask: How can religious unity be achieved without sacrificing ethnic diversity and the cultural richness that accompanies it? That question takes on crucial political importance the moment that representative institutions become necessary both to satisfy religious needs and to safeguard civil rights.

Islam as a Political Issue

Despite lack of any original intent to organize themselves into a unified community, Muslims were actually taking a first step toward collective organization in France when they set up places of prayer (*masjids*). Later came demands for recognizable mosques that would symbolize the definitive presence of Islam in French society. As of now, only five mosques stand—those in Paris, Mantes-la-Jolie, Evry, Lille, and Lyon—for more than four million Muslims, because efforts to build additional structures have aroused such fierce resistance. Petitions for construction were routinely ignored or refused by town mayors. Civil rights were even denied. In 1989, in Charvieu-Chavagneux, the municipality knocked down a building without consideration for the Muslim prayer room located within; in 1990, in Libercourt, the mayor called for a local referendum on the construction of a mosque in clear violation of French law, which forbids local votes on religious matters.

The political attitude toward Islam in France is, however, gradually moving away from hostility for two major reasons. First, the peaceful operation of the major mosques built during the past decade has defused fears in the political arena that such meeting places pose threats to public order. Politicians and sometimes the citizenry are ready to accept these mosques as part of the French landscape. The home minister himself played a prominent role in opening ceremonies in 1994 for the new mosque of Lyon. Moreover, the efforts of astute mosque leaders to foster communication and understanding are paying off. Free meals for the poor during the month of Ramadan and conferences and debates involving intellectuals, journalists, and politicians—to cite two examples—have opened mosques to the non-Muslim world. It is no wonder that the committee board of Lyon and mosque leaders in other cities, such as Evry and Lille, are now recognized in local political negotiations.

Second, panic over the imagined rise of homegrown Muslim extremism has convinced politicians and bureaucrats of a need to improve rapport with their nation's Muslim population. After the headscarf affair of 1989, which alerted the politicians to the grow-ing appeal of Islam to French-born Muslim youth, came the death of Khaled Kelkal in 1995. This young, French-born citizen of Algerian extraction was pursued and killed by police for his suspected part in a terrorist bombing campaign in Paris. His death raised the specter of alienated Muslim youth in rundown suburbs, turning to violent Islamist groups that result in a rebel subculture. Caught up in the swell of public fear, politi-cians have been pursuing their new policy guidelines and improved relationships with Islamic leaders in the hopes that France will maintain the political loyalty of its young Muslims.

Moreover, now that authorities have set aside their ideological objections to accept-ing Islam, they recognize the practical need for new Islamic institutions. As Islam takes root in French soil, its institutional requirements increase. The same Muslims who used to view themselves as "sojourners" within an alien society cannot, in what is now their new homeland, justify compromising religious practice out of pragmatic necessity. Be-yond mosque construction, communal activities such as distribution of *halal* meat and allocation of Muslim sections within local cemeteries required that they deal with French authorities. With Islam, institutionally speaking, in infancy—that is, lacking a civil au-thority at the national level—the French government has found itself awaiting the emer-gence of a unified Muslim organization. Recognizing this power vacuum, North African states exploited their historical ties to France and strove for influence over Franco-Muslims for their own political gain. For decades, their efforts were supported by successive French governments, who viewed their influence as a safeguard against radical Islam.[4] Now that the Muslim community is becoming recognized as a bona fide component within French society, official attitudes have changed. Authorities resent activism by North African states as interfering in French domestic affairs and construe it as counterpro-ductive to any effective organization of the Muslim community. In their own move to-ward greater activism, the French government created the Council of Reflection on Islam in France (CORIF) in 1990. This council, which met under the supervision of the home minister, gathered leaders from major Islamic associations all over France, including the French Federation of French Muslims (Fédération Française des Musulmans de France) and the Federation of Islamic Associations from Africa, Comorros, and the West Indies (Fédération des Associations Islamiques d'Afrique, des Comores et des Antilles), as well as lesser-known Turkish associations. Because ethnic differences have predis-posed many Muslim leaders, loosely speaking, to confuse defense of ethnic solidarity with defense of Islam, council representatives fell victim to infighting on nonreligious grounds. As a result, the council was permanently suspended, even though it has never been officially dissolved. The resolve of the French government, however, to curb North African hegemony over Franco-Muslims remains stronger than ever.

In December 1999, Minister of Interior Jean-Pierre Chevenement decided to begin a new attempt to organize French Islam. But, prior to any consultation process or project, the major Muslim associations, mosques, and religious authorities have been required by the minister to sign a declaration that is a kind of reminder of obligations and rights of Muslim according to the Constitution and the 1905 Law of Separation of Church and State. This initiative has been unanimously criticized by the main leaders of the community as suspect of the civic loyalty of Muslims and therefore a humiliation to them.

The Privatization of Islam

Within the academy, an initial total disregard for Islam has given way to a misunderstanding that resonates with the xenophobic distrust that has pervaded French society as a whole. Remarkable as it now seems, sociologists during the 1960s and 1970s actually studied North African immigration without even acknowledging the Muslim heritage of the immigrants concerned.[5] Having finally taken notice, these sociologists and their colleagues in political science[6] have misconstrued the increasing visibility of Muslims and their institutions as a sign that Islam is a phenomenon unto itself, impervious to those powerful secularizing[7] forces that have been shaping French life for generations. Few voices have been heard to the contrary, affirming that Muslims are—like everybody else—subject to the laws that characterize sociopolitical change.[8] Few voices[9] have stated that the traditional Islamic devotion of parents is giving way to ever more individualized[10] and privatized[11] expressions of religiosity by their children.

For Muslim immigrants, settlement in France has essentially meant exilic isolation from natural modes of transmission that has resulted in a cultural gap between parents and children. That gap is more pronounced for North Africans than for any other migrant group in France.[12] Limited in means as members of the French working class, these parents have lost crucial battles against dominant French educational, cultural, and social institutions in their struggle to inculcate the cultural values of their home countries. Most notable among their defeats has been abandonment of the Arabic language, in response to which a "vernacular" Islam (not only in France but also in Europe) has arisen, whose sermons, literature, and public presentations are conveyed in various languages. Indeed, second-generation North African Muslims have usually received precious little religious education either within or outside the family. At home, they were exposed to minimal Islamic observance by parents who, thinking themselves to be only temporary residents within France, compromised and neglected Islamic prescriptions. Nor did any Qur'anic schools exist when these twenty-five- to thirty-five-year-olds were growing up. (The situation is different now because those Islamic associations that emerged in the 1980s have developed numerous programs of Qur'an study.) Last but not least, exile has broken the collective chain of transmission within rural North African communities, where religious instruction is provided by the extended family, as well as the parents.

As it is true for a majority of French people of Christian background, many young Muslims are now relating to Islam as "consumers." They are choosing which rules and tenets of their religion to embrace and which to dismiss. Their freedom to choose continually provokes questions of purpose; they demand personal meaning as a prerequisite to religious observance. On a philosophical level, they search within Islam—especially with better education and greater upward mobility—for ethical and moral values to guide the course of their lives. Drawing a distinction between those who merely believe and those whose belief leads to practice, they have broadened the term "believer." For them, it includes those who, like themselves, acknowledge the legitimacy of Islamic rules and values without observing. This redefinition of believer allows them to remain a bona fide part of their parents' community. It facilitates their participation in Islamic holidays, feasts, and commemorations of life-cycle events, such as births, marriages, and deaths, without feelings of shame, guilt, or conflict. Exactly as they have done for themselves, they permit their children—that is, France's third Muslim generation—the right to decide their own level of observance.

Individualization of Islam, however, does not proceed without limits. It remains constrained by two traditional factors, namely the practice of circumcision and the prohibition against intermarriage for females. In the first case: even though not included among the "five pillars of Islam," the circumcision of children endures even for the most assimilated of Muslims as an ultimate connection to their Islamic origins. In the second case: because Islamic law assigns name and religion to children on the basis of patrilineal descent, women who marry non-Muslims do more than violate Islamic law. They dishonor their families, set themselves up for crises of personal identity, and cut their children off from family, community, and origin. Therefore, Muslim women who achieve personal autonomy through professional advancement are more likely to choose discreet sexual relationship and cohabitation with non-Muslim men than civil marriage.[13]

Islam as a Social Movement

To the surprise of many French sociologists of religion who once considered secularization to be the inevitable outcome of individual choice, a number of young Franco-Muslims are choosing strict religious observance, rather than wholesale abandonment of Muslim attachments, as an expression of personal autonomy. Although their involvement with Islam is a very recent phenomenon and they still constitute a fairly small minority, their numbers are growing. Their practice of Islam, however, does not simply represent a spiritual return to the religion of their fathers. Preferring to distance themselves from parental practices that seem more superstitious than informed, they pursue what they call the "real Islam." Sometimes they undertake study on their own; in other cases they appeal for help and instruction to intellectuals and students from Arab countries, many of whom are members of the Muslim Brotherhood, such as the Mouvement Islamique Tunisien (MIT) of Rached Ghannouchi in Tunisia or the Algerian Islamist movements. (Despite their political activism in their own countries, these intellectuals and students tend not to use Islam as a means of political propagandizing among young Muslims in France. Rather, their main concern is preservation of Islam among new generations who might otherwise be assimilated into western culture.) Some of these newly religious young adults are finding in Islam a credible alternative to marginalized lives, resulting from unemployment, drugs, alcohol, and delinquency. Others, who question the value of progress and modernity, especially among the educated and successful, are discovering a sense of belonging they cannot achieve within a society whose schools, political parties, trade unions, and professions have failed to provide a collective sense of common good.

Besides those who return to Islam as a religious devotion exist others whose Islamization represents a sublime exercise of personal choice such as their parents could never in their wildest dreams have contemplated. Through a collective identification that can stand minimally supported by practice, these young Muslims are choosing to validate and support a heritage whose practices they may not realize through their own daily conduct. They logically enough invoke their Islam in protest against those undesirable social conditions that have been exacerbated by postcolonial discrimination. For them, it is the most promising of options, following the failure of collective actions that included the civil rights and antiracist movements of the 1980s,[14] such as the "Beur" movement.[15] Their Islamic involvement enables them to work in the secular domain for social change through associations that emphasize education as a major vehicle of religious, as well as personal, growth.[16] Hence, they open neighborhood meeting places, rather than mosques, where they provide tutoring and cultural enrichment to school-age children, encouragement toward voter registration for disenfranchised young adults, and lectures open to all community members on civic matters, as well as on Islamic issues.

Independent of the specifics of their Islamic identification, young French Muslims appear to have forged a new conception of citizenship. By disentangling political and national identifications, they have reconciled loyalties that still stand in mutual contradiction in their parents' eyes. They accept French political values, such as liberty and democracy, while discounting certain periods in French history, such as the colonial past under which their parents suffered. Politically speaking, they identify themselves locally; they include themselves within the communities in which they were born and raised, while downplaying their French nationality. Nor do these young Franco-Muslims necessarily define themselves as Arab. They may, in fact, criticize political circumstances in their parents' countries of origin as freely as they do those within French society. They are often called overly westernized by relatives in North Africa who misunderstand their individualized religious observance and their political outspokenness against North African regimes. Such criticism distances them still further from feelings of global Arab membership.

Nevertheless, young French Muslims to varying degrees do remain in accord with their own personal histories of discrimination, prone to episodes of collective identification that blend Arab with Muslim. At a minimum, all have experienced pejoratives based upon the socioeconomic status of their ethnicity and have faced categorization as foreigners, despite possessing French nationality by birth. Such discrimination promotes a sympathetic identification with other Muslims, both Arab and non-Arab, who have been similarly oppressed—whether in France, in their country of origin, or in the worldwide Muslim community. The greater the degree of injustice perceived, the more likely they are to rise in staunch defense of Muslim victims, Arab or not. This response was particularly visible during the Gulf War, when French Muslims voiced strong solidarity with the Iraqi people, despite their fears that they might be suspected of disloyalty toward France.[17] Currently it involves solidarity with struggles in areas like Palestine, Bosnia, and Kosovo.

Through their redefinition of citizenship, young French Muslims are participating in changing French politics, which traditionally has permitted only public interest groups based upon nonethnic and noncultural origins.[18] Their activities, with their emphasis upon culture and ethnicity, predominate among similar ventures within other minority groups, such as Jews, Corsicans, Armenians, Basques, and Britannies. Taken as a whole, these activities are catalyzing a transfer of political identification from the national level to the local level.

Grassroot Young Muslims Organizations

In the transfer of political identification to the local level, the most significant development lies in the propagation of new forms of citizenship that emphasize civil, rather than the civic, dimensions. The civic dimension is grounded in the allegiance to centralized, universal political institutions and to public authorities. It is expressed most often through institutionalized channels, such as voting, but also through activism in parties and unions. In contrast, the civil dimension of citizenship involves more local forms of participation that are rooted in "nonpolitical" issues: the neighborhood, academic failure, crime . . . and now Islam. Thus, civility is founded on a recognition of diverse groups within the social body, as well as on a common attachment to the social order. Civil-minded Muslims, for example, are creating grassroots organizations to counter marginality and exclusion and to overcome apathy and political inertia. Their example is demonstrating that the separation of French citizenship from membership in ethnic and religious groups is no longer crucial to political activism, even though that separation lies at the core of the political contract between the individual and the national community, which emerged from the Revolution.

These young Muslims are working toward a reconciliation of their commitments to Islam and to the national collectivity. Their civil actions may be seen as a positive reaction to their alienated and conflicted status as "illegitimate children of France." They have learned from their predecessors with the "Beur" movement, who were consumed by similar tensions between ethnic and nationalistic loyalties. Like the Beurs, they have created organizations from the shared interests of young people who live in the same neighborhood; unlike them, they unite on the basis of a precise criterion: Islam. Their religious unity bypasses the strategic difficulties of their predecessors, who, vacillating between social and ethnic self-identification, emphasized shared experiences of social constraint and exclusion over common North African origin.

"Beur" organizations aimed chiefly to encourage young people's social involvement in the local environment. They initiated a process of mobilization centered on neighborhood ties whose goals were not to change lives but rather to provide consumer goods and leisure activities and to fight against symptoms of social exclusion, such as addiction and crime. Leaders of today's Islamic organizations are preoccupied with the same goals, but with one major difference—they are not torn between political action and social activism. They differ from earlier Beur activists, whose actions were constrained by dependency on public funding and aspirations to political recognition and career advancement in the public service sector. Today's Muslim activists have opted for voluntary social activism. In the process, they are rekindling a spirit of voluntarism within poor neighborhoods.

They are also redefining themselves in relationship to Islam. Theirs is an experience of solidarity with Muslims throughout the world. Their sense of Islamic brotherhood is promoting a cooperative spirit that never existed among Beur associations, which reacted to each other as rivals in the competition for government funds. For this reason, their attempts to organize at the national level may in the long run have a better chance of success than did similar efforts by their predecessors.

Efforts at National Leadership

The new local Islamic organizations are establishing both new sites and new forms of action without regard for the competition between representatives of "official Islam" who are vying to lead the "second religion of France." In consequence, a gap is widening between them and the representatives of official Islam. In Lyon, for example, leaders of the Grande Mosque have little relationship with, and even less influence over, local Muslim youth groups. Thus, young Muslim activists are forging their own independent structures and methods of action at both the local and the national levels. To raise religious consciousness, they rely heavily on audio- and videocassettes and lectures, as well as on brochures, magazines, and books. As they circulate their materials, members of Muslim organizations from all over the country come to know and recognize one another.

Sometimes this mobilization occurs by means of proselytism. This is the case with Tabligh wa Daʿwa, better known in France as Faith and Practice. This movement, founded in India in 1927 as Tablighi Jamaʿt by Mawlana Muhammad Ilyas, seeks to spread Islam and foster respect for Quʾranic law in its literal interpretation. It adheres to the following principles: profession of faith, prayer, the knowledge and commemoration of God, respect for all other believers, and sincerity. The members of Tabligh, who renounce all political activity, particularly in Europe, are organized in national sections composed of several subdivisions. A branch of Tabligh has existed in France since 1972. Its activities take place in the mosques it controls, and in many other settings, through missionary activities. These efforts put into practice a major principle of Tabligh, namely devoting one's time to spreading the faith. These small outings in the member's immediate environment should be distinguished from pilgrimages, which take members throughout France and Europe.

Although this movement is gaining adherents, most of the young individuals engaged in Muslim activities did not come to Islam by this means. The forms of discourse and action of the Union of Islamic Organizations of France (UOIF) are much more effective. Transplanted intellectuals, most of them Tunisian, founded this organization in 1983. They had close ties with the Islamic Tendency Movement, which later became known as Ennahda, founded by Rached Ghannouchi (exiled in London). Some of them came from North Africa for university studies and then remained in France to work and start families. They began to make connections with the immigrant world, which had until then been unfamiliar to them, during the first "headscarf affair" of 1989. Since then, they have undertaken a series of efforts to organize a French Muslim minority. Professors, students, and businessmen, the leaders of the movement are part of the emerging Muslim French elite. They promote the strict observance of Islam, as well as openness toward other cultural and religious sectors of French society. Since the organization's founding, most of the original leaders have retired. When the administrative council was modified in December 1995, a new group of leaders surfaced, most of Moroccan origin and living in Bordeaux. Today, the UOIF claims 200 local organizations of different statuses: fifty are active, fifty are "friends," and one hundred are sympathizers.

UOIF functions on both the national and the regional levels. On the national level, the General Assembly elects an executive bureau, which then elects a president. On the regional level, member organizations elect twelve city delegates, who choose a regional representative. Since 1994, regional conferences have occurred in Acquitaine and in the Southeast region of France. The organization's most significant accomplishment is its annual congress in the outskirts of Paris, which features different lectures and roundtables. This event attracts several thousand young people from all over France, who gather for three days of festivity and study. Its other important achievement has been the founding of an Islamic university institute. UOIF leaders were among the first to understand the critical importance of training Imams in France. They founded the European Institute of Human Sciences, including an institute for Imams and Islamic educators. With about eighty students—the majority of them French—it has not yet shown itself capable of producing religious leaders in France, chiefly because public authorities often view it with mistrust. In 1997, the institute's first graduating class of Imams included only four people, of whom one was a woman. In addition, the institute conducts yearly summer seminars for those unable to pursue the complete program of study.

Beyond the training of Islamic leadership, educating Muslim youths is UOIF's chief priority. For this purpose, the organization created French Muslim Youth (JMF) in 1992. This group's members are men and women between the ages of eighteen and thirty. Its leaders are young men, students, or upwardly mobile professionals. Their operation is decentralized. Today there are six federations, one in Paris divided in three sections (Dreux, Evreux, Montfermeil), as well as five federations in other regions, such as Lille, Nantes, St. Nazaire, Cholet, and Marseille. They see themselves more as a consciousness-raising movement than as providers of services. They do, however, organize conferences (at the local level) and forums (at the regional level), where guest lecturers speak on assorted subjects. In 1996, one of these forums addressed the theme "Young People and Belief." Several UOIF members lectured. More than 300 young people, with an average age of twenty, gathered at this forum. They crowded into the conference room to hear the remarks of Hassan Iqouissen, the first president of JMF and a history student from Lille. A change in leadership occurred in JMF over the summer of 1996, when a sociology student from Nantes, Farid Abdelkrim, became president.

The JMF section in central France held a forum, entitled "The Islam We Need," on March 29, 30, and 31, 1997. It brought together about 5,000 participants. The lecturers included a representative from the Education League and a manager from the secretariat of the Episcopacy for Relations with Islam (SRI). This is how the new president of JMF described the organization:

> Though the word of God, we try to build a future here. But although JMF claims to take the word of God as its main point of reference, that does not mean that we privilege God's law over the law of the republic. To be a good Muslim, one must be a good citizen. We are in France, not Bangladesh or the United States. There are specific circumstances the Muslim must take into consideration, because he has decided to live here. We must not resort to simplistic formulas: "I don't give a damn about France." We cannot live on the margins of French society. The main objective of JMF is to educate, through lectures, publications and seminars. From this standpoint, JMF has a civilizing influence. I am deeply convinced that I can bring something more to my society. I have been given a mission, a role. We should not see this in terms of proselytism but in terms of relationships with people and means of remedying the problems that plague our society.

Other organizations, targeting specific categories such as students and women, exist, as well. The Islamic Students' Union of France, which changed its name to Muslim Students of France in 1996, has headquarters in Bordeaux. The older French Association of Islamic Students (AEIF), founded in 1963 by Professor Mohamed Hamidullah, drew its original membership from foreigners studying in France. Since then, some young people of immigrant origin have joined the organization. The League of Muslim Women, a satellite organization of the UOIF, is a premiere women's group.

All of these groups use the same sort of language. Their discourse emphasizes education as a means of attaining the true Islam. This education must be reconciled with integration into French society. Members seek to maintain their dignity and to study Islam without becoming detached from French society. Members also should not feel obligated to cut themselves off from Muslims who are less observant, as leaders try to explain. The organizations' activities in suburban housing projects bear some analogy to the young Catholic workers movements of the 1940s and 1950s, which attempted to distance their members from the influence of Marxist ideology through similar methods of evangelism: preserving religious values by educating members in the workplace. Today, housing projects, rather than factories, form the setting for such efforts. Still, they share the aim of strengthening individuals and groups through faith. Today, however, the challenge lies in resisting social disenfranchisement, not the pull of a competing ideology such as Marxism.

This new collective action in the name of Islam is also different in that it draws from models and references unfamiliar to the West. Most young Muslim activists look to the Muslim Brothers movement and its founding figures, such as Hassan al-Banna, for guidance and inspiration. As they do, the doctrine of Muslim Brothers is gaining ground in Europe. Insofar as it does so without undermining political order, one must acknowledge that same doctrine as an increasingly positive force for social change and cultural integration. It should be viewed as a return to the sources of the organizational doctrines of Hassan El Banna, before they took a political turn in Egypt and throughout the Muslim world. From this perspective, its dissemination in Europe does not respond to the same logic as it does in the Arab world. Hence, the flow of ideas from the Muslim Brotherhood within Europe does not follow the same logic that applies in the Arab world. In Europe, it answers an existential need for greater familiarity with Islam. It revives a spirit of reform similar to the one that characterized the Islamic world during the nineteenth century and resurrects old question concerning the compatibility of Islam and modernity.

The New Islamic Landscape of France

The Islamic landscape in France is divided between two poles. The first represents the different ethnic and national currents that claim to promote Islam. The second is situated in a more universalist perspective, inspired by the Muslim Brothers' doctrine. It is also important to take note of the vast movement of brotherhoods and mystic groups, although they appear to attract few young Muslims of Arab origin.

The ethnic-national side of the spectrum includes the Mosquée de Paris, whose history and intrigues have been endlessly examined, as well as the mosques of Evry and Mantes la Jolie. Other important organizations, which appeared during the early 1980s, are characterized by the national origins of the people or groups they represent. The National Federation of French Muslims (FNMF) was founded in December 1985 by a French Muslim convert. It has established itself as the main rival of the Mosquée de

Paris, promoting a French Islam freed from the influence of countries of origin. Daniel Youssouf Leclerc, who served as director of the organization during the first "headscarf affair" of 1989, espoused this view charismatically. According to the federation's directors, it has more than 500 local associations; this claim is difficult to verify. During 1995, Moroccans came to dominate its leadership, when Mohamed Bechari became president.

The National Tendency-Islamic Union, founded in France in 1981, recruits mostly from the Turkish population. It is connected with the Welfare Party (Refah) and with Millî Görüş, both of an Islamist orientation. The Islamic Association of France appeared in 1984. Most of its members, as well, are of Turkish descent, and it is considered the French wing of the radical Islamic groups in Germany directed by Hamalledin Hocaoglou, or "Kaplan," the former Mufti of Adana. Finally, the Federation of Islamic Associations of Africa, the Commoros, and the West Indies (FIACA: Fédération des Associations Islamiques d'Afrique, des Comores et des Antilles) and the Coordination of Muslim Associations of the Countries of Asia and the Indian Ocean occupy positions around the ethnic-nationalist pole.

On the fundamentalist side of the spectrum are UOIF, UJM, and JMF, as well as independent organizations such as the Addawa mosque, founded in 1967 in Paris. It has gradually gained a reputation as one of the important sites of Islam in the capital and beyond. Its renown is mostly an outgrowth of the personality of its director, Larbi Kechat, an intellectual of Algerian descent who earned a degree in history at the Sorbonne. He has encouraged open-mindedness and exchange through the activities of a cultural center, which regularly organizes conferences that bring together academics and representatives of non-Muslim religious traditions. These conferences feature sometimes conflicting points of view on different social subjects. Kechat also manages a publishing company, Confluent, which produces audio- and videocassettes and books. Plans to renovate and expand the mosque, which currently accommodates more than 3,000 people, have been approved by neighborhood officials but await the mayor's approval. He was put under House arrest in Folembray in November 1993, when Algerian Islamist networks in France were being dismantled. His arrest prompted the creation of an extensive committee of supporters. On March 17, 1977, a bomb exploded in front of his mosque. No one has claimed responsibility for the attack. According to Kechat, the police, long seeking a pretext to search the mosque, arrived quickly after the attack and stayed for hours. The police investigation continues.

Between these two poles, which could be labeled "fundamentalist" and "traditionalist," the beginnings of a liberal Islam are developing. Soheib Bencheikh represents this new trend. Mufti of Marseilles and son of the deceased Sheikh Abbas, who was superintendent of the Mosquée de Paris from 1982 to 1989, he has spoken widely on *laïcité* and Islamic reform. He gained renown in the non-Muslim community, especially in the media. Bencheikh does not hesitate to consider all Muslim law dependent on historical and cultural context, and thus subject to constant revision: "Every generation, every group inhabiting a region, reads into the Qur'an its own concerns and aspirations. . . . Many Qur'anic verses urge Muslims to renew their understanding, and above all not settle for the results their ancestors produced."[19] Building on this argument, Bencheikh argues that many prescriptions are not applicable in modern societies, particularly veiling: "Muslims must let each other know that in Islam, the injunction to fortify oneself with science and knowledge is more important than the injunction to wear the veil wherever the two are opposed. This is the case, right or wrong, in the public schools, where education clearly takes precedence over the veil. This is the very spirit of Islam. It is the logic at the core of Islamic law."[20] This sort of argument is paradoxical in that it refers to a certain reality of French Islam, when in fact many of these Muslims do not identify with an overly liberal interpretation of Tradition. In other words, even if secularized Muslims do not actually respect the law, they still prefer to have authorities who articulate it.

The Issue of Pluralism

The French citizenry now finds its Islamic presence large enough to threaten its ideal for public life, that is, the balance it has struck among its three major pillars: unity, respect for religious pluralism, and liberty of consciousness. As a result, the French are rethinking their basic notion of pluralism. Pluralism can no longer mean equal opportunity in socioeconomic advancement for deprived groups. Instead, it must refer to political balance between the need for recognizing ethnic and cultural differences at the institutional level and the need for maintaining political and cultural cohesion throughout the nation. Neither French politicians nor French citizens are prepared to address the implications of pluralism so defined. Most French citizens still identify French unity with loyalty to nation and state elevated above all others. They fear the consequences of any national debate on pluralism that might, by dividing the nation along lines of irreconcilable ideological difference, strengthen the National Front political party, which has already preyed upon racism and xenophobia to mobilize support in favor of a white and Catholic France.

Pluralism, however, is not a phenomenon isolated within French national boundaries; it interfaces with transnationalism. Franco-Muslims necessarily maintain solidarities and linkages with Islamic cultures and movements beyond France. If not for education and training in foreign Muslim countries, few leaders would exist at all within the French Muslim community, given their limited resources for clerical study within France.[21]

While the transnational dimensions of Islamic membership are generally seen by French society exclusively as sources of political risk and international instability, the reality is otherwise. Religion, in general, and Islam, in particular, can facilitate social integration, notwithstanding the modern imagination's difficulty perceiving religion as a vehicle for cooperation and progress. Allegiance to Islam is indeed allowing French-born Muslims to integrate into French society in a way their parents cannot. It is providing them with a collective narrative that celebrates the triumph of a tradition throughout the ages, thereby healing the colonial wounds that their parents bear in memory. It is also renewing their commitments on an abstract level to humanitarian values and on a pragmatic level toward making France a better place for Muslims and others alike. Only when secular citizens accomplish for themselves theoretically what France's new Muslims have accomplished for themselves practically—reconciliation between religion and modernity—will they appreciate how Franco-Muslims are creating a new civic-mindedness through Islamic identification that may benefit the national community at large.

Notes

1. Samuel P. Huntington, *The Clash of Civilizations and the Remaking of World Order* (New York: Simon & Schuster, 1996).

2. A comparison between Algerian and Portuguese migrants reveals that Portuguese migrants gathered their families together in less than twenty years, whereas Algerians took almost half a century. For a long time, Algerian migration was exclusively composed of single men. Only at the beginning of the 1960s did families begin arriving in France. Belkacem Hifi, *L'immigration algérienne en France: origines et perspectives de non retour* (Paris: L'Harmattan, CIEM, 1985).

3. Jocelyne Cesari, *Etre musulman en France: associations, militants et mosquées* (Paris: Karthala, 1994).

4. Because Algeria, as part of colonial France, provided the vanguard for North African emigration, it has sought the dominant role in this competition for influence. The history and operation of the Paris Mosque, which has been under Algerian control since 1982, illustrates Algeria's ongoing entanglement within the Franco-Muslim community and French diplomatic affairs. At the end of World War I, French authorities built a mosque in Paris in tribute to those colonial Muslim troops that had fought for France. Construction was supervised by a company in Algiers that could fulfill Islamic requirements for financing and managing holy places through funds, free from loan-derived interest. Algeria rapidly seized control of the project, despite initial contributions by Morocco and Tunisia. Independence in 1962 began a conflict between Algeria and France for mosque ownership that still continues. Although Algeria dramatically strengthened its claims for ownership in 1982 when an Algerian citizen was successfully installed as mosque rector, civil war in Algeria throughout the past six years has diminished its concern with the Paris mosque.

5. For an inventory see François Dubet, *L'immigration: qu'en savons-nous? Un bilan des connaissances* (Paris: La Documentation Française, 1989). See also Tawfik Alla, Jean Paul Buffard, Michel Marie, and Tomaso Reggazola, *Situations migratoires* (Paris: Galilee, 1977); Juliette Minces, *Les travailleurs étrangers en France* (Paris: Seuil, 1973); Abdelmalek Sayad, "Les trois âges de l'émigration algérienne en France," *Actes de la recherche en sciences sociales* 15 (June 1977): 59–76; Larbi Talha, *Le salariat immigré dans la crise* (Paris: CNRS, 1989).

6. Gilles Kepel, *Les banlieues de l'islam* (Paris: Seuil, 1987), and Annie Kreiger-Krynicki, *Les musulmans en France: religion et culture* (Paris: Maisonneuve-Larose, 1985).

7. Secularization is the movement toward a social order whose ideologies, practices, and institutions derive from values held without religious justification and reference. Carried to its logical conclusion, it would result in the total disappearance of religious influence from social life. See major theories of secularization: James A. Beckford and Thomas Luckmann, eds., *The Changing Face of Religion* (London: Sage, 1989); Karel Dobbelaere, *Secularization: A Multidimensional Concept* (London: Sage, 1981); Jeffrey Hadden and Anson D. Shupe, eds., *Secularization and Fundamentalism* (New York: Paragon House, 1989); Thomas Luckmann, *The Invisible Religion: The Problem of Religion in Modern Society* (New York: Macmillan, 1967); and David Martin, *A General Theory of Secularization* (Oxford: Blackwell, 1978).

8. Felice Dassetto and Albert Bastenier, *L'islam transplanté* (Anvers: éd. EPO, 1984); Bruno Etienne, *La France et l'islam* (Paris: Hachette, 1989); and Cesari, *Etre musulman en France*.

9. Jocelyne Cesari, *Musulmans et républicains: Les jeunes, l'islam et la France* (Brussels: Complexe, 1998).

10. Individualization refers to the appropriation of rights to personal choice in matters of religious belief and practice. Its logical outcome is a shift away from authoritative traditions—in both interpretation and practice—toward idiosyncratic constructions of religious lifestyle. It transforms institutionalized religion into a common well from which each person draws with his own vessel for his own purposes in accord with his own needs.

11. Privatization refers to the restriction of religious practice to the private sphere and the relegation of religious values and rules to a secondary and compartmentalized role in the conduct of daily life.

12. Hélène Malewska-Peyre, *Crise d'identité et déviance chez les jeunes immigrés* (Paris: La Documentation Française, 1982).

13. By contrast, despite the reluctance that young Muslim men voice toward mixed marriages on grounds of cultural incompatibility, the latest national statistics indicate that the number of marriages across religious boundaries is growing far faster for them than for their female counterparts. See Jocelyne Streiff-Fenart, *Les couples franco-maghrébins en France* (Paris: Le Centurion, 1990).

14. Those failed movements began with protest, public disorder, and reactive violence against racist murders and what they, second-generation Franco-Maghrébians, perceived as police racism. The political support the protestors received helped to change the direction and meaning of their collective action. It resulted in significant public funding from France's socialist government, which catalyzed the formation of local associations by these protestors. The aid these associations received not only indirectly legitimated the permanent settlement of North African migrants in France but also helped establish a fragile young Muslim elite—those recipients of publicly funded jobs in social service who, independent of professional qualification, were ill prepared for their newly awarded opportunities for social advancement.

Of all government programs, the Social Action Fund (Fonds d'action sociale), which was created in 1958 to facilitate housing and social integration for Algerian migrants, now serves as the major conduit for financial support to North African associations. It remains an important partner to large municipalities, which find themselves formulating ethnically connoted urban policies.

15. "Beur" is a slang expression in French for Arab.

16. In full cognizance of public guidelines for financial allocation, young North Africans originally developed plans of action that emphasized ethnic origin over religious identification. Their collective presentation as members of an ethnic minority, however, in no way meant that ethnicity was a predominant factor in their daily lives or their social interactions.

17. Jocelyne Cesari, "La guerre du Golfe et les arabes de France," *Revue du monde Musulman et de la Méditerranée*, no hors série (1991): 125–29.

18. For example, during the 1989 local elections, the leaders of an association called FRANCE PLUS managed to place candidates on different slates. They argued that persons of North African origin should hold elected office as representatives for a legitimate component of French society. They negotiated their rosters with different political parties, ranging from left to right (excepting, of course, the National Front). Leaders of other North African associations created their own rosters through alliances with various minorities (e.g., women and non-Muslim migrant groups).

The leaders of FRANCE PLUS also created autonomous electoral rolls for the parliamentary elections of March 1993 that were based exclusively on ethnic criteria. Their efforts were not successful; their candidates won only 1 percent to 2 percent of the vote.

The term "Franco-Maghrébins," defined as "French coming from North Africa," was born of these political campaigns. It was used in an effort to access political and financial resources on an ethnic basis. That effort, however, was unsuccessful, mainly because it required too many political compromises.

19. Souhab Bencheikh, *Marianne et le Prophète: l'islam dans la laïcité francaise* (Paris: Grasset, 1998).

20. Ibid., 186–87.

21. As a consequence, however, of their training abroad, they are often ill prepared to address the specific needs of Franco-Muslims who live as a minority. Within the small circle of the Islamic elite in Europe, however, an innovative reflection on the adaptation of the Islamic law (*Shari'a*) to minority conditions is just now starting. These scholars are highlighting the flexibility of the law and demonstrating its compatibility with secular and democratic rules.

3

The Turks in Germany:
From Sojourners to Citizens

Barbara Freyer Stowasser

Historical Roots of German Conceptions of
Nationhood and Citizenship

German history, because of the nation's geographic location in the center of Europe in an expanse with few natural boundaries and at the crossroads of ancient continental and transcontinental trade and migration routes, has been a canvas of migration and immigration movements. Given the complex political structures, interrelationships, and shifting boundaries of the central European states, these movements involved not just in-migration by non-Germans into German-held territories or German assumption of political control over non-German territories but also massive out-migration by Germans, especially toward the East, during the high Middle Ages and again during the early modern period. The latter created enclaves of German language, culture, and national identity in the Slavic East, just as enclaves of Polish language, culture, and national identity came to exist in Eastern Prussia. To the nineteenth-century intellectual formulators of nationalist thought in both Germany and Poland, this historical record of maintaining a distinctive ethnocultural identity in areas of ethnoculturally mixed populations did much to furnish the outline of a differentialist model of "nationhood,"[1] while neither side had the institutional framework of a unified state within which to develop the notion.

Germans' understanding of statehood differed markedly, for example, from that of the French. The essentially political concept of French nationhood developed within the territorially and institutionally centralized framework of the pre- as well as post-1789 French state, where French political unity provided the basis for the definition of French cultural unity, including policies of assimilation of cultural minorities and foreign immigrants. In contrast, the German concept of national identity, itself a step away from the concept of nationhood, first took tentative form during the medieval and early modern periods of the "Holy Empire of the German Nation." The latter, however, provided neither an administrative framework nor a state-anchored focus for its formulation. Made up of well more than 300 independent states until 1848, Germany developed its notion of national identity "between supernational Empire and the subnational profusion of sovereign and semisovereign political units,"[2] where "the conglomerative pattern of state building in polycentric, biconfessional, even (in Prussia) binational Germany was the historical matrix for a more differentialist self-understanding."[3]

Eighteenth-century German Romanticism was, at least initially, in part an aesthetic, culture-critical response to the rationalist and universalist paradigm of the French-centered Enlightenment. It moved around the time of the French Revolution into the area of social philosophy. With the outbreak of war between France and Prussia in the 1790s and, especially, Napoleon's conquest and occupation of much of Germany during the first decade and a half of the nineteenth century, it became thoroughly politicized. The Napoleonic wars transformed both the French and the German constructs of "nation," both now transmuted into parallel variants of the new ideology of "nationalism" but with the old structural differences still in place. While nationhood in France was fused to the institutional realities and was thus a political fact, nationhood in Germany was sharply distinct from the institutional realities of statehood and therefore was an ethno-cultural fact.[4] In France, the notion was assimilationist. In Germany, it was differentialist.

Germany's early nineteenth-century nationalist thinkers were largely intellectuals, civilian spokesmen of a nation in search of a state. Nation, to them, was an historically rooted, organic being sui generis, that is, an organism endowed with its own specific genius or spirit (*Volksgeist*) manifested in language, culture, custom, law, and the state. The state thus "derived from" the nation, but—to some—was also a precondition of its ultimate expression. When the exponents of Prussian realpolitic, however, did create a German state toward the end of the nineteenth century, their creation maintained the inherited order of separate dynastic or corporate substates. Contrary to what many had hoped for, the (Kaiser-)Reich was not a nation-state with a unified citizenship, and its state-ist framework failed to integrate the German ethnocultural understanding of nationhood. These disappointments remained available for political exploitation during the Weimar Republic, and especially during the Third Reich.[5]

Several manifestations of the traditional German construct of nationhood remain characteristic of the present state. First is the legal notion that citizenship is based on blood ties, that is, descent from German parents—*ius sanguinis* as opposed to the *ius soli*, under which citizenship is based on something more "territorial," such as birth, residence, or other circumstantial criteria. Both postwar German states, and the new Germany since 1990, have continued to adhere to this "ethnic" definition of citizenship. From it, second, flows the still extant political notion that "Germany is not a country of immigration," by reason of which no German legal code of immigration has been promulgated. However, the new German nationality (or citizenship) law of 1999 that went into effect on January 1, 2000, is making inroads into areas formerly ruled by these traditional legal and political constructs.

Immigrants, Migrants, and Foreign Labor to the End of the Second World War

Large numbers of immigrants from neighboring countries arrived in Germany during the seventeenth and eighteenth centuries, partly to escape religious persecution at home and partly to find land and work made available by the rulers of the many German principalities and kingdoms. These Swiss, French, Austrian, Bohemian, Polish, Dutch, Swedish, Italian, and other immigrants were given citizenship rights. In the nineteenth century, Germany's economic development and rapid industrialization intensified both internal migration and also immigration from abroad. The former was at first primarily focused on the industrial sector (such as the Ruhrgebiet), and the latter on agricultural jobs (mainly in Prussia). These foreign migrants, however, were now considered temporary workers only, and at the end of the nineteenth century the by-then unified German state had developed a system of one-year work and residence permits that were to ensure rotation and prevent permanent settlement.[6]

During the First World War, well over two million foreigners worked in Germany in agriculture and industry. These, however, were now mainly coerced laborer, among them 1.4 million migrants forced in 1914 to remain in Germany and to work for the German state against their will, as well as one million prisoners of war. Both before and during the Second World War, the Third Reich expanded and radicalized this system of exploitation. It forced the slave labor of more than fourteen million foreign workers and several million prisoners of war and concentration-camp victims, with the death rate by starvation, exhaustion, or disease reaching 50 percent among all three groups.[7]

Immigrants, Migrants, and Foreign Labor since the Second World War

Between 1945 and German unification in 1990, nearly twenty million people migrated or immigrated into the Federal Republic, the former "West Germany."

German Refugees

Immediately after the war, more than eight million refugees who had been expelled from the territories of the 1937 German Reich and East Europe arrived in Germany. They were joined by three million refugees from the German Democratic Republic, "East Germany," who fled to the West between 1945 and 1961, when the construction of the Berlin Wall and tight control over the East-West border prevented further large-scale migration. As these refugee populations were of German background, they more or less automatically and instantly acquired FRG citizenship and became full members of the West German political, social, and economic systems.[8] While legally they were true immigrants, they neither considered themselves as such nor, to my knowledge, were they officially categorized by that name.

Foreign Workers

The second wave of postwar migrant, legally nonimmigrant populations arrived between the mid-1950s and the early 1970s. They were the foreign laborers whom the German government recruited abroad to meet the needs of its expanding economy. Perceived and promoted as a short-term, temporary measure to sustain and enhance Germany's economic growth, the policy to invite these "guest workers" into Germany was largely developed[9] by the executive branch of the then-Christian-Democrat-led government in Bonn. German political parties, government agencies, labor unions, agricultural and industrial employers, and cadres of the media supported the recruitment policy on the assumption that it was a temporary measure undertaken for the benefit of the German economy. Governments of south European, southeast European, and North African countries with labor surpluses likewise supported the system for economic reasons of their own. These included hopes of lessening domestic unemployment, budgetary benefits through workers' remittances sent from abroad, and the expectation that exported unskilled workers would return home as semiskilled or skilled after having worked for a period in Germany's modern industrialized economy. As a result, a number of recruitment treaties were signed by Bonn and the governments, respectively, of Italy (1955), Spain (1960), Greece (1960), Turkey (1961 and 1964), Morocco (1963), Portugal (1964), Tunisia (1965), and Yugoslavia (1968).[10] Large numbers of German recruitment and employment offices were established in these "sender nations." In the case of the non–European Union (at that time, the non–European Economic Community) countries, these treaties stipulated a permit system by which newly recruited foreign workers were initially awarded one-year work permits, while EEC workers could obtain less restricted contracts.[11] Even in the case of non–EEC workers, however, the German government never implemented an official "temporary" or "rotation" policy. Thus, longer-term sojourns, which most employers preferred, could be negotiated with the appropriate residency-granting bureaucratic offices on the local level from the start, albeit initially for one year at a time.

Then came the exclusivist FRG 1965 Foreigners Act, which stipulated that rights of entrance and residence of foreign workers depended on "the interests of the German state." These German policies, with their own original, restrictive hiring patterns, along with the 1965 Bonn reminder of the fragility of their work situation in Germany, directly affected the workers from non–EEC countries. This was especially true during the 1966–1967 temporary downturn in the German economy, when labor migration from abroad was largely halted. Anticipating problems of re-entry, it was mainly the non–EEC workers, and among them mainly the Turks, who early on chose to extend their contracts by all available bureaucratic/legal means instead of rotating in and out of the Federal Republic. The trend was facilitated in 1971 when, possibly under pressure from the Federation of German Trade Unions, which desired to maintain control over all foreign workers, the Social-Democratic government in Bonn issued a new Ordinance on Work Permits. That ordinance permitted non–EEC foreigners with a five-year employment record to apply for special five-year work and residence permits.[12] At the end of the 1960s, labor recruitment abroad had also again intensified, especially in non–EEC countries. In the case of the Turkish workers, the two factors of high recruitment rate and their tendency to remain in Germany resulted in an increase of Turks in the German labor force from 11 percent in 1965 to 23 percent in 1973, 29 percent in 1980, and 34 percent in 1990. By contrast, Italians, for example, represented 31 percent in 1965 but only 10 percent in 1990.[13]

The period of official German foreign-labor recruitment lasted until the "recruitment halt" (*Anwerbestopp*) of November 1973, itself a function of a major decline in the German economy in the wake of the oil embargo. The halt was accompanied by a program of financial incentives designed to motivate the foreign workers to leave Germany. Some did choose to leave,[14] while others who had already brought their families to Germany opted to stay. The 1973 recruitment halt actually increased the size of their communities, as the remaining guest-workers increasingly took advantage of Germany's right-of-family-unification laws.[15] In 1973, 11.6 percent of the German workforce and 6.4 percent of the population were foreigners; by the mid-1980s, foreigners constituted 7.7 percent of the workforce but 7.4 percent of the population, while the Turkish share in both categories increased steeply. By 1990, 34 percent of all foreign workers, and 32 percent of the foreign resident population, were Turks. In the early 1990s, almost two million Turkish citizens lived in Germany.[16] Contrary to what the German legislators had had in mind, the 1973 recruitment halt actually increased the number of foreigners in Germany. It also transformed the status of the original migrant laborers into that of resident aliens and changed the national and social profile of the foreign community as a whole.[17]

From the beginning, the German trade unions had insisted on integrating the foreign workers into the regular structures of wages and benefits. Since the 1970s, generous social support services such as unemployment benefits, children's allowances, medical insurance, access to vocational training and the like rendered residence in Germany financially attractive to the guest workers.[18] To many Germans, these workers represented a drain on the German budget that the original architects of the recruitment system had not foreseen. It has also been argued, however, that by 1973–1974 the migrant/immigrant workers were no longer merely an industrial reserve but had become structurally integrated into the labor market, paying back more into the system than they received through social services and public facilities.[19] Successive governments both before and after 1973 have struggled with these issues, with the Left (Social Democrats, Greens) usually in favor of opening up the German system more fully to the foreigners and the Right (Christian Democrats) in favor of tighter controls. Both sides framed their arguments in terms of the German economy. Even the 1990 federal Foreigners Act, passed by a CDU-led government after the economic upswing of the 1980s and just before German reunification, which considerably expanded foreigners' residency rights as well as eligibility for naturalization, reaffirmed German control over the issuing of work permits.[20] Since the latter were especially crucial to foreign workers' family members, mainly spouses and work-age children arriving in Germany under the family-reunification scheme, such policies were harmful to what had de facto become a legally recognized minority of resident aliens. The question of work permits is bound to enter a new phase as part of the major changes entailed in the new German nationality (or citizenship) law of 1999. Its core was first proposed by the Social Democrat/Green coalition government of Gerhard Schroeder, who was elected in fall 1998. After a protracted and emotional debate, Parliament in 1999 passed the new law that inter alia reduced the required residency of new citizens to eight years and granted limited dual citizenship to foreign children born in Germany, under certain conditions. The law thus opened the door to citizenship for three million (including 900,000 Turks) of Germany's 7.4 million foreign residents.[21]

Asylum Seekers

A third wave of migration or immigration into Germany in the late 1980s and early 1990s involved sizeable numbers of ethnic German resettlers from the East (*Aussiedler*), who were given preferential rights in the FRG because of their ethnic backgrounds. In larger part, however, the new arrivals of these decades were non-German asylum seekers admitted under Germany's constitution-based, very liberal asylum laws, promulgated to signal the Federal Republic's intention to distance itself from the shameful victimization of foreigners by the Third Reich. During the early 1990s, more than half of the asylum seekers per annum (mainly from Eastern Europe, Africa, and Asia) who sought admission to an EEC/EU country were "taken in" by Germany, at least on a temporary basis, until the validity of their claim of political persecution by their home state could be determined.[22] While in economic, political, and legal terms the asylum seeker question is largely independent of the issue of "guest workers," including the presence of Turkish "guest workers" in Germany, the two have become linked in popular perception. This has served to heighten and intensify a German public sense of malaise at "too many foreigners in our midst."[23] By the early 1990s, rising unemployment and economic fears about the national cost of supporting skyrocketing numbers of refugees and asylum seekers, linked with fears about rising crime rates among foreigners, had produced waves of xenophobia and some acts of violence against foreigners carried out by radical fringe groups. Support for the numerically marginal New Right parties, with their anti-immigration platforms, also increased in some regions.[24] The presence of guest workers in Germany, which had become a political issue during the economic downturn of 1966-1967 and again in the wake of the 1973 oil crisis, became an even greater concern in the next decade. It was arguably the demographic and economic realities and perceptions created during the late 1980s by the liberal asylum policy that caused immigration and the treatment of foreigners to emerge as Germany's most persistent and contested political concerns. The fall of the German Democratic Republic in 1989 and German reunification in 1990 only temporarily lessened the intensity of the national debate. It soon flared with increased urgency since the New Laender (states of the former East Germany), because of the former regime's segregationist practices, came with little or no experience of Germans relating to foreigners. The result after reunification was an atmosphere of intense xenophobia, especially among the young, that erupted in acts of violence and also found imitation in the Old Laender (states of the former West Germany), where the targets often were Turks.[25]

The Founders of the Turkish Community in Germany: The First Generation

The Turkish migrants who arrived in Germany between the early 1960s and the mid-1970s were largely urbanized or semiurbanized, skilled and semiskilled workers. Their exodus from cities and towns in Turkey was contrary to the intention of the original Turkish planners, who had anticipated a system of direct rural-to-foreign migration of unskilled labor.[26] The early contract workers were predominantly male.[27] Having left their families behind in most cases, the early migrants were also de facto a bachelor population who found housing either in company-provided dormitories or privately rented, shared apartments, the latter mainly in rundown and overcrowded apartment houses.

Literacy and Language

The majority of first-generation Turkish workers in Germany were doubly isolated in their new life because of language and literacy problems. Their native language was a local Turkish dialect. Few had received a formal education beyond the rudimentary level in Turkey, and thus most were not able to read Turkish newspapers. Their physically demanding jobs in Germany, which rarely required linguistic competence, left them little time to expand their knowledge of Turkish beyond the dialectal level or to develop a knowledge of German as a workable second language. Their social life was largely confined to interaction with other Turks who came from similar backgrounds, which did not help them to develop new language skills or social contacts. In the beginning, very few Turkish radio or television broadcasts were available to the Turkish community in Germany. Sometimes a migrant worker's children would act as his translators of newspaper articles on world events. This situation changed with the arrival of videos and satellite transmission, especially the latter, connecting the first-generation migrants with events in Turkey and the world by way of the spoken Turkish word.[28]

Housing

According to federal regulations, German recruiting companies had to provide housing for their foreign workers. Frequently this consisted of large barracks or hostels located in the vicinity of the workplace. Regulations issued in 1971 by the Federal Ministry for Labor and Social Affairs and in 1973 by the West German Parliament amended previous general housing laws and guidelines to specify the legal maximum of dwellers per unit of space, as well as the legal minimum of sanitary and cooking facilities. According to a 1971 regulation of the Board of the Federal Labor Office, construction of workers' hostels qualified for government financial support under certain conditions. Later literature on the subject, however, has questioned whether application of the official housing laws and guidelines was ever truly monitored and whether such and similar federal financial aid policies were ever truly implemented.[29] While the hostels were by definition for the use of "single," employed foreign workers only, workers with families had to look for lodging elsewhere (as, indeed, did many "single" workers). Forced to find living space in order to obtain residency permits, foreign workers often discovered that low-cost housing was in short supply. They and their families often had to settle in rundown apartments, ancient working-class tenements in inner-city areas that quickly turned into ghettos.[30] Overcrowding, especially in the case of "single" workers, has been ascribed to the first migrants' desire to spend as little on rent as possible in order to remit as much of their wages as possible to their families back home. Equally responsible, however, were the high rents charged by landlords who exploited their tenants and their tenants' situation. Overcharging of foreign worker renters for poor or substandard housing by German landlords has continued to the present. Turkish families in metropolitan areas still live predominantly in inner-city ghettos, often in slum dwellings for which they are charged higher rent than Germans would be charged for similar properties. As recently as ten years ago, one in three Germans, but four out of five non-Germans, lived in overcrowded housing.[31] Landlord greed, contributing to the exclusion of the majority of Turks from housing integration into German society, remains one of the faces of German ethnic discrimination.[32] In addition, a state (Laender) housing policy adopted in 1975 placed restrictions on foreign worker immigration into urban areas with high percentages of foreign residents. Cities with more than a 6 percent foreign worker population could apply to the state government for designation as an "overburdened settlement area," while those with foreign worker populations of more than 12 percent could legally assume this designation without application.

By 1977, this policy had rendered five of the largest West German cities off limits for foreign worker settlement.[33]

Jobs

Most of the first-generation workers recruited abroad under bilateral sending-country and host-country agreements were given recruitment contracts. In practical terms, these signified both the workers' job security for the duration of the contract and their limitation to the job designated in the contracts, which for the majority meant unskilled labor in the manufacturing industry. The legacy of the original labor recruitment policies is still evident today. Even though Germany's economic and occupational structures have undergone profound changes, most of the foreign workers (and especially the Turks) who were originally hired as unskilled or semiskilled labor have remained in unskilled or semiskilled jobs, while many Germans have advanced from blue-collar to white-collar employment.[34]

The jobs first performed by the workers recruited abroad were often physically demanding, many were potentially hazardous to the workers' health, and most were dirty. This job profile has persisted; according to a 1993 statistic, Turks figured prominently in employment in foundry work, plastic production, car manufacturing, fish processing, leather processing, hotel and catering services, and cleaning services.[35] The share of Turks working in manufacturing jobs in 1993 remained high at 53.4 percent, by far the highest even among non-German workers, while the increase to 19 percent in their share of service-sector employment was well below the 26 percent increase among non-Germans overall.[36] Unlike their early situation under recruitment contract or even during the years immediately following the 1973 recruitment ban, however, Turkish workers by the early 1980s had become especially vulnerable to unemployment, which has forced them to hold on even to unattractive or only marginally tolerable jobs. By 1994, Turkish unemployment figures had risen more sharply than was the case even with other foreign labor groups; 18.9 percent of Turkish workers were unemployed, compared to 15.5 percent of all foreign workers and 8.8 percent of Germany's total workforce.[37]

An Angry Roadmap?

In 1985, the leftist German journalist Günter Wallraff shocked the German public with a book entitled *Ganz Unten* ("In the Pits," or "Way Down"),[38] in which he reported his experiences when impersonating a Turkish worker called "Ali Levent." Disguised with a partial wig and "dark contact lenses," the reporter took on a number of mainly illegal minimal-wage jobs, confronted German institutions, and escaped detection by Turkish coworkers whose cause he championed. The incompetence of the German police saved his ploy, with the help of a corrupt and powerful German industrialist whom he successfully hoodwinked into negotiating a criminal deal with some bogus atomic plant representatives. Among the targets of Wallraff's wrath are the (late) Bavarian CSU chairman Franz Josef Strauss (with whom he also had a bad relationship during his "real life" journalistic career); the international food chain McDonald's, which he accuses of cheating and poisoning the German eating public while exploiting its employees; an illegal construction firm that neither registers nor insures its workers; the Catholic Church, where several hypocritical priests refused his application for baptism; and even the Bhagwan sect, where he was also belittled and rejected. His experiences of dehumanization increased with a visit to a German undertaker where, as a terminally ill and jobless Turkish worker, he bargained for his own burial.

Wallraff's worst experience came during employment in the Thyssen (Germany's largest) foundry. Work there is devastating to the health of the foreigners, as they are deprived even of standard safety equipment. Forced to work upward of ten-hour shifts without adequate breaks, in an atmosphere of cruelty, derision, and xenophobic jokes, in the end the workers find that their wages are not paid in full or even on time. But the threat of unemployment is even worse, because, even for the most dismal living accommodations (he records the case of a Turkish family of eleven crowded into a 100-square-meter apartment), slumlords evict tenants who fail to pay their rent on time. The exploitation Wallraff describes involves a number of German poor, as well. Foreigners and natives are jointly portrayed as victims of a corrupt German economic system controlled by faceless institutions—Thyssen's, or the pharmaceutical industry with its dangerous experiments on unsuspecting "volunteers"—and also their representatives, the unscrupulous, venal, neo-Nazi individuals with whom Wallraff, as "Ali Levent," enters into working relationships.

German reaction to Wallraff's book was positive among the extreme Left of the mid-1980s. The majority of the German reading public, however, rejected the book's political confrontationalism and its bipolarization along class lines. It also took a dim view of the sensationalist journalism that rendered its author famous for a while, so the publication failed to call forth the German guilt and moral reform that may have been the author's intention. Among the Turkish critics of the text were those who objected both to its Marxist ideology and to the "image" of the Turks that it put forward. The Turkish feminist Aysel Özakin rejected Wallraff's paradigm as one of "pity," where "pity" becomes a means of stabilizing cultural dominance, "the most refined form of contempt." For Özakin, Wallraff's and the German Left's approach to ethnic minorities suffered from their tendency to lump all foreigners together as a uniform, inferior group, while exempting themselves from responsibility.[39]

Religion

The German-Turkish government contracts that stipulated the conditions of early foreign workers' recruitment in 1961 and 1968 did not include, nor foresee the need of, host country obligation to provide for the foreign workers' religious needs. The governments following the 1961 Democratic Party ouster in Turkey were strongly secularist, and both they and the Germans regarded religion as a matter of private conscience that had no public policy or planning implications. As a consequence, those in the first generation of Turkish workers were pretty much on their own in matters of ritual and worship. Several factors, some evident from the beginning and others occasioned by later social and political developments, worked against these early official expectations.

First was the fact that the majority of recruited workers, even the urbanized or recently urbanized, came from traditional backgrounds. Religion for them was a much greater part of life and identity than the Turkish secular regimes supposed. At the same time, the marginalization and alienation that the recruited workers experienced in German society caused them to place even greater emphasis on religion as part of their identity. Communal prayer became a solidarity building ritual. Since mosques were scarce at the beginning, the workers held their prayer meetings in private quarters or in public rooms in hostels or workplaces, if permission could be obtained from the appropriate administration. There were no official Muslim theological experts to organize or oversee these activities, but the members of the individual groups took turns as Imams to lead the prayer. They interpreted and debated religious issues with one another within the framework of their inherited tradition, which was mainly the Sufi-tinged Islamic paradigm of their Anatolian roots.[40]

A second factor underscoring the importance of tradition for these Turkish workers was the increasing numbers of their families who arrived in Germany under the German family-reunification law. The presence of family served to greatly enhance and strengthen the appeal of, and to, religious tradition in shaping domestic life in Germany as the (mostly male) Turkish workers now became heads of households. While their original out-migration had often provided their spouses who were left behind in Turkey with greater decision-making powers, the situation in Germany after family re-unification involved redefinition of family authority and jurisdiction both for spouses and for children. "Normal" generational conflict and uneven and, in the children's case, accelerated degrees of acculturation combined to call forth an increased emphasis by Turkish parents, especially fathers (sometimes also Turkish older brothers) on Islamic values, customs, and social rules. This has been called the use of "lived Islam" as a device to legitimate and prop up the patriarchal family. Similar dynamics were and are at work within Turkish neighborhoods.[41]

Third, and simultaneously, within this growing community of Turkish Muslim expatriates in Germany emerged large numbers of self-help organizations, often with an Islamic bent, later replaced by Islamic organizations and associations, that provided a growing array of services to the community. Among the latter were religious instruction, Arabic instruction, sales of religious books and videos, literacy courses for older individuals, and help in dealings with German bureaucrats, employers, teachers, and physicians.[42]

The fourth and also simultaneous factor came into play during the late 1970s and 1980s. Western Europe in general and West Germany in particular became an arena where Turkish (and other) Islamic organizations could openly take shape and engage in sociopolitical activities, even if only on the level of registered corporations, from which they were then barred in Turkey. The results were twofold: (1) Turkish Islamic (and also some nationalist right-wing) leaders and their followers developed some strong organizational, recruitment, and publication activities in Germany that served to consolidate their Turkey-centered efforts while in exile; (2) Turkish Islam in Germany grew into the maze of multitudinous, well-organized, often competing, and partially opaque official or semiofficial corporations and associations that it is today.

Identity and Citizenship

A 1990 amendment to the Foreigners' Law gave the Turkish workers, as it did all other foreign nationals, the right to apply for a permanent residency permit after eight years.

After ten years of residency, they were entitled to apply for German citizenship but had to demonstrate German language proficiency and a modicum of cultural assimilation, as well as consent to renouncing their own original citizenship. Very few Turks took advantage of this opportunity.[43] The complex psychological state of first-generation immigrant Turks is often referred to as *Heimkehrillusion*, the illusion of returning to the homeland, which though rarely acted upon while they are alive underlies the wish of a majority of immigrants to be buried in their native soil. A German study of Turkish burial practices in Munich between 1989 and 1993 revealed that 96.2 percent of Turkish migrants who lived and died in Munich were buried in Turkey, even though two cemeteries in the Munich city area had Islamic sections. Special consular services, specialized undertakers' services, and financial aid provided by, for example, the Turkish-Islamic Association of the Institute for Religious Affairs, have been made available to facilitate the transfer of bodies for burial in the home country. Interviews with Turkish migrants revealed that their choice of a final resting place was seen as a return to the family network that they had left behind in favor of an often traumatic emigration.[44]

The Second and Third Generations

Family reunification changed both the social and the age profile of the Turkish community in Germany. In the mid-1970s, and before the legal age limit for family reunion of children was set at its present level of sixteen years, 60 percent of the new arrivals from Turkey were under the age of eighteen.[45] This rendered the Turkish minority on average younger than the German population, a situation that has continued because the Turkish birthrate in Germany (2.6 children) is double the German rate (1.3).[46] Even though Turkish youths and children were given access to German public education and training programs, the majority of second- and third-generation Turks continued to work in the unskilled or semiskilled sectors of the economy. A significant number advanced to the status of skilled labor, but they held a very small percentage of white-collar jobs.[47] In addition, and unlike their "recruited" elders, these young Turks born in Turkey or Germany have had to compete in the German labor market, which since the economic decline of the early 1980s has meant high unemployment.[48]

Education

In Germany, education is a prerogative of the state. The individual states hold primary constitutional authority over educational policy within their territory, but a considerable degree of federal coordination occurs through a permanent working group of educational ministries. As part of West German reform of its general education and university systems in the 1960s, the secondary school level underwent a number of changes. This did not, however, result in the fusing or even linking of vocational training with academic education, as several Social Democratic-Liberal (SPD-FDP) educational reform proposals in the 1960s and 1970s had intended. Vocational training remained the responsibility of employers in part-time company schools (*Lehrwerkstätten*) or else was done through a special educational track (*Berufsschule*). At present Germany has three types of secondary schools. The *Hauptschule*, successor to the old eight-year *Volksschule* designed to offer access to apprenticeships in the crafts and industry, is now the least prestigious, as well as the least preferred, among secondary schools. Second is the *Realschule*, which opens doors to more prestigious apprenticeships, as well as to white-collar jobs. Third, the *Gymnasium* prepares students for university education.[49] A study of the educational opportunities of Turkish children in Germany highlights the continuing class-based nature of the German educational system.[50] Turkish children and adolescents are doubly disadvantaged in that the majority of them attend only the *Hauptschule*, as opposed to German children, and a considerable percentage leave (even) the *Hauptschule* without a certificate. Even though by the 1990s the majority of foreign children had been born in Germany, and one in four second-generation non-Germans thought of himself as German, language problems played a large role in this negative balance.[51] Critics have also leveled blame at the lack or inadequate availability of German preschool facilities, which in Germany are run privately. Concerning schoolchildren, the expectation is that parents will help with homework, which most often foreign parents are unable to do. Lack of private study space in the home, as well as the overly rigid and confining German teaching system,[52] also contribute to the problems. Some minority voices, however, have tried to take into consideration other factors such as Turkish parental expectations and the kinds of communal and family pressures their children face when making educational choices.[53]

Over the past decades, both the individual German states and the Federal Standing Conference of Ministers have issued multitudinous educational policies specifically targeted at immigrant children. Some of these try to provide for the linguistic and cultural assimilation of foreign children within the German school system. Others emphasize, at least as a parallel goal, that the children (also) need to maintain their linguistic, cultural, and historical ties to the homeland.[54] The Berlin model and the Bavarian model represent these two alternatives. The integrationist Berlin model, with its emphasis on preparatory language courses for non-German speakers and coeducation of students from all backgrounds, has been criticized for its philosophy of "Germanization" of foreign children. Critics also point to its high dropout rate, lack of focus on multiculturalism, adherence to traditional German curricula, and policy of leaving instruction in the foreign students' language and native culture to elective afterschool courses organized by their respective embassies or consulates.[55] By contrast, the Bavarian model offers access to standard, German-taught classes only to foreign students who are proficient in German, and then only at their parents' request. For the majority, instruction is provided in the students' native language from teachers appointed and often salaried by the home country. This model has been criticized as "segregationist" and denounced for producing students with "functional illiteracy in both languages."[56] In actual fact, the educational policies in the various other German states now fall somewhere between these two models.

Language and Literature

In contrast to their elders—whose language proficiency is in (usually dialectal) Turkish that they have come to pepper with German words denoting "official" work- and bureaucracy-related concepts—the young Turks of the second and third generation have acquired considerable degrees of German language proficiency. Depending on their level of acculturation and/or education, a minority is literate in both languages. Some have mastered "Standard" ("High") German in addition to a fluent "domestic" Turkish for family use, while many speak German more fluently than they do Turkish, although both languages in their repertoire are of the dialectal variety. The considerable extant literature on these phenomena has recorded and analyzed patterns of language mixing that can produce a hybrid *"parole"* that disregards the *"langue"* grammar of both of its components. In addition, numerous instances of "code-switching" have also been recorded.[57] In a 1995 German publication entitled *Kanak Sprak*, the leftist Turkish writer Feridun Zaimoglu[58] presents samples of what he calls the intensely personalized rhetoric of this generation between cultures, whose language is "a sort-of Creole . . . with secret codes and signs" that produces speech in the manner of the Rap Free-Style-Sermon.[59] The book is rendered by the author entirely in dialectal German. It presents what appear to be monologues by a group of Turkish-German figures on the margins of German society, including a rapper, an Islamic fundamentalist, a sociologist, a petty criminal, a poet, a pimp, a gigolo, a mechanic, an unemployed worker, a transsexual, and a patient in a psychiatric institution. The book's themes and spirit are strongly reminiscent of Wallraff's 1985 journalistic report, *Ganz Unten*. Like its predecessor, this publication also gained fame and acceptance among readers of the radical Left, while the majority of the reading public reacted negatively to its sensationalism and political confrontationalism.

The formation of a Turkish middle class in Germany has been a slow process. Yet the increasing numbers of Turkish professionals, intellectuals, artists, filmmakers, and writers who work in Germany, usually through the medium of the German language, do not necessarily see themselves as representatives of the Turkish migrant community even when they are writing about its plight. Certainly they do not wish to see their work stigmatized as "guest art." Works where elements of both German and Turkish culture are fused can be statements of rebellion against dominating, official features in both.[60] As opposed to the narrative of negative personal experience (*Betroffenheitsliteratur*) of the early years, which was most often written in Turkish, younger Turkish writers tend to write in German, both for their own and other minority communities and also for the larger German reading public. In their best-selling novels, writers such as Güney Dal (writing in Turkish)[61] and Emine Sevgi Özdamar (writing in German)[62] probe the many facets of Turkish identity, often with devastating humor. In Özdamar's work, memories of Turkish history, religious traditions, regional peculiarities, and family and neighborhood idiosyncrasies are interwoven with events of life in the West, where they provide a deeper notion of self.

Identity and Citizenship

Even higher levels of integration into the German educational system concomitant with increasing "standard" German language proficiency have not erased the barriers that exist between foreign and German children or young adults who attend the same school or work in the same workplace. In many cases, persons of foreign descent who were born in Germany report that they cross a cultural threshold when leaving home in the morning to do their day's work. Then they cross another cultural threshold at the end of the day when they return home to socialize with their family, neighbors, and friends who are of an ethnic background identical or similar to their own.[63] Young Turks in Germany share many qualities, interests, and aspirations with their German cohorts, such as strong generational tastes in fashion, music, and dancing. But, because of their self-perception as "outsiders," the question of identity appears to loom larger with them than it does with the German youth. The revised Foreigner's Law of 1990 gave foreigners born in Germany the right to acquire German citizenship at or after age eighteen, provided they give up their own. As increasing numbers of young Turks who took that option have continued to feel excluded from the majority culture, the question of their identity has continued to be problematic. The new nationality/citizenship law of 1999 that took effect on January 1, 2000, facilitates the acquisition of German citizenship for much larger numbers of Turkish and other non-German residents by making it available after eight years of legal residence in the country. The law's most innovative provision is the granting of dual citizenship to foreign children born in Germany, provided that at least one parent had been a German resident for eight years; however, by age twenty-three, the children must decide whether to keep German citizenship or that of their parents.[64] Acceptance as citizens will certainly have an impact on the self-perception of many second-, third-, and by now fourth-generation Turks that so far has remained colored more by alienation than by a sense of belonging and integration.

Religious Education

In 1996, there were 379,093 school-age Turkish children and adolescents in Germany, most of them enrolled in public schools.[65] Until February 2000, no Islamic group in Germany had been granted the same official status as the Roman Catholic and Protestant churches, which (also) meant that Islamic religious instruction, unlike instruction in the Christian denominations, could not be offered as part of the regular school curriculum. After a protracted legal battle that began in the early 1980s to allow the teaching of Islam alongside Catholic, Protestant, and "secular" studies, the federal court in February 2000 ruled to grant the Islamic Federation (Islamic Federation Berlin, an umbrella organization of twenty-five Turkish Muslim groups) the right to teach Islam in the state-run sector, after which Berlin announced that Islam will be offered as "an option in religious education in Berlin schools." Mainly because of the membership of Islamist groups in the Federation, the court's decision was highly controversial among both Germans and Turks.[66]

Education in Germany being a regional matter, the various states have designed a number of different formulas for integrating religion into public education, usually arrived at in consultation with representatives of the Christian churches. No Islamic group, however, has been officially recognized as representative of all Muslims and thus legally empowered to commence similar discussions with the Laender governments. Two basic models have been developed so far. One, the Nordrhein-Westfalen model, offers "religious instruction for female and male Muslim pupils" through the tenth grade on a voluntary basis, within the framework of extra lessons given to Turkish children in

Turkish. Teachers are hired by the state government, the materials are developed in Germany, and the emphasis lies on the specific situation of Turkish children in Germany.[67] The other model, followed in Baden-Württemberg, Berlin, Bremen, Hamburg, Saarland, and Schleswig-Holstein, is labeled "religious instruction on the basis of Islam for Muslim pupils." It includes the teaching of religious and language subjects and works on a voluntary and after-hours basis. But the program is offered by Turkey, teachers are employees of the Turkish state, instruction is in Turkish, and course materials are developed in Turkey (with a focus on life in Turkey), while the German schools contribute access to their facilities and sometimes some financial aid.[68] Shortly after its inception in 1994, the Nordrhein-Westfalen model was vigorously opposed by the Central Council for Muslims in Germany, which first applied in 1995 to the Federal Ministry of Culture for the introduction of Islamic instruction taught in German as a curricular requirement in all German schools. The Islamic Council for the Federal Republic of Germany, the Turkish-Islamic Union for Religious Affairs, the Association of Turkish Cultural Centers (Süleymanci), and the Islamic Association of Millî Görüş cosigned the application, the first such united effort among Islamic groups in Germany.[69] Following the February 2000 federal court decision in its favor, a third model of Islamic instruction will shortly be developed in Berlin by the Islamic Federation.

The only Islamic elementary school in Germany to date was founded in Berlin in 1989 and is now funded by the Berlin government. In addition to a general curriculum, it offers classes in Islamic religion and Arabic language.[70] Outside the German school system altogether are the Koran schools ("Koran courses") offered at all mosques in Germany. They are sponsored by a large number of different Islamic groups and organizations, some of which—such as the Islamic Association of Millî Görüş, the Association of Islamic Cultural Centers, and the associations of Fethullah Gülen—also offer religious instruction on weekends and holidays and during school vacations at their own boarding school facilities. Depending on the organizer, the Koran schools teach either an Islamic orthodoxy or a more modern, politicized Islam, neither of which considers the students' special situation in Germany and is in fact often hostile toward integration.[71]

Until the problem of religious instruction at German public schools is solved, Koran schools are bound to remain popular among the Turkish and other Muslim foreign residents; presently they enroll about 10 percent of all Muslim children and youths in Germany.[72] Whether because of a greater awareness of modernity and a higher educational level than that of their parents or because of their exposure to Islamic instruction at any of these institutions, some young Turks in Germany have become what has been dubbed "postmodern Muslims." This means that they are developing a more intellectual knowledge of their scripture and religion than their elders, by studying Arabic, reading the Qur'anic text, and debating its tenets, the latter most often in German. Spiritually, intellectually, and culturally, they accept Islam as part of their identity, in both a modern and an ancient sense. Such an interest in Islam is expressed even by some secularists, such as the Turkish novelist Emine Sevgi Özdamar, who in her pseudoautobiographical novels[73] records her own study of Arabic as a reconnection with her deepest, pre-Republican Anatolian roots. For these young Turks in Germany, traditional dress codes can be fulfilled by wearing modern West European leisure wear in a certain manner (such as the blue jeans and headscarf combinations popular among some young Muslim women) that are symbolic of their belief that religious commitment is compatible with modern life.[74] The relationship of these groups with the more traditionalist and/ or ideologically committed Islamists, however, remains as problematic as it is with the many Turkish youths of secular orientation.

Islamic Religious Organizations in Contemporary Germany

At present, the connections between Turkish Islam in Germany and Islam in Turkey are hard to read. While the major associations are largely organized and directed from Turkey, many others are locally based, and a number of Islamic groups in Turkey are even said to be financed and supported from Germany. About 20 percent of the now more than two million Turks residing in Germany are said to be Alevi and to have their own organizations.[75] Islamist organizations are said to number twenty-two, which includes groups linked to Islamist cadres in Algeria, Palestine, and Iran. The most prominent Turkish groups regarded as "extremist" are the Association of Islamic Congregations and Societies (the group of the late Cemalettin Kaplan) and the Islamic Association Millî Görüş (National View), founded in the 1970s by followers of Necmettin Erbakan.[76] Taken together, all Islamic associations and organizations, many of which are now joined into umbrella organizations, are said to number about 2,000. Many are legally incorporated and enjoy nonprofit status. Affiliation of groups and organizational connections, however, are said to be "opaque," as are many of the associations' chosen, and changeable, names, and their membership figures.[77]

In addition to Kaplan's Association of Islamic Congregations and Societies and Erbakan's Islamic Association Millî Goruş, the following Turkish-Islamic groups and umbrella organizations are active in Germany: the Turkish-Islamic Association of the Institute for Religious Affairs (which represents the official State Islam of Turkey), the Islamic Council for the Federal Republic of Germany (linked to Millî Görüş), the Central Council of Muslims in Germany (said to be Saudi-funded), the Association of Turkish-Islamic Cultural Organizations in Europe, the Nakshbandi order, the Association of Islamic Cultural Centers (Süleymanci), and the Islamic Association Jama'at al-Nur (Nurcus and followers of Fethullah Gülen).[78] While divisions and competition persist, some organizations have lately begun to cooperate, pooling resources as well as coordinating efforts to seek representation on the elected advisory councils for foreigners that operate on the local level in many parts of Germany. The main common goal is to establish Islam as a legally recognized religion in Germany, which would place religious instruction into the German public school curriculum, facilitate mosque building, and provide many other rights in public and private life. Most of the groups are also in favor of introducing dual citizenship in Germany.[79]

A Glimpse of the Future

Most of these goals now seem within reach. Germany's new interior minister, Otto Schilly, expressed his support for granting Islam in Germany the same official status as that held by the Roman Catholic and Protestant churches, thereby making it eligible for government funding. If this plan were to be approved, Islamic religious instruction would be introduced into the German public school curriculum.[80] Furthermore, the new immigration law proposed by the Social Democrat/Green government elected in fall 1998 would grant citizenship at birth to all children born in Germany, provided that at least one parent was born in Germany or arrived there before age fourteen and holds a residence permit. (The Greens wanted to award citizenship to all children born to foreigners holding residence permits, but the Social Democrats were not willing to go that far, at least for now.) Non-Germans born elsewhere would be able to apply for German citizenship after eight years of legal residence. And dual citizenship would be tolerated, even though it would not be encouraged. Of all the contested provisions in this proposed new immigration law, the issue of dual citizenship remains the most controversial.[81] Yet the transition from an ethnicity-based concept of nationality to a liberal republican one is now well under way.[82] As it involves profound psychological shifts on the part of large segments of the German population, however, the full integration of citizens of foreign descent into German society—the full transformation of Sojourners into Citizens—is bound to require time and generational change.

Notes

1. Rogers Brubaker, *Citizenship and Nationhood in France and Germany* (Cambridge, Mass.: Harvard University Press, 1992), 5.
2. Ibid., 4.
3. Ibid., 5.
4. Ibid., 4.
5. Ibid., 8-13.
6. Wesley D. Chapin, *Germany for the Germans? The Political Effects of International Migration* (Westport, Conn.: Greenwood Press, 1997), 3-6. According to Ray C. Rist, *Guestworkers in Germany* (New York: Praeger, 1978), 57-59, thousands of nineteenth-century Polish miners actually did remain in the Ruhr area and eventually took German citizenship.
7. Eva Kolinsky, "Non-German Minorities in Contemporary German Society," in *Turkish Culture in German Society Today*, ed. David Horrocks and Eva Kolinsky (Providence: Berghahn Books, 1996), 71. See also Chapin, *Germany*, 7-8, and Rist, *Guestworkers*, 59-60.
8. Chapin, *Germany*, 8-9. Even higher figures are given by Rist, *Guestworkers*, 5, 60-61.
9. For the 1938 Foreigner Police Ordinance and the 1933 Ordinance on Foreign Workers, cf. Chapin, *Germany*, 10.
10. Chapin, *Germany*, 11, and Rist, *Guestworkers*, 61.
11. Rist, *Guestworkers*, 22-24.
12. Chapin, *Germany*, 11-15.
13. Kolinsky, "Non-German Minorities in Contemporary German Society," 82; cf. Rist, *Guestworkers*, 65-66.
14. Kolinsky, "Non-German Minorities in Contemporary German Society," 82.
15. While in 1961 20 percent of all foreign workers had members of their families with them in Germany, by 1975 that figure had risen to more than 50 percent. In the first two years after the recruitment ban alone, 550,000 family members, including 40,000 juveniles, immigrated to Germany; they were, however, not issued work permits if they arrived in Germany after November 30, 1974 (Rist, *Guestworkers*, 115-17), and certain cities with a high percentage of foreign residents were declared off limits for family reunification (P. L. Martin, *The Unfin-

ished Story: Turkish Labor Migration to Western Europe, with Special Reference to the Federal Republic of Germany [Geneva: International Labour Office, 1991], 30–31).

16. Kolinsky, "Non-German Minorities in Contemporary German Society," 82–83.

17. Kolinsky, "Non-German Minorities in Contemporary German Society," 82, and Chapin, *Germany*, 16–18.

18. Rist, *Guestworkers*, 33.

19. Rist, *Guestworkers*, 34 and 112, cf. 53 and 120–32.

20. Chapin, *Germany*, 18.

21. *The Economist*, 31 Oct. 1998.

22. Chapin, *Germany*, 18–24.

23. In practical terms, the division between old-time "guest workers" and new "asylum seekers" may not even always be clear, as many would-be migrant or immigrant workers from abroad, including Turkey, to whom the former opportunities of German labor recruitment are now lost and the opportunities of family reunion lessened, have also swelled the ranks of the asylum-seekers. Chapin, *Germany*, 19–20.

24. For a full analysis, cf. Chapin, *Germany*, 53–91.

25. David Horrocks and Eva Kolinsky, eds., *Turkish Culture in German Society Today* (Providence: Berghahn Books, 1996), "Introduction," XV–XVII.

26. The reason for the "deviation" from this plan was, in part, that the recruiting country, in addition to placing generic "anonymous" work requests, also had the right to place individual-specific "nominative" requests that were beyond the authority of the Turkish employment service; thus, during the years of the most active in-migration into Germany, the German recruitment office managed to contract three-quarters of all skilled workers who migrated out of Turkey. The majority of migrants were either of urban background or, if of rural origin, had previously migrated to and found work in a Turkish city, which meant that they were generally more skilled, literate, and mobile than their rural counterparts (Rist, *Guestworkers*, 91–97). Many of the data on the Turkish workers in Germany presented in this chapter are taken from Rist, whose analysis in turn relies on a number of primary studies of the subject, especially the work of Nermin Abadan-Unat and Ayshe Kudat.

27. According to Rist, the ratio of Turkish male to female workers migrating to Germany between 1969 and 1973 was roughly four to one, lower than elsewhere, mainly because Germany had put in special requests for female workers. *Guestworkers*, 95–97.

28. Dursun Tan and Hans-Peter Waldhoff, "Turkish Everyday Culture in Germany and Its Prospects," in *Turkish Culture in German Society Today*, ed. David Horrocks and Eva Kolinsky (Providence: Berhahn Books, 1996), 143–44.

29. Rist, *Guestworkers*, 151–53.

30. Kolinsky, "Non-German Minorities in Contemporary German Society," 96.

31. Elçin Kürsat-Ahlers, "The Turkish Minority in German Society," in *Turkish Culture in German Society Today*, ed. David Horrocks and Eva Kolinsky (Providence: Berhahn Books, 1996), 125.

32. Kürsat-Ahlers, "Turkish Minority," 124. Cf. Rist, *Guestworkers*, 151, 158–61, 171, 174–75.

33. Rist, *Guestworkers*, 78–79.

34. Kolinsky, "Non-German Minorities in Contemporary German Society," 93–95.

35. Kürsat-Ahlers, "Turkish Minority," 126.

36. Ibid., 127.

37. Ibid., 125.

38. Günter Wallraff, *Ganz Unten* (Köln: Kiepenheuer & Witsch, 1985).

39. Sabine Fischer and Moray McGovern, "From *Pappkoffer* to Pluralism: On the Development of Migrant Writing in the German Federal Republic," in *Turkish Culture in German Society Today*, ed. David Horrocks and Eva Kolinsky (Providence: Berhahn Books, 1996), 14.

40. Cf. Yasemin Karakasoglu, "Turkish Cultural Orientations in Germany and the Role of Islam," in *Turkish Culture in German Society Today*, ed. David Horrocks and Eva Kolinsky (Providence: Berhahn Books, 1996), 157–60.

41. Tan and Waldhoff, "Turkish Everyday Culture," 139–40, and Karakasoglu, "Turkish Cultural Orientations," 160–61.

42. Karakasoglu, "Turkish Cultural Orientations," 166; Ursula Spuler-Stegemann, *Muslime in Deutschland: Nebeneinander oder Miteinander* (Freiburg: Herder Verlag, 1998), 108.

43. Kolinsky, "Non-German Minorities in Contemporary German Society," 91–92.

44. Thorston Blach, *Nach Mekka gewandt* (Kassel: Arbeitsgemeinschaft Friedhof und Denkmal, 1996), 54–58, 70.

45. Of the new arrivals, spouses as well as working-age children had to wait four years before seeking legal employment. Kolinsky, "Non-German Minorities in Contemporary German Society," 90.

46. Ibid., 89.

47. Ibid., 95.

48. Kürsat-Ahlers, "Turkish Minority," 126.

49. Thomas Faist, *Social Citizenship for Whom? Young Turks in Germany and Mexican Americans in the United States* (Brookfield: Ashgate, 1995), 198–204.

50. While "no racially and ethnically separate systems of schooling and job training evolved in Germany during the twentieth century . . . social citizenship rested upon a class-based system of preparation for the working world. German apprenticeship and university education evolved as separate spheres of post-secondary education and training that were unconnected, quite unlike the comprehensive high school in the United States." Faist, *Social Citizenship*, 202. Cf. Rist, *Guestworkers*, 183. Other critics have blamed German educational policy for having a nationalist focus when they decry the fact that Turkish students who complete the German educational system in Germany still have to apply for university admission within the rubric of non-German applicants (Kürsat-Ahlers, "Turkish Minority," 130–31).

51. Kolinsky, "Non-German Minorities in Contemporary German Society," 101–3.

52. Kürsat-Ahlers, "Turkish Minority," 130.

53. Tan and Waldhoff, "Turkish Everyday Culture," 138–40.

54. Rist, *Guestworkers*, 187–205.

55. Ibid., 187–205, 226–30.

56. Ibid., 206–22.

57. Cf., for example, Günter Rückert, *Untersuchungen zum Sprachverhalten türkischer Jugendlicher in der BDR* (Pfaffenweiler: Centaurus Verlagsgesellschaft, 1985).

58. Feridun Zaimoglu, *Kanak Sprak, 24 Misstöne from Rande der Gesellschaft* (Hamburg: Rotbuch Verlag, 1995); *Kanake* is a contemporary racist German epithet applied to foreigners, especially Turks, that has all the denigrating connotations of "nigger" or "spic." Forty years ago the word *Kanake* meant something like "rascal" or "wild man." It appears to have acquired its present meaning of a racist slur with the arrival of large numbers of foreign workers and settlers into Germany. *Sprak* is a dialectal equivalent of *Sprache*, "language." According to Zaimoglu, second- and third-generation Turkish children have adopted the epithet as a confrontational symbol of their identity: "they carry it with a proud defiance." 9.

59. Ibid., 13.

60. Tan and Waldhoff, "Turkish Everyday Culture," 148–49.

61. Güney Dal and Emine Sevgi Özdamar, *Europastrasse 5*, trans. Carl Koss (München: Piper, 1990).

62. Emine Sevgi Özdamar, *Mutterzunge: Erzählungen*, 2nd ed. (Köln: Kiepenheuer & Witsch, 1998); *Das Leben ist eine Karawanserai* (Köln: Kiepenheuer & Witsch, 1992); *Die Brücke vom Goldenen Horn* (Koln: Kiepenheuer & Witsch, 1998).

63. Cf. Kolinsky, "Non-German Minorities in Contemporary German Society," 103, and Kürsat-Ahlers, "Turkish Minority," 117.

64. *Washington Post*, 9 Jan. 2000.

65. Spuler-Stegemann, *Muslime in Deutschland*, 235.

66. *Arabia.On.Line*, http://www.arabia.com/article/0,1690, ArabiaLife-14447, 00.html. This article emphasized that some members of the Federation are known for extremist activities and agendas and that even the conservative Turkish press was reacting negatively to the court's decision. The article soon disappeared from the *Arabia.On.Line* home page.

67. The Nordrhein-Westfalen model was vigorously opposed by the Central Council of Muslims in Germany, which is said to have applied with the Federal Ministry of Culture for introducing Islamic instruction taught in German as a curricular requirement at all German public schools; the Islamic Council for the Federal Republic of Germany, the Turkish-Islamic Union for Religious Affairs, the Association of Turkish Cultural Centers (Süleymanci), and the Islamic Association of Millî Görüş, are said to have cosigned the application, the first such united effort ever. Spuler-Stegemann, *Muslime in Deutschland*, 242-45.

68. Karakasoglu, "Turkish Cultural Orientation," 164-65.

69. Spuler Stegemann, Muslime in Deutschland, 242-45

70. An Islamic secondary school was established by the Islamic Center in Munich, and since 1995 there has been a Saudi King Fahd Academy in Bonn; but instruction at the former is in both Arabic and German and at the latter in Arabic only. Spuler-Stegemann, *Muslime in Deutschland*, 236-37.

71. Cf. "Was lernt man in einer Koranschule? Themen eines Lernprogramms extrem-islamistischer Tendenz," in *Begegnung mit Türken, Begegnung mit dem Islam: Ein Arbeitsbuch*, ed. Hans-Jürgen Brandt and Claus-Peter Haase, vol. 4 (Hamburg: Rissen, 1984), 83-102, which reproduces "exam questions and their correct answers" obtained from a Millî Görüş–affiliated Koran school in Hamburg. This document combines emphasis on traditional articles of the faith with a glorification of the Ottoman Empire and the condemnation of secularism in Turkey and worldwide.

72. Spuler-Stegemann, *Muslime in Deutschland*, 240-41.

73. Especially *Das Leben ist eine Karawanserei*, and *Mutterzunge*.

74. Karakasoglu, "Turkish Cultural Orientation," 173-74.

75. Spuler-Stegemann, *Muslime in Deutschland*, 51-56.

76. Ibid., 73-91. Extremist but not religious are the left-extremist PKK (Kurdish Workers Party), the now outlawed Turkish *Devrimci Sol* (Revolutionary Left), and the right-extremist Grey Wolves. Ibid., 69-71.

77. Ibid., 103-8. For example, the Islamic Center Aachen and the Islamic Center München belong to two different branches of the Muslim Brotherhood, while the Islamic Center Hamburg is the theological and political headquarter for all Shi'ites in Germany.

78. Ibid., 11-126, 138-46.

79. Cf. Karakasoglu, "Turkish Cultural Orientation," 175-76.

80. *Christian Science Monitor*, 3 Dec. 1998.

81. *Economist*, 31 Oct. 1998.

82. *New York Times*, 16 Oct. 1998.

4

Islam in Switzerland: Fragmented Accommodation in a Federal Country

Hans Mahnig

For many observers Switzerland is a puzzling example of a nation-state. It consists not only of four different cultural groups—75 percent of the country's Swiss population speak German, 20 percent French, 4 percent Italian, and 1 percent Ratho-Romanic[1]—but it is also divided into twenty-six territorial units, the so-called *cantons*, which have significant autonomy in a variety of policy fields such as education, police, and taxes. It is primarily through its federalist institutions that the country succeeds in accommodating its cultural diversity. According to the federalist principles, the Swiss parliament is divided into two chambers, the *Nationalrat* (the representatives of the people) and the *Ständerat* (the representatives of the cantons). In order to become law, a bill must be supported by a majority in each chamber.[2]

Traditionally a multicultural society, since the end of the nineteenth-century Switzerland has also become a country of immigration.[3] Since 1945 it has had one of the highest immigration rates in Europe. Today, about one-fifth of its population is foreign born,[4] a figure twice as high as that of the United States and considerably higher than that of Canada, two traditional immigration countries. From 285,000 in 1950 (6.1 percent of the total population), the number of foreigners living in Switzerland has now increased to 1,368.000 (19.2 percent).[5] During the 1950s and 1960s most of these immigrants came from Italy and Spain. But, more recently, there have been increasing numbers of migrant laborers from the former Yugoslavia, Portugal, and Turkey and of asylum seekers, mainly from Sri Lanka but also from the former Yugoslavia and Turkey. The most sizeable foreign groups are the Italians, Portuguese, Spaniards, and former Yugoslavians. The majority of the countries of origin of immigrants in Switzerland are members of the European Union.[6]

Despite its multicultural character, Switzerland has not yet recognized that it is an immigration country, and it has no real immigrant policy on the federal level. The claims for such a policy have always been rejected with the argument that the integration of immigrants was the duty of the cantons.[7] As a matter of fact, the cantons, and also the municipalities, are responsible for the inclusion of immigrants and their children in two major domains: school and citizenship. The public school (*Volksschule*) is organized by the cantons, which means that persons from outside Switzerland as well as Swiss from other linguistic regions within the country are required to adapt to the dominant local language. The cantonal authorities, however, favor quite different policies toward immigrant children. The distinctions among their strategies correspond roughly to the major linguistic split in Switzerland: German-speaking cantons tend to set up specific and separate institutions for immigrant children, whereas French- and Italian-speaking cantons try to integrate them quickly in the mainstream institutions.[8]

Swiss citizenship is strongly rooted in the municipalities. The federal Constitution stipulates that in order to get Swiss citizenship one first has to become a citizen of a municipality and then of a canton. A candidate for naturalization must first seek federal authorization for naturalization from the federal Office of Police. Once he is in possession of this document, he has to ask the right of citizenship (*droit de cité*) of a municipality.[9] While the federal Constitution says only that in order to apply for Swiss citizenship one must prove that he has lived legally for twelve years in the country, the municipalities have the right to establish additional criteria, which are frequently grounded on an ethnocultural logic.

The cantons also play a crucial role in determining the relationship between state and religion. Again, while the federal Constitution guarantees religious freedom to all citizens, which obliges local communities to respect religious neutrality and to treat the different religious groups on equal terms, cantons are autonomous in their relationship with the churches. Because Switzerland is also a multiconfessional country—some cantons in the past were Catholic, others Protestant—the historical conflicts between different confessions on the one hand and between religion and state on the other led to quite different results.[10] Thus, today there are twenty-six ways of defining the place of religion in public life, from a relatively close relation between state and church in some cantons to a complete separation in others.[11]

Nevertheless, in practically all cantons religious communities are recognized as corporations under public law (*öffentlich-rechtliche Körperschaften*), a status that gives them the right to receive public subsidies. This treatment, however, is almost everywhere reserved for the Christian churches. The Jewish community is recognized by only four of the twenty-six cantons in this way, Islam by none of them.[12] Unlike the Jews, who never tried to question this situation openly, Muslim immigrants in recent years have begun to challenge the traditional relationship between state and churches in several ways.

Muslims in Switzerland

The presence of Muslims is a comparatively recent phenomenon in Switzerland; at the beginning of the 1970s fewer than 20,000 were living in the country. Over the past twenty-five years, however, their number has multiplied. The federal census of 1980 counted 56,600 Muslims, and that of 1990, 152,200 (see table 4.1). Because the census—which takes place every ten years—is the only instrument that asks about religion, there are no more recent official data available. Estimates suggest that today between 200,000 and 250,000 Muslims are living in Switzerland, which is between 2.8 percent and 3.5 percent of the total population. Therefore, Islam has become the second largest religion of the country after Christianity.[13]

The national and social composition of Muslims living in Switzerland is regionally quite heterogeneous. In the French-speaking part of the country, many come from Arabic countries (mostly from Northern Africa) and belong to the middle classes. In the German-speaking part, the majority are foreign workers from Turkey and the former

Table 4.1. Muslims living in Switzerland according
to the federal census (1970–1990)

	Total Number	% of Total Population
1970	16.353	0.3%
1980	56.625	0.9%
1990	152.217	2.2%

Source: Bundesamt für Statistik, *Mohammedanische Bevölkerung in der
Schweiz*, Bern, 1991, and Bundesamt für Statistik, *L'évolution de
l'appartenance religieuse et confessionelle en Suisse*, Bern, 1997.

Yugoslavia.[14] In 1990 almost 80 percent of all Muslim foreigners came from these two
countries (42.8 percent from Turkey, 36.4 percent from the former Yugoslavia), followed by persons from the Maghreb (4 percent%) and from Lebanon (3.3 percent).[15]
Only some 5 percent claim Swiss citizenship. As is true elsewhere in Europe, the immigration of Muslims to Switzerland is an urban phenomenon. Seventy-three percent of
Muslims live in cities,[16] and, because most of them arrived as foreign workers, the initial expressions of an Islamic life emerged in poor neighborhoods. At the beginning of
the 1990s, scholars estimated that about sixty mosques existed in Switzerland, almost
all of them established in converted apartments or stores. Today there are more than a
hundred. Because of the very liberal legislation in this domain, most of the mosques
and Islamic centers in Switzerland are organized as associations;[17] some of them are
also set up as foundations, a legal form that gives the founding members of the organization more control than they would have in an association.

The religious organization of Muslims differs according to their ethnic and national
origin. Turkish Muslims, for example, are divided by the ideological and political divisions of their home country. When in the 1970s the Islamic movement Millî Görüş
was established in Germany, some of the Turkish Muslims in Switzerland joined this
organization. But the activities of the Diyanet, the Turkish directorate of religious affairs that sends Imams to the Turkish diaspora, attracted other Turkish Muslims to
adhere to this state-controlled form of Islam.[18] Turkish groups such as the Sufi Süley-
mancilar and the Nurcu confraternity also play a role in the Turkish Muslim community in Switzerland.[19]

For a long time these first manifestations of an Islamic life were invisible in the public
space. During the 1980s the media became interested in the new religious minority, but
until quite recently Islam has remained "an almost complete mystery"[20] for Swiss society. One of the reasons for this phenomenon, as several scholars have observed for
Europe in general, is that Muslim immigrants began to address religious claims to the
European host societies only at the moment when they abandoned the idea of returning "home." In other words, the affirmation of their religious identity for many Muslims is a way of settling in Western societies.[21] Because their immigration is more recent in Switzerland than in other Western European countries, accommodation is still
in an early stage. However, during the past decade Muslims have increasingly addressed
claims to the authorities, who have begun (rather reluctantly) to take them into account.
The most important of these claims concern the setting up of Islamic cemeteries, the
building of mosques, and the formal recognition of Islam as a religious community.

At the same time that Muslims have begun to articulate their demands to Swiss society, public opinion has become increasingly hostile to Islam. One reason for this is international politics. Political events such as the Islamic revolution in Iran and the civil war in Algeria had significant impact on the perception of Islam in Switzerland. Studies show that the Swiss media provide mostly negative pictures of Islam.[22] A second reason is the fact that during the past few years the drug market in Switzerland has increasingly become dominated by dealers from the former Yugoslavia, especially Kosovo. The negative impact of this phenomenon on the perception of immigrants in general is made worse by the fact that the majority of people from Kosovo are Muslims.[23] There is actually a tendency in the media and in public opinion to attribute the problems of Muslim immigrants in Switzerland to their religious difference.[24] This "ethnicization" of what are mostly social problems has a detrimental impact on the chances of Muslims to be naturalized. Many municipalities have recently refused to give Swiss citizenship to Turks or Albanians, whereas members of other nationalities (for example, Italians or Spaniards) are not faced with such problems.[25]

It is predictable that "the carving of Islamic space"[26] in Switzerland will be a long and difficult process for three primary reasons. First, the Muslims are ethnically and socially very heterogeneous, and many religious differences and political conflicts separate their organizations. Like Muslims in other countries,[27] they have difficulties determining a common strategy and speaking with one voice in front of Swiss authorities. Second, the negative perception of Muslims in public opinion and on the part of many politicians makes them the object of discrimination and unequal treatment. Finally, the federalist Swiss political system requires that Muslims address their demands to the local authorities, who choose quite different strategies to include—and often also to exclude—them.

A closer analysis of the accommodation of Islam in Switzerland needs therefore to focus on the cantons. The following illustrations of the ways in which Muslims and Swiss authorities interact on the local level in the three cantons of Geneva, Neuchâtel, and Zurich will give the reader an idea of what different paths the establishment of Islam in Swiss society will take.

Geneva: The Question of *Laïcité*

Geneva is the Swiss canton where Islam is the most publicly visible. The reason is not the number of Muslims living there—today about 15,000—but their social composition: the middle classes are more strongly represented and students, diplomats, and intellectuals play a more important role in the Muslim community than they do in German-speaking cantons where most of the Muslims came as foreign workers. However, the Muslim community is fragmented in an important way because of the history of Islam in Geneva.[28]

Antagonisms within the Muslim Community

In 1961 Saïd Ramadan, the son-in-law and one of the first disciples of Hassan al-Banna, the founder of the Organization of the Muslim Brothers in Egypt (1928), established the first European branch of this association in Geneva. Arriving in 1958 with other refugees fleeing the repression of Nasser's regime in Egypt, he created the Centre Islamique des Eaux-vives, which became one of the central Islamic institutions in Geneva. Saïd Ramadan's son, Hani Ramadan, is the actual director of the center, and his brother Tariq is one of the most important Islamic intellectuals in Switzerland.[29] However, Saudi Arabia, which supported the center in the beginning, in the 1970s decided to establish its own Islamic institution, both because it wanted to be highly visible in a city of international organizations and because relations between Saudi Arabia and the Muslim Brothers on an international level were deteriorating.[30] In 1978, the mosque of Petit-Saconnex was inaugurated by King Khaled of Saudi Arabia, which is the only mosque in Switzerland recognizable as such by its architectural form. The mosque is part of the Fondation Culturelle Islamique du Petit-Saconnex, financed by Saudi Arabia. It attracts about 2,500 Muslims from all social origins for the Friday prayer,[31] and the Foundation offers Islamic and Arabic courses for children and adults. There are also classes aimed at a non-Muslim public that wants to know more about Islamic culture and history.[32] Most of the members of Geneva's international institutions and most of the diplomats from Muslim countries go to the mosque.

The Centre Islamique des Eaux-vives provides Islamic courses for children and adults, as well as language courses for Muslims who do not speak French. It organizes conferences on Islam and publishes a number of reviews. Its library is used mostly by Muslims from the Maghreb, but it also attracts a number of Turks. Students from Arabic countries, who are critical of Saudi Arabia, avoid the Foundation and come to the center. Thus far, the ideological differences between the two institutions have prevented members of the Muslim community from adopting a common strategy to promote their aims.[33]

On the other side, the authorities of Geneva have never tried to set up a dialogue with Islamic organizations to address the different issues and concerns that emerged during the past decade. In Geneva there is a strict separation between the state and the churches. The idea of *laïcité*, the principle of neutrality of the state toward all religious communities, is—as in France—a deeply entrenched tradition, and almost all conflicts that have arisen between the authorities and representatives of the Muslims have been related to this issue.

The Debate on the Relation between State and Religion

The first of these debates took place over an Islamic cemetery. In 1978, at the same time as the establishment of the first mosque, a first Islamic cemetery in Switzerland was created. To be precise, it was not an autonomous cemetery but an isolated area—a so-called *carré musulman* (Muslim quarter)—on the communal cemetery of Petit-Saconnex.[34] In 1992, however, a new member of the city government responsible for cemeteries restricted access to the cemetery, explaining that only Muslims who had lived in the city of Geneva would now have the right to be buried there. Declaring himself committed to the principle of *laïcité*, he decided at the same time that the existing *carré musulman* should not be enlarged or replaced. In spite of the fact that the decision was criticized, it was maintained during the 1990s. Muslim representatives, considering the setting up of a new Islamic cemetery as one of their most important claims, tried to look for a solution in other cantons or even in neighboring France, as the Jewish community of Geneva had done.[35] However, with the arrival in 1999 in the city government of a new *conseiller administratif* responsible for cemeteries, a member of the socialist party who has a more open conception of *laïcité*, the setting up of a new cemetery seems to be once more possible.

The question of *laïcité*, however, has been so far the most politicized with regard to the headscarf. In 1996, the department of public education had asked a Muslim teacher not to wear her headscarf in the classroom. The teacher, a Swiss who converted to Islam in 1991, had worn it for several years without any difficulties. It became an issue only when a visitor to the school informed the authorities. The Swiss authorities argued that while Muslim pupils in Geneva are normally allowed to wear the headscarf in the class-room, the teachers (whether Swiss or foreign) as representatives of the state must con-form to the principle of religious neutrality.[36] In the fall of 1996 the cantonal executive, to whom the teacher had made appeal, confirmed the decision, insisting that an agent of the state cannot wear visible religious signs.[37]

The decision provoked the protest of many Muslim leaders in Geneva. Hani Ramadan condemned it as discriminatory because it focused on the *visibility* of religious signs. According to him, the decision was "against the principles of constitutional states, which guarantee to everybody the freedom of religion and conscience." "The *laïcité*," he added, "cannot mean, in a multicultural state, that its citizens, whatever their function is, have to dissimulate their beliefs and their faith."[38] Tarik Ramadan adopted a similar posi-tion, underscoring the fact that Christian and Jewish symbols never had been prohib-ited.[39] However, the federal court confirmed the decision of the authorities of Geneva in November 1997. In its sentence, the court balanced the guarantee of religious free-dom with the principle of limiting the demonstration of religious convictions in public space. The crucial question, therefore, was whether the headscarf was a *fundamental expression* of the teacher's religion. The federal court denied this, saying that wearing a headscarf was not a fundamental right protected by the principle of religious freedom.[40] Not only Muslims challenged this interpretation; Catholic priests criticized the decision as based on a dogmatic view of the state's neutrality.[41] The teacher decided to appeal to the European Court of Human Rights in Strasbourg, where as of this writing the case awaits judgment.

In the summer of 1999, another conflict concerning the same issue arose. Three Muslim medical students working at a hospital of the University of Geneva were asked to remove their headscarves because the students were employed by a public institu-tion. Once more, the decision was heavily criticized by representatives of Islamic orga-nizations. One of their arguments was that the authorities were hindering the access of Muslim women to education. The Fondation Culturelle Islamique encouraged the three women, who were its pupils, to go to court.[42] There has not been a decision so far.

In sum, dialogue and negotiation between cantonal authorities and Muslim groups in Geneva about the place of Islam in society hardly exist. One reason for this is the strong tradition of separation between state and religion, which transforms the ques-tion—on the political level—rapidly into an ideological one. A second reason is the an-tagonism between the Islamic organizations that have so far kept them from looking together for common solutions and a common strategy toward the authorities. The specific relation between state and religion in Geneva, however, as well as the intellectual resources of the Muslim community there, have produced the most far-reaching reflections in Switzerland of the place of Islam in a secular society. Tariq Ramadan, who at the beginning of the 1990s also founded the Foyer Culturel Musulman as a place of dialogue between Swiss society and young Muslims,[43] can be considered one of the leading figures promoting the birth of a European Islam.[44] According to Ramadan, the Swiss Constitution, within the legal framework of other western democracies, permits the complete affirmation of a Muslim identity.[45] The discrimination against Muslims derives from false interpretations of these constitutional guarantees, sometimes grounded in xenophobia. Ramadan believes, therefore, that the challenge to Muslims is to develop within this framework a new European Islam.[46]

Neuchâtel: Integration through Negotiation

Between 3,000 and 3,500 Muslims are living today in the canton of Neuchâtel. As everywhere, multiple ethnic and political differences explain the existence of a variety of Islamic organizations. Among ten such organizations are the Islamic associations and foundations of the Turks and Bosnians, Islamic centers set up by immigrants from the Maghreb, and an organization of Muslims from India and Pakistan. Two groups also exist for the purpose of uniting the different organizations, including one for women only.[47] Nevertheless, Muslims in Neuchâtel are a quite discrete community and have so far refrained from articulating their demands clearly in the public space.

The Idea of an Intermediary Institution

As in Geneva, there is a strict separation between church and state in Neuchâtel. However, like other associations with humanitarian or social aims, churches have the status of organizations of public interest (*statut d'utilité publique*), which allows them to receive public funding. Because this means of recognition involves a difficult process (on a formal level, the cantonal parliament decides on a request) and for Islam would require the unification of the Islamic groups in one organization, Islam has so far not been accorded this status. The situation, though, has been judged unsatisfactory by the Muslims, as well as by the cantonal authorities, and other ways of recognizing Islam have been sought. In 1996, the office of the delegate for foreigners of the canton commissioned a study of possible solutions. The study concluded that many of the difficulties Muslims have in Neuchâtel could be resolved if a permanent dialogue between Islamic organizations and the cantonal authorities could be institutionalized. According to the report, such a dialogue could help the authorities to understand better the specific claims of Islamic groups in order not to interpret them as extremist demands. It could also help the representatives of the Muslims to become aware of the constraints of the legal framework on the cantonal and the federal level in order not to consider refusals of their claims by the administration as discriminating against Islam.[48]

Because of the traditional separation between state and churches, no institution existed that could have been charged with creating such a dialogue. However, some years earlier the cantonal authorities had already set up a working community for the integration of foreigners (Communauté de Travail pour l'Intégration des Étrangers, or CTIE) in order to improve the relations between immigrants and the canton in general. They decided, therefore, in 1996, to set up a specific group for Muslims (Groupe de Contact "Musulmans") within the framework of the CTIE. The principle of representation is the following: all Islamic organizations can send one of their members to the Groupe de Contact "Musulmans," where members of the cantonal authorities and of civil society are also represented. The group, which meets regularly, has the task of establishing a permanent link between the Muslims and the local authorities. The underlying philosophy of this approach is that the difficulties of Muslims have to be interpreted within the wider scope of the problems of immigrants in general.[49] The aim of the integration of immigrants (*intégration des immigrés*), which is considered to be a process of mutual adjustment through permanent negotiation, has therefore also become the ground for the authorities' policy toward Muslims.

This open attitude has historic roots. Neuchâtel and Jura are the only cantons in Switzerland to have given local voting rights to non-Swiss; foreigners with a permanent residence permit living for one year in Neuchâtel can participate in local elections and voting.[50] So far this legal opportunity for immigrants has not led to the setting up of specific "migrant parties," and there are no indications of a specific "Muslim vote."

Negotiating Compromise

The new institution was accepted by the Islamic organizations and has dealt with many problems since then. In the 1990s, the most important claim of Muslims, as in Geneva, has been the setting up of an Islamic cemetery.[51] The establishment of isolated burial areas on communal cemeteries, as well as of private confessional cemeteries, is prohibited by the constitution of the canton on the grounds that it is discriminatory (see discussion on Zurich). The Jewish cemetery in La-Chaux-de-Fonds is the only exception to this rule. Thus, the question cannot be resolved without a legislative change. So far the matter is still being explored.[52]

Another problem the new institution has taken up is the question of how to produce *halal* meat. This question has particular complications in Switzerland, because, contrary to other European countries, the Confederation legally prohibits the slaughtering of animals before they are knocked unconscious. The Muslims of Neuchâtel are therefore forced to import *halal* meat from France, which is an expensive procedure. To resolve the problem, the Groupe de Contact "Musulmans" asked for several meetings between Muslim representatives and the veterinary office of the canton in order to see whether there might be possible compromise between the federal law and the Islamic prescription that the animal must not be unconscious before being slaughtered.

The philosophy of integration through exchange and mutual adaptation has had other outcomes. The already quoted study from 1996 reported that the public holds a very negative view of Islam.[53] Therefore, the office of the delegate for foreigners supports initiatives for a better mutual understanding between Muslims and the majority population. For example, it organized two weeks of cultural activities under the title "Être Musulman dans le Pays de Neuchâtel" (Being Muslim in Neuchâtel), which has proved to be a very successful event. Newspapers covered the initiative extensively, and Muslim organizations considered it an important step toward the recognition of Islam by the local society.

The question of laïcité, also a founding principle in Neuchâtel, has so far been treated in a pragmatic way and has not led to the ideological struggles that have taken place in Geneva. Nevertheless, the issue has become politicized. In 1998, the teachers of a primary school in La-Chaux-de-Fonds, together with Neuchâtel, the most important city of the canton, protested against the wearing of the headscarf by a Muslim girl, and the issue became a major debate in the local press.[54] The cantonal authorities, however, decided that the girl had the right to wear the headscarf. This decision corresponds to the "headscarf policy" of almost all of the cantonal education authorities in Switzerland.

The establishment of a permanent institution in which Muslims, as well as members of the authorities, are represented in Neuchâtel has been significant in lowering tensions over how Islam should be accommodated in Switzerland. In spite of the fact that Muslims are scattered in many different organizations, the creation of the Groupe de Contact "Musulmans" has begun a process of negotiation and debate that has opened opportunities to find pragmatic solutions.

Zurich: The Impact of Politicization

There are about 35,000 Muslims living today in the canton of Zurich. The first of them came thirty years ago from Near Eastern countries and from the former Yugoslavia; later Muslim immigrants arrived from Turkey, Albania, Bosnia, and Pakistan.[55] The Muslim community of the city of Zurich consists of about 15,000 persons representing three main linguistic groups: the Turkish, the Bosnian, and the Albanian.[56]

The oldest organization of Muslim migrants in Zurich is the Stiftung Islamische Gemeinschaft Zürich (Foundation for the Islamic Community of Zurich). Established in 1975 by Muslim students from the Polytechnic School and the University of Zurich, its principal aim was to provide a common room for the Friday prayer. Its president, the Egyptian Ismail Amin, a former professor at the University of Zurich, has become the leading figure in the struggle to unite the different components of the Muslim community in Zurich in one organization (see later discussion). Today, some eleven Islamic communities can be distinguished according both to the nationality of their members and to political disputes in their countries of origin: five of them are Turkish, two Arabic, one Bosnian, one Kosovo-Albanian, one Pakistani, and one Ahmadi.[57] Coming from Pakistan, the Ahmadi group in 1946 founded a missionary station in Zurich. Though there were almost no Muslims living in the city at that time, the Ahmadiyya movement in 1964 built the first large mosque in Switzerland, which became its European headquarters.[58] The city council apparently believed that the mosque would be perceived as a symbol of the city's liberalism and tolerance and therefore would attract investors from Arab countries. That has not been the case, however, because the Ahmadiyya movement is considered by orthodox Muslims to be a heterodox sect with which they will not associate.

The most important Islamic institution in Zurich is the Islamisches Zentrum (Islamic Center), established in a building owned by the Arabic Emirates but administered by the Foundation Islamic Community Zurich. About 500 persons come to the Friday prayer, mostly immigrants from west and north Africa, Egypt, Somalia, the Arabian Peninsula, Pakistan, and Malaysia. The Imam, who was employed by the Fondation Culturelle Islamique in Geneva before coming to Zurich, is from Morocco; the language spoken in the Islamic Center is Arabic.[59] Nevertheless, Muslims so far have not become a visible minority in the city because they are not concentrated in specific neighborhoods and because most of their mosques are established in industrial areas.

The Muslims' Claims

In 1989, the director of education of the canton published for the first time a circular concerning Muslim pupils, which recommended that they be excused from school for the 'eid al-fitr celebration at the end of the month of Ramadan and that they be allowed to honor their Islamic food prescriptions. Nevertheless, it insisted that Muslim girls attend all classes (including sport instructions) and that the integrative principle of the popular school—to be a school for all—had to be preserved. In 1992 a new circular confirmed this position, which also included toleration of the headscarf of Muslim girls. Therefore, the headscarf has never become a political issue in Zurich. However, when a Turkish father asked that his daughter be exempt from the swimming instruction in school, he was refused first by the director of education and then by the cantonal government. The father appealed to the federal court, which ruled in 1993 that the cantonal authorities were wrong and that the Islamic prescription regarding modesty was more important in this case than the obligation of swimming instruction. The federal court asked therefore that the canton suspend the swimming requirement for the Muslim girl, especially because the father agreed to take his daughter to private swimming lessons.[60]

Nevertheless, the case was thoroughly debated in the legal literature, as well as in the newspapers, as an example of the issues to be faced in the integration of Muslims in Switzerland. Some years before, the federal court had already ruled against the authorities of Zurich, when the cantonal director of justice objected to organizing Friday prayer in a prison where 20 percent of the inmates were Muslims (a percentage that can be explained by the fact that at this time Albanians from the Kosovo, the majority of whom were Muslims, were heavily involved in drug dealing). According to the federal court, this decision violated the principle of equal treatment.[61]

In both conflicts, Muslims succeeded in having their claims respected because they made use—as individual persons—of the legal system. However, there are also *collective* claims made by Muslim organizations in Zurich, the most important being for the setting up of an Islamic cemetery, the construction of a central mosque, and the public recognition of Islam.[62] The third demand is linked to the special relation between the state and the churches in the canton of Zurich. The Reformed Church was the state church of the canton until the beginning of the nineteenth century. In 1831, the process of separation between the state and the Reformed Church began, but it was only in 1963 that the Catholic Church was recognized on equal terms as a corporation under public law (öffentlich-rechtliche Körperschaft), a status that confers the right to receive public subsidies.[63] Therefore, to be recognized as a corporation under public law would put Islam on equal terms with the Christian churches.

In January 1994, in a meeting between different immigrant groups and the city council, a member of the Stiftung Islamische Gemeinschaft transmitted the three demands mentioned to the municipal authorities. In their response, the latter made it clear that they wanted to deal with only *one* Islamic organization, which should represent all the

Muslims living in Zurich. Therefore, although there were some disagreements and tensions among the different communities, they began to engage in negotiations for a common association, and in 1996 they decided to form together the Vereinigung der Islamischen Organisationen in Zürich, or VIOZ (Association of Islamic Organizations in Zurich). Ten of the eleven communities belong today to the VIOZ; the Ahmadiyya movement is not permitted to participate.

At the beginning, the VIOZ tried to promote all the three aims together—the establishment of the cemetery, the construction of a central mosque, and the public recognition of Islam—but the Islamic cemetery became quickly the most important issue on its agenda. Because there is no cemetery in Zurich where Islamic burial prescriptions can be observed, today about 90 percent of their dead are transferred by Muslim families to the countries of origin at very great expense.[64] Already in the middle of the 1970s, the Stiftung Islamische Gemeinschaft asked the help of the municipality in establishing an Islamic cemetery, but the response of the authorities was negative. Their arguments were of a practical nature—they considered, for example, that burying the dead in a shroud and not in a coffin transgressed hygienic regulations. The Muslims, believing that these reasons were only superficial and that there was no political will to support their demand, abandoned it.[65] Only when the municipality showed openness to the Muslims' demands at the beginning of the 1990s did they put the issue back on the agenda.

Struggling for Recognition: The Issue of the Islamic Cemetery

In February 1994, the Muslim communities chose a committee of representatives to negotiate with the city council of Zurich; a month later they met with the mayor, who promised to support their demands. The prevailing idea at this time was to establish a separate area for the graves of Muslims in an existing cemetery.[66] However, a cantonal decree on cemeteries forbids the establishment of separate burial areas in communal cemeteries. This provision has to be understood as a historic legacy of the struggle against religious discrimination. The prohibition against distinguishing burial areas according to confessions was meant to protect religious minorities from being excluded in the communal cemeteries.[67] The decree in principle can be changed by the cantonal executive, but the concerned authorities informed the mayor that they were not willing to change the article. Therefore, the project of a private cemetery was chosen. Because the climate toward immigrants in general became increasingly unfavorable during this period, the mayor asked the Muslim organizations to prepare the project silently and discreetly. The project became a public issue only when, in November 1995, the municipality decided to sell the Muslim representatives an area near an already existing cemetery in the neighborhood of Altstetten, at the periphery of the city.

With the publication of the decision in the press at the beginning of 1996, local politicians from the Schweizerische Volkspartei, or SVP (Swiss Popular Party), a populist right-wing party, began to mobilize against the project, trying to enlarge their constituency by leading a xenophobic campaign against the Islamic cemetery. One of their main arguments was the fact that the graves of Muslims are "eternal" because the dead cannot to be removed, whereas normally a grave on a public cemetery is replaced by another one after twenty-five years. In fact, because of a general lack of space in Swiss cemeteries, most cantons in Switzerland demand the removal of the graves after a certain time period. Thus, the SVP presented the Muslims' demand as a claim for more extensive rights than the Swiss have. Even though this in fact was not true—Muslims agreed to reuse the old graves—the opponents of the cemetery declared in advertisements and pamphlets that Christian tolerance was being "shamelessly abused" and that Swiss would become strangers in their own country.[68] Faced with this campaign, the mayor and the Catholic and Protestant priests of Altstetten organized information meetings, where they defended the project as an answer to a legitimate problem and a question of treating Muslims on equal terms.

Meanwhile, the different coordination meetings between Muslim representatives and municipal administrations had produced concrete results. The price of the burial place had been fixed, and the official name, Islamischer Friedhof Zürich (Islamic Cemetery of Zurich), had been chosen. Because the Muslim communities did not have enough money to buy the cemetery, they planned to collect funds from Arab countries; the president of the VIOZ was charged with the job of contacting Arab embassies and consulates. However, the project failed. The reason was not the political opposition—even though some politicians tried to keep the question on the agenda, the emotional atmosphere in Altstetten calmed down[69]—but the failure of the Muslim communities to find the necessary funds. The Arab countries were not willing to finance an Islamic cemetery, because, they argued, that this was an interior problem of Switzerland. By the end of 1996, it became clear that the Muslims would not be able to get the necessary money—only $100,000 US were collected, whereas the total costs of the burial place were estimated at about three to four times that amount. In November 1997, the project was finally abandoned.

The failure to set up a private cemetery for Muslims brought back the question of a change of the cantonal decree on cemeteries. In June 1997, the mayor of Zurich sent a letter to the cantonal authorities, asking to discuss the possibilities of reforming the article. He based his request on a juridical analysis by a former federal judge, who came to the conclusion that the provisions of the Swiss Constitution obligated local communities to help religious minorities to establish their own cemeteries, either by giving them the possibility of establishing their own burial places or by according them separate areas in already existing cemeteries.[70] The cantonal authorities were nevertheless very cautious and organized a consultation procedure that invited municipalities and religious communities to give their opinions on a possible change in the decree. During the same time, in May 1999, the federal court rejected the appeal of a Swiss Muslim against his municipality, which had denied him a grave without time limit in the local cemetery. On the grounds of this judgment, although in the consultation procedure a majority of participants expressed themselves in favor of a change, the cantonal authorities decided in September 1999 to leave the article as it was.[71]

This decision has been heavily criticized, especially in light of a decision around the same time by the city of Bern to establish an Islamic quarter in a communal cemetery. That decision, critics argued, showed that such a project was possible if it was preceded by a process of dialogue and compromise.[72] Thus far, however, the authorities of the canton of Zurich have refused a dialogue with the Islamic organizations on the question.

The accommodation of Islam in Switzerland has so far not become as politicized an issue as it has in some other European immigration countries.[73] One reason for this is that Muslim immigration in Switzerland is more recent than Muslim immigration elsewhere in western Europe. Another is that, up to now, the heterogeneity of the Muslim population living in Switzerland has prevented Islamic organizations from speaking with one voice and adopting a common strategy to address their claims to the Swiss authorities. These claims are very similar to the demands of Muslims in other European countries, the question of setting up Islamic cemeteries being today the most urgent. Several attempts to establish a common representative organization on the federal level have been made, but they have not succeeded so far. A third reason for the absence of politicization of the question in Switzerland, however, is the country's political system. Federalism is responsible for the fact that most of the claims of Muslims are treated on the local level and that they rarely appear in the arena of national politics.

Therefore, the "carving of Islamic space" in Switzerland will be the result primarily of local politics. The examples of the three cantons presented here show that the decentralized system in place in Switzerland leads to quite different responses and to a fragmented accommodation of Islam. However, in several cases, Muslims have also appealed to constitutional principles, challenging local decisions they considered discriminatory, and the decisions of the federal court have therefore become an important factor in the definition of the rights of religious minorities in Switzerland. Often these decisions have favored the claims of Muslims against the policies of local authorities and against public opinion.[74] In other cases, however, the federal court has rejected the Muslims' demands.

Today, some observers believe that the existing legal framework is sufficient for the accommodation of Islam in Switzerland,[75] whereas others think that Swiss legislation needs to change and that "certain collective provisions will be necessary in the near future in order to satisfy minority demands."[76] This debate is only beginning, and it is not yet possible to know the concrete political and legal outcomes of the struggle of Muslims for the recognition of Islam in Switzerland. In any case, Switzerland's institutional settings, as well as the attitude of its politicians and public opinion, will have to change in order for Islam to have a possibility of being treated on equal terms with other, previously established religions.

Notes

I would like to thank the persons who gave me important information during the writing of this text: Sarah Burkhalter, Matteo Gianni, and Hani Ramadan (Geneva); Thomas Facchinetti (Neuchâtel); and Ismail Amin, Taner Hatipoglu, and Peter Wittwer (Zurich).

1. The Ratho-Romanic are a cultural minority speaking a Romance language. Consisting of about 50,000 persons, they live in the canton of Graubünden.

2. See for example Wolf Linder, *Schweizerische Demokratie–Institutionen, Prozesse, Perspektiven* (Bern: Verlag Paul Haupt, 1999), 135–59.

3. Gérald Arlettaz, "Démographie et identité nationale (1850–1914): la Suisse et la 'question des étrangers,'" *Etudes et Sources* 11 (1985): 83–180.

4. Werner Haug, *Vom Einwanderungsland zur multikulturellen Gesellschaft* (Bern: Bundesamt für Statistik, 1995), 28.

5. *Neue Zürcher Zeitung*, 12–13 Feb. 2000.

6. *Die Ausländer in der Schweiz–Retrospektive Bestandesergebnisse* (Bern: Bundesamt für Ausländerfragen, 1997).

7. Hans Mahnig, "La question de l'intégration ou comment les immigrés deviennent un

enjeu politique—une comparaison entre la France, l'Allemagne, les Pays-Bas et la Suisse," *Sociétés Contemporaines* 33, no. 34 (1999): 31.

8. Christina Allemann-Ghionda, "Schule und Migration in der Schweiz: Zwischen dem Ideal der Integration und der Versuchung der Separation." *Schweizerische Zeitschrift für Soziologie* 23, no. 3 (1997): 354.

9. See Pierre Centlivres, *Devenir Suisse* (Genève: Georg Editeur, 1990).

10. See Louis Carlen, "Das Verhältnis von Kirche und Staat in der Schweiz," in *Handbuch des katholischen Kirchenrechts*, 2nd ed. ed. Joseph Listl et al. (Regensburg: F. Pustet, 1999), 1308–23.

11. Ueli Friederich, "Einführung in das schweizerische Staatskirchenrecht," in *Kirche und Staat im Umbruch*, ed. Adrian Loretan (Zürich: NZN-Buchverlag, 1995), 19–32.

12. Louis Carlen, "Das Verhältnis von Kirche und Staat in der Schweiz," 1310; see also Liz Fischli-Giesser, "Die öffentlich-rechtliche Stellung 'anderer' Religionsgemeinschaften," in *Kirche und Staat im Umbruch*, ed. Adrian Loretan (Zürich: NZN-Buchverlag, 1995), 161.

13. Marcel Heiniger, "Daten zu Muslimen und Musliminnen in der Schweiz," *Tangram— Bulletin der Eidgenössischen Kommission gegen Rassismus* 7 (1999): 79–80.

14. Hartmut Fähndrich, "Unverträgliche Mentalitäten?—Muslime in der Schweiz," in *Blickwechsel—Die multikulturelle Schweiz an der Schwelle zum 21. Jahrhundert*, ed. Simone Prodolliet (Luzern: Caritas-Verlag, 1998), 249–52.

15. Marcel Heiniger, "Daten Zu Muslimen und Musliminnen in der Schweiz," 79.

16. Ibid.

17. Christoph Peter Baumann and Christian Jäggi, *Muslime unter uns—Islam in der Schweiz* (Luzern: Rex-Verlag, 1991), 69–73.

18. Patrick Haenni, "L'islam pluriel des musulmans de Suisse: engagement et distanciation de 'l'autre intérieur,'" *Tangram—Bulletin der Eidgenössischen Kommission gegen Rassismus* 7 (1999): 12–15.

19. Ibid., 13; see also Christoph Peter Baumann, ed., *Islam in Basel-Stadt und Basel-Land* (Basel: Vorabdruck des Projekts *Führer durch das religiöse Basel*, 1999).

20. Patrick Haenni, "Musulmans de Suisse et religion: d'un islam à l'autre," in *Minorités chrétiennes et musulmanes—aspects religieux*, ed. Jacques Waardenburg, *Cahiers de l'Université de Lausanne* 4 (1995): 10.

21. For this hypothesis see for example Gilles Kepel, *Les banlieues de l'islam—naissance d'une religion en France* (Paris: Seuil, 1991), 9–19, and Steven Vertovec and Ceri Peach, "Introduction: Islam in Europe and the Politics of Religion and Community," in *Islam in Europe The Politics of Religion and Community*, ed. Steven Vertovec and Ceri Peach (Warwick: Centre for Research in Ethnic Relations, 1997), 21–24.

22. Waseem Hussain, "Feindbild Islam: die Verantwortung der Redaktionen," *Tangram— Bulletin der Eidgenössischen Kommission gegen Rassismus* 2 (1997): 33–36.

23. Nada Bokovska, "Feindbild Jugo," *Tages-Anzeiger Magazin* 19 (1999): 22–29.

24. Hartmut Fähndrich, "Glauben und glauben lassen, nicht glauben und nicht glauben lassen—c'est la vie, et la vie est dure." *Tangram—Bulletin der Eidgenössischen Kommission gegen Rassismus* 7 (1999): 9–11.

25. See, for example, *Neue Zürcher Zeitung*, 13 March 2000.

26. Yvonne Haddad, "Towards the Carving of Islamic Space in the West," *ISIM Newsletter* 1 (1998): 5.

27. For France see for example Jocelyne Cesari, *Etre musulman en France aujourd'hui* (Paris: Hachette, 1997), 177–90; for Germany, Peter Heine, *Halbmond über deutschen Dächern—Muslimisches Leben in unserem Land* (München: List-Verlag), 1997, 112–33.

28. For the history of Islam in Geneva see Adama Bamba, *Introduction à la connaissance de l'islam et des musulmans dans le pays hélvétique: le cas de Genève* (Genève: Institut Universitaire d'Études du Développement, Université de Genève, 1992).

29. See for example their portrait in *L'Hebdo* 19, May 1998.

30. Haenni, "L'islam pluriel," 9, and Bamba, *Introduction à la connaissance d'islam et des musulmans*, 29–39.

31. *L'Hebdo* 19, May 1998.

32. Bamba, *Introduction à la connaissance d'islam et des musulmans*, 34–36.

33. Ibid., 32–33, 43.

34. Sarah Burkhalter, *La question du cimetière musulman en Suisse* (Genève: CERA-Editions, 1999), 27–28; see also Sarah Burkhalter, "La question du cimetière islamique en Suisse: quels enjeux pour la communauté musulmane?" *Revue Européenne des Migrations Internationales* 14, no. 3 (1998): 61–75.

35. Burkhalter, *La question du cimetière musulman en Suisse*, 28, 71.

36. *Tribune de Genève*, 7 July 1996.

37. *Journal de Genève*, 17 Oct. 1996; *Tribune de de Genève*, 17 Oct. 1996.

38. Hani Ramadan, "Foulard à l'école: les musulmans sont scandalisés," *Tribune de Genève*, 21 Oct. 1996.

39. Tariq Ramadan, "A propos du voile islamique, deux prises de position," *Journal de Genève*, 17 Oct. 1996.

40. *Journal de Genève*, 20 Nov. 1997.

41. *Tribune de Genève*, 20 Nov. 1997.

42. *Le Temps*, 15 July 1999.

43. Haenni, "L'islam pluriel," 27.

44. His numerous publications include, for example, Tariq Ramadan, *Les musulmans dans la laïcité: responsabilités et droits des musulmans dans les sociétés occidentales* (Lyon: Tawhid, 1994), and *Peut-on vivre avec l'islam? Le choc de la religion musulmane et des sociétés laïques et chrétiennes: entretiens avec Jacques Neirynck* (Lausanne: Favre, 1999).

45. Tariq Ramadan, "Islam en Suisse: etats des lieux et perspectives," *Tangram–Bulletin der Eidgenössischen Kommission gegen Rassismus* 7 (1999): 24–28.

46. Tariq Ramadan, "L'islam d'Europe sort de l'isolement," *Le Monde Diplomatique* (avril 1998): 13.

47. Thomas Facchinetti, "Musulmans à Neuchâtel ou musulmans neuchâtelois?" *Tangram–Bulletin de la Commission fédérale contre le racisme* 7 (1999): 62.

48. Yvan Kaenel, *La population musulmane du canton de Neuchâtel–pour un dialogue entre les associations musulmanes et le canton de Neuchâtel*. Zurich: Rapport du bureau du délégué aux étrangers, 1996, 17.

49. Facchinetti, "Musulmans à Neuchâtel," 63.

50. Andreas Cueni and Stéphane Fleury, *Etrangers et droits politiques–l'exercise des droits politiques des étrangers dans les cantons de Neuchâtel et du Jura* (Bern: Commission nationale pour l'UNESCO, 1994).

51. See Hassan Mutlu, *Le tissu associatif des communautés étrangères dans le canton de Neuchâtel–problèmes, besoins et demandes des associations* (Neuchâtel: Institut de Sociologie et de Science Politique, 1995), 140.

52. See Burkhalter, "La question du cimetière musulman en Suisse," 63–72.

53. Kaenel, *La population musulmane*, 15–16.

54. See for example *Express*, 27 Jan. 1998; *Nouveau Quotidien*, 2 Feb. 1998; *Tribune de Genève*, 12 Feb. 1998.

55. Angelika Lüthi and Leonhard Suter, *Musliminnen und Muslime in Zürich–Eine Dokumentation* (Zurich: Kirchlicher Informationsdienst kid, 1999), 3.

56. Peter Wittwer, "Muslime in Zürich: Unruhe um Ruhestätte." *IRAS-Panorama* 1 (July 1996): 7–8.

57. Lüthi and Suter, *Musliminnen und Muslime*, 5-6.

58. Oswald Eggenberger, *Die Kirchen, Sondergruppen und religiösen Vereinigungen–Ein Handbuch* (Zürich: Theologischer Verlag Zürich, 1994), 232-33.

59. *Tages-Anzeiger*, 3 Jan. 1995.

60. Walter Kälin, "Grundrechte in der Einwanderungsgesellschaft," in *Blickwechsel–Die multikulturelle Schweiz an der Schwelle zum 21. Jahrhundert*, ed. Simone Prodolliet (Luzern: Caritas-Verlag, 1998), 37-39.

61. *Tages-Anzeiger*, 14 Nov. 1987.

62. Ernst Hunziker, "Allah an der Limmat," *Unizürich–Magazin der Universität Zürich* 2 (1996), http://www.upd.unizh/magazin/2-96/muslime.htm.

63. Ernst Rutz-Imfhoof, "Zum Verhältnis von Kirche und Staat im Kanton Zürich," in *Kirche und Staat im Umbruch*, ed. Adrian Loretan (Zürich: NZN-Buchverlag, 1995), 51-52.

64. Nuri M. Yüksel, *Konzeptstudie für islamische Friedhöfe in Zürich* (Zürich: Islamisches Zentrum, 1995), 1.

65. *Tages-Anzeiger*, 5 Jan. 1996.

66. For an account of the struggle for an Islamic cemetery in Zurich see Hans Mahnig, *Contradictions of Inclusion in a Direct Democracy–The struggle for Political and Cultural Rights of Migrants in Zurich*. Paper for the UNESCO-MOST program " Multicultural Policies and Modes of Citizenship in European Cities," Swiss Forum for Migration Studies, 1999, 21-26.

67. Niccolò Raselli, "Schickliche Beerdigung für 'Andersgläubige,'" *Aktuelle Juristische Praxis* 9 (1996): 1104.

68. *Neue Zürcher Zeitung*, 20-21 April 1996.

69. *Tages-Anzeiger*, 20 Dec. 1996.

70. Raselli, "Schickliche Beerdigung."

71. *Neue Zürcher Zeitung*, 15 Sept. 1999.

72. See *Der Bund*, 19 Sept. 1997 and 14 Aug. 1998, as well as *Der Bund*, 12 Nov. and 15 Nov. 1999.

73. See Patrick Haenni, "Dynamiques sociales et rapport a l'Etat–l'institutionnalisation de l'Islam en Suisse," *Revue Européene des Migrations Internationales* 10, no. 1 (1994): 183-98.

74. Kälin, "Grundrechte in der Einwanderungsgesellschaft," 49.

75. Ibid., 49.

76. Joanna Pfaff-Czarnecka, "Let Sleeping Dogs Lie! Non-Christian Religious Minorities in Switzerland Today," *Journal of the Anthropological Society of Oxford* 29, no. 1 (1998): 48; see also Joanna Pfaff-Czarnecka, "Collective Minority Rights in Switzerland?" *Tsantsa* 4 (1999): 199-203.

5

Integration through Islam?
Muslims in Norway

Kari Vogt

A fifteen-minute walk from the Parliament and the main street, Karl Johan, in the center of Oslo, brings the visitor straight to the Muslim sections of the capital. Until 1960, the eastern parts of the city, Grønland and Grünerløkka, were areas largely inhabited by the Norwegian working class. These areas were invaded by immigrants from the third world during the 1970s and discovered by wealthy Norwegians in the 1990s. Today the settlements are still mixed; there are no neighborhoods that are exclusively inhabited by immigrants. The Muslim minority is still a part of the center of the city, not isolated in the suburbs as is the case in many other cities in western Europe. There are thirty mosques and associations concentrated in these eastern sections of Oslo, and, in 1995, Oslo was the first of the Scandinavian capitals to erect a mosque specifically built for that purpose. There are around fifty mosques and Islamic organizations across the country, two-thirds of which are in the Oslo area.

Most of the immigrants coming from the third world are Muslims, and "immigrant" has almost become synonymous with "Muslim." The numbers speak for themselves: out of Norway's total population of 4.3 million, 1.5 percent today are Muslims. The concentration is greatest in the cities of eastern Norway, with Oslo as the "Muslim capital," where approximately 10.5 percent of the population come from the third world. In some primary schools in eastern Oslo, 80 to 90 percent of the pupils are immigrants, the majority Muslims.

The rapid establishment of mosques and the increase in their membership gained the media's attention in the first half of the 1990s. Public statistics showed that the number of members more than doubled in five years, from 19,200 members in 1990 to 40,500 in 1995. The most recent statistics, from 1998, show 46,500 members.[1] Since 1996, Islam has come to represent the largest faith community outside the Norwegian church, the Evangelical Lutheran Church.

It should be noted, however, that, in Norway, religious preferences are not registered; only nationality is. Norway has never had a census on religious preference as Sweden had in 1930.[2] On the basis of the statistics of the national background of the population, a realistic estimate of people with Muslim background would be approximately 67,000 to 70,000 individuals. In addition there are some 450 to 500 Norwegian converts to Islam, a group that became visible in the Muslim community in the beginning of the 1990s.[3]

The Norwegian government's funding of religious communities gives a unique overview of mosque membership. According to the law pertaining to religious communities,[4] all such communities receive funding per member. In Norway, the money is paid directly to the mosque or congregation, not to umbrella organizations that redistribute the money, as in Sweden. In 1999, the amount per individual was around NKr. 208 per year. It is therefore very important for each mosque to ensure that all members are registered, as the number of members determines the mosque's funding. Yet such funding arrangements can only partly explain the large number of mosque members and the continually increasing number of congregations.

Today as many as 70 percent of the Muslim population are members of a mosque. This high level of organization, however, is limited to Sunni Muslims. If we assume that at least 70 percent of Iranians and 50 percent of Iraqis are Shi'i Muslims, and then add Pakistani Shi'i, as well as small Shi'i groups from the Middle East, it adds up to approximately 19 percent of the Muslim population in Norway. Only about 10 percent of them are organized in mosques or other Islamic organizations. One obvious reason for this is that a large group of Iranians are not religiously active; others may keep away from the mosque because they do not accept the political-religious ideology that pervades the Shi'i centers.

When it comes to the registered nationalities, Pakistanis dominate the statistics. Today the largest seven ethnic groups are as follows: Pakistanis (21,950), Bosnians (12,084), Turks (10,279), Iranians (9,818), Moroccans (5,923), Somalis (5,893), and Iraqis (4,394).[5] Understanding the phases of immigration can provide insight into the history of the Islamic organizations.

Phases of Immigration

Immigration from the third world is a relatively new phenomenon in Norway. The entry of migrant laborers began later in Norway than in either Sweden or Denmark. Because of the Norwegian oil boom, however, the labor migration lasted longer than those in other European countries. Young men from South Asia, Morocco, or Turkey took industrial or service jobs that Norwegians left because of an improved job market. The year 1967 marks the beginning of a new era when the first group of ten Pakistani men arrived Oslo. After this, the number increased rapidly.

In 1975, Parliament passed a law that was intended to prevent further immigration. The official argument was that, in order to treat the immigrants equally and to be able to provide acceptable material standards of living for those who had already arrived, immigration had to be limited. Strict external control aimed at ensuring successful internal integration. Three exceptions were made: refugees, family members of immigrants, and experts, mostly in the oil industry. The growth of the Norwegian economy presented the government with a dilemma. How could immigration be restricted at the same time that labor was much needed for the Norwegian offshore industry? Thus, the numbers of immigrants continued to grow, despite the 1975 law. One of the ways around the law was through the liberal interpretation of the regulations for family reunion.

While labor-related immigration was the prevailing trend in the 1970s, in the 1980s and 1990s immigration was dominated by refugees and asylum seekers, as was true in most other western European countries. The majority of immigrants from the third world arrived in the country after 1975, despite the fact that Norway tried to follow a more restrictive policy than either Sweden or Denmark. The question of degree of openness toward refugees entering the country became one of several quandaries for the Norwegian government. Strict regulations would seem to be in conflict with Norway's ideal of an open, democratic and multicultural society. It is not surprising, however, that the economic pressure of increased immigration on the welfare state soon became a controversial political issue. The populist Progressive Party, which enjoyed rapid growth after 1997, has demanded that an "immigration account" be established in order to show "how much immigrants cost the Norwegian society." So far, such demands have been rejected.

The Labor Party, the major political force in Norway during the past fifty years, has promoted the vision of a society with a maximum of social, economic, and political equality. This vision has not been as expansive in Norway as in Sweden, however, where the government's responsibility for the individual's welfare has been even more comprehensive. Since the 1970s, Norway's positive view of equality has also included a strong emphasis on women's right. The Gender Equality Law was passed in 1978, and since 1979 a Gender Equality Ombudsman has seen to it that the law is enforced. Thus, legislation regarding the granting of citizenship to the immigrants, and proving them with the right to vote, work, and participate in higher education, reflects the extent to which the goals of integration and indicators of equality have been attempted by the Norwegians.

The Norwegian Framework

In cultural and religious terms, Norway has been a relatively homogeneous country with a firmly established state church system.[6] The state is "religious" in the sense that the king is the head of the church (as confirmed in §4 of the Constitution), and half (originally all) of the members of the government are required to be members of the Lutheran Church (§12b); Parliament still elects bishops. Religion has been a concern for much of Norway's history. In 1814, the fathers of the constitution found it necessary to state explicitly that neither Jesuits nor Jews should have access to the kingdom. The ban on Jews was lifted in 1851, while the ban on *Societas Jesu* was not abolished until 1956. It was not until 1964 that the principle of religious freedom was specifically stated as part of the constitution. And, until 1969, only Lutherans were allowed as teachers of religious education in primary schools.

The state church system has been characteristic of the three Scandinavian countries, with few internal differences. What is typically Norwegian is the Law of Faith Communities (*Lov om trudomssamfunn*) of 1969, with later amendments. The Church of Norway is financed by the general tax bill (there is no separate church tax bill), and the state offers exactly the same amount of money per member to other faith communities— Muslims, Jews, Buddhists, or Humanists—as to the state church. The paradox is that, by doing so, the state finances its own vigorous opposition in the religious field. In general, faith communities outside the Lutheran Church have been able to express themselves freely and to organize their efforts without interference from the authorities. Freedom of religion, however, has been relative in the sense that religious practice must not interfere with public order. During the 1990s, as we shall see, some remarks made by representatives of the Muslim communities were considered to be in conflict with this public order.

The only citizenship requirement today is that a person must have lived in Norway for at least seven years. Only four years are required if one is married to a Norwegian citizen. This, of course, also holds for spouses who are brought from the home country, which has made the way to citizenship shorter for many. Dual citizenship is normally not allowed, but in practice there is a great deal of flexibility, and the issue is currently being debated. Those with permanent citizenship appear to attach less importance to attaining Norwegian citizenship as a means for easing daily life, although a few immigrants desire Norwegian citizenship as a means of facilitating their move to another, more attractive western country. As many as 95 percent of those who received Norwegian citizenship in 1995 were non-Westerners; in that year, Iranians were the largest single group, with 1,400 people acquiring Norwegian citizenship.[7] By comparison, only 10 percent of Pakistani immigrants changed to Norwegian citizenship as soon as they were able. The apparent hesitance of Pakistanis when it comes to changing citizenship is often attributed to their close contact with their homeland.

All foreign citizens who have lived in Norway for at least three years and who are eighteen years of age or older, have the right to vote in local elections. Only parliamentary elections require Norwegian citizenship. This arrangement was debated in Parliament toward the end of the 1970s. The line of argument, which followed the Swedish debate in detail, was that a true democracy cannot accept having a large number its residents unable to influence local politics in the place where they live and work.[8] The right to vote in local elections was awarded to citizens of the other Nordic countries in 1978; only in 1983 did all residents obtain this right. The political sympathies of immigrants from the third world, often determining their participation in elections, have been concentrated in the parties on the left, with a clear preference for Labor.[9] This may be changing now. The Christian Democrats, who in 1995 did not receive a single vote from immigrants from the third world, today seem to get at least a few Muslim votes because of the party's emphasis on family values and moral values in general.[10] The elections are not yet fully analyzed.

It is was not until the municipal and county elections in September 1999 that a new consciousness could be seen among Muslims in Oslo with regard to their numerical strength. The pressure from the populist Progressive Party, with its clear anti-Muslim stance, seems to have had a unifying internal effect. For the first time, the intense election campaign efforts were directed toward Muslims; national politicians from the Conservative Party and the Labor Party visited the mosques, and the Islamic Council arranged a meeting with politicians from all parties. As a result, seven out of a total of fifty-nine members elected to the Oslo City Council were of Muslim background. A few days later, Muslim immigrant politicians commented to the daily newspaper *Aftenposten*: "We are a power factor."[11]

In 1997, a comprehensive survey on living conditions among nonwestern immigrants was published.[12] In this survey, Turks, Pakistanis, Iranians, and Somalis represented the Muslim population. The survey also provided the following kinds of information: the level of education is lower among immigrants than among Norwegians—an estimated

15 percent had university or college education, as compared with 34 percent of Norwegians. The proportion of educated Turks and Pakistanis is especially low; not surprisingly, Iranians are the best educated. It must be added that while first-generation immigrants often have problems adjusting to the educational system, second-generation immigrants seem to be more "goal-oriented in their education than students with two Norwegian-born parents."[13] Two surveys from 1998 also indicate that second-generation immigrants have higher ambition levels with regard to education: 42 percent of non-western immigrant students are planning to take higher education compared to 38 percent of Norwegian students.[14] The most important objective of the integration policy, of course, is to ensure that people get the opportunity to work and gain economic independence. This goal is far from being reached. While only 44 percent of immigrants are employed, 79 percent of Norwegians have paying positions. The gender imbalance is also noticeable, especially among Pakistanis, whose participation in the workforce is low in any case. It should also be added that increasing attention has been given to employers' discrimination against women who wear headscarves, with several cases of discrimination having been reported during the past two years. In one area, Muslim immigrants did score higher than Norwegians, namely active engagement in religious associations and organisations.[15]

Information about and analyses of organized Muslim religious activities are virtually nonexistent. While the living conditions of immigrants have been thoroughly researched since the 1970s, religious and ideological commitment, ritual practice, and the emergence of Islamic institutions remain the least examined part of the immigrants' lives. Although there has been some research on Pakistani Muslims' religious practices and ideologies, our knowledge of the Turkish, Arab, and African mosques is highly inadequate. There are reasons to believe that these groups should not be considered in isolation. They have been in mutual contact since the beginning of the 1970s, and various forms of coexistence and cooperation have developed through intricate patterns of exclusion and inclusion.

Emergence of Islamic Institutions

The two first welfare organizations for immigrants were established in Oslo in the early 1970s, and Oslo also became the center for Islamic organizations.[16] The welfare organizations included religion as a part of their cultural activities and organized Eid celebrations and *tarawih* prayers during Ramadan in premises rented for the occasion. These celebrations were very popular and actually served to blur the distinctions between Sunnis and Shi'is. From the very beginning, the Pakistani Workers' Welfare Union had a board comprising both Sunni and Shi'i Muslims, and the same people can be found on the boards of the mosques some years later.

In 1972, the Pakistanis in Oslo joined forces to find more permanent accommodations for their religious activities. The first mosque was opened in 1974 as the Pakistani Deobandi-oriented Islamic Cultural Center, with ties to the political party Jamaat-i Islami. It still exists and today has 2,078 members. The establishment of the first Barelwi mosque followed a few years later, in 1976. Today, it is the largest Muslim congregation in Norway, with 5,737 members. Numerically, the two Pakistani Barelwi mosques dominate, and two of the new Pakistani Barelwi organizations are represented. World Islamic Mission in Oslo has a loose connection to the organization with the same name, led by Shaykh Noorani, who also is the leader of a branch of the political party Jam'iyatul Ulama-i Pakikstan. Idara Minhaj ul-Qur'an, a centralized and politicized organization with head-quarters in Lahore, opened a branch office in Oslo in 1990 and is today the third larg-est mosque in Norway. Taher Qadri, Idara's founder, is simultaneously the leader of the political party Pakistan Awami Tareek.

Arabs and Africans (West Africans and Somalis) remained members of the Paki-stani Islamic Cultural Center until they founded their own mosques toward the end of the 1980s. The largest Arab mosque was opened in 1987, the two African mosques in 1989. Neither Africans nor Moroccans have mosques outside Oslo, in contrast to the other groups, which have branch offices in most of the larger Norwegian cities. Arabs and Africans, to a large extent, tend to be ideologically representative of a moderate Islamism. They generally are associated with politicoreligious groups such as the Ikhwan al-Muslimun and the Tunisian an-Nahda party. The Algerian FIS has its official spokes-person in Oslo, and Hizb al-Tahrir has a handful of supporters.

Turks, among the first immigrants to arrive in Norway, have always kept to them-selves. While Arabs and Africans attended Pakistani mosques, the Turks organized their own religious activities. The first Turkish mosques were established in Oslo and Drammen in the beginning of the 1980s. Toward the end of the decade, the group split into three ideological fractions, and today the Diyanet (Diyanet Iserli Baskanligi), Süleymanlis (Islam Kultur Merkesleri Birgligi), and Milli Görüş have their own mosques. (Nurculuk, with a relatively large number of supporters in Sweden, has few members in Norway.) Diyanet members make up the majority; Süleymanlis are second in size and are led from the main administrative office in Stockholm; Milli Görüş adherents make up only a small minority.

The Tabligh movement came from Sweden to Norway in 1977, and it carries on its recruitment mainly among Pakistanis and Moroccans. Tablighis work quietly in the background; during the 1900s they made a degree of progress in propagating their mes-sage in Norway. Today, there are nine Tabligh mosques in the country. A few dozen Norwegian-Pakistani youth are currently receiving their Islamic education in Dewsbury, England. Oslo has had a small Albanian mosque since 1989; Bosnian refugees quickly organized themselves upon their arrival in Norway, and today the Islamic Society of Bosnia and Herzegovina consists of 5,000 members. The Islamic Bosnian community is affiliated with Islamska Zajednica and has *reis ul ulema* in Sarajevo as its head.

Meanwhile, the Shi'i community has also been growing. The Pakistani-dominated Anjuman-e Husseini was founded in 1975.[17] From 1975 to 1994, there was only one Shi'i congregation. With the arrival of some Iraqis and a few religiously active Iranians, however, a conflict regarding the Pakistani domination of the mosque board arose. After an initial split in 1994, the Shi'i community in Oslo now is divided into five different congregations, grouped according to language and ideology.

Mosques in Norway, as elsewhere in western Europe, are centers of many different kinds of activities. They function as important social arenas for first-generation Muslims and as the place where children receive instruction in Qur'an and various other subjects. During the early years of Muslim presence in the country, women were almost absent from the mosques. Today, a greater emphasis is put on women's participation, but with great variations between the different mosques and ethnic groups. The participation of women in the Eid prayer can be seen as a symbolic expression: at the largest Arabic mosque (1,337 members), women have joined the Eid prayer since 1997, a change that came about because of the pressure applied by the mosque's women's group. Today, women from other mosques (mostly Turkish and African) come to the Arabic mosque to take part in the prayer. A small group of Norwegian women converts have also taken the initiative to translate Islamic literature into Norwegian. Within a far more traditional framework, the Turkish Süleymanlis have their own women's mosques, one in Oslo and one in Drammen, and female preachers are invited from abroad to these mosques during Ramadan. Women are represented on boards of both the largest Arabic mosque and the Bosnian mosque in Oslo. One of the new Shi'i centers, established in 1997, has given women the right to vote, but there are no women representatives on the board.

Muslims in Norway represent a number of different ideologies. As previously mentioned, in the Arabic-speaking environment various shades of the "Islamic Movement" dominate. The largest Arab mosque community is led by members of Ikhwan al-Muslimun, a small group in Norway that is ideologically and administratively linked to Stockholm. With few exceptions, the activists represent moderate points of view on public issues and are more concerned with demonstrating solidarity with their Muslim brothers at home than with the Muslims' integration into Norwegian society. Yet members of the Ikhwan still demonstrate a certain degree of local commitment. The typical "Norwegian" Muslim Brother has completed his technical studies in Oslo, has his home in a middle-class suburb, and votes for the Socialist Left Party with the argument that it is fighting for a more just distribution of welfare services.

Books and brochures by Mawlana Mawdudi, Hasan al-Turabi, Muhammad and Sayyid Qutb, and others are distributed in the mosques. Yusuf al-Qaradawi's popularity is growing, aided by the fact that a few of his books are easily available in English. The religious programs broadcast by the TV Jezira channel gather many viewers among Arabic-speaking Muslims in Norway, adding to Shaykh Qaradawi's repute. A few books are also translated into Norwegian, primarily several written by Mawlana Mawdudi. There are also several Norwegian translations of books published by the Islamic Foundation in Leicester, Great Britain. Syyed Sabiq's *Fiqh us-Sunna* and Ahmad ibn Naqib al-Misri's *Companion of the Traveller* are widely circulated. Several English translations of Qur'an commentary are available from Pakistan; otherwise, this literature is generally read in Urdu. However, the religious videos, available in a plethora of languages, are more popular than books; the large mosques have a great selection of videos for rent and sale. Efforts are put forth to make more Islamic literature available in Norwegian, but currently the selection is limited. There is a handful of children's books, the most original contribution being "Muslim Songbook for Children" with a cassette, produced by Muslim women in Oslo. In addition, al-Turabi's *Women in Islam* and Ikhwan al-Muslimun's book of prayers are currently being published in Norwegian.

In addition to the small Jamaat-i Islami- and Mawdudi-oriented groups, Pakistani Islam in Norway is totally dominated by Sufi brotherhoods. Chishtiyah and Quadiriyah are in the majority, while one small mosque gathers Naqshbandi-Murids. Pakistani Barelwis are linked to *pirs* in the Punjab province. The largest Barelwi mosque in Oslo has close connections to Mihr Ali Shah's shrine at Golra Sharif, Punjab, and *pirs* from Punjab come to visit several times a year. Currently there are two Imams in Norway, who claim *pir* status.

The West Africans are divided between Qadiriyah and Tijaniyah, the latter representing the majority, and a small group of Iranian members of Ni'matullah have their own small *khanaqah* in Oslo. Unlike in Sweden and Denmark, the Sufi movement generally has not recruited Norwegian converts. The one exception is Ni'matullah; a handful of Norwegian converts have been initiated by Javad Nurbaskh in England.

In sum, the Muslim community is highly fragmented, with some cooperation between ideologically related mosques. Symptomatic of this fragmentation is the fact that not even in Norway have the Muslims been able to agree upon a common date for Ramadan. The Barelwi groups, however, have been unified on certain issues and since 1985 have cooperated in regard to arrangements related to *mawlid al-nabi*; the largest Shi'i mosque takes part in the planning and implementation of an annual procession through the streets of Oslo.

New Organizations in the 1990s

An emerging, new feature in this picture consists of the organizations that recruit across all mosque communities, that is, across language groups, ideology (e.g., Barelwi-Deobandi), and confession (Shi'i-Sunni). Three relatively large organizations are the primary actors, all with clear social objectives; integration of Muslims into Norwegian society is an important part of their agenda. In addition, there are two youth organizations: Muslim Student Society (Muslimsk Studentsamfunn, 1995), which recruits Muslim students at the University of Oslo, and Muslim Youth Norway (Muslimsk Ungdom Norge, 1996), which gathers second-generation Muslims between the ages of thirteen and twenty-five. Both these organizations are small but active.

Islamic Women's Group Norway (Islamsk Kvinnegruppe Norge, or IKN), founded in 1991, is today a rapidly growing organization working effectively around the country. It tries to respect all Islamic regulations, offers a variety of activities, such as swimming classes and various other sports, and also does awareness raising. Through these efforts, IKN has reached groups that have not been reached by public authorities.

The charitable foundation Urtehagen, also founded in 1991, runs three Muslim kindergartens in Oslo (the only ones in the country), a youth club, and an Islamic independent school for youth (one-year courses in practical subjects) that opened in 1998 for a small group of students. Urtehagen's activities are run with state support. Both the Islamic Women's Group and Urtehagen are managed by converts—this in contrast to Islamic Council Norway, dominated by born Muslims.

Dealing with issues concerning relations to the Norwegian society, the countrywide umbrella organization Islamic Council Norway (Islamsk Råd Norge) is considered to be the Muslims' official voice. Since its establishment in 1993, ICN has managed to gather twenty-one mosques with a total of some 25,000 members, almost half the number of all organized Muslims in Norway. The Council is one-of-a-kind as an umbrella organization without any competition from other Muslim groups. A few larger mosques that still stand outside ICN have chosen to give the Council power of attorney to act on their behalf in certain important matters.

The Council has an interesting profile. It is run by lay people—*ulama* do not play prominent leadership roles—and two of the large mosques in Oslo have chosen to be represented by women. The working language is Norwegian, and the board members, with a variety of of cultural backgrounds, have lived in the country for a long time and speak the language well. After a referendum in 1997, ICN was opened to Shiʻi Muslim representation. The Council has managed to attain a position of prominence. When the Norwegian government needs to discuss issues involving the Muslim community, it turns to the Council; when the prime minister wanted to meet representatives from the Muslim community in April 1999, he chose to visit ICN and the largest Barelwi mosque.

Islamic Council has continued the work of the welfare organizations from the 1970s to the present. There are now enough burial sites for Muslims, and access to *halal* meat has been temporarily ensured. (Ritual slaughtering has not been a common issue for Jews and Muslims in Norway; the Jewish minority is small [1,041 individuals] and imports all kosher products.) The council has put a great deal of effort into negotiating for a Qurʾan school project, which is aimed at providing a pedagogically acceptable and modern Qurʾanic education for children. The most important issue, as we shall see, is the struggle for the right for exemption from the new mandatory subject in elementary school, "Religious Knowledge and Ethical Education."[18]

Who Has Religious Authority?

One major issue for the Islamic community in Norway is that of who speaks on behalf of the Muslims. Quite another issue is who has internal religious authority in questions regarding faith and practice. Who should one listen to in questions of *fiqh*? Who determines what it means to be a good Muslim in Norway? These concerns are complex, as is reflected in the number of different mosques and organizations. The real authority regarding the *fiqh* question is found outside Norway. No local *alim* has acquired a significant enough reputation that it is likely he would be consulted by people outside his own narrow circle. If a difficult case emerges, the local *ulama* consult authorities in the home country.

For several reasons, the Imams are not a strong group. They generally have a poor command of the Norwegian language, which makes communication difficult not only with Norwegians but also within the Muslim community. A study of the language competency of twenty Imams in the Oslo area shows that only eight have a good command of Norwegian. Of the remaining twelve, two attended language classes; the others, who have lived in Norway for ten years or more, are unable to communicate in Norwegian or read a Norwegian newspaper.

The mosques have different policies regarding Imams. The Pakistani Idara Minhaj ul-Qurʾan employs its own Imams, all of them educated at the organization's college in Lahore. The selection of a person takes place outside Norway, and the Imam is employed for only four or five years at a time. The Turkish Diyanet has the same policy, and in the past ten years there have been several Turkish Imams who do not speak any language other than Turkish. On the other hand, Süleimalis have started to give Imam education to boys who are born and brought up in Norway; thus far, it is the only organization that has made this choice.

The Imam's authority is limited in several ways. If he is not employed by an organization, the relationship between the Imam and the mosque's board will be one of loyalty, as the board has elected the Imam and been responsible for his residence permit.

The Ministry of Justice since 1993 has increasingly restricted the granting of residence permits to Imams. The Ministry now demands "expert status," hoping to increase the general level of competency. "It is a requirement that . . . the Imam is a specialist in Islamic jurisprudence . . . not only *hafiz*."[19] The Norwegian government allots permanent residency to religious leaders provided that they can document formal education and practice. It is an increasing desire, on the parts of both the Norwegian government and several of the mosques, that personnel should be qualified. During the 1990s the trend has been for employed Imams to be better qualified than their predecessors.

Three Issues

Since 1989, three issues have dominated the public debate and colored the relationship between Norwegian society in general and the Muslims. The first was the Salman Rushdie case, which in Norway spawned an unusual series of events. Second, questions about Muslim marriages have been heatedly debated after 1997. The third and final issue concerns religious education in schools. The last two issues are far from resolved, and the ways in which they are finally concluded may have far-reaching consequences.

The first Muslim umbrella organization was created in 1989, when the Pakistani Barelwi organizations and the single Shi'i congregation in Oslo united and brought a court case against Salman Rushdie's Norwegian publisher. The intention was to halt the publication of *The Satanic Verses* by invoking the Norwegian legal provision concerning blasphemy and insult. However, the Muslims gave up the case at an early stage, realizing that there was very little chance of success. In 1993, the case took a dramatic turn when Salman Rushdie's Norwegian publisher was shot in an assassination attempt. The publisher survived, but the event created an extra-tense relationship with the Muslim minority. Islamic Council issued a moderate statement, but in 1996 a small group of Imams publicly expressed their support for Ayatollah Khomeini's *fatwa*.[20] Although the Muslims insisted that they would at all times keep within the bounds of Norwegian law, a majority of the intellectual and political establishment wanted the Muslim leaders to come forth with a public rejection of the *fatwa*. According to §13 of the Law of Faith Communities, communities that in one way or another infringe upon public order can be denied economic support. The Imams were required to explain their position, and, carrying the Holy Qur'an, dressed in traditional headgear and *shalwar-kamis*, they met with the representatives of the district governor. The Holy Qur'an, they insisted, was their only guide, and obedience their obligation.[21] This was only one of several incidents showing that there was no common platform for mutual understanding. The threat to stop economic support was never implemented, but the issue is still open for debate: can the state support (religious) communities that, seen through Norwegian eyes, do not respect the most elementary democratic principles of freedom of speech and legal protection of the individual?

The second major concern relates to Muslim marriages, also highlighted by a specific case. In 1997, when a young Moroccan woman was abducted to her home country to be married off by her parents, a comprehensive debate over arranged marriages versus forced marriages broke out. The particular case ended with a disturbing court battle in which the parents were sentenced for abduction; a larger issue was that the focus of the debate was set on the living conditions of second-generation immigrants.

The question of arranged marriages versus forced marriages set off a debate in the Parliament in 1998, and a plan of action against forced marriages was made public the same year. In the autumn of 1999, a new case exploded. At the same time that Amnesty International published its report about violence against women in Pakistan, a Norwegian television program presented a probable, but unconfirmed, case of at least one young Norwegian-Pakistani woman who was killed in Pakistan because she refused to marry a partner of her parents' choice. Norwegian security companies reported that they were being employed by young Muslim women in Norway who were seeking protection against their own families. The extent of the problem is not documented, but questions about "honor killing" of young women and the use of force in choice of spouses was put on the agenda for national debate. This is also true for the Muslim community, where the right to arranged marriages is insisted upon, but—perhaps not surprisingly— the use of force is characterized as "un-Islamic."

The third and final issue relates to the question of freedom for religious minorities, a topic of current interest after the introduction of the new subject "Religious Knowledge and Ethical Education" in the schools. It should be noted that in Norway the private schools system is weak; only 1.5 percent of children in Norway attend private schools, which receive funding from the State. Unlike Sweden and Denmark, Norway does not have a Muslim primary school. The application for a state-supported Muslim primary school was turned down in 1995 by the Labor Party (in power until 1997); Labor's concluding argument was that such a school would obstruct the process of integration.

The background for the present conflict is as follows. Until 1969, only Evangelical Lutheran religious instruction was offered in state schools; after that year, the students were given three options: (1) confessional education, (2) neutral life stance education, or (3) full exemption. In 1995–1996, Labor was the primary force behind the new and compulsory version of religious education in primary schools. Since 1997, everyone has been required to take a class titled "Religious Knowledge and Ethical Education," with exemption possible only in those hours of religious practice such as church visits or singing of hymns. The choice of alternative education is no longer available.

The Muslim community has been heavily involved in the demand for the right to exemption, and Islamic Council Norway is playing a central role by bringing the case to court. The Muslims brought a case against the State in October 1999 but lost. This well-prepared case has, however, brought ICN into close cooperation with all other faith communities in Norway. Since 1996, ICN has taken part in the organized effort made by Jews, Buddhists, Baha'is, Christians, and Humanists to ensure that students gain the right of exemption.[22] In addition, since 1993 ICN has worked with the Norwegian Church (Den norske kirke) in the so-called Contact Committee (Kontaktutvalg), where this case has been discussed.

Integration through Islam?

The number of Muslim communities established in less than thirty years and the history of the mosques bear witness to a strong will to recreate a Muslim life on foreign ground. The first striking impression is one of diversity and vitality. At the same time, internal splitting and fragmentation into increasingly smaller units, and communication problems—both within the community and externally with the larger society—have been unavoidable and to some extent have disturbed the development of the Norwegian Islamic community.

The largest ethnic groups have created close networks, often with a high degree of internal social control. Technically, these groups are free from the legal systems of their home countries, and from their religious-political initiatives and religious authorities. Nonetheless, there is still a long way to go before we can speak of an "individualization of religion," and a situation where religious engagement "*s'éprouve comme choix et comme foi*," as the French researcher Olivier Roy expresses it.[23] Still, state funding has created a certain degree of autonomy in relation to benefactors in the Muslim world. Mosques and Islamic institutions are not obscure underground organizations; on the contrary, they have a high degree of visibility and are forced to maintain some contact with the surrounding society. And some of the new organizations are displaying potential for change and development; the will to solve problems and the ability to cooperate with various public agencies has been convincingly expressed at several occasions.

There are few signs of an ideological *aggiornamento*, and to date there is no religious or intellectual elite.Yet, this is not the complete picture. The young people of the second generation, in the process of being educated or on their way into professions, are just starting to make their marks, even in the religious organizations. Some of them are acutely aware of the shortcomings of the first generation and have the background needed to make their own contributions. And a small minority today—which includes both first and second generations—talks about the need for a "new *fiqh*," adapted to western conditions and relevant to a "Norwegian Islam" that integrates the values of the society of which the Muslims have now become a part.

Notes

1. *Kulturstatistikk. Den norske kyrkja 1998, og trus- og livssynssamfunn utanfor Den norske kyrkja, per 1.Januar 1999* (Oslo: Statistisk Sentralbyrå [Norwegian Bureau of Statistics]).
2. Cf. A. S. Roald's contribution in this volume (chapter 6).
3. The number of converts was estimated to be approximately 400 in 1995 by Lena Larsen in her unpublished master's study on Norwegian converts to Islam, University of Oslo, 1995.
4. Law of Faith Communities of 1969 (Lov om trudomssamfunn og ymist anna).
5. *Aktuelle befolkningstall. Innvandrerbefolkningen 1.januar 1998.* Statistics Norway, 2/99.
6. Cf. O. Leirvik. "State, Church and Muslim Minority in Norway," paper presented at the conference *Dialogue of Cultures*, Berlin, April 21-23, 1999.
7. K. Vassenden, ed., *Innvandrere i Norge. Hvem er de, hva gjør de og hvordan lever de?* (Oslo: Statistisk Sentralbyrå, 1997), 57-58.
8. Ibid., 199.
9. Ibid., 207.
10. This remark is based on personal communication with Muslim voters.
11. *Aftenposten*, 20 Sept. 1999.
12. Cf. S. Blom, E. Gulløy, and A. Ritland, *Levekår blant innvandrere 1996.* Dokumentasjonrapport med tabeleer. Oslo: Statistisk Sentralbyrå 97/6.
13. T. Jørgensen, "Utdanning," in *Innvandere i Norge. Hvem er de, hva gjør de of hvordan lever de?* ed. K. Vassenden (Oslo: Statistisk Sentralbyrå, 1997), 107.

14. T. Øya, *Generasjonskløfta som ble borte, Ungdom, Innvandrere og Kultur* (Oslo: Cappelens Akademiske Forlag, 1997), 92.

15. Vassenden, *Innvandrere i Norge*, 188.

16. All information on the Muslim community in the following section of this article is taken from my book on Muslims in Norway, *Islam på norsk. Moskeer og islamske organisasjoner i Norge* (Oslo: Cappelen, 2000).

17. The Shi'i community in Norway has not yet received the attention it deserves. A detail: the year 1974 for the founding of Anjuman-e Husseini is given by three other researchers: N. Ahlberg, *New Challenges–Old Strategies, Themes of Variation and Conflict among Pakistani Muslims in Norway* (Helsinki: TAFAS 25, 1990); R. Natvig, "Les musulmans en Norvege," in *L'islam et les musulmans dans le monde*, ed. M. Arkoun, R. Leveau, and B. Jisr (Beirut: Centre Culturel Hariri, Recherches et Documentation, 1993); and S. Østberg, *Pakistani Children in Oslo: Islamic Nurture in a Secular Context*, Ph.D. diss., University of Warwick, Institute of Education, 1998. In citing 1975, I rely on the information given to me by the founder of Anjuman-e Husseini, Mustaq Naqi, who in turn was relying on his diary.

18. It is interesting to note that the official English translation of the title of the subject does not emphasize the Christian aspect as does the Norwegian; the Norwegian name is "Kristendomskunnskap med religion og livssynsundervisning," the direct translation being "Knowledge of Christianity with an Introduction to Religion and World Views."

19. *Religiøse ledere og lærere–arbeidstillatelse etter utlendingsforskriftene §3 annet ledd, bokstav A*, Det Kongelige Justis- og Politidepartement, 2 Sept. 1993.

20. Verdens Gang, 17 Jan. 1996; Verdens Gang, 19 Jan. 1996.

21. This incident received considerable attention in the media and is referred to in *Rapport fra arbeidsgruppen for trosforhold*, Kommunal- og arbeidsdepartementet, mai 1996, 18.

22. Cooperation committee on belief and life stances (Samarbeidsrådet for tro- og livssyn), founded in 1996.

23. ". . . expresses itself as personal choice and faith"; O. Roy, "Naissance d'un islam européen," *Esprit* 1 (1998): 10.

6

From "People's Home" to "Multiculturalism": Muslims in Sweden

Anne Sofie Roald

The last census in Sweden in which Swedes were asked to designate a religious affiliation took place in 1930.[1] At that time, fifteen persons indicated that they were Muslim. Since then, the number of Muslims in Sweden has increased dramatically. Immigration from Muslim countries to Sweden began just after World War II, when Turkish-speaking Tartars came from Finland and Estonia. The Tartars established the first Islamic congregation in 1948. In the beginning of the 1960s, the first wave of Muslim labor immigrants entered Sweden. It consisted mainly of young Turkish, Yugoslav, Albanian, and Pakistani men who came as industrial workers to contribute to the rapidly growing manufacturing businesses. This first wave of immigration was marked by the transitoriness of adventurous youths whose main aim was to return to their homelands after having built up a fortune in Sweden. With the legal restriction of labor immigration in 1967, this pattern changed to one of chain migration, with many young Muslim men marrying spouses from their homelands and remaining in Sweden.

Liberal Swedish refugee policies also led to the arrival of many different Muslim refugee groups. During the 1980s, a stream of refugees from Iran and Iraq (including many Kurds from both nations), as well as from Lebanon, entered the country. They were followed in the 1990s by Somalis, Bosnians, Albanians from Kosovo, and more Iraqi refugees. For many refugees, Sweden was more an intermediate station (a station en route) than a permanent residence, giving them sojourner status. What has been understood as a lack of interest on the part of many refugees in learning Swedish properly and in integrating into Swedish society by getting a job or involving themselves in welfare work or political activities often has been seen as a result of the refugees' being in this kind of intermediate state. It must also be asked, however, whether language and integration problems are to be blamed solely on a lack of interest on the part of the immigrants or whether it is in large part a result of the "inaccessible" Swedish social structure.

The largest groups of Muslim immigrants in Sweden today consist of Iranians and Bosnians, followed by Turks and the Arabic-speaking groups (Iraqi, Lebanese, Palestinian, Syrian), Albanians, and Somalis. Southeast Asians constitute a small contingent, in contrast to the situation in the two other Scandinavian countries, Norway and Denmark, where the Pakistanis are a particularly substantial force. Within the Muslim community in Sweden, many of the prevailing international religiopolitical directions are represented. In the Arab community, the Muslim Brotherhood, the *salafi* trend, the *habbashi* movement, and liberal Islamists with no particular group identity are active. In the Turkish community, the Millî Görüş, Süleymanci, and Nurcu movements provide the primary affiliation. Among the Somalis, the *salafi* trend is strong, a result of the fact that many of the Somali scholars have been educated in Islamic institutions in Saudi Arabia.

In contrast to many other western countries, where Muslims who had come to pursue postgraduate studies have often decided to remain and become part of the intellectual elite, in general Muslims in Sweden are not well educated. While the proportion of Muslims who are highly educated varies from one ethnic community to another, immigrants in Sweden in general have a lower level of education than do ethnic Swedes.[2] There are several reasons for this, including the fact that the main wave of immigrant labor consisted of unskilled workers. This situation has been exacerbated by the problems immigrants encounter in mastering the Swedish language. Highly educated Muslim immigrants and refugees tended to go to English- or French-speaking countries, where they did not have to learn a new language in order to get a job and in that way become integrated into society.

While it is generally true that Muslims, like most other immigrants, belong to the poorly educated stratum of society in Sweden, there are certainly exceptions. Among the Iranians, for example, there are many highly educated persons. However, most Iranians who came to Sweden as refugees in the 1980s had run away from the Islamic religious leadership and can therefore be classified as "cultural" or "ethnic" Muslims, rather than Muslims in a religious sense.[3] The same is true for parts of the Iraqi community, many of whose members obtained their university degrees in Eastern Bloc countries. Within the Bosnian group, there are also quite a few individuals who are highly educated.

It is interesting to note that the work of the Swedish researcher Åke Sander on the religiosity of Swedish Muslims indicates that many immigrants from Iran and Iraq are less religiously inclined than those from many other Muslim immigrant groups.[4] In his investigation, he administered a questionnaire that contained items pertaining to religious activities and belief. In his sample, he discovered that approximately 50 percent of Iranian and Iraqi respondents stated that they did not believe in God, nearly the same percentage expressed that they were not interested in Islam, and very few reported that they performed the daily prayers.[5] It is mainly in these two groups that the more highly educated Muslims can be found. Sander's findings seem to indicate not that it is not the entire Muslim community that belongs to the low-educated stratum of society, but, rather, that many of those Muslims who are directed toward an Islamic lifestyle do.

It is difficult to determine exactly how many Muslims are living in Sweden today. Some researchers such as Sander suggest that there are approximately 200,000, while others, particularly Muslim leaders, claim that there are nearly twice that number. It is also difficult to estimate how many Swedes have converted to Islam, but I estimate that the number is between 1,000 and 3,000. In 1999, the Swedish population was estimated at nearly nine million people, which makes the Muslim population between 1.8 percent and 3.5 percent of the whole. Sander estimated that in 1996 approximately 1.5 million, or approximately 15 percent of the population, was immigrant.[6] There are various official definitions in Sweden of the term "immigrant." In some statistical reports an immigrant is defined as a nonnaturalized individual living in Sweden; in other reports there is a distinction between first-generation immigrants (born outside Sweden) and second-generation immigrants (those born in Sweden). In the discussion that follows, the term "immigrant" designates both first-generation and second-generation immigrants, as this is the most common understanding in contemporary Sweden.

While it is sometimes useful for authorities, researchers, and even the public to talk about Muslims as a homogenous group, the primary drawback of this is that generalizations often tend to discredit the Muslim group as a whole. For example, pointing to "Muslim practice" while discussing a practice common within marginalized groups can sometimes lead to a negative portrayal of the whole Muslim community. As Norbert Elias has observed, established groups tend to "attribute to its outsider group as a whole the 'bad' characteristics of that group's 'worst' section—of its anomic minority."[7] In contrast, Elias notes that "the self-image of the established group tends to be modeled on its exemplary, most 'nomic' or norm-setting section, on the minority of its 'best' members."[8] In the Swedish context, such a stigmatization of the Muslim community's "worst" section creates problems for the Muslim community, particularly the second and third generations and converts, as it influences the self-image of the Muslim group as a whole.

Part of the stigmatization of Muslims is caused by the problem of identity. It is often the case that, in the process of formulating one's own identity, one tends to point out those elements in oneself that are in opposition to "the other." Thus, Muslims tend to portray themselves first and foremost as Muslims in their cultural encounters with Swedish society, rather than as members of a national group or as having a certain professional affiliation, since being Muslim is their most conspicuous contrast to the Swedish Christians. The degree of "Muslimness," however, receives less attention, and Muslims are often perceived by others as a homogenous group with Islam as the common degrading factor.

"Ethnic Swedes" tend to manifest one of two attitudes toward the Muslim community. On the one hand, the government and the authorities in general have responded positively, in the sense that the Muslim refugees have been "taken care of" (omhändertagna). Housing and daily needs are met through the social security system, and instruction in the Swedish language is provided free of charge. On the other hand, the idea that the authorities "take care" of the immigrants without making any demands on them is extremely frustrating to many "ethnic" Swedes. The letters-to-the-editor columns in various Swedish newspapers often feature comments about foreigners in general, and Muslims in particular, who live "good lives" on the backs of "hard-working Swedes." It is interesting to note that it is retired Swedes who are often most upset, probably because of their feeling that they are being deprived of the benefits of the "Swedish welfare program," which have in recent years been shrinking.

In the official debate about immigrants in contemporary Sweden, the Muslim immigrant has become the immigrant per definition. In the following, therefore, one should be aware that the discussion of immigrant policy and strategy to a great extent pertains particularly to the Muslim situation.

Swedish Citizenship

During the first wave of immigration, in the 1960s, the Swedish authorities reformed their immigration and settlement policies.[9] The citizenship policy was changed in 1963 to allow immigrants to become Swedish citizens after a residency of more than five years in the country. Although the point was not stated explicitly in the law, the citizenship guidelines suggested that immigrants should be able to speak and understand Swedish.[10] They were also expected to renounce their former citizenship. The reason for this, as explained to me by a civil servant in charge of issuing passports, was to safeguard the rights of Swedish citizens in foreign countries. Another reform, introduced in 1976, granted immigrants with more than three years' residence the right to vote and to stand for local elections. In the 1980s, the law of citizenship was reformed again; the authorities removed the guideline that an immigrant should have a substantial knowledge of the Swedish language. In the 1990s, the law of citizenship was debated once more. One issue that has received a great deal of commentary recently is whether to allow dual citizenship, that is, the right to maintain citizenship in one's country of origin while becoming also a citizen of Sweden.[11]

"The People's Home"

The policy of the Swedish state toward immigrants thus has been one of paternalistic "caretaking"; although the material needs of immigrants are provided, full integration into society has been difficult. The much-debated establishment of the National Office of Integration in the late 1990s indicates the difficulties the state faces with regard to the integration of immigrants into Swedish society. In 1976, Sweden appointed the first minister of immigration. By 1999, the ministry had been split into two sections, mainly because of the decrease in the number of refugees admitted. One section deals with residence permits and similar administrative issues, and the other handles coordination of immigrant affairs, an indication of the state's emphasis on integration of immigrants into Swedish society.

In 1974, the government proclaimed a freedom-of-choice policy for "members of linguistic minorities domiciled in Sweden" between "retaining and developing their original cultural identity and assuming a Swedish cultural identity."[12] Theoretically speaking, this notion of multiculturalism seems to be in opposition to the Swedish reality, with its segregation between "ethnic" Swedes and immigrants in all aspects of social life. The Swedish authorities' attitude of "caretaking" may be seen within the framework of Swedish history over the past century, with its dominating ideal of "the People's Home." Mauricio Rojas is a researcher who has tried to look for reasons for this peculiar feature of Swedish society. A South American economic historian who has lived in Sweden since 1974, Rojas is one of the few active immigrant participants in the integration debate in Sweden.[13]

In his book *The Rise and Fall of the Swedish Model*, Rojas discusses the concept of "the People's Home" (*folkhemmet*). According to Rojas, the idea of "the People's Home" has prevailed in twentieth-century Sweden as a consequence of the vast modernization process Sweden went through from 1870 to 1950. Rojas sees the concept more as a bridge between old times and modernity than as a modern break with earlier Swedish history. He identifies two ideological contradictory positions in "the People's Home" in modern Sweden. Swedes are seen either as subject to the control of the social state or as citizens emancipated by a "strong society," and there is an obvious tension between submission and freedom, which has characterized 500 years of Swedish history.[14] In the 1920s, the Social Democratic Party developed its social project of "the Good Home," later identified as "the People's Home," the goal of which was to create a welfare society with equal opportunity for all. It was structured on the ideal of "functionalism," in which life and society are seen as consisting of basic functions that become the basis of planned actions.[15] However, as Rojas shows, such a dream of a planned society presupposed "an ethnically homogeneous population, a strong national state, an expanding industrial economy, and a technological and an organizational development of the kind epitomized by the term Fordism."[16] These are, according to Rojas, factors that existed at a certain point of Swedish history but that have all changed in contemporary Sweden, with its transition from an industrial to a postindustrial society.

For the present study, it is the idea of ethnic homogeneity that is of importance. The ideology of "the People's Home," with equal opportunity and similar patterns of behavior for all, however, still lingers in a society where the material and physical conditions have dramatically changed.[17]

The sociologist Åke Sander holds views similar to those of Rojas regarding the integration of immigrants in Sweden. Both researchers base their perceptions on the prevailing idea of conformity in Swedish society. Sander does not speak in terms of "the People's Home," but he emphasizes the Swedish notions of equality and uniformity, both of which have their roots in the Social Democratic dream of "the People's Home." Sander sees the integration of Muslim immigrants as a huge problem. In his view, it is not that Muslims do not want to integrate but that the Swedish structure does not allow them to do so. As he has observed, Sweden has been built on the notion of "One nation, One people, One religion."[18] He links the segregation of Muslims in Sweden to this idea of "a common culture and religion, including common manners, norms and value system, as well as a common way of thinking in general."[19] He further argues that the state's proclaimed "multiculturalism," where equality, freedom of choice, and partnership are important ingredients, is understood differently by Swedish non-Muslims and by Swedish Muslims. Whereas Swedes in general understand multiculturalism mainly by the principle of equality, meaning "equality between universal individuals regardless of culture, ethnicity, race, religion and gender,"[20] Muslims tend to see multiculturalism in terms of equal right to freedom of choice. For them this translates into the requests for special rights pertaining to religion, ethnicity, and cultural expressions. According to Sander, for Swedish authorities the ideal of "multiculturalism" means that public life should be characterized by equality, meaning similarity, while religious and cultural expressions should be confined to the privacy of the home. Thus, while the authorities advocate an integrationist model, in reality they hope for a high degree of assimilation.[21] Sander's arguments are echoed by the Pakistani-British sociologist Muhammad Anwar when he speaks of how integration in Britain is understood in different ways by the majority society and by the immigrants. Anwar believes that immigrants understand "integration" as "acceptance by the majority of their separate ethnic and cultural identity." From a majority point of view, however, "integration" reflects the "ideology of the dominant group,"[22] which conveys the notion that "any group unabsorbed, or not assimilated, is considered to upset the equalization of social relations in the society."[23]

"The People's Home" notion of equality and equal opportunities for everybody in Sweden has turned into an idea of uniformity or homogeneity. It is this concept of uniformity that prevents the integration of many immigrants. The possibility of employment for women who wear headscarves, for example, is limited because employers fear that salespeople or cashiers with headscarves would be offensive to "ethnic" Swedish customers. Similarly, employers are reluctant to employ persons with dark complexions, as they are afraid their potential customers will go elsewhere.

Repatriation Programs for Refugees

Because of the large influx of refugees over the past two decades, the Swedish government has initiated programs to facilitate the return of those who wish to repatriate after conditions in their countries of origin have stabilized. Many of the Palestinian and Lebanese who came in the 1980s, for example, thought of Sweden as a temporary place of refuge and intended to go back as soon as the situation became settled at home. The government, however, has no actual plan for this refugee group. In my discussions with Lebanese refugees who have been in Sweden for more than ten years, I found that most, although not totally giving up the dream of "returning home," have more or less accepted the idea of remaining in Sweden. Most of them give as their reasons that in Lebanon there are no jobs and that their children would find the transition difficult because the Arabic school system is much "harder" than the Swedish. Most of the Palestinians who came to Sweden used to live in refugee camps in Lebanon, and they now regard Sweden as the only country where they could possibly live outside Palestine. Some of the Lebanese, however, have built houses in Lebanon with the dream of going back. Similarly, few of the Turkish labor immigrants of the 1960s and 1970s, whose salaries were in large part sent back to housing projects in Turkey, have actually repatriated. The parents have come to realize that their children, who have been brought up in Sweden, now regard Sweden as their homeland.

As the return program for Lebanese refugees is not very encouraging, the Swedish authorities have concentrated their efforts for repatriation on the Bosnians, the Kosovo-Albanians, and the Somalis, among the Muslim refugee groups. Approximately 45,000 Bosnians came to Sweden in 1992–1993; of these, some 1,700 Bosnians returned to Bosnia during the second half of the 1990s. The National Office of Integration, through its repatriation program for refugees, organizes bus tours to Bosnia from Sweden where refugees can meet with local authorities in Bosnia in order to arrange for housing, employment, and so on. The Swedish authorities agree to pay for the trip home and to provide a certain amount of money for each person in the family. The money is supposed to last for a couple of months while the refugees get ready to cope with the new surroundings. As the refugees leave, they have to renounce their Swedish permanent work and stay permits, but if they return within one year they will get the permits back. According to the civil servant I spoke with, the surrender of the Swedish permit creates an element of uncertainty for the refugee, and it may cause some refugees to decide against repatriating.

There is also a repatriation program for the Kosovo-Albanians, both those who came to Sweden during the war in Bosnia in the early 1990s and those who came to Sweden during the NATO bombing of Kosovo. Few in the first group had any wish for repatriation, whereas those in the second wave were forced to repatriate because their stay permits were limited to eleven months. The program for the Somalis has been less substantial. Given the unstable situation in Somalia, the refugees themselves are reluctant to participate because of the uncertainty of their futures at home; similarly, the Swedish authorities do not want to invest resources in such a project when the outcome is still so uncertain.

Religion: Religious Belief or Religious Practice?

Many of the obstacles Muslims face in their cultural encounters with Swedish society seem to relate to the definition of religion. Freedom of religion was not introduced in Sweden until 1951. Before that time, certain legal restrictions were placed on persons who belonged to faiths other than Christianity. Until the end of the nineteenth century, for instance, it was possible to expel dissidents from the "Right Faith."[24] Currently, Swedish society is built on a secular world view, in which religion has no part to play in official life and religion and religious expression are considered personal matters. To have a religious world view is acceptable as long as it is kept within the private domain. The idea of Sweden as a secular society is well established and may be one reason for the hostility toward the religious force Muslims represent in Swedish society.

The legislation on freedom of religion promotes the "privatization" of religion. According to the law, "Every person has the right to freely practice his/her religion as far as s/he does not disturb the peace of the society or cause public offense." Thus, for instance, the male Sikh who wants to wear a turban or a knife in public as part of his religious obligation transfers religion into the public domain, which is not acceptable according to the Swedish standard. Muslims and Jews who require properly slaughtered meat (halal or kosher) run into trouble because Swedish legislation forbids the prescribed method of slaughtering animals.[25] The problem of religion versus religious practice becomes one of definition, and the question is how far one can practice one's religion before it is regarded as causing public offense.[26] Moreover, many Swedish researchers have raised the question of whether the Swedish Law of Religious Freedom supports freedom *from* religion, rather than supporting freedom *of* religion.[27]

The Swedish ideal of "equal opportunities" has led to strong support for "gender equality," which culminated in the establishment of the Office of the Equal Opportunities Ombudsman (jämställdhetsombudsman) in 1980. The ideal of gender equality has contributed to the negative response to Islamic women's dress. Covered Muslim women are seen as victims of patriarchal structures, as well as of oppressive male relatives. The Swedish reaction to women's headscarves has been intense and emotional. When television channels or newspapers latch onto a story about headscarves, they may engender a debate that goes on for weeks. A local populist right-wing party in Malmö, a town in the south of Sweden that has a relatively high Muslim population, has even raised the issue of the Muslim headscarf as a public offense. The case started in the late 1990s when a representative of the party proposed a ban on headscarves in the debate on the budget in the local government. He argued that, if headscarves were forbidden, Muslims would move out of Malmö and the town's expenses for social allowances would decrease, allowing it to balance its budget. Later, he also argued that women with headscarves cause public offense, apparently based on the Law of Religious Freedom. At the time, the party's proposals were depicted in the media as ridiculous. It is obvious, however, that in a tense situation, the Law of Religious Freedom may be interpreted elsewhere in a similar way, and external signs of religious affiliation can easily be said to cause "public offense."

In contrast is the 1994 Law against Ethnic Discrimination, which defines "ethnic discrimination" as the unfair treatment of a person or a group because of race, color of the skin, national or ethnic origin, or confession of faith.[28] It is interesting to note that the formulation "confession of faith" (*trosbekjennelse*) is used, rather than "religious affiliation" (*trostillhörighet*). The Law against Ethnic Discrimination might be regarded as more forceful than the Law of Freedom of Religion, since the Swedish authorities established the position of Ethnic Discrimination Ombudsman in 1988.

State Financial Grants

Part of the motivation for Sweden's support of multiculturalism is its desire to challenge the monopoly of the Lutheran State Church. As a result, the confessional teaching of Lutheranism in schools has been replaced by a curriculum based to a great extent on comparative religion and ethics. The state also began to provide financial assistance to religious congregations besides the state church. The negotiation for such financial assistance started in 1964, and in 1971 independent Christian congregations obtained financial allowances for the first time. The Commission for State Grants to Religious Communities (SST) was established as a result of a parliamentary decision, but it was not until 1974 that "immigrant religions," meaning non-Christian religious congregations, were included into the system of state grants. The first Muslim confederation eligible for a state grant, United Islamic Organizations in Sweden (Förenade Islamiska Församlingar i Sverige [FIFS]), was established in 1974. Today three Muslim confederations are entitled to state grants; other confederations, including the Shi'i, have applied for the same status.

Some Muslims are critical of the way the state money has been distributed, since it is funneled through Muslim confederations led mainly by Turkish and Arab Muslims. While many local organizations belong to one regional confederation or another, some organizations have chosen to remain independent, as they regard the confederations to be too centralized. These independent organizations have also had difficulties in obtaining state grants. Other confederations have also had trouble being accepted, since the application procedure goes through the Islamic Council for Cooperation (Islamiska Samarbetsrådet [IS]), established in1988, whose members are from the established Muslim confederations, which often see their economic and power hegemony threatened by new confederations.

Muslim leadership thus emerges from the Muslim confederations. Three separate councils have been established to function as bridges between the state and Swedish Muslims, with the Islamic Council for Cooperation as the overarching body. Arabic- and Turkish-speaking first-generation Muslims, along with members and sympathizers of the Muslim Brotherhood and Millî Görüş, run the Council of Swedish Muslims (Sveriges Muslimska Råd [SMR]), which was established in 1990. The Swedish Islamic Council (Islamiska Rådet i Sverige [IRIS]) was established in 1986 (reestablished 1991) and is mainly run by Turkish first-generation Muslims, with members and sympathizers of Suleymanci movement. Representatives from the two latter councils are usually invited to participate in discussions concerning immigrants in general and Muslims in particular. For instance, in the spring of 1999, the main daily Swedish newspaper *Dagens Nyheter* started a series of reports about young immigrant girls who quit the senior level in school in order to get married. The minister of integration and the minister of education established a committee with representatives from various immigrant confederations and councils such as the two Muslim councils mentioned, along with Orthodox Christians, the Roma group (Gypsies), and others, to try to find solutions.

Segregation of Living

In other Scandinavian countries, as in many other European countries, Muslims often live in ghettos in the inner cities, where they become part of the inner-city economy. The situation is different in Sweden, where most immigrants live in the suburbs of the three biggest towns. The inner cities are usually the expensive housing areas, whereas the suburbs consist of concrete apartment blocks, with several families on every floor. Although it is clear that the segregation of living (or the "enclavisation" of society) is not a conscious policy of the Swedish authorities, it is still a policy, insofar as nothing is done to stop it. The consequence of this policy is that in some suburban schools few pupils have a proper knowledge of the Swedish language. In some classes, there may be one or two pupils from "Swedish" families, while in others there are often none at all. There is massive unemployment among the population of these immigrant suburbs, and few immigrants have primary or even secondary contacts with ethnic "Swedes." This influences their ability to speak the Swedish language properly and to understand the cultural codes of Swedish society, both essential in order for immigrants to integrate into the labor market and into society in general.

It is often argued that immigrants themselves prefer to live in these areas, as they feel secure in an environment where other individuals belong to the same ethnic or religious group. However, many immigrants who live in these areas tend to move to other areas as soon as they have established their own economic position apart from state allowances. Moreover, many Muslim immigrants have told me that, when they have tried to find apartments in more "ethnic" Swedish areas, the housing companies, even the municipal ones, say that they have no free housing at the moment. One Palestinian man who speaks Swedish well but with an obvious accent described how an "ethnic" Swede had called the same person at the municipal housing company right after the Palestinian had been refused and was told that there were free apartments in the desired area. Immigrants in general feel that the same is true for education, where, particularly at the upper secondary level, immigrant children usually end up in typical "immigrant schools."

The immigrant suburbs are usually well off in material terms. The apartments are often vast and well equipped, and outside there is an abundance of greenery. A case in point is Rosengård, a well-known and often-cited suburb of Malmö, the third largest town in Sweden. Rosengård represents the same social pattern that can be found in the suburbs of all the big towns in Sweden. Malmö is distinguished by its relatively high percentage of immigrants, particularly Muslims, and therefore illustrates various aspects of immigrant social structure in Swedish society. A Swedish television reporter recently commented that Sweden is the most segregated country in western Europe, and Malmö is the most segregated town in Sweden.[29] According to the 1998 statistics, approximately 27 percent of Malmö's population is composed of immigrants. Malmö is an old immigrant town; its early immigrants, who came particularly from South America, Turkey, and the Balkans, still live there. That means that many are third-generation immigrants, constituting a substantial force that is not accounted for in the statistics. Muslims are calculated to be approximately 20 percent of the population.

According to a 1997 statistical report, 77 percent of Rosengård's 20,000 inhabitants are immigrants. By 1999, this number had risen, as "ethnic" Swedes moved out and immigrants moved in. On the one hand, this is a result of the desire of many immigrants to live where they feel a sense of belonging; at the same time, it reflects a conscious policy on the part of both private and communal housing companies. According to a 1999 statistic, 33 percent of Rosengård's population is unemployed. That does not include persons who are enrolled in special employment programs such as educational projects or who have jobs as probationers in various companies, efforts that are devised as means of keeping the employment rate down. It is difficult to say how many of the immigrants in Rosengård are Muslims, but one civil servant estimated that they constitute approximately 60 percent of the population. The schools in the suburb have various constellations according to the dominating ethnic group. In one of the schools in the area, for instance, of some 1,200 pupils, approximately 80 to 90 percent are Muslim, and, of the rest, many belong to the Roma group. The director of this school has taken this situation seriously and has employed teachers of Muslim origin and introduced ritually slaughtered meat for school meals. Other schools are less Muslim dominated, but as a rule the Muslim pupils tend to be the biggest group in all schools in the area. Few schools, however, have followed the example of engaging Muslim staff or providing ritually slaughtered meat for their pupils.

In Rosengård, almost all social needs are provided for: there is a big shopping center, a medical center (with doctors, dentists, nurses, and child welfare services), a library, a social welfare office, employment agencies, Swedish courses for immigrants, and a district council where all political decisions for the district are made. There are also large shopping centers in the surrounding area, with McDonald's restaurants where Muslim children can even get Happy Meals with fishburgers, instead of hamburgers. On the two Muslim festivals, these particular McDonald's restaurants are filled with celebrating Muslims. Because of the facilities in the area, there is no specific need for these immigrants to have business in the inner city. A Danish colleague visiting Malmö remarked that she was surprised that almost no Muslim headscarves were to be observed in the town center. In Rosengård and in the surrounding shopping centers, however, Muslim women wearing headscarves are a common sight.

Rosengård is marked by a "non-Swedish touch," with immigrant shops of various categories, restaurants and snack bars with Palestinian *falafel*, and *halal* meat slaughtered in a *dhabiha* (here: ritual) manner. This pattern of "ethnic enclaves" is not exceptional, as such ethnic areas are common among immigrants in many countries such as Britain, America, Germany, and France. The difference in Sweden, however, is the way immigrants are invisible in the inner cities—in the daily life of ethnic Swedes—and are "exiled" to suburbs where ethnic Swedes rarely have any business. The question is whether or not this has to do with a wish to keep peace and order, with every disturbing element either hidden away or eliminated in one way or another.

It seems that the immigrant suburb system fits well with what Rojas refers to as a dream of the planned society. Further, such a system, where immigrants are kept out of sight of most ethnic Swedes and taken care of materially, reflects one part of the opposition that Rojas has observed in Swedish society, namely that Swedes are "subjects under the thumb of the social state."[30] The other aspect, namely that of the Swedes as free citizens, is also evident in the arguments put forward in the segregation debate about the importance of free choice of living for the individual. The immigrant, on the one hand, is subject to the paternalistic state, protected and "taken care of," while the individual's freedom has been well provided for, as there are no apparent restrictions on where the individual should live. The local housing companies seem to be the underlying force in enforcing such decisions, but their strategies are difficult to uncover. In the proposal for the plan of action for promoting integration that the municipality of Malmö distributed to various immigrant organizations and local authorities for consideration, one of the proposed measures was that the municipality should open a dialogue with the housing companies in order to prevent "ethnic discrimination" in the housing market.

The problem with such segregated living is that the social status of one generation will be inherited by the next. Muslim children in such areas do not properly learn the language or the social codes of the majority society because of their lack of contact across ethnic borders. Furthermore, as the environment conserves traditional Islamic and cultural expressions, rather than open them for a "Swedish Islam," integration into the majority society becomes difficult.

Muslim Leadership

I have discussed Muslim leadership in terms of the Muslim confederations and councils, which are supposed to work as bridges between Muslims and Swedish society. The question, however, is whether these councils really represent the Muslims. The representatives who meet with the authorities are more often than not first-generation men who usually work and act within Muslim communities, rather than having a broader contact with majority society. Moreover, the same first-generation men are often representatives in multiple confederations and councils. This has created an understanding, particularly among the second and third generations and among the Muslim women's organizations, of the Muslim leadership as a hierarchical and patriarchal power structure with little room for renewal.

On the local level, various leaders and Imams belong to local congregations. More often than not, ethnic groups have their own congregations. The Muslim leaders are therefore working ethnically, in the sense that the Arabic-speaking Imam serves the Arabic-speaking congregation, the Turkish Imam the Turkish congregation, the Kurdish Imam the Kurdish congregation, and so on. There have been difficulties with gathering the various Imams in order to centralize the Muslim expertise. Many Imams come to Sweden especially in order to serve an ethnic congregation. They rarely learn Swedish, as they tend to keep within their own ethnic groups. This creates serious difficulties, as few Imams can speak or read Swedish, and they rarely have any common language in which to communicate.

The lack of knowledge of the local language on the part of their leaders is only one part of the problem Muslims in Sweden face. Although there are some "ethnic" Swedish Imams and also some highly educated Muslim immigrants, with knowledge of Swedish society and its cultural codes, who act as Imams, many Imams have very little knowledge of Swedish society. They are therefore often ill equipped to help solve the problems of their congregations. Because these Imams live within the Muslim communities, with little external contact with majority society, they tend to regard the problems faced by members of their congregation within the narrow framework of their local Muslim community or to relate them to life in their countries of origin. Moreover, as such leaders tend to "live in religious books," instead of living in the Swedish reality, Muslims who work and act in the majority society find it difficult to relate their proposed solutions to real life. This is less true for the first-generation Muslims, as they often live within the same frame of reference as these Imams, but it is particularly true for the second- and third-generation Muslims who relate to the larger society in one way or another.

Religious authority is not easily exercised in Swedish society, even by Muslims. More often than not, Swedish Muslims look for religious authority to their countries of origin or to other western immigrant countries, or they find it in religious programs on the innumerable satellite channels sent from various parts of the Muslim world. In Rosengård, one can see that nearly every balcony has a satellite dish, and by looking at the direction of the dish one can actually tell the Arabs from the Turks or the people from the Balkans. One journalist called these satellite dishes "the ears to the immigrants' native lands."[31]

In Qatar, in December 1998, I met with the producer of the call-in program *Life and Islamic Law* (al-hayat wa ash-shariʿa) at the Arabic satellite channel al-Jazeera, where the famous Islamic scholar Yusuf al-Qaradawi answers questions every week. The questions vary from how to perform daily worship to how to deal with a changed society in the migration situation. The producer noted that the calls usually come from Europe, saying particularly that he got many calls from Sweden every week. This indicates the strongly felt need for proper leadership not only for Swedish Muslims, but also for Muslims in Europe, in general.

Education

As mentioned earlier, Muslim children tend to be the dominant group in governmental schools in "immigrant areas." In talking to teachers in such schools, I have experienced the great frustration they feel in their encounter with Muslim pupils and their parents. There are some issues where Muslims and Swedish teachers are on a collision course. For example, sometimes teachers do not find it acceptable that adolescent Muslim girls do not shower after sport classes. The girls refuse to take a shower in accordance with Islamic law, which stipulates that grown Muslims should not expose themselves naked in front of others; the shower facilities in the Swedish schools cannot provide such privacy. The teachers' insistence in this matter seems to be grounded in the ideal of "the People's Home," where the stress on equal opportunity has become a stress on uniformity. The shower facilities in school might be seen as giving all the pupils, regardless of class or social status, equal opportunities to "keep clean and proper." The possibility of "equal opportunity," however, has turned into a compulsion, where everybody is forced to be "equal" or to act in a similar fashion. The issue of showering in school seems to be a symptom of the general frustration with the situation within what have been called "immigrant schools," that is, governmental schools in dense immigrant areas, rather than something of inherent real importance. School showers have become the battlefields where "ethnic" Swedes and Muslims can try each other's strength.

Other issues of conflict in "immigrant schools" are far more serious. The problem of authority and discipline in the Swedish schools in general seems to be a source of severe frustration. I believe that much of the teachers' frustration with immigrant children is a symptom of their concern over the school situation in general. The "immigrant schools" seem to embody the discipline problem in an extreme form. The problem of authority becomes especially apparent in the case of adolescent Muslim boys who, in the eyes of the teachers, not only show a lack of respect but also show abusive tendencies, particularly toward female teachers. I believe this problem originates in different views of authority in the home and in society. Whereas many Muslim children have their roots in countries where parental authority is strong, authority in Swedish school is built mainly on an ideal of mutual respect between the teacher and the child. The adolescent Muslim boy may well understand this latter practice as weakness. Teachers with whom I have discussed this problem understand the Muslim boys' lack of respect in terms of hostility toward the female sex, seemingly interpreting it in view of their presuppositions and prejudices toward Islam as a religion. It is, however, important to be aware that it is not only in "immigrant schools" that there is a growing authority problem. Even in schools with mainly "ethnic" Swedish children, the problem of authority has become manifest. It seems that the pedagogical ideal of mutual respect between teachers and pupils has failed, and immigrants have become the scapegoats.

These problems have been interpreted in various ways. Some believe that they originate in class identity and educational standards, as many Muslim parents in Sweden are not well educated and do not see the necessity of scholarly knowledge for their children. Others feel that, lacking knowledge of the Swedish language, as well as of the society and its cultural codes, Muslim parents tend to pay less attention to their children's school situations than they might have in their countries of origin. Indulgence on the part of parents is seen by some teachers to be manifested in the indifference many Muslim parents show about coming to the parent-teacher association meetings to discuss their children's development in school. Even when specific issues arise, teachers complain that Muslim parents often refuse to come and discuss the matter. In the conflict among teachers, Muslim pupils, and parents, the pattern of Elias's established group/outsider group becomes obvious. Many parents do not share the attitude described here, but it is the group's "worst" section that tends to become the "Muslim norm" in the eyes of the teachers.

In October 1999, Hans Persson, head of the educational board in the town of Malmö, proposed that the allowances of immigrants who depend on social benefits and who live in other parts of Sweden be stopped if the immigrants moved to Malmö. The reason he gave was that 45 percent of all schoolchildren in Malmö have immigrant backgrounds, and many of them belong to newly arrived refugee groups. Nearly half of Malmö's school children are in need of extra support, and the local budget is unable to bear the financial burden. Persson wants to halt further immigration into the city in order to be able to concentrate on those children who are already living there and to try to provide them with the best possible help. Persson's move indicates the problem Malmö faces as a town with a heavily immigrant population. Many immigrants who live in small localities in other parts of Sweden, particularly Muslims, want to move to Malmö in order to be part of a broader ethnic and religious community.

The reaction to Persson's initiative was mainly one of anger and accusation; some even indicated that he had a racist motive. However, many of his opponents did say to the media that, although they were opposed to Persson's proposal, they regarded it as a result of a great concern for the future of children in Malmö, rather than as a proposal with racist overtones. On an official level, Social Democratic politicians refuted Persson's claim, supporting citizens' freedom of choice, even when they are living on social benefits. This reaction supports the Swedish ideal of freedom as the best of things,[32] which is part of the ideal of "the People's Home." It is interesting to note how the tension between submission and freedom is particularly apparent in the school arena. On the one hand, there is the shower issue, where teachers enforce equality for all pupils without any regard for religious prescriptions. On the other hand, when freedom of choice about where to live is at stake, individuals' freedom is accentuated, even though most of the debaters agree that segregation has an obvious harmful effect on society.

The issue of children's education seems to be the stumbling block for many Muslims, who regard Sweden as a society where young people have the utmost personal freedom and where youngsters show no respect to adults. In Elias's terminology, Muslims tend to pick out the "worst" section of Swedish youth and make it a generalization for all.[33] This seems terrifying for those Muslims who come from parts of the world where values of respect for elders are nurtured. The fear drives their wish to establish private Muslim schools. They hope these schools will provide Muslim children with a sound environment where they will be able to establish an Islamic identity built on an Islamic ethic and will prevent the children's being exposed to sexuality and to other dangers, such as drug and alcohol abuse, that are pervasive in western society.

Some private voluntary-aided schools with alternative pedagogical approaches or with a religio-ethnic direction were established as early as the 1940s, indicating Muslim dissatisfaction with the public school system. It was not until 1992 that Swedish authorities came to accept voluntary-aided Muslims schools, where the state finances a large part of the school's expenses. While local governments generally oppose the establishment of voluntary-aided Muslim schools, the national authorities tend to support them. Muslim schools are rapidly increasing, and every year the number of new applications for establishing such schools increases.

Many Swedes are fiercely opposed to Muslim private schools because they think such schools will necessarily promote a further segregation of Muslim immigrants within Swedish society. They cite Muslim children's unsatisfactory progress in learning the Swedish language as the main argument against such schools. Moreover, some Muslim schools have been criticized for maintaining too low an intellectual level, and even within the Muslim community there are some who prefer to send their children to governmental schools. Muslim intellectuals, however, state that, as long as severe segregation in daily life continues to be a characteristic of Swedish society, the national constellation of children in the public schools in the "immigrant areas" will be the same as in Muslim schools. Thus, they say, there is no difference between Muslim schools and "immigrant schools" with regard to the immigrant children's language and intellectual development. As most Muslim private schools also have Swedish-educated teachers, mostly non-Muslims, the Muslim intellectuals argue that the difference between the public schools and the Muslim schools is one of Muslim leadership and environment only.

The main aim for Muslims involved in Islamic educational activities in Sweden is to maintain an Islamic identity. Apart from the establishment of formal educational institutions, many Muslims are active in nonformal educational activities. These activities range from traditional Qur'anic readings to study circles in a traditional Swedish style. Locally, the Muslim organizations have informal weekend schools where children are taught to read and write Arabic and recite and memorize the Qur'an. Many Muslim organizations have established contact with the boards of local "immigrant schools" and may use the schools' rooms for their weekend activities for free. Some Muslim organizations provide weekly circles for Islamic teachings for both men and women in the community.

Education is also carried out through the growing number of Muslim women's organizations in Sweden, many of which have an active information program. They sponsor lectures at various levels about Muslims and Islam, directed to both Muslims and non-Muslims, that serve as a bridge between Muslims and Swedish society. These organizations are helping women find their own voices and are very attractive to a number of women. The boards of other Muslim organizations are in general male dominated. The lack of female influence in these organizations has encouraged women to establish their own groups, and, in the Swedish context, many local women's activities have mushroomed. The notion of "equal opportunities" in the Swedish program often tends to favor women's movements and actions. This is particularly true for Muslim women, who generally are seen as being oppressed. Swedish authorities are thus eager to financially support activities, which can be regarded in terms of Muslim women's integration into Swedish society. Moreover, while many male-dominated Muslim associations are ethnically segregated, Muslims women's organizations are more international in composition and include Arabs, Pakistanis, Turks, and so on. In some women's organizations Shi'i Muslims even work side by side with Sunni Muslims, a constellation that is rarely found in male-dominated organizations. Many Swedish converts are active within various Muslim women's organizations. Thus, activities are much in line with Swedish traditions, such as outdoor activities for women and children, pottery making for girls, summer camps in the woods, and so forth.

Family Relations

The most fundamental change for immigrant Muslims who come to Sweden is in gender relations. Coming from countries where family relations are determined within a traditional Islamic framework, Muslims may experience cognitive dissonance in their perception of the world because of the emphasis in the Swedish context on gender equality.[34] Because many Muslim families are on social welfare, the husband's traditional role as the provider of the family changes dramatically. Statistically, Muslims have a high divorce rate. However, many Muslim couples get "deceptive" divorces through the Swedish legal system in order to increase their state allowances, while at the same time remaining Islamically married. In Sweden, the divorced father's allowances for his children are paid by the state if he is on social welfare. It can therefore be profitable for a family with many children, as is the case for most Muslim immigrant families, to get such a divorce. As a result of such practice, Muslim intellectuals have started a discussion with local Muslim authorities to consider letting "a Swedish divorce" automatically lead to "an Islamic divorce."

Muslims perceive the pattern of gender equality and the program of equal opportunities in two ways. On the one hand, as women become economically independent through state allowances and social benefits, the possibility of a woman's obtaining a divorce increases. With the growth of relational problems due to changes in role patterns and general Muslim unemployment, many Muslim women choose to divorce their husbands. Thus, the Swedish social program liberates many Muslim women living in miserable marriages, and the generous state allowance and the social benefit system allow them to live an economically decent life. Moreover, as within educational institutions there are equal opportunities for men and for women, and for rich and for poor, Muslim women who would not normally have the possibility for higher education in their countries of origin have the chance to obtain higher education in Sweden.

On the other hand, many Muslims may see western policies favoring gender equality and equal opportunities as compulsion and, thus, repression. Since many Muslim women believe that their first obligation is to serve their husbands and children, the emphasis on work is perceived as a compulsion. Swedish authorities, eager to lower the unemployment rate, have created educational and employment opportunities designed especially for women, including courses in Swedish, computer training, and various practical skills such as motor mechanics and welding.[35] They see these as offering women the possibility of escaping the domestic sphere. Many Muslim women do not want to participate in such programs, not only because of their home responsibilities but also because they are not interested in learning these kinds of skills. Swedish authorities do not understand this reluctance, as it goes against the general Swedish idea of the importance of paid labor. Muslim women, unfortunately, find it difficult to turn down these opportunities because, if they do, they will lose their monthly state allowance.

Political Participation

The political maps of the Scandinavian countries are quite similar but are different from those of other parts of the world. The Swedish Conservative Party is no more conservative than the Democratic Party in the United States, whereas the Social Democratic Party, which was dominant during most of the twentieth century, has gradually moved to the right in the past few decades. This has created a political situation where there is no great polarity between the main parties.

The Social Democratic Party has more or less had a monopoly on Muslim votes until recently, because Muslims see the Social Democrats as supporting the state allowances system in contrast to the Conservative Party, which some Muslims see as favoring restrictions on benefits. To some extent, this is due to language difficulties—Muslims may link the word "social" in "Social Democrats" to the institution of social benefit. However, by the end of the 1990s, the Social Democratic Party's monopoly had ended. One of the main reasons was the growing Muslim awareness of the Social Democratic Party's family policies, which many Muslims believe contribute to the loosening of family ties in Sweden.

The two main Muslim strategies—creating separate Muslim institutions and joining Swedish institutions—are exemplified in the Muslim political approach. On the one hand, leaders of the Council of Swedish Muslims have stressed the importance of specific Muslim institutions, and this has been the approach of the Muslim Confederations.[36] Members of the confederations kept out of politics for a long time, but in the late 1990s the Council of Swedish Muslims called for the establishment of the Islamic Political Assembly (Politisk Islamisk Samling). The first paragraph of the statutes of this political organ state that the board of the Assembly has "no right to pass a resolution which is contrary to a decision taken by the Council of Swedish Muslims."[37] This is yet another example of how the official Muslim leadership in Sweden attempts to centralize its power over Swedish Muslims. Although the Assembly has professed to be independent of the Swedish political parties, it has been linked to the Social Democratic Party because it has provided certain services such as political education for the Assembly's members. In contrast, many Muslims outside the confederations have decided to join Swedish political institutions, and many of the established Swedish political parties now have Muslim members.

While relatively few immigrants in general, and Muslims in particular, vote, the political scene has recently been set for a fight for immigrants' votes. The Social Democratic Party has one female Muslim in Parliament. The small Environment Party has started recruiting among immigrants; recently it has been successful in placing many immigrants on the party board and has nominated immigrants for both local and regional elections. Independent Islamic activists have recently joined the established parties, and in Rosengård, for instance, many Muslims have joined either the Social Democratic Party or the Conservative Party. It is important to note that recently one of the leaders of the Social Democratic Party proposed that immigrants be allocated quotas for leading political positions.

Reflections

The question that persists in light of the matters raised in this essay is why integration of immigrants in Sweden has met such difficulties. Why is there still a profound problem of "enclavization" of Swedish society, despite the considerable financial resources the government has put into various integration projects? It is obvious that the issue is complex and multifaceted. One clear reason, however, seems to be the failure of the government to see the necessity of a fundamental reform of the labor market. Second, there is a need to combat the partly unconscious and partly conscious discriminatory attitudes that dominate contemporary Swedish society. Success in the latter would entail a re-envisioning of Sweden as a nation and a new understanding of what it means to be "Swedish." Attention also must be given to improving the situation of immigrant schools in order to create a strong educational grounding for future generations. Most of these schools are not providing the children with enough Swedish language instruction to prepare them to enter a profession in a future Sweden. This concern, and the need to re-establish the authority of teachers in Swedish schools, is a serious matter that must be addressed both by the Swedish authorities and by Muslims themselves.

Success in these efforts is far from guaranteed. Muslims correctly perceive that they are subject to the definitions and decisions of others, and to a great extent they are powerless to determine their own futures. Many Muslims, however, even those living in segregated areas, feel comfortable in Sweden, and they do not react to their situation in the same way as "ethnic" Swedes and Muslim intellectuals do. Thus, the assessment of the Muslim situation as positive or negative becomes a matter of perspective.

Many of the second- and third-generation Muslims will probably end up understanding Islam in terms of Swedish cultural processes. Furthermore, there is an increase in the number of "ethnic" Swedes and other immigrants who convert to Islam. The converts and the new generations of Muslims incorporate local Swedish cultural components into their religion. These Muslims are moving into positions of influence in the Muslim communities because of their knowledge of Swedish society and its cultural codes, which may well mean that in the near future a genuinely "Swedish" form of Islam will emerge. This has been defined by researchers as the "blue-yellow" Islam, referring to the color of the Swedish flag.

One of the main problems today for Swedes as a whole seems to be the change in locus of authority. Sweden has been marked by a strong state authority for generations, and the society has been regarded as the main actor in most aspects of life. In the era of globalization, decisions that have a direct bearing on Sweden and Swedish politics, however, are increasingly made in other parts of the world. Swedes have been used to looking to society as the driving force. It is difficult to change such an attitude as the state weakens and individuals have to carry the main responsibility for their own lives. This is increasing obvious, for example, in the discussion of the educational system, where people tend to look to society for help instead of regarding themselves as society.

The consequences of the increasing weakening of the state also impinge on Muslim communities in Sweden. The first-, second-, and third-generation Muslims are mainly socialized into a system of "caretaking," where the state has taken the responsibility for meeting daily needs, as well as for providing for secondary needs, such as education and jobs. With the change in the economic situation and in the role of the state, it becomes necessary for Muslims to get more involved in Swedish social activities. Furthermore, the ideal of the "People's Home," which has been a prominent feature in Swedish politics and which is regarded by some researchers as one of the main obstacles to the integration of immigrants, may loosen its power in the changing circumstances. This opens the way for further integration of Muslims into Swedish society.

Migrants in general might be regarded as energetic and inventive individuals, since the process of leaving one's homeland and family involves breaking the traditional bonds of one's social universe. As integration of immigrants in Sweden to a great extent has been a matter of employment, it is of importance to consider the immigrant issue in this perspective. The aspect of power in the Swedish "caretaking" project is apparent. If they continue to rely on such "caretaking," Muslim immigrants will remain powerless, with other people thinking for them, deciding their futures, and defining their status. The opening up of opportunities for Muslims to assume responsibility for part of their own problem solving will counter the current pattern of looking to the dominant society for help, instead of taking an active role, both individually and communally. There are various positive examples of Muslim immigrants who have managed to start their own enterprises, often with the whole family involved on various levels. This may well be the future for Muslim immigrants in Sweden, but to reach this point, attitudes on the part of both the Swedish authorities and the Muslim communities will have to change.

Sweden is no longer subject to a high rate of immigration. As recent legislation makes it difficult even for refugees to enter the country, the great immigration wave of the late 1980s and the early 1990s, with a daily flow of new immigrants entering the country, is history. Furthermore, the five-year limit for obtaining Swedish citizenship will turn a great number of Muslim immigrants into Swedish citizens in the near future. In less than two generations, there will not be many individuals who can be classified as "immigrants," in the Swedish authorities' sense of the word. It is all the more urgent, therefore, that the present patterns of "enclavisation" in Sweden be ended and that new models be developed that will lead to a stable society.

Notes

1. Pia Karlsson and Ingvar Svanberg, *Moskeer i Sverige En Religionsetnologisk studie i intolerans och administrativ vanmakt*. Serien Tro och Tanke 7/95. Uppsala: Svenska Kyrkans Forskningsråd, 1995, 14.

2. Pieter Bevelander, Benny Carlson, and Mauricio Rojas, *I Krusbärslandets Storstäder: Om Invandrare i Stockholm, Göteborg och Malmö* (Kristianstad: SNS Förlag, 1997), 40. See also SCB (Statistiska Centralbyrån), *Utbildning för utrikes födda* (Örebro: SCB, 1995), 4.

3. Åke Sander, "The Road from Musalla to Mosque," in *The Integration of Islam and Hinduism in Western Europe*, ed. W. A. R. Shadid and P. S. van Koningsveld (United Kingdom: Kok Pharos, 1994), 68–69.

4. Sander's investigation was done in the early 1990s, before the Bosnian refugees came to Sweden and the result does therefore not say anything about this group.

5. Åke Sander, *I vilken utsträckning är den svenska muslimen religiös* (Gothenburg: KIM, 1993).

6. Åke Sander, "The Status of Muslim Communities in Sweden," in *Muslim Communities in the New Europe*, ed. Gerd Nonneman, Tim Niblock, and Bogdan Szajkowski (London: Ithaca, 1996), 273.

7 Norbert Elias, *The Established and the Outsiders: A Sociological Enquiry into Community Problems* (London: Sage, 1994), xix.

8. Ibid.

9. Jörgen S. Nielsen, *Muslims in Western Europe* (Edinburgh: Edinburgh University Press, 1996), 82.

10. SOU (State's Official Reports), Stockholm: Regeringskansliet (Government's office). 1999: 34, 137–42.

11. Ibid., 137–42.

12. SOU (State's Official Reports), *Investigation of Immigrants 3*. Stockholm: Regeringskansliet, 1974. See also Sander, "The Status of Muslim," 288.

13. Mauricio Rojas, *The Rise and Fall of the Swedish Model*. London: Social Market Foundation, 1998.

14. Ibid., 10.

15. Ibid., 51.

16. Ibid., 90.

17. Ibid., 90. Where, as Rojas puts it, "the foundations of our stately home have been remorsely undermined, but the home still stands, it lives in the form of increasingly anachronistic institutions, structures, attitudes, and nostalgic dreams."

18. Sander, "The Status of Muslim Communities," 272.

19. Ibid., 273.

20. Ibid., 274.

21. Ibid., 276.

22. Muhammad Anwar, "Religious Identity in Plural Societies: The Case of Britain," *Journal of the Institute of Muslim Minorities Affair* 2, nos. 2–3 (1987): 110.

23. Muhammad Anwar, *Pakistanis in Britain: A Sociological Study* (London: New Century, 1985), 9.

24. Åke Sander, "The Road from Musalla to Mosque," 63.

25. Sweden is one of three European countries where the ritual slaughter of animals is forbidden. (The two other countries are Switzerland and Norway.) There is a discussion going on in Sweden about whether the reason for the banning was purely anti-Semitism or whether the goal of the ban was the protection of animal rights. The ban was introduced in Swedish law in 1938, whereas Norway introduced the law in the mid-1920s. Recently, ritual slaughter has been accepted if the animals are drugged before being slaughtered. Muslims, however, disagree on whether meat of drugged animals is acceptable to eat. In the late 1990s, this discussion faded away. The great majority of Muslims in Sweden accept such meat, and *halal* meat is no longer a big issue in the contemporary debate.

26. This question was raised by a Muslim researcher in one of the major newspapers in Sweden in relation to Article 18 of the Declaration of Human Rights. Pernilla Ouis, ""Ersätt rättigheterna med mänskliga skyldigheter," in *Sydsvenska Dagbladet*, 7 June 1998, Malmö.

27. See, for instance, Pia Karlsson and Ingvar Svanberg, *Religionsfrihet i Sverige* (Lund: Studentlitteratur, 1997).

28. Swedish Law, 1994:134, §1.

29. Swedish Television 2, *Reportrarna*, 19 Oct. 1999.

30. Rojas, *Rise and Fall of the Swedish Model*, 10.

31. Aje Carlbom, "Allahs tårar: Islam som integrerande kraft i stadsdelen Rosengård." Papeer presented at the SAND conference, Lund University, 1998.

32. Rojas, *Rise and Fall of the Swedish Model*, 10.

33. Elias, *The Established and the Outsiders*, xix.

34. Eva Hamberg, "Migration and Religious Change," in *Religion and Social Transition*, ed. Eila Helander (Helsinki: University of Helsinki, 1999).

35. Students enrolled in these training programs are not counted in unemployment statistics.

36. Islamic Political Assembly, *Statutes for Islamic Political Assembly*, Stockholm (n.d.).

37. Ingvar Svanberg and David Westerlund, eds., *Blågul Islam? Muslimer i Sverige* (Blue-yellow Islam? Muslims in Sweden). Nora: Nya Doxa, 1999).

7

Globalization in Reverse and the Challenge of Integration: Muslims in Denmark

Jørgen Bæk Simonsen

The current debate on globalization is taking place in the social sciences, as well as in the humanities. Quite often it is impossible to understand fully how scholars use the concept. Sometimes globalization is projected as a *cause* intimately linked to increasing economic cooperation on the global scale. In this respect it refers to the locally, regionally, or internationally unpredictable consequences of decisions taken by multinational companies on where to invest surplus capital or when to transfer investments from one region of the world to another. Such decisions may cause dramatic social and political changes in the regions involved,[1] as is the case when one hegemonic political system decides that the time has come to introduce a new world order and uses its power to implement its decision.[2] Other times the concept is used to refer to the *consequence* of change(s) intimately linked to modernization, itself a concept with several meanings.[3]

Old Wine—New Bottles?

This lack of clarity and specificity may reflect the fact that, throughout history, human cultures have been exposed to the same kind of paradoxical phenomena. The best example, perhaps, is the spread of the so-called great world religions as they gained support by ordinary people in parts of the world that had no direct economic, political, or social links to the regions in which the religions initially were born. When Christian missionaries, for example, transplanted the original Middle Eastern religion to Europe, people converted. The process of conversion slowly challenged social and political structures based on time-specific interpretations of earlier traditional religions, which generated further changes at all levels.

That is how all the great world religions originally spread. Later, other ways of expansion were added, often linked to political and religious struggles in parts of the world converted to one of the new world religions. This was the case in the seventeenth century, when Europeans brought groups of Christians to North America at the same time that the Catholic Church tried to increase the numbers of Catholic Christians in what is now Latin America. Another example is the establishment of the Jewish religion in the United States, which was the historical result of anti-Semitic pogroms organized by the Russian government from the early 1880s on. Nearly two million Jews left Russia and parts of Eastern Europe; most settled in America.

The transplanting of a number of religions from their areas of origin to other parts of the world took place because individuals decided to convert, and because institutions of various kinds were established that made it possible to accelerate the conversion already begun. These developments often had important political consequences, as when the Roman emperor decided to make Christianity the official religion of the Roman Empire. Thus, during the Middle Ages it was possible for intellectuals in Europe to create a European Christian tradition, even though Christianity originated in the Middle East.

When the phenomenon of globalization is discussed at the turn of the twenty-first century,[4] however, these facts are often ignored, as if globalization had no historical precedent. Needless to say, the integration of any local economic system into the global one is far more complicated now, at the beginning of the new millennium, than ever before. The speed and visibility of changes set in motion in all parts of the world illustrate dramatically how globalization is linked to the concept of modernization, the introduction of new technologies of information, and so forth.

Whether globalization is the *cause* or the *consequence* of change, it seems to be a generally accepted presumption that, in the very near future, those who will be most dramatically confronted with its political, social, and cultural consequences are the countries in the so-called two-thirds world. The West has not been able to fully understand the political reactions of the rest of the world as a result of the increasing economic and cultural pressures to which it is exposed. This has been apparent in Muslim countries ever since the advent of modern European imperialism. Two reactions set in: one expressed a need for defense in the form of *jihad*,[5] and the other called for a critical revitalization of Islam. Revitalization was first formulated and expressed by the intellectual elite, and later picked up as a means of social mobilization by movements such as the Muslim Brotherhood. Islamism is a modern sociocultural phenomenon that cannot be attributed to one cause only, but it is beyond doubt that increasing external pressure plays an extremely important role.[6]

This, however, is only one side of the story. In the long run, the West as well will be confronted with and challenged by the consequences of globalization. This has clearly been the case in Europe during the past two decades; the number of people immigrating to Europe from the two-thirds world has been steadily increasing. The reactions of politicians, intellectuals, and citizens in general to the changes in the streets are quite similar to those formulated by individuals and groups in the rest of the world. In all cases, the need to preserve the authentic local cultural tradition in face of the pressure these same traditions are experiencing as a result of globalization is given a very high priority.

Islam Transplanted—Muslims in Denmark

Islam is now, at the beginning of the twenty-first century, the second-largest religion in Denmark. Its approximately 150,000 adherents, composed of both sexes and all age groups, make up a little less than 3 percent of the total population of the country. Danish Islam is now well established, with some sixty mosques situated all over the country, along with seventeen private Muslim schools and a large number of different organizations. The various needs of the Muslim community are accommodated by such services as Islamic banks, *halal* food shops, travel agencies that offer special fares for persons going on the annual pilgrimage to Mecca, companies that offer courses for young Muslim women who want to get their driver's license, sport clubs with lessons for women only, and so forth.

The presence of Islam in Denmark historically is due to two different factors. The first is the immigration of workers to meet a labor shortage in the country, and the second is the need for political asylum for Muslim refugees who have been exposed to oppression in their home countries. While both factors have served to increase the number of Muslims in the country, they are rooted in quite different circumstances.

The first movement was initiated when Danish companies were in dire need of more workers in the late 1960s. No more workers were to be found locally, as men were fully employed and all women who wanted to join the workforce at that time had already done so. The increasing demand could be met only by bringing in immigrant workers. From 1967 until late 1973, Denmark pursued a very liberal immigration policy, as a result of which Muslim workers from the periphery of Europe began to arrive in the country. As the economy of the West from early 1973 onward showed the first signs of crisis, Danish trade unions put pressure on Parliament to curb further immigration. This was achieved by passing a law in November 1973 that put a total stop to further immigration of workers into the country. The immigrants who already had jobs, however, were desperately needed, and, in order to encourage them to stay, Parliament, in the spring of 1974, passed another law making it possible for those who had permanent permits issued before November 1967 to bring their families to join them. The unification of the families took place throughout the following decade.

The second constituency of Muslims in Denmark began to appear in the early 1980s. These were the refugees who came seeking asylum from several countries. Iranians fleeing the new Islamic regime after the revolution of 1979 were the first of this stream of refugees; they were followed in the mid-1980s by stateless Palestinians escaping the civil war in Lebanon in general, and Beirut in particular, as a result of the Israeli invasion in 1982. In the late 1980s, Iraqis constituted the largest number of refugees, as did Somalians during the 1990s. Political asylum is granted by decision of the Danish authorities, and persons who obtain asylum are guaranteed by the state the right of having their families unified in Denmark. Approximately 52 percent of the Muslim in Denmark at the beginning of the year 2000 were political refugees, with the other 48 percent being migrants or children or grandchildren of migrants.

In looking at the issues and concerns facing Muslims in Denmark, we must bear in mind that, from the very beginning, both workers and refugees were accepted and that for the most part those in the immigrant group were actively endorsed by the Danish state. Parliament has accepted and permitted immigration in order to secure industrial workers, and the state has granted political asylum upon application because Denmark prides itself on being a liberal political entity in which human rights are embedded in the constitution.

From Majority to Minority

Islam in Denmark is far from homogeneous, with immigrants and refugees often disagreeing as to which interpretations of Islam are correct and holding different views on how to be a good and upright Muslim. The establishment of Islam in Denmark was gradual and slow, with the various ethnic Muslim groups generally operating quite independently. The local mosques established from the early 1970s onward were organized by Turks for Turks, or by Pakistanis for Pakistanis.[7] As the number of Muslims in Denmark grew, new groups upon arrival quickly established their own mosques, their own Qur'an schools, and their own private Muslim schools, profiting from the experience of earlier Muslim groups.

In only one case was a mosque established for the benefit of several different national groups. In the early 1970s, a number of Muslim diplomats tried to persuade Danish authorities to donate a building to be converted into a mosque for the benefit of the immigrant Muslim workers in the greater Copenhagen area, but the authorities declined. As a result, the Muslim embassies launched their own initiative and in 1976 established the Islamic Cultural Center in a building bought by a committee set up by the various Muslim embassies. For several years, the mosque was the biggest in the country, and various Muslim embassies guaranteed that they would pay the cost involved in running the center. Thus, the Libyan-sponsored organization al-Da'wa al-Islamiya for several years paid the salary of the Imam working at the center, but that support was lost in the late 1980s.[8] Another Islamic organization, the Rabitat al-Alam al-Islami (Muslim World League), sponsored by Saudi Arabia, runs two mosques in the Copenhagen area established in buildings bought by the League.[9]

For a long time, the immigrants held onto their original hope that they would be able to return to their country of origin as soon as they had saved enough money to ensure the financial security of their families. As time passed, however, the possibility of fulfilling this dream became increasingly remote. Many of the immigrants were persuaded that it would benefit their families as a whole if the children were educated in Denmark. A prolonged stay, it was argued, would provide the opportunity to increase family savings. The stay for most became longer and longer. The political refugees, too, soon were forced to realize that their stay in Denmark was to be a more permanent one than first expected. The political situation in the Islamic Republic of Iran stabilized, with the Khomeini supporters in total power after 1982. The civil war in Lebanon was ended with an agreement negotiated in 1989 by all parties involved except the Palestinians. The political regime in Iraq seems to have an enduring grip on power, and, although the civil war in Somalia has ended, the political situation remains unresolved.

Therefore, the Muslims have had to learn to accommodate to a life in Denmark, where Islam in general and Muslim traditions in particular continue to be viewed as something new, strange, and culturally foreign. While in their country of origin the various Muslim groups were used to being part of a majority, this was no longer the case in the new setting. They found themselves reduced to a minority, and as such in a subordinate position vis-à-vis the surrounding non-Muslim Danish society.

Not surprisingly, the discourse formulated by the Muslim groups during the 1970s and most of the 1980s was a defensive one. This defensive attitude was characteristic of the mosques run by the immigrants, as well as those run by the refugees. The Muslim minority groups established themselves independently along ethnic lines, with very limited communication taking place across those lines. No serious effort was made to organize for mutual benefit. This had primarily to do with the point of reference: for both immigrants and refugees, the myth of returning home, even as the hope of its realization became dimmer, made in-depth communication with the other Muslim groups or the surrounding non-Muslim majority superfluous. As a result, a great deal of emphasis was laid on maintaining relationships with the country of origin: by mail, by phone, by sending money back to parents and other family members, and, for the immigrants themselves, by frequent visits to and spending holidays in the home country. Little or no energy was invested in establishing closer relations to the surrounding society, as it was agreed upon that the stay was to be a temporary one.[10]

Since the middle of the 1970s, when the unification of the immigrant families made Islam more visible in Danish society, Muslims have been forced to conduct their daily life in a society dominated by the norms, values, and existing rules of the dominant culture. Parents of school children and Imams of the local mosques have wanted to keep communication and interaction with the surrounding non-Muslim society to a minimum, as that society was deemed a challenge to the ways in which Islam traditionally has been interpreted. Muslim parents, both immigrant and refugee, have articulated their fear that their children will be too much influenced by the norms and values of the surrounding Danish majority.[11] As Danish society in general, as well as the immigrants themselves, upheld the myth that Muslims would eventually return home,[12] only a few concerted efforts were made to include the immigrants in the larger society. The most direct link between the immigrants on the one hand and Danish society on the other was the law passed in 1976 that forced all immigrants to send their children to school.[13] In the long run, this was to have profound consequences for all: the children, their parents, and the society as a whole.

The concept gradually formulated by the state to facilitate interaction between the immigrants and the surrounding Danish society was *integration*, by which a number of host countries in Europe found the means to solve the challenge presented by their new and "different" populations. Integration for the host society meant that it listed the obligations that the immigrants and the refugees had to fulfil if they were to be recognized by the majority as truly integrated. In general, however, the immigrants and refugees saw this arrangement as very one sided. While they were asked to adapt to social rules and norms decided upon and developed by the majority, in no concrete way was the majority or its institutions ready to negotiate those rules and norms as a result of conversations with the Muslim minority. No initiative was taken in the public schools, for example, to call attention to the fact that a growing number of the children came from families with religious values and traditions different from those of the dominant, in this case Danish, society. Muslims perceived the conversation about integration to be strictly in the hands of the majority and its institutions, formulated without inviting the Muslims to participate in the dialogue. The Muslim parents were talked *to*, not *with*.

At the beginning of the twenty-first century, some sixty local mosques are to be found in Denmark. All the local mosques are established in buildings not originally constructed for religious purposes. Only one was built to be a mosque from the beginning; to the regret of many Muslims, this mosque is run by the Ahmadiyya movement, which they consider not to be part of orthodox Islam. Muslims are allowed to establish private schools, and at the beginning of the year 2000 there were seventeen in existence. Most of them are located in the greater Copenhagen area, but during the past few years private Muslim schools also have been established in Århus and Odense, the second and the third largest towns in the kingdom. Recently a group of young educated Muslims has been active in trying to organize some kind of higher Islamic teaching in Denmark, but so far the initiative has not borne fruit. In one mosque, a young Turk functions as Imam and delivers his Friday sermons in Danish.

The Majority and the Myth of Tolerance

Social changes are interpreted in various ways by different groups. Many Danish citizens regard the changes that have taken place since the middle of the 1970s as a threat to the homogeneity of their society. From the early 1980s on, Islam and Muslims generally have been considered to be a problem all over Europe. Among the reasons for this are the fact that Muslim refugees continue to flow in steady streams from politically and economically troubled countries, that the number of Muslims in Europe is growing because of the continued unification of the immigrants' families, and that the general economic recession has brought about the rise of unemployment in the various European countries.

To these factors have been added the concerns generated among Danes by their observation of the issues that arise when Muslims try to live their lives in a non-Muslim social setting. In all cases the Muslims have been described as presenting a problem. It is a problem that they try to keep their distance from the surrounding Danish society. It is a problem that Muslim wives do not participate socially in different activities outside the realm of the nuclear family. It is a problem that Muslim children often are unable to speak Danish when they start school at the age of six or seven years, and so forth. In every instance it is the presence of the immigrants and the refugees that is seen as the cause of the problem, with no responsibility assigned to Danish society and institutions themselves to work toward its solution.

The appearance of new groups with different social behavior has challenged the historical homogeneity of Danish society in very concrete ways, with the result that a feeling of being threatened has been growing since the middle of the 1980s. As a result, part of the majority has focused on the necessity of taking initiatives to sustain Danish traditions that are seen to be under ever-expanding pressure as the number of foreigners grows. According to the worst scenario, in the not-too-distant future Danes will be reduced to a minority "in their own country," a fear often held by right-wing politicians who oppose further immigration of foreigners into Denmark.

In this respect Denmark has been undergoing the same kind of transformation as the rest of Europe. All countries in what used to be western Europe have experienced the establishment of Islam within their traditional national borders. For some this is a consequence of a colonial heritage, as is the case for Great Britain, France, the Netherlands, and, to an extent, Italy and Spain. For others it is a consequence of the expanding European industry during the 1960s and 1970s and the need for foreign workers, as was the case in countries like Germany, Sweden, and Denmark.[14] During the 1980s and 1990s, a flow of political refugees from parts of the Islamic world applying for political asylum had consequences for many countries. These factors have had similar results all over Europe. In general, the reaction to the common challenge (what I call globalization in reverse) is structurally the same in all European countries, although small differences can be observed related to the particular national culture of the country in question.

Religiously and linguistically, Denmark has always been characterized by an extremely high degree of homogeneity. Because of the particularities of social background, educational levels, and other socioeconomic factors, Danish culture on the surface may appear to differ from one group to the other, or from one part of the country to the other. Until recently, however, the differences in reality have been superficial, representing little more than slight variations of a value system all groups and individuals have in common.

Like other Protestant European countries, Danish society became secularized during the twentieth century, and the role of Christianity in the public sphere, as well as in culture and politics in general, was continuously reduced. This secularization was recognized and even accepted by most Danes. Now, however, it is being challenged by Muslims who are in the process of organizing their lives and their routines in the country. They exhibit in their social behavior and in their religious practices certain values and rules that are obviously different from those of the Danish majority. This kind of globalization in reverse is proving to the majority that not only the poor countries of the two-thirds world pay a price in this process. The West has been challenged on its own geographical territory, as well.

The Challenge—Will the Liberal Polity Survive?

At the beginning of the new millennium, the public debate in Denmark is in a kind of blind alley. In public confrontations, on television and radio, in daily papers and weekly magazines, people critical of immigrants and refugees have organized to defend what they refer to as true and authentic Danish traditions and values. It is ironic to see how often they formulate an approach to the changes in society that in both substance and structure is identical to that formulated by the immigrants and the refugees when they first arrived several decades ago. The defensive discourse initially articulated by the Muslims reinforced social behavior characterized by lack of interaction with the surrounding society. The Danish majority reacted to this by assuming that the Muslims were simply unable to integrate in a modern pluralistic society. Less than two decades later, the very same majority started formulating a discourse in which they want to keep *their* culture from being challenged by others. At the same time, a growing number of Muslims living in the country have begun a new offensive discourse in which they regard themselves as an integral part of Danish society.[15]

As a result of their rising fears about the loss of integrity of Danish culture, some Danes are making a concerted effort to throw suspicion on young Muslims born in Denmark. These young people have been brought up in the country; ever since they started in school they have been part of the new emerging multicultural Danish society that is so vehemently criticized by some of the majority population. They are fluent in Danish, many of them are well educated, and they are equipped to fulfil the demands posed by the surrounding society. Nevertheless, they are still met with suspicion by the majority. During the summer of 1999, Danish media once again focused on an item that has been under intense discussion ever since the first Muslim families were unified in the middle of the 1970s, namely the headscarf. Most of the Danish majority population interpret the headscarf as a sign of male dominance and female suppression and as clear proof of the inability of Muslims to modernize. This interpretation is upheld in spite of arguments put forward by young Muslim women who argue just the opposite.[16] These women have abided by most of the demands formulated by the Danish society: they have learned the language, they have finished school, and they have continued their education by taking a variety of technical courses. But still they are classified as a "problem," now because they want to wear a headscarf.

On June 5, 1999, ceremonies were held all over the country to celebrate the 150th birthday of the Danish Constitution of 1849. In these ceremonies it was stated again and again how Danish society had developed a genuine tradition for tolerance and openness vis-à-vis the surrounding world. To a certain extent, this seems to be right. Tolerance was demonstrated as different social groups in society began to develop new styles of living in response to the increase in the general standard of living after World War II. From the late 1960s, for example, it was socially acceptable for a man and a woman to live as an unmarried couple. A few years later, lesbian women and homosexual men were legally allowed to marry. The depth and the extent of the claimed tolerance, however, was dramatically challenged when the immigrants and refugees began to arrive in greater numbers.

It has been obvious ever since that the idealistic picture painted by the Danes does not mirror reality. Many citizens are not at all pleased to see how the previous homogeneous society has been transformed into a multicultural, multilingual, and multireligious one. The challenge is serious, and what is at stake is something very precious: the survival of the liberal cultural tradition and the open tolerant political atmosphere gradually developed and expanded in Denmark, as well as in the rest of Europe since the French revolution in 1789. The vehement reaction all over Europe to the globalization in reverse has fostered the beginnings of a dichotomy within the various European countries, one that differentiates between "us" and "them." By referring to an "authentic" culture, politicians, supported by a growing number of their constituencies, try to secure exclusive rights and privileges for the ethnic majority that are not to be enjoyed by others. That raises the question, To what degree is the majority willing to pass on to new members of society rights regarded as inalienable according to the values embedded in their liberal constitutions? Judged by developments during recent years, the future of the political culture held in such high esteem by Danes and Europeans alike is seriously threatened.

Ironically, the threat is not coming from the Islamic world as often predicted in the media and in books and articles written by intellectuals from the West.[17] The threat comes from within, a result of globalization in reverse that is bringing people from without into established western cultures. Right-wing political groups have gained momentum all over Europe and have forced more liberal parties to pursue a policy of steadfastness. The result is indeed a paradox in itself. In order to save a European identity characterized by tolerance, openness, ability to change, and willingness to adopt to new challenges, European governments launch political initiatives that in the end threaten the very same liberal political tradition. By insisting that potential future members of society are not really part of the entity in which they live, by excluding them with rules and regulations that stress their difference, rather than their belonging, the majority makes it impossible for the minority to be recognized. At the same time, they are attempting to stop the flow of history, denying the obvious fact that social norms and rules always have changed. Were this not true, Europe and the West would never have become Christian!

Perhaps the greatest paradox is the timing of these rules and regulations, coming at a time when European nations are struggling for greater unity and economic cooperation through the European Union (EU). Now a growing number of laws valid in individual countries are determined not by the respective governments (in this case the Danish national parliament) but by the various EU institutions. Yet, Danish politicians—like politicians all over Europe—are still referring to a nation-state seriously eroded and invalidated by global economic integration and by social, cultural, linguistic, and religious globalization in reverse.[18]

The situation thus seems to have come full circle. A number of scholarly books and articles since the early 1980s have posed the question whether Islam is compatible with democracy. The question raised by the arrival of a small number of Muslims in Europe at the edge of the new millenium seems to be the opposite: Will the supposed cradle of democracy, that is, Europe, be able to include Muslims living in the West as fully recognized members of a multicultural, multireligious, and multilinguistic society where they are empowered by the same political, cultural, and linguistic rights as the rest of society?[19]

Notes

1. Alex E. Fernández Jilberto and André Mommen, *Regionalization and Globalization in the Modern World Economy: Perspectives on the Third World and Transitional Economies* (Routledge: London, 1998); Satya Dev Gupta, *The Political Economy of Globalization* (Boston: Kluwer Academic, 1997). For a more critical view, see Paul Hirst and Grahame Thompson, *Globalization in Question* (Cambridge: Polity, 1999).

2. David Armstrong, *Revolution and World Order* (London: Clarendon, 1993); Haifa Jawad, ed., *The Middle East in the New World Order*, 2d ed. (London: Macmillan, 1997).

3. Bryan S. Turner, *Orientalism, Postmodernism and Globalism* (London: Routledge, 1994); Staffan Lindberg and Arni Sverrisson, *Social Movements in Development: The Challenge of Globalization and Democratization* (New York: St. Martin's, 1997).

4. James Foreman-Peck, ed., *Historical Foundations of Globalization* (Cheltenham: Edward Elgar, 1998).

5. Rudolph Peters, *Islam and Colonialism: The Doctrine of Jihad in Modern History* (The Hague: Mouton, 1979); John Obert Voll, *Islam: Continuity and Change in the Modern World* (Boulder, Colo.: Westview Press, 1982).

6. Mir Zohair Husain, *Global Islamic Politics* (New York: Harper/Collins, 1995).

7. Jørgen Bæk Simonsen, *Islam in Denmark: Muslim Institutions in Denmark, 1970–1989* (Århus: Århus Universitetsforlag, 1990).

8. Ibid., 115.

9. Ibid., 103.

10. Jørgen Bæk Simonsen, *From Defensive Silence to Creative Participation—Muslim Discourses in Denmark* (forthcoming).

11. Bæk Simonsen, *Islam in Denmark*, 145ff.

12. The Danish parliament, in debates about migration policy in the early 1970s, voiced the same approach to the immigrants. They were here for a while and would eventually return as the need for them would disappear. Cf. David Coleman and Eskil Wadensjö, *The Migration to Denmark: International and National Perspectives* (Copenhagen: af Spektrum, 1999).

13. Legally the law requires not that children go to school, only that they be taught. This can be done either in a state-run public school, by the parents themselves, or in a private school.

14. Jørgen S. Nielsen, *Muslims in Western Europe* (Edinburgh: Edinburgh University Press, 1992); Ingmar Karlsson, *Islam and Europe* (Stockholm: Wahlström & Widstrand, 1994); Gerd Nonneman, Tim Niblock, and Bogdan Szajkowski, eds., *Muslim Communities in the New Europe* (Reading: Ithaca Press, 1996); Lars Pederesen, *Newer Islamic Movements in Western Europe* (Aldershot: Ashgate, 1999).

15. Jørgen Bæk Simonsen, "A Means to Change or Transform Images of the Other—Private Arab Schools in Denmark," in *The Arabs and the West: Mutual Images*, ed. Jørgen S. Nielsen and Sami A. Khasawnih (Amman: University of Amman Press, 1998).

16. Connie Carøe Christensen and Lene Kofoed Rasmussen, *Choosing the Headscarf: Young Women in Political Islam* (Copenhagen: Forlaget Sociologi, 1994).

17. Samuel P. Huntington, *The Clash of Civilizations and the Remaking of World Order* (New York: Simon & Schuster, 1996); V. S. Naipul, *Beyond Belief: Islamic Excursions among the Converted Peoples* (London: Vintage, 1999).

18. Zygmunt Baumann, *Globalization: The Human Consequences* (New York: Columbia University Press, 1998).

19. Lisbet Christoffersen and Jørgen Bæk Simonsen, eds., *Visions of Freedom of Religion, Democracy and Ethnic Equality* (Copenhagen: Nævnet for Etnisk Ligestilling, 1999).

8

Muslims in Italy

Maria Adele Roggero

From a historical point of view, the Italian peninsula has been exposed to Islamic influence since the beginning of the Muslim age (seventh century C.E.), initially through acts of piracy from North Africa, then with the full-fledged Muslim conquest of Sicily and part of southern Italy. Throughout the Middle Ages, Islam continued to make its influence felt in Italy through traders, travelers, and plunderers, with its effects felt in commerce, language, and culture. From the last decade of the eighteenth century to about 1940, this direct contact was renewed, in this case in reverse, by Italy's colonization of certain areas of Africa inhabited by Muslims.

This essay describes a more recent, that is, post–World War II, phenomenon that has characterized much of contemporary Europe, that is, Muslim immigration. Over the past twenty years, this immigration has reached a very significant level, both numerically and in terms of its cultural impact. Muslim immigrants are interacting with all aspects of Italian society: religious, social, occupational, educational, cultural, institutional, and so on. Muslim immigrants in some cases are even influencing the conversion of Italians to Islam.

Analysis of European Migratory Waves

Unlike many other parts of Europe, where immigration began seriously only after the Second World War, Italy did not become a destination for Muslim immigrants until the 1980s. The country began to be aware of a Muslim presence at a time when there was already a sizeable Muslim presence in other European countries.[1]

Muslim immigration to Europe began in the 1950s during the postwar reconstruction and continued throughout the 1960s, stimulated by the strong economic growth of European countries. Usually a country received immigrants from its former colonies: France from Algeria and Morocco, for example, Great Britain from Pakistan and other Commonwealth countries, and Germany from Turkey on the basis of bilateral treaties. This explains why, in many European countries today, new immigrants join communities made up primarily of people who came from specific countries; thus, these communities tend to be more homogeneous. At the earlier stage, immigration was considered a transitory event motivated by purely economic reasons. Consequently, the policy of absorption was minimal, and Islam generally manifested itself through language and traditions.

Toward the mid-1970s, the immigration flow changed radically as a result of the economic recession started by the oil crisis. Local unemployment led often to increasing hostility toward the new immigrants. At the same time, the immigrants lost the dream of returning to their countries of origin. Often the economic crisis in the home country was even worse than that in the host country, meaning that a decision to return home would have been financially very difficult, as would a possible return to Europe, especially because of emerging national policies that limited the entry of immigrants. As a result, the process of absorption accelerated. Families got reunited, the number of the women increased, and, with the growth of the new generations, new problems arose and new needs had to be met. All of this caused a variety of new forms of interactions with the different sectors of the host society and its institutions. The heads of the households were afraid that their families would lose the cultural and religious characteristics of the home country, and they began to create places of religious socialization to transmit their faith to the new generations. They put particular efforts into opening prayer halls and Qur'anic schools in the attempt to maintain their authority and to protect their children from contamination by western culture. In this period, we also witnessed the rebirth of Islam in the countries of origin through the growth of Islamic movements that provided economic assistance to the Islamic centers in Europe.

It is against this background, then, that Europe in the 1980s experienced a new migratory wave. The new immigrants, persons who have been driven to emigrate for economic or political reasons, are much more diverse in terms of their places of origin than were those who came earlier. Usually the immigrants want to go to countries that are easily accessible either because they have no laws concerning immigration (a situation that pertained in the first years of this refugee immigration) or because there is considerable flexiblity in enforcing them. Italy, along with Spain and Greece, is one of the most favored targets of this wave of immigrants. While earlier waves of immigrants were mainly illiterate (or semiliterate) and came from rural areas, the more recent arrivals are often young, urban, and literate (though often with a fairly low level of education). Furthermore, most of the new immigrants have grown up in the period often characterized as the "Islamic awakening."

Muslims in Italy: Analysis of Statistical Data

The Islamic presence in Italy, then, became most evident in the late 1980s. According to the official statistics, in 1992 there were some 304,000 Muslim immigrants in Italy, which amounted to approximately 29 percent of the total legal immigrant population. At the end of 1998, their numbers had increased to more than 436,000, and they constituted nearly 35 percent of the immigrant population as a whole.

Table 8.1 shows the sixteen largest groups of Muslim immigrants legally resident in Italy as of the end of 1998, categorized according to national origin.[2] These statistics do not take into account either illegal immigrants or Muslims who obtained Italian citizenship.

Since illegal immigration in Italy is high—two laws had to be passed (in 1996 and in 1998-1999) in order to give resident status to some illegal immigrants—it is estimated

Table 8.1. Muslim population in Italy

State of Origin	Muslims in Italy	% of the Total Number of Muslims
Morocco	145,843	33.4
Albania	67,000	15.8
Tunisia	47,261	10.8
Senegal	35,897	8.2
Egypt	25,553	5.8
Algeria	13,324	3.0
Pakistan	11,320	2.5
Bangladesh	11,201	2.5
Somalia	10,818	2.4
Iran	6,814	1.5
Turkey	6,630	1.5
Nigeria	6,447	1.4
Yugoslavia	6,500	1.4
Bosnia	5,339	1.2
Iraq	4,519	0.9
Macedonia	4,126	0.5

that the total number of Muslims in Italy is about 600,000, including the 7,000 to 10,000 Italians who have converted to Islam. Of this number, about half live in northern Italy, 29 percent in central Italy, and the remaining in southern Italy and on the islands. Islam is, therefore, the second largest religion in Italy after Catholicism, even if for the moment it is still mainly a religion of foreign residents and not of citizens.[3] The table clearly shows the range of origin of the Muslim immigrants. In other European countries, most Muslim immigrants come from two or three nations, but in Italy there are at least nine major countries of origin, including Morocco, Albania, Tunisia, Senegal, Egypt, Algeria, Pakistan, Bangladesh, and Somalia, with small numbers coming from a range of other countries. At present the largest number of Muslim immigrants come from Morocco, although the number from Albania is steadily increasing. Some 20 percent of the North Africans are women, and about 30 percent of the Albanians. The Senegalese population, on the contrary, is composed almost exclusively of males, even though the numbers of Senegalese Muslims continue to grow.

These demographic data present a very complex picture in terms of both the circumstances of immigration and the ways in which the faith of Islam is practiced. Groups that are trying to take root in the host country coexist with groups that still consider their stay in Italy to be transitory. Muslims coming from Morocco, Tunisia, and Albania seem to be more interested in putting down roots in Italy. Statistics show that they are the most interested in family reunification, and they also have the highest number of children enrolled in the Italian school system. In terms of faith practices, the traditional Islam of the Moroccans is different from the Islam practiced by the Murides and Tijani brotherhoods of Senegal and from the secularized Islam of the Albanians. It is also the case that living in a pluralistic nation generally allows the immigrant more freedom to practice his branch of Islam as he chooses than was the case in the country of origin.

A Classification of Italian Muslims

Since Islam in Italy is a recent reality, it is, of course, still evolving. It is very hard, therefore, to suggest a classification that takes into account all the internal changes within the Italian Islamic community. Such changes are caused by the diversity represented in the social, ethnic, and national origins of its members, by the variety of their religious practices, and by the kinds of relationships that they establish with other members of their faith.[4] The following categorization may suggest some general ways in which to understand the diversity of the Italian Muslim community:

1. *Laicism or secularism.* Some Muslims in Italy, often those originally from Arab cultures, while identifying themselves with Islam, do not choose to actively practice the faith. This is also true of Albanians who, after a long period under a Marxist regime, have lost touch with much of their specifically Muslim heritage.

2. *Private or religious devotion within the family.* This approach emphasizes the private and family aspects of religious life. Islam is seen as the religion of the father, mother, and family and is characterized by personal attitudes of piety and ethics and strict adherence to alimentary rules, particularly in regard to the prohibition of certain foods. Muslims who practice in this way usually try to adapt to the surrounding culture, often aiming at integration into Italian society but at the same time maintaining religious customs. Sometimes such customs are adjusted to suit the needs of the host society. Participation in mosques is irregular, partly because most Italian mosques are run by Imams who preach an integralist and traditionalist Islam. Many Moroccan families follow this kind of privatized Islam.

3. *Orthodoxy and communitarianism.* Muslims of this persuasion regularly frequent a mosque and tend to participate in groups in which religion plays a unifying role. In this way they serve as defenders of the Islamic system, as well as preservers of specific religious values, such as those related to family reproduction. Religion in this context plays an important role in self-identification. From the figures concerning mosque attendance it can be estimated that some 10 to 15 percent of Italian Muslims, mostly from the Maghreb, fall into this category.

4. *Militancy.* This approach stresses a fusion of religion, society, and politics and characterizes what are sometimes referred to as "fundamentalist" or "neofundamentalist" groups with small revolutionary elements on the fringes. Adherents represent a numerical minority but are able to exert considerable influence on the whole of the Muslim community in Italy because its members run many of the mosques.

5. *Brotherhoods.* A deeply religious form of Islam is practiced by many Senegalese within the Muridi and Tijani brotherhoods. They do not seek other collective forms of religious expression. Many native Italians who have converted to Islam are attracted to the Muslim brotherhoods.[5]

How Islam Becomes Visible within Italian Society

The mosque is the central place of observant Islam. It is not a holy place in the Christian sense, but it provides Muslim space within the larger secular state and a concrete and visible way for Muslims to evidence their presence. It is also the place where discussions about Islam take place, where proponents and critics of particular interpretations can take the opportunity to make their views known.[6]

Islam in Italy is following the same organizational evolution that it followed in other European countries, but at a much faster pace. The rapid increase in the number of mosques is one manifestation of that activity. Until the 1970s, there was only one mosque in Italy, located in Rome. Today there are more than sixty mosques all over the country and at least 120 to 150 other places designated for prayer. The term "mosque" (*masjid*) is used to indicate the *jami'*, the prayer hall that is recognized as the proper place for holding the Friday noon *salat* (ritualized prayer) and sermon. Sometimes the mosque structure includes other rooms for religious activities, such as a Qur'an school, a library, a bookstore, or even a facility for the sale of Islamically acceptable food.

Only three of the mosques in Italy have been conceived and built as such. The great mosque of Mount Antenne in Rome, the largest mosque anywhere in Europe built at the initiative and with the backing of the Arab embassies in Italy, was inaugurated in June 1995. The mosque "del Misericordioso" (al-Rahman) in Milan, opened in 1988, is one of the most important and influential centers in Italy. The mosque of Omar in Catania, opened in 1980, was built at the initiative of a non-Muslim lawyer with Libyan financial support.

In most cases the Imam who runs the mosques belongs to the category of "self-proclaimed," rather than having been specifically and Islamically trained. Generally Imams have not been sent by a state or by traditional and official religious institutions (Islamic universities, of course, do not as yet exist in Italy). Therefore, they do not have a precise formation in the Islamic sciences. Rather they are leaders who have emerged out of a group of immigrants who feel the strong need to safeguard their traditions in the new cultural environment. These leaders are, above all, guardians of traditional Islamic beliefs concerning women, the family, the state, society, and education. Since they have not been well educated in Islamic legal sciences, they often have difficulty reinterpreting Islamic laws in a modern environment. In spite of this, they often become official spokesmen of the community in interaction with local institutions. It is a new component of Islam that Imams are increasingly called on to perform many of the functions that are not traditional to that role but that are similar to those performed by pastors and priests in the Christian context.

Qur'anic schools near mosques are costantly growing in number. Usually they provide instruction on Sunday mornings for the religious formation of children and adults. There are also some Islamic schools that adopt the scholastic program of the country of origin for the children of Muslim immigrants who intend eventually to return to their country of origin. There are Egyptian schools in Milan and in Torino, for example, and a Tunisian school in Mazara del Vallo, in Sicily. In terms of public schooling, in recognition of the growth in the number of foreign students in recent years, the Italian government is making a great effort to adapt the scholastic environment to the new reality. On the whole, there is a good deal of flexibility in the public schools for the accommodation of the special needs of students from different cultures and religions. No major decisions have been made at the national level concerning the presence and particular needs of Muslim students in Italian schools; at the local level, however, solutions have been reached for special problems such as absences during Muslim festivities, the wearing of the veil by girls in the classroom, gender separation during physical activity, and the kinds of food provided for school meals.

Another important issue for Muslims all over Europe is proper disposal of the body after death. While some Muslims prefer to pay for their bodies to be sent back to their country of origin to be buried in accordance with Islamic tradition and prescription, they do have the possibility of being buried according to Islamic ritual in several Italian cities. Burial places for Muslims can be found in the main cities of north and central Italy, and occasionally also in provincial cities. They are separate places in local cemeteries given to Muslims for burial according to the Muslim ritual.

According to Islamic law, animals must be butchered in carefully designated, acceptable (*halal*) ways. There are many shops in the principal cities of northern Italy, Rome, and Naples at which Muslims can buy *halal* food. Many of these shops simply import such meat from France, but there are now attempts to prepare it appropriately within Italy itself. In Torino, for example, an agreement was made to butcher animals in the public slaughterhouse according to appropriate Muslim ritual. Occasionally protests are raised by some animal rights groups about the method used to slaughter the animal (by cutting its throat), especially on the occasion of the 'Eid al-Adha feast at the end of Ramadan, when a lot of meat is consumed.

The publication of books, magazines, and other materials for the Muslim population in Italy, as in other European countries, is a growing industry. It is carried on mainly by Italian converts, who have the language skills and are better acquainted with Italian rules of printing and the media. Magazines are almost all bulletins of the various Islamic associations and centers. Most are printed in the Italian language, with religious and political content, as well as information about the life of the Islamic community. Their frequency of publication, as well as the ways in which they are distributed, is very inconsistent. Recently some Muslim groups have begun to use the internet to spread information about their activities and about Islamic beliefs and practices.

Islamic Associations

Two main Islamic associations dominate the sphere of activity of Muslims in Italy. These are as follows:

1. *The Centro Islamico Culturale d'Italia* (CICI), *or Italian Islamic Cultural Center.* Begun in 1969, the Center is responsible for the construction of the big mosque of Mount Antenne in Rome, built on 30,000 square meters of land donated by the city of Rome. It is run by a council of ambassadors from Islamic countries who answer to the Muslim World League and, consequently, to Saudi Arabia. (The League controls most of the Islamic centers in Europe.) The CICI is the only Islamic center in Italy that has received official Muslim World League recognition as "Ente morale di diritto privato," a private civic association.

2. *The Unione delle Comunità e delle Organizzazioni Islamiche in Italia* (UCOII), *or Association of Islamic Communities and Organizations in Italy.* Founded in 1990, UCOII is one of the new players on the scene of Italian Islam. It was created out of the union of various older groups. Among these are the Centro Islamico di Milano e della Lombardia (CIML), or Islamic Center of Milan and Lombardy, founded in 1976, one of the best organized in the country and claiming to represent popular Islam, and the Unione Studenti Musulmani in Italia (USMI), or Association of Muslim Students in

Italy, which is the country's oldest Muslim organization, founded in 1977. Today the USMI is declining in importance due to changing proportions in the number of students and workers, but it is still one of the most prolific producers of Muslim leaders. Ten regional Islamic centers are affiliated with the UCOII, on which other centers at the municipal level that constitute local networks depend. The group acts on the cultural and social levels as it pursues the aim of directing *da'wa* (mission) toward the Italians. It organizes pilgrimages to Mecca and publishes a magazine, titled *Il Musulmano*, edited by an Italian convert. The UCOII has more contacts with the media than any of the other organizations.

Many other groups have been founded at the local and national levels, some in an attempt to solve the difficult matter of who will represent Islam in an agreement with the Italian state. Among them are:

1. Comunità Religiosa Islamica Italiana (COREIS), or Islamic Italian religious community.
2. Associazione Italiana per l'Informazione sull'Islam (AIII), or Italian Association for information about Islam, one of the most noted associations of Italian converts, with its central office in Milan. It engages in scientific research on the relations between Islam and the West, and runs courses on Islamic formation. It is opposed to the UCOII, which it accuses of integralist behavior.
3. Associazione Musulmani Italiani-Istituto Culturale della Comunità Islamica Italiana (AMI-ICCII), or Italian Muslim Association-Cultural Institute of the Islamic Community in Italy. It was started in Naples in 1982 at the initiative of a Muslim of Somali origin, backed by Saudi Arabia. The association claims to be the legitimate representative of Islam in relation to the Italian state because it is spread across the country and because it has the highest number of members with Italian citizenship. It defines itself as moderate and nonfundamentalist, tending toward the apolitical and moral conduct of the Tabligh Jamaat and of the theological and judicial current *wahabita*. It denies the Muslim legitimacy of both the COREIS (which it defines as an agnostic and syncretist cult) and the UCOII (which it defines as fundamentalist).
4. The Center of Metaphysical Studies Rènè Guènon in Milan, an association with mystical tendencies created and guided by Italian converts.
5. The Islamic University of Casamassima, in Bari, an as-yet-unfulfilled project to found the first Islamic university in Italy. The promoter is an Italian convert who has conceived the university as a center for the preparation of leadership for Italian mosques.

At this point in the evolution of Islam in Italy, various Islamic states are trying to exert their influence on their citizens living in Italy by backing associations that promote cultural activities, publish magazines, and run mosques and Islamic schools. Libyan *da'wa*, for example, has financed the construction of the mosque of Omar at Catania and mantains ties to the association Unione Islamica in Occidente (Islamic Union in the West) of Rome. Egypt, through an Imam from Al-Ahzar University in Cairo, controls the Istituto Culturale Islamico (Cultural Islamic Institute) of Milan, which operates a parallel school, recognized by the Egyptian Consulate, for the children of Egyptians who eventually plan to return to Egypt. Tunisia, through the Associazione Culturale Islamica (Cultural Islamic Association) of Palermo, controls the state-owned mosque of Palermo, entrusted by the regional government of Sicily to the Tunisian government.

The Tunisian govenment also controls the school of Mazara del Vallo, where the children of Tunisian immigrants attend classes taught by Tunisian instructors who follow the state-sponsored Tunisian curriculum. (This is a unique case in Italy and is a result of the high number of Tunisian fishermen in the area.) Morocco tries to control the various self-run mosques, especially in southern Italy, through its embassy.

The Brotherhoods

Other Muslim organizations in Italy include numerous Sufi brotherhoods. They follow a more spiritual kind of Islam, in contrast to the Sunnis, who have a more legalistic understanding of the faith. Spiritual Islam is based on asceticism, sometime even esoterism, ecstatic rituals, a cult of the founder, and the saints. The more active brotherhoods in Italy include national organizations, as well as small regional groups.

The largest national brotherhood is the Muridiya, whose membership is made up mainly of Senegalese Muslims living in Italy.[7] Their doctrine is basically a "mysticism of work," to which they attribute the same value as to prayer. The *shaykh*, the highest religious leader, performs the duty of the prayer in conjunction with other leaders on behalf of everybody, while the other members (disciples) dedicate themselves to work. The Murids maintain strong links with their centers in Senegal and often organize travel to Italy for famous *marabuts* (spiritual leaders) to obtain advice to enrich the spiritual life of their members and sometimes even economic help for those in need. The tomb of the Holy Founder in Senegal is the target of annual pilgrimages. Murids have *dahires* (prayer rooms and meeting centers) throughout Italy. Important *dahires* are located in Milan, Brescia, Quercianella, and Genova, with others also found in Torino, Rome, Naples, Riccione, Cagliari, and in other places where there is a concentration of Senegalese immigrants.

Italy also has a variety of local brotherhoods. Many Italian converts are organized in small local groups that generally try to avoid publicity. Among them are the Turkish Naqshbandiyya, with members in the regions of Piedmont, Lazio, Sardinia, and Liguria; the North African Ahmadiyya-Idrissiyya; the Spanish Shadhiliyya Darqawiyya; and the Jerrahi-Halveti of Turkish origin, guided by an Afghan sufi who has lived in Italy for many years.

Outside Movements

Other kinds of movements influenced from abroad are active in the Italian contex, as they are in other parts of Europe. Generally, they mix religion with sociopolitics and aim to restore the integral practice of Islam in society, often in contrast to the policies of their country of origin. The most important of these movements in Italy are as follows:

1. The Jama'at al-Tabligh is of Indian origin. It aims to reinvigorate the faith and religious practice of Muslims. Members organize itinerant *da'wa* and preach the observance of Islamic rules in everyday life, in the family, and in the mosques, although they avoid direct intervention in political life. The Tablighis are present in some of the major cities of northern Italy.

2. The Jama'at-i Islami is a famous political-religious movement of Pakistani origin, founded by Abu'l A'la al-Mawdudi, whose writings have been translated in Italian by USMI. It is a full-fledged religious political party that pursues the strict application of the *shari'a* and seeks the establishment of an Islamic state and has contacts with Wahhabi Islam. The organization runs some prayer rooms in the principal Italian cities.
3. The Muslim Brotherhood is a movement, founded in Egypt in 1928, whose members have periodically been persecuted by the Egyptian state. It is composed of a moderate wing and a more violent wing. Many of its members are refugees in Europe. In Italy it has a number of sympathizers, as well as some groups of full-fledged members in the big cities.
4. Milli Görüş is a political religious movement of Turkish Muslims, whose European center is in Köln in Germany. It preaches a rigorous observance of the *shari'a*. It is present in small Turkish communities in Northern Italy.

It is interesting to note that among these groups there is no representation of Albanian or East European Muslims, even though they are fairly numerous in Italy. The reason is that, as has been noted, having been ruled for many years by Marxist regimes, these immigrants have slight if any identification with religion. It will be very interesting to see how this situation evolves and what kinds of relationships develop between the orthodox Sunnis and the East European Muslims.

Official Recognition by the Italian State

The Italian constitution proclaims equality among its citizens without distinction of gender, race, language, political opinion, or personal or social conditions (art. 3). In article 19, the constitution guarantees its application to those persons present on Italian territory. Every Muslim in Italy can "freely practice his/her religious faith in every form, individual, or associated, make propaganda and practice in private or, unless they involve rituals contrary to public morality." Article 8 establishes that the relationship of the religious groups with the state must be "regulated by law on the basis of agreements with their representative." Thus far, the Italian state has signed agreements with the Valdesi (1984), the Adventists (1988), Assemblies of God (1988), the Hebrew Community (1989), the Union of Italian Buddists (1999), and the Italian Jehovah's Witnesses (2000).

With time, these agreements have helped new religious communities to be accepted by the host country, both judicially and socially. This explains why the Muslim organizations are putting forth a good deal of effort to obtain such official recognition. For a community of immigrants, many of whom do not have Italian citizenship, such agreements are an important step in the official recognition of its rights, as well as of its cultural identity. These agreements are also important for religious groups, especially insofar as they create a potential channel for public financing through the system of redistribution of tax receipts (.8 percent of income tax [IRPEF] payments may be directed to such organizations as may be desired by the representative). They can also give some flexibility to city regulations concerning the construction of places of worship, and similar issues.

At the present moment, there are many obstacles to reaching such an agreement. Among them are the realities that most Muslims are foreigners whose cultural, linguistic, family, and even economic ties are abroad, that Islam is a religion whose religious and social aspects often are incompatible with the Italian legal system, and that the Islamic community is still new in Italy and still unable to present a homogeneous image of itself.[8] At this time, there is still no official representation of the Islamic Italian community. In Italy the issue is not so much the fact that there are many different representations of Islam and that there is no religious hierarchy per se as it is the rivalry that divides them and the claim they all make to represent all the Muslims in Italy. It is important, therefore, to allow time for the relationship among the various Islamic groups to develop.

At the time of this writing, three drafts of agreements are under scrutiny by the Office of the Prime Minister. These have been presented by UCOII (1992), by AMI (1994), and by COREIS (1996). They seek a same structured agreement like that signed with the Jewish community, addressing the following specific demands:

1. Assocation of land for mosques and other religious purposes
2. Allocation of land for the construction of cemeteries
3. *Halal* (regulated by Islamic rules) food served in public places (e.g., hospitals, schools)
4. Slaughterhouses regulated by Islamic law and controlled by religious elements
5. Freedom of dress code for women in public places
6. Respect for Ramadan, the month of fasting
7. Respect for the time of daily prayer
8. Observance of Friday as a holiday and the feast days of ʿeid al-fitr and ʿeid al-adha and other holidays
9. Religious assistance in the prisons, hospitals, and military bases (as other religions have)
10. Gender separation in the schools, at least for physical activity
11. Possible alternative religious teaching to Muslim students in public schools
12. Legal recognition of the possibility of opening private Muslim schools
13. Freedom to express the Muslim point of view on ethical, social, and public problems
14. Civic recognition of Muslim marriages
15. The possibility of applying Islamic law in family relationships such as marriage, repudiation, rights over children, rights relating to inheritance, and so on
16. Deduction of the *zakat*, or ritual charity, from taxes.

Some of these demands are already met by the present law, such as provision of acceptable food in schools, religious assistance in hospitals and prisons, Islamic slaughterhouses, and freedom of dressing in accordance with their religion. Other demands can be accommodated without problems, such as the preparation for the burial of the dead body according to Islamic ritual. The request for alternative religious instruction in the schools poses the problem of who will teach it. The problem of creating private Islamic parochial schools is less complex and can be resolved. The main problem concerns the civic recognition of Muslim marriages; there are too many differences between Islamic law and Italian law (e.g., regarding poligamy, divorce, repudiation, rights over inheritance, and rights over children).

The use of the veil in public places, in schools, in the workplace, and on the pictures of official documents is not forbidden by Italian law, on condition that the face can be recognized. Therefore, it is possible to wear both the *chador* and the *hijab*, the veil used in the Maghreb (North Africa), the place from which most Muslim immigrants come. There are no reports of discrimination against Muslim women in the workplace, at school, or anywhere else because of the veil.

The Role of Italian Converts

The role of local converts is particularly interesting in the development of Islam in Italy.[9] This can be clearly seen by looking at the positions they have achieved in the associations, in the brotherhoods, and in the Islamic culture of Italy as a whole.[10] The presence of converts in the Islamic network accelerates and reinforces the process by which Islam is establishing itself in the West, and in some ways it directs it, changing its aim or at least the way that aim can be achieved. Converts play a role of cultural mediation in various ways. Stefano Allievi points out some of the elements of this cultural mediation:

1. Imparting knowledge to immigrants about the pluralistic society in which they live and what it means to be a minority in that society
2. Sharing a network of political, institutional, and religious ties
3. Providing information both within the group (through publishing) and outside (maintaining relations with the media, conferences, publications, and explaining Islamic beliefs in a way understandable to Italian culture)[11]
4. Demonstrating the dignity of the Islamic community. It is especially gratifying for the members of the immigrant Muslim community, especially if they are low on the social scale and poorly educated, to see westerners, especially if they are educated and financially well off, embrace their religion. It proves the universality of their religion and demonstrates that it is not just a faith belonging to underdeveloped areas of the world or immigrants from these areas.

It seems clear that converts will play an important role in the future in the transition between an Islam that is a guest in Europe and a European Islam, especially in judicial and theological elaboration, and in adapting religious practice to European culture. When there is a second and third Islamic generation in Italy, as is now the case in many other European countries, the situation of Italian Islam will become more normalized.

Mixed Marriages

One of the consequences of the settlement of immigrants in Italy is the increase in mixed marriages. In Italy today there are some 150,000 mixed marriages, 10 percent of which are Islamic-Christian. Even though only a small percentage (20 percent) of these are celebrated with a religious rite, the increase in the number of Islamic-Christian couples worries the Catholic Church, which fears the conversion of Christians to Islam and the Islamic education of the children of mixed marriages. Recent declarations by the Italian Catholic bishops call for greater prudence in giving permission for Christian-Islamic mixed marriages. Muslim leaders share the same concern when mixed couples ask to celebrate their marriage in the mosques.

Islamic-Christian dialogue and exchange thus still face many difficulties. On the national and international level, there are some Christian institutions, such as the community of Saint Egidio and Pontifico Istituto di Studi Arabo Islamici di Roma (Papal Institute for Islamic-Arab studies in Rome), which are active in interfaith relations. At the level of the local diocese, however, the administrative bodies constituted for the dialogue are more concerned with preventing relationships that might lead to marriage than with initiating friendly dialogue. The few attempts at interfaith conversation are made informally or by little groups and movements. Muslim groups also are not very interested in interreligious dialogue for the moment because they are too busy with internal problems. Only some of the converts seem to be interested in having exchanges with Christians.

Italy, which until recently was a country of emigration and at certain times was the greatest reserve of manpower of Western Europe, in the past twenty years has been the target of immigration in which the Muslims occupy a very significant position. This movement is still very much in process, and it is difficult to predict how it will develop. What is certain is that in Italy, as in other western European countries, the presence of Islam is not a temporary phenomenon. Islam will be a permanent part of the Italian cultural landscape. In recent years Italy has been trying to develop laws (most recently in 1998) to regulate the flow of immigration and to fight illegal immigration, which is often fed by organized crime. Nonetheless, especially in certain regions of northern Italy, the use of immigrant manpower has become indispensable in certain industries and services. This situation is likely to continue because Italy has the lowest birthrate in the world (1.4 percent).

Even more than other Europeans, Italians have always thought of themselves as a monocultural and monoreligious population. They are thus reacting to this new situation with a sense of deep uncertainty and, at times, even fear. Unfortunately, this fear is often exaggerated and twisted by the media and by local politicians. Single episodes become generalized, so that it is easy for the public to forget that the great majority of immigrants work honestly, pay taxes, and wish to integrate themselves into Italian society. Part of the reason for the fear often expressed about Islam is the stereotype of the religion as a vehicle of cultural obscurity, fanaticism, and terrorism. International reports about various conflicts, terrorist attacks, and violence in Islamic countries contribute to the tension. This creates an environment of suspicion that risks becoming a self-fulfilling prophecy, because it pushes the Muslims in Europe to isolate themselves.

Almost all of the members of this first generation of Muslim immigrants have low levels of education, hold menial jobs, and must constantly fight for survival. The coming generations will need to seriously consider their own identity as a minority and their role in a pluralistic society, a situation that in most cases differs dramatically from that which pertains in their countries of origin. Tariq Ramadan, one of the leaders of the young European Muslims, identifies six main topics that he thinks the young generations of European Muslims must attend to:

1. *Islam and laicism.* In what way are the faith and the spirituality of Islam influenced by the laicism of the European society? Will Islam undergo the same kind of historical-critical revision that has influenced Christianity?

2. *European Islamic identity.* The first generation carries with it the culture of the country of origin, but who is the European Muslim? Can one be a European Muslim, or must one remain Egyptian Muslim, Moroccan Muslim, and so on? Is it possible to maintain a Muslim identity in European culture? Is it possible to free Islam of its oriental cultural characteristics?

3. *Religious practice in Europe.* What remains of the religious identity once it is stripped of its cultural background? What is the role of the mosque? What are the fundamental practices, and how they will change in contact with European culture?

4. *Islam and the law.* What relationship can be developed with local authorities? Can European laws accommodate Muslims? Will there be opposition, and isolationism?

5. *Citizenship and participation.* Once citizenship has been acquired, to what extent should Muslims participate in European social and political life, at least at the local level?

6. *Promotion of a European Islamic culture.* What contributions can Muslims make to the development of a new European culture?[12]

These are the kinds of problems that must be dealt with in the near future by Muslims in Italy as well as in the other countries of Europe.

Notes

1. For an analysis of European immigration see Felice Dasseto and Albert Bastenier, *Europa: Nuova frontiera dell'Islam* (Roma: Edizioni Lavoro, 1988); Stefano Allievi and Felice Dasseto, *Il ritorno dell'Islam: I musulmani in Italia* (Roma: Edizioni Lavoro, 1993).

2. *Elaborazione Caritas Roma Dossier/Statistico Immigrazione su dati del Ministero dell'Interno e dell'Istat.* The data concerning the religious affiliation are based upon the percentage of the original country.

3. In Italy law 91 of 5 Feb. 1992 establishes that the child who has at least one Italian parent is a citizen by birth. A foreigner can obtain citizenship if he or she is married to an Italian citizen and has been residing in Italy for at least six months or has been married for at least three years, unless the marriage has been voided. Citizenship can be granted to a foreign citizen up to eighteen years of age who was born and raised in Italy if he or she requests it within one year after reaching that age. The President of the Republic has discretionary power to grant citizenship to foreigners who have been living in Italy for at least ten years.

4. Chantal Saint-Blancat, *L'Islam della diaspora* (Roma: Edizioni Lavoro, 1995), 105–7.

5. For further informations see ibid.; see also Felice Dasseto, *L'Islam in Europa* (Torino: Edizioni Fondazione Agnelli,1994); A. Pacini, "I musulmani in Italia, Dinamiche organizzative e processi d'interazione con la società e le istituzioni italiane," in *Musulmani in Italia, la condizione giuridica delle comunità islamiche*, ed. S. Ferrari (Bologna: Il Mulino, 1996).

6. Stefano Allievi, "L'Islam in Italia profili storici e sociologici," in *L'Islam in Europa: lo statuto giuridico delle comunità musulmane*, ed. S. Ferrari (Bologna: Il Mulino, 1996).

7. Ottavia Schmidt di Friedberg, *Islam, solidarieta e lavoro: I muridi senegalesi in Italia* (Torino: Edizioni Fondazione Agnelli, 1994).

8. Allievi, "L'Islam in Italia."

9. See Stefano Allievi, *I nuovi musulmani: I convertiti all'Islam* (Roma: Edizioni Lavoro, 1999).

10. Ibid., 213.

11. Ibid., 220.

12. Cf. Tariq Ramadan, *Etre musulman en Europe* (Lyon: Tawhid, 1999).

9

Islam in the Netherlands

Thijl Sunier and Mira van Kuijeren

As is true of most western European countries, the Netherlands has witnessed the emergence of Islam as a result of large-scale immigration. Over the past twenty-five years, somewhat more than 700,000 immigrants and refugees from Islamic countries have settled in the Netherlands. Today they constitute 4.5 percent of the total population of 16 million. Turks form the largest group (300,000), followed by Moroccans (252,000), Surinamese (35,000), Pakistanis (5,000), and a few thousand Moluccans. Most of them came as migrant workers. In more recent years, a growing number of Muslims have arrived as refugees from countries such as the former Yugoslavia, Somalia, Iran, Afghanistan, and Iraq.

For a long time, hardly anyone realized that, with the influx of so-called guest workers, a new religion had also entered the Netherlands.[1] Initially, Islamic practices remained hidden behind the walls of the boarding houses where the single male immigrants lived. On special occasions such as Ramadan, Muslims were sometimes able to make use of factory halls or churches to perform their religious duties and to celebrate their holidays. It was really only on these occasions that the Dutch citizenry sensed their presence. Until the end of the 1970s, the government and the society considered the presence of Muslims a temporary phenomenon. Islam was brought to Europe as "cultural baggage" by immigrant laborers who would soon return to their home countries. The few who stayed permanently, they assumed, would gradually assimilate into Dutch society, which itself was in the middle of a process of secularization and modernization.

A quarter of a century later, the idea that Islam is a kind of residue from former societies that would soon "dry up" or fade away has at least partly been seen to be false. In the early 1970s, there were only a few provisional places of Muslim worship. A decade later, some 100 permanent mosques had grown up across the country, a number that has now increased to more than 400.[2] In other respects, too, Islam has become more visible to the outside world. Muslim families have settled in the old quarters of the main cities, where they have opened their own shops and teahouses. Children attend the public schools, and in 1988 the first Islamic primary school was started. Currently there are more than thirty Islamic schools. In many fields, special arrangements have been made to enable Muslims to live according to Islamic prescriptions. It is clear that in the past twenty-five years, Islam has gained a foothold in Dutch society. Muslims have managed to create a religiocultural infrastructure and to give Islam a public face. This has been referred to as the institutionalization of Islam.[3]

In this chapter we first focus on the conditions under which this institutionalization process has taken place in the Netherlands and, more generally, how the Netherlands has dealt with the new religious and ethnic diversity over the past decades. The Netherlands, like other western European countries, grants religious freedom to all religious denominations. The possibilities for Muslims to set up a religious infrastructure are generally conditioned by constitutional principles of freedom of religious worship and the separation of church and state. The argument put forward here is that, in addition to these general principles, in each country there are specific conditions and circumstances that produce considerable differences with respect to the place of religion in society and the model of civic incorporation.[4] This not only structures the way in which institutionalization takes place but also shapes the ongoing debates about the place of Islam in society.

Religion and the Dutch State

Apart from the general principles of freedom of religion and the separation of church and state, there are three main constitutive factors that have influenced the place of Islam in Dutch society. The first is the constitutional principle of religious equality. The Dutch Constitution of 1983 stipulates that all religious denominations are equally valued.[5] Although this principle of equality actually dates back to the liberal Constitution of 1848, the idea was reinforced and reformulated in 1983, when all financial and other ties between the churches and the state were severed. An important aspect of the equality principle is that the Dutch system does not apply the principle of religious recognition and registration, as is true in Belgium or Germany. Thus, there are no religious denominations in the Netherlands that formally have more privileges than do others. Equality means equal treatment in similar situations. Although there still remains a good deal of inequality between established denominations like the Reformed and the Catholic churches and "new" religions like Islam and Hinduism, this principle of equality has offered Islamic leaders legal and political leverage to demand equal treatment and, in some cases, extra provisions in order to be able to catch up with established denominations.

The second factor relates to the era of pillarization that shaped Dutch society and the political landscape from the 1920s until the 1960s. The Dutch pillar system is one of the more complicated aspects of Dutch political history. During those forty years, Dutch civil society consisted of two pillars, a Catholic one and a Protestant one. In addition, there was a Socialist movement and a so-called Liberal sphere.[6] These politico-ideological blocks determined, to a large extent, the political relations in the Netherlands; they also, however, fragmented the Dutch population. The two confessional pillars comprised more that 50 percent of the Dutch population and ran through all social classes. They had their own political parties, trade unions, schools, universities, media, and all kinds of other associations. The churches were at the heart of these pillars. The Socialist movement, not a pillar in the literal sense, was actually organized as one, although it had its political base mainly in the labor class. These three blocks were organized from top to bottom and exerted great influence on their rank-and-file. The ruling elite of the Liberal sphere was economically the strongest faction in society, but it did not have a social-organizational base like the other three blocks. To a certain extent, it also represented a category of people who were not affiliated with one of the three other blocks and who adhered to the principles of the liberal Constitution of 1848.[7] Although these kinds of politico-ideological divisions were not unique to the Netherlands, they served to almost completely shape and determine the political relations during that period. Dutch society was characterized by a political (in some critiques, rigid) stability that contributed to a sense of "natural" character. Despite the divisions, there was a strong feeling of belonging to one nation. The different political and ideological blocks were considered more or less equal and balanced. Social conflicts were resolved and neutralized by closely cooperating ruling elites at the top of the four blocks. It is mainly because of the rigidity of the system from the 1920s and the 1960s that political changes were slow to develop in the Netherlands. For that reason, the system continued to shape political relations for a considerable period of time, even after the Second World War.

By the 1960s, the system ceased to function as it had, and most sections of civil society experienced a process of decategorization and a breakdown of the pillar structure. Although the societal forces that sustained the pillarization process are today almost completely replaced by the centralizing mechanisms of the modern welfare state, the juridical remnants of the system do still play a role in some crucial areas. The most important is the Dutch school system, which is still largely pillarized. The particular (*bijzondere*) school system continues to operate parallel to the public (*openbare*) schools and receives equal support from taxes; at the same time, it maintains relative autonomy, making it a crucial element in educational politics. These principles of equality with respect to education were officially effectuated by the constitutional changes of 1917, the so-called pacification laws. Public education is organized and administered by the state. Particular schools, which are usually confessional, have their own administrative boards. Most of these confessional schools were of Christian (Catholic or Protestant) origin. In addition to that, there were some Jewish schools and "Free schools" (anthroposophical), which grew in number after the Second World War. Since the waves of postwar immigration, Islamic and Hindu schools have been added to the list.[8] Although there is today a steady increase in public schools, the majority of pupils at primary schools are still enrolled in particular education. It is important to recognize, however, that the basic core curriculum is similar and obligatory in all types of schools. This curriculum is the responsibility of the state. The difference between public and particular schools is mainly a matter of educational method, extracurricular activities, and amount of religious education.

Other activities organized on the basis of juridical provisions originating in the pillar system are pastoral welfare work in hospitals and prisons and various kinds of public broadcasting. Muslims can relatively easily make use of these provisions. Since the end of the 1980s, a little more than thirty state-financed Islamic primary schools and one secondary school have been founded in the Netherlands. Despite the fact that discussion about the implications of secularization has taken place even in many confessional schools, the system is one of the most delicate issues in Dutch politics.

The third factor concerns Dutch minority policies. Muslims are generally considered immigrants, and as such they are subject to specific requirements and aims of the Dutch minority policies that have been set up and developed since the early 1980s. Key to these policies are the concepts of permanent residence and integration of immigrants into Dutch society, in light of a (limited) recognition of cultural diversity. Thus, Muslims have the right to set up their own religious infrastructure, and they can make use of the juridical provisions that enable them to found their own schools, with the understanding that this should in no way hamper their integration into society.

The shifting interplay between these constitutive factors over the past decades has rendered particular meaning to the typical Dutch model of citizenship. In the following sections we first give an historical account of general developments in the past two or three decades. We then illustrate one particular aspect of the discussions about immigrant Islam that offers good insight into the complexity and sometimes contradictory aspects of Dutch political culture, namely the ongoing debate about the wearing of the headscarf in public places.

Muslims, Migrants, and Citizens

Until the end of the 1970s, the cultural and religious backgrounds of immigrants did not play any significant role in debates about their position in society. Immigrants were defined in terms of ethnic origin, but this was of no political consequence. Officially, the Netherlands did not yet conceive of itself as an immigration country. Immigrants were seen primarily as temporary laborers who would return to their countries of origin. Policies were based on this idea of temporariness. The creation of religious facilities was therefore considered to be something that should be completely left to private initiative. No special policies were needed.

Toward the end of the 1970s, important developments took place. The number of immigrants increased considerably, primarily because of family reunions. These families settled in the old quarters of the main town centers. Although the vast majority of the Muslims still hoped to return to their country of origin, the actual return was usually postponed. Many immigrants had no alternative other than staying in Holland because of financial constraints. Religious activities increased, and organizational structures began to grow up, creating an increased need for religious facilities and especially for qualified religious personnel. Many mosque organizations developed into real centers for immigrants, with teahouses, shops, and other facilities. The first attempts were made by various local Muslim associations to work together, to improve communication, and to coordinate activities. The number of religious organizations grew steadily. It was, however, a development that hardly caught the attention of Dutch society.

Toward the beginning of the 1980s, a turning point was reached. For the first time, the government acknowledged that the idea of temporariness was, for most immigrants, unrealistic. It began to be recognized that the majority of the immigrants would stay in the country permanently. In 1983, the government issued a report in which the outline of a new policy was formulated. It was at this point that the concept of "integration with the preservation of identity" (*integratie met behoud van identiteit*) was introduced.[9] Immigrants were granted basic rights to live according to their own cultural backgrounds; at the same time, they were expected to integrate into society. This became the typical Dutch trajectory to full citizenship. "Integration" was narrowed down to "participation" in the central sectors of society: labor, housing, and education. Along with this concept of integration, the term *achterstand* (best translated as "deprivation") made its way into the discourse. Failure to integrate was equated with *achterstand*, and vice versa. Equality meant "equality of starting positions," not "similarity."[10]

An important aspect of this new discourse was that a relation was constructed between integration on the one hand and cultural background on the other. "Guest workers" were now called "ethnic minorities," "cultural minorities," or "ethnic groups," and later on "allochtonous." In other words, a shift in the definition of the situation took place. From an economic category, immigrants came to be seen in terms of a cultural one.

Cultural background thus became a relevant factor in integration policies. During the 1980s, the government adopted a lenient attitude toward cultural specificities. In the first place, there was the general notion that culture and religion are basic properties of human beings. The Netherlands, with its history of pillarization, had always been a society that supported religious pluralism, and the general feeling was that it should live up to that ideal. In addition, the relevance of cultural background to one's well-being should be acknowledged. In the trajectory to full citizenship, the relevance of culture and religion for the people concerned was recognized as an important psychological outlet. Immigrants should have time to adapt to their new circumstances, and this could best be accomplished in "their own circles." Organizations of immigrants were considered to function as bridges between individuals and society in order to ensure a smooth integration. As such, they gained more significance in the integration process. They were politically and ideologically incorporated into the government's policies. Also, Islamic organizations were considered important to immigrant identity, and their activities were judged in terms of their function in the process of integration. Organizations could now apply for subsidies to develop activities for their rank-and-file members, provided these activities sustained the integration process. This has been described as the "migrantization" of Islamic organizations.[11] One of the consequences was that the number of such organizations grew disproportionately during the 1980s.

Despite this political climate favorable for the growth of Islamic organizations (as immigrant organizations), there was a simultaneous concern about the attitude of Muslims and their organizations toward the principles and priorities of integration programs developed by the government. The new policies of integration took shape at a time during which some rather dramatic events were taking place in the Islamic world itself, such as the revolution in Iran and the assassination of the Egyptian president Anwar Sadat. These events resulted in a tremendous increase in the number of publications about Islam and its adherents. Suddenly immigrants from countries like Turkey and Morocco were "discovered" as Muslims. A new cultural category called "Muslim immigrants" began to emerge. For convenience's sake, people with completely different backgrounds were lumped together as the possessors of "Muslim culture." Since it was mainly Muslims who faced problems of deprivation with respect to housing, labor, and education, "Muslim culture" carried a specific meaning.

Islam increasingly became the explanatory factor, not only for specific (collective) behavior of Muslims but also for the kinds of societal problems they face. This "Islamization of the discourse" in many cases led to some sort of narrowed awareness: "when one wants to know what goes on in the head of a Muslim then one should study Islam." All other possible explanations were in fact reduced to "the" Islam.[12] Although this line of thinking was not found explicitly in official documents, it was part of public discourse on Islam as expressed in newspapers and magazines, as well as in statements by individual politicians in Parliament and on television. Besides that, there was a growing interest in Islam and its adherents among welfare workers and other people working with and for Muslims in various situations.

Consequently, a specific image of Islam based on the idea that Muslims are the least integrated of the immigrants became prominent. Just as the country itself was on the way to eliminating religion as a binding force in society, a new religious group had appeared and asked for provisions that had almost disappeared in Dutch society. And it was representing not just another religion, but one known for its antimodern character, one whose adherents are seen as passive, fatalist people who are turned inward and who find it difficult to keep up with the pace of modern society and who for that reason easily fall back on their faith. One of the main objections to the formation of Islamic schools is that they cause undesirable isolation of young children; Islam enforces rules upon them that prevent them from taking part in society.

The origin of this image is related to the so-called rural bias. Because most of the first-generation Muslim immigrants came from a rural background, the very word "Muslim" suggested a rural image. Rural habits and Islamic prescriptions were seen as woven together into the fabric of the religion as a whole. Despite the potentially negative tone in this type of discourse, boundaries between "them" and "us" have not been seen by the Dutch to be impermeable. The image, rather, suggests a kind of understanding, compassion, and even inclusiveness. Muslims are not fundamentally excluded as a separate category; they are seen as constrained by their faith, which enforces rules upon them. But these problems can be overcome through systematic socialization; the boundary between Muslims and the rest of society may be temporary, provided certain conditions are fulfilled.

As a result of the political and ideological developments that took place in the 1980s, a new type of Islamic leadership emerged. These leaders had lived in the Netherlands for a relatively long time; they knew society quite well and acted as intermediaries between Muslim immigrants and Dutch society. They were entrepreneurs rather than "ideologues" and were oriented toward mobilizing as many resources as possible. They successfully made use of their contacts with Dutch policymakers and institutions. They emphasized that Islamic organizations must be considered as the main forms of self-organization among immigrants. These leaders increasingly took part in discussions on the position of immigrants in Dutch society, and as opinion leaders they were influential in defining the situation. They represented the Muslim populations to society as a whole and articulated the needs that existed among Muslims and what it means to be a Muslim in a non-Islamic society. By stressing the foreign character of Islam as part of a specific cultural heritage, they were able to convince policymakers that certain facilities were required.

Toward the end of the 1980s, because of several particular developments, a change took place. The lenient attitude toward the preservation of cultural identities and the prominent role that had been given to immigrant organizations came under pressure. In an advisory report, the influential Scientific Board of Government Policies (WRR) warned the government about the continually weak socioeconomic position of minorities.[13] Unemployment figures among immigrants remained relatively high, and educational results remained below the expected levels. The conclusion was that integration was bound to fail unless the government put more emphasis on the struggle against poverty and deprivation, even at the cost of cultural multiplicity. Integration gradually came to have a more individualized connotation. Notions of the collective integration of certain minority groups were replaced by the stress on an individual trajectory to full-scale integration into the "hard" sectors of society. More than before, participation in the central institutions of society became key term in the integration policy. General programs for combating poverty and deprivation gradually replaced specific programs targeted to specific groups.

In addition, the image of Islam itself changed considerably. More or less as a direct consequence of the Rushdie Affair, a new type of image made its way into the public discourse. This image is far from harmless and links Muslims in the Netherlands to the violence in the Middle East. Muslims are conceived as a fifth column that may be a threat to society. The ongoing debate about growing fundamentalism among immigrants, the alleged connections between Muslims here and fundamentalist groups and regimes in the Middle East, and the perceived strong orientation of Muslims toward their country of origin are all the results of this alleged association.

The main difference between the new understanding and that which underlay the first model is that boundaries are now seen to be impermeable. In this new view, Muslims constitute a different "brand." They will never become part of Dutch citizenry unless they abjure their religion completely. They do not fit in the Dutch nation, since it is not the preservation of culture that they aim at but transnational political activism. One of the leaders of the Dutch conservative party said in 1991 that he considered Islam to be the main threat to European liberal civilization. Muslims, therefore, must be carefully monitored.[14]

At the turn of the new century, there seem to be two main, contrasting positions in the public debate about cultural diversity, multiculturalism, and Islam in the Netherlands. The first one is a slightly revised version of the neoliberal view on individual rights. It envisions society as being made up of individuals who have equal relations to the state. Integration means an individual trajectory into the central institutions of society, and equality is defined on an individual level. Cultural diversity, therefore, is subservient to this principle. Members of religious or ethnic collectivities cannot claim specific collective rights on the basis of cultural peculiarities with respect to their position in society, since this would jeopardize equality. At this point the approach is reminiscent of the French republican model; it does not, however, mean that cultural peculiarities are to be discarded completely. The state should acknowledge that culture can have an important impact on the well-being of the individual, so there must be room for cultural and religious expression. But, at the same time, all individuals must have a moral responsibility toward the nation as a whole. They should enter into a sort of social contract with the state and with society and subscribe to the liberal principles central to the nation-state.

Distinct from the French model in which citizenry is defined as a territorial community and where civic incorporation is based on the *jus soli* principle, and from the German model by which the understanding of nationhood and citizenship is based on descent,[15] this Dutch version of citizenship can be described as "contained pluralism," or "plural equality." The model is in some respects similar to the American "nation of nationalities" in that the Netherlands is today acknowledged as an immigration country with immigrants from different ethnic backgrounds, although in terms of the integration trajectory it follows the French assimilationist logic. The assumption is that, through a coherent program of economic and educational measures, structural inequality between immigrants and native Dutch society should disappear. Once this is accomplished, everybody can take part in society on an equal basis without having to deny ethnic or religious specificities. According to this argument, when material equality is achieved, ethnic differences will become irrelevant and may eventually fade away completely. The Dutch term "allochtonous," referring to the ethnic minorities, in fact contains all these elements. It refers not to culturally distinct collectivities but to equal and distinct individuals.

The other view hinges on the idea that the history of pillarization in the Netherlands offers a relevant framework for the development of a model that grants certain collective rights to religious groups. According to this view, it is unrealistic to deny the fact that the Netherlands is a multicultural society. Although the collective emancipation of religious denominations at the beginning of the twentieth century led to a fragmentation of society into confessional blocks, at the same time it contributed to the building up of the Dutch unified nation. The pillars were the principal integrative devices in the Dutch nation-state. In a modern multicultural society, new ethnic or religious collectivities can integrate into society in a similar way. Supporters of this view question the fear of neoliberals that an emphasis on ethnic and religious autonomy jeopardizes the integrity and unity of the nation. Recognition of religious diversity and certain collective rights granted to religious denominations, it is argued, will in no way infringe upon the goals of the governmental policies of civic integration (*inburgering*).[16]

Each of these positions invokes different principles and emphasizes different aspects of Dutch political culture. As a consequence, each gives different meanings to concepts like equality, freedom, emancipation, and integration. The recent debates about multiculturalism clearly reflect these different positions. In order to elucidate this, let us now look more closely at some cases with respect to a seemingly controversial aspect of Islamic identity: the headscarf.

The Headscarf Debates: Between Ideals and Pragmatism

For many Muslim women, the wearing of a scarf is an essential part of their identity, although there always have been and still are many discussions on whether it is an absolute religious requirement and how its use should be interpreted. Women wear different types of scarves or veils; some cover only the hair and others the whole face. In the Netherlands, most Muslim women who dress Islamically wear a scarf that covers only the hair and ears. The scarf, of course, is not the only element of Islamic dress; many Muslim women feel that they also should wear clothes that cover all of their bodies, except their faces and hands. In Holland as elsewhere, however, not all Muslim women believe that it is incumbent on them to wear Islamic clothing. The children of the early guest workers, who were often born and raised in the Netherlands, do not necessarily adopt the Islamic style of clothing, and girls as well as boys often can be seen wearing western clothes.

Since the 1980s, several so-called headscarf affairs have taken place in the Netherlands. These have varied from relatively small discussions in public schools to national debates, although they have never reached the extent of the controversies in France, where a large part of society, including politicians and intellectuals, have been involved in discussion.

The first headscarf affair in the Netherlands took place in Alphen aan den Rijn, a town in the province of South Holland, in January 1985. The city council decided that girls should not be allowed to wear scarves in public primary schools, because these scarves would impede the integration of Muslim girls with other pupils in the classroom. Muslim parents protested the decision. They organized themselves into a committee and sought to discuss the issue with the council, but the council refused because it did not consider the committee to be an official representative body. The community then decided to contact an expert on Islam from the University of Leiden, who would be able to give them advice on the delicate matter. This specialist concluded that the wearing of an Islamic scarf is neither essential nor absolutely necessary to exercise Islamic duties. This was, of course, the answer that the city council wanted, since it supported the council's decision.

However, protests continued, by local Muslim organizations and also by the national organization for foreigners (NCB). This led to a discussion in Parliament, where the minister of education was questioned about the matter. He had to admit that it was not up to a city council to interpret the Qur'an and to judge the importance of a scarf for Muslims. Consequently, the city council saw no other option than to reverse the measure. Girls were allowed to wear scarves in public school again. This case illustrates some important things. First of all, the argument of the city council that integration of Muslim girls was possible only if they renounced the headscarf points to the growing concern in those years about the results of the integration programs. Taking off the headscarf was seen as a sign of integration, whereas wearing the scarf was a sign that integration was somehow being hampered. Thus, religious symbols became conflated with policies related to the integration of minorities.

Second, the case shows that, in those years, self-representation of Muslims was still very rudimentary. While there were some official representative organizations, Muslims themselves were at that time barely able to raise issues themselves, since their representatives, if any, were almost never consulted. Third, this case shows the typical Dutch way of solving these kinds of cultural problems. Instead of asking Muslims themselves, the matter was referred to "experts." Although this is still a common practice, more and more young Muslims, most of them born and raised in the Netherlands, demand that they themselves be asked. They consider the wearing of the headscarf such a personal issue that it should not be a matter for external "experts" to decide.

The reaction to the initial decision by the municipality was certainly not expected. It was one of the first cases of "Muslims talking back." The relative ease with which the municipality gave in also shows that the question about headscarves was an issue that had not been thoroughly discussed internally. After this incident, which took place relatively early in comparison to France, where the Creil debate broke out in 1989 (see chapter 2), no other significant debates on female dress took place. Since there was no official national guideline regarding the veiling of girls in schools, communities and schools generally could decide for themselves, within the boundaries of the principles of religious freedom, what their regulations should be.

In the 1980s, the Alphen aan den Rijn incident was a novelty, but the fact that there were no other incidents in the Netherlands, as was true in France, does not imply that there were no problems. In many schools throughout the country, discussions arose with Muslim girls on practical issues. For example, there were girls who refused to take their scarves off during physical education, chemistry, and handicraft lessons, despite the argument of some teachers that wearing them might be dangerous. Some pupils indeed took their scarves off during these courses, but others did not. Usually, a solution was found; the girls wore tighter scarves or bathing caps to diminish the practical danger. Swimming lessons, which are compulsory in Dutch primary schools, have also caused some discussion. Muslim girls sometimes do not want to swim in bathing suits that leave large parts of their body uncovered, nor do they want to swim in the presence of boys or men. In most cases, this has been resolved through discussions among parents, community members, and teachers. In several large cities, separate swimming lessons for girls have been organized. Instead of bathing suits, Muslim girls sometimes wear less revealing old-fashioned clothing.

These relatively small skirmishes have continued since the beginning of the 1990s. Solutions seem to be found more easily now, however, as most schools have experienced and know what to expect of their Muslim pupils. There is, in other words, an increase in argumentative skills on both sides, not least because the media have given a great deal of attention to such issues. Incidents have been documented and publicized, and in general the debates are now conducted in a more sophisticated way.

In the 1990s, another factor arose to complicate the discussion, namely Islamic "fundamentalism." In September 1994, another major headscarf affair broke out at a secondary private school, the Protestant-Catholic Baandert College, in the town of Heemskerk, in the province of North Holland. Two female pupils of Turkish descent were refused admission because they wore headscarves. The school's headmaster stated that he considered the Islamic veil a sign of Islamic fundamentalism and of the inequality between men and women in Islam. After lengthy discussions among the schoolteachers and the board, the school finally accepted the girls, but it still stressed its concern about the position of women in Islam. It was the first time that a school had openly raised such issue related to the religion of its pupils. Arguments about practicality or about integration were replaced by arguments about principle.

In November 1994, another problem arose at a public secondary school in Vlaardingen, a town in the suburbs of Rotterdam, when two Muslim girls of Turkish descent refused to take off their headscarves during physical education. The school's headmaster argued that headscarves constituted a practical danger during these classes and that the girls should take them off. He emphasized the fact that it was not an antireligious argument, for Muslim girls were allowed to wear clothes with long sleeves and trousers during physical education. After discussions between the school officials and the father of the two pupils, with the help of a school inspector of Turkish descent, a compromise was reached: the girls were allowed to wear scarves, provided they were tight enough to allow the girls to move freely during the course. Again, a solution was found in compromise.

Another issue came to the fore as a result of an incident in December 1999 at the Caland-lyceum in Amsterdam, namely the status of public schools in relation to the pillarized educational structure in the Netherlands. Seven "well-integrated" female Muslim pupils asked the school for permission to pray in a vacant classroom during school break. The school's headmaster refused this on the grounds of the public character of the school. Praying was said to be something that one should do at home, not in a public school. To stress the fact that he was not anti-Islamic, he added that his school was very considerate of the duties of Muslim pupils during Ramadan, allowing them to go home early during this month. The pupils insisted that prayer is an Islamic religious duty, that they were not bothering anyone, and that all they were asking for was the key to a classroom.

A debate arose in the press and also among Dutch politicians, who were reluctant to make statements about the issue. A great range of arguments was put forward. Those in favor of allowing the prayer said that a refusal would cause the Dutch Muslims to ask for their own Islamic secondary schools, which could mean an end to integration in public schools and the complete segregation of Muslim pupils. Others pointed out in the name of equal opportunity that facilities for prayer existed in many workplaces and that a school should provide for the same. But most politicians agreed with the headmaster's arguments, fearing that allowing the prayers would open the door to the demands by pupils of different religions and nationalities, which would undermine the general rules in public schools.

Several cases are known of female Muslim teachers who have applied for jobs but were not accepted because of their headscarves. Muslim women teachers are regularly asked to take off their headscarves in front of the class. In Islamic primary schools, it is of course no problem if a teacher is veiled. On the contrary, even non-Muslim teachers are sometimes asked to wear headscarves inside the school because such practice is in accordance with the prevailing moral code.

Besides problems in schools, Muslims in the Netherlands often encounter problems in the sphere of work. Although it is legally forbidden to discriminate against a person because of his or her religion, employers still face such problems, for example, when a Muslim employee asks for time and facilities for prayer during worktime, appropriate food choices in the lunchroom, time off for the observance of Ramadan and other religious holidays, and, of course, permission to wear a headscarf. Numerous cases are known of Muslim women having problems on the job because of their headscarves. Some employers argue that a veiled woman is not good for business or that a woman with a headscarf will discourage clients. In Dutch supermarkets, one seldom sees a veiled employee. Employment agencies often note on their information sheets if a candidate is veiled. There is a very well-known case of a doctor's assistant who was fired because she insisted on wearing the headscarf. These commercially oriented arguments show that many companies in the Netherlands are ready to give in to existing prejudices in society. In general, it is difficult to accuse these employers of discrimination and violation of the first act of the Constitution, because they can always argue that there were better candidates for the job.

Nevertheless, since the passing of the law on equal treatment in 1994, which is based on the first act of the Constitution, there have been some 300 *reported* cases of its violation. Twenty of these cases deal with wearing the headscarf. The Commission for Equal Treatment (*Commissie Gelijke Behandeling*), which was created in 1995, handles the incoming complaints. Although the commission does not have the same jurisdiction as the court, its decisions have some binding force for the parties involved. Besides, one can always go to court to challenge one's dismissal from a job. In most cases, the aggrieved person is juridically backed by one of the so-called semi-official antidiscrimination offices that one can find in every city in the Netherlands or, of course, by a regular lawyer.

In general, it can be said that wearing the Islamic veil is not a huge problem in the Netherlands. There have been several headscarf affairs in schools, and there still are many problems in workplaces, but most of the cases have been resolved through compromise. This does not mean, of course, that Muslim women who wear veils are completely accepted by Dutch society. On the contrary, many Dutch believe that the veil is a sign of oppression and that Muslim women are all slaves of their husbands. Emancipation is considered a necessary development, and that implies taking the scarf off. This paternalistic and highly simplistic view is widespread in the Netherlands, even among the highly educated. But the cases also show that the general lack of clear regulations with respect to ("new") religious symbols and practices in the Netherlands often leads to unclarity and inconsistency with respect to decisions taken. The proverbial Dutch consensus society always leaves room for endless debates without clear solutions.

A very interesting new development is that, toward the end of the 1990s, young Muslims increasingly began to take part in these debates. They are confronted with stereotypes that they consider not applicable to them and feel that they have to account for their Islamic identity and correct the errors in the dominant image.[17] There seems to be a growing self-awareness among young Muslim girls of Turkish and Moroccan decent, born and raised in the Netherlands, who have deliberately chosen to wear headscarves as a sign of their religious convictions. They argue that wearing a scarf is a democratic right that has nothing to do with their attitudes toward Dutch society. They want to distance themselves from the image of the poor immigrant who has nothing but his or her faith and to show that Islam and modernity can go together quite well. These Muslimas are becoming increasingly visible in universities, higher professions, the media, and (local) politics. It is very possible that they will become the spokespersons for the young Muslim women in the Netherlands in the future. In contrast to their mothers, these young women consider themselves to be Dutch citizens of foreign descent, with the same rights as the other Dutch people. They also see no reason why full participation in the central institutions of society cannot go together with religious conviction.

Young Muslims in the Netherlands today are finding their way in Dutch society very well. They increasingly display the appropriate skills to be able to cope with society's growing complexity and to meet the requirements of modern culture. Muslim identities are not necessarily bound only to traditional social networks of families and fellow countrymen, and the traditional definitions of concepts such as "culture," "community," and "ethnicity" are no longer adequate to describe the various roles being played by the Muslim community in the Netherlands.

Notes

1. Before the Second World War, there were already small Muslim communities in the Netherlands, made up of immigrants from the former Dutch colonies of Indonesia and Surinam. The University of Leiden is renowned for its archives of old Islamic texts, since it was the principal place where administrators for the colonies were trained. The Netherlands once dominated the most populous Muslim area in the world. Yet it was not before the large-scale postwar immigration that Islam took root in the public imagination.

2. When we speak of 400 mosques, we refer to registered public places designed for worshipping with an Imam and with a more or less permanent character, run by an Islamic organization. Most of these places are, however, not recognizable as mosques from the outside. They are housed in factory halls, former churches, rebuilt ordinary houses, and so on. Currently,

there are a little more than thirty purpose-built mosques in the Netherlands, of which twenty-five are recognizable as such, with minarets and a dome.

3. Nico Landman, *Van mat tot minaret: De institutionalisering van de islam in Nederland* (Amsterdam: VU Uitgeverij, 1992); Jan Rath, Kees Groenendijk, and Rinus Penninx, *Nederland en zijn Islam* (Amsterdam: Het Spinhuis, 1996); Thijl Sunier, *Islam in Beweging: Turkse jongeren en islamitische organisaties* (Amsterdam: Het Spinhuis, 1996).

4. See, for example, Rogers Brubaker, *Citizenship and Nationhood in France and Germany* (Cambridge, Mass.: Harvard University Press, 1992); Yasemin Soysal, *Limits of Citizenship: Migrants and Post-national Membership in Europe* (Chicago: University of Chicago Press, 1994).

5. The first article of the Constitution, the so-called antidiscrimination article, stipulates that all who find themselves within the boundaries of the Netherlands must be treated equally in equal situations. Discrimination on the basis of race, religion, gender, or conviction is forbidden. This article forms the basis of a series of laws on equal treatment.

6. Jews did have their own institutions at that time, but they did not form a religious pillar in the strict sense of the word. Their number was too small, and, more important, they did not play a role in the political struggle that resulted in the pillarization structure. Jews were, however, granted basically the same rights as other religious groups.

7. The origin of the Dutch pillarization structure dates back to the Dutch history of religious emancipation at the end of the nineteenth century. Pillarization was in fact the unintended consequence of strategies in which sociopolitical organization, ecclesiastical structure, and religious ideology were interwoven. Siep Stuurman, *Verzuiling, Kapitalisme en Patriarchaat* (Nijmegen: SUN, 1983), 307. An important characteristic of the system was the strong emphasis on sovereignty of the pillars. Especially the two confessional pillars demanded that the state not interfere in any way in matters that were related to the daily life of the rank-and-file. Education especially has always been, and still is today, a field that was considered to be under the jurisdiction of the pillar. The pillarized character of the school system and probably the whole pillarization as such resolved around the so-called school struggle. See Hans Knippenberg, "The Ethnicity of National Integration: Religion, Education and Politics in the Netherlands," in *Netherlands Journal of Social Sciences* 35, no. 1 (1999): 37–53. This struggle was a reaction to the educational ideals that were at the basis of the liberal Constitution of 1848, which bore great resemblance to the French system. The confessional blocks managed at the beginning of the twentieth century to create their own school system almost completely independent of state control.

8. Currently there are twelve registered types of schools (including public ones), mostly of Christian origin. New initiatives and requests for founding a school are evaluated mainly according to technical educational criteria. Should a group of people with a hitherto unknown or unregistered religion ask for permission to set up a school, their request will be submitted to "experts" who must validate the "genuineness" of the religious denomination. In the city of The Hague, this led to a conflict when the municipality refused to comply with a request by one branch of Hinduism on the grounds that there was already a Hindu school (of another type). Hendrik Jan Schwencke, "Schoolstrijd in Den Haag. Veranderingen in de religieuze cultuur van Surinaamse Hindoes in Nederland," in *Migrantenstudies* 10, no. 2 (1994): 97–111. According to the registration list, there is only one type of Hinduism. A recent report by the governmental Educational Advisory Board recommended that the government abolish the religious consideration and confine itself to purely educational criteria. Interestingly, the Board invoked the constitutional principle of equality to sustain its argument.

9. Ministry of Internal Affairs, *Minderhedennota* (Den Haag: BiZa, 1983), 38–42.

10. The proper Dutch term used here is *gelijkwaardig*, meaning "of equal value." The idea behind this is that, while a Muslim and a Christian, for example, are not thought equal, they are "of equal value." The term denotes the political principle that, ideally speaking, differences

in religious or ethnic background should in no way affect a person's legal, political, or social rights in society.

11. Sunier, *Islam in beweging*, 8.

12. Jan Rath & Thijl Sunier, "Angst voor de islam in Nederland?" *Kritiek. Jaarboek voor socialistische discussie en analyse 1993–1994*, ed. W. Bot, M. van der Linden, and R. Went (Utrecht: Stichting Toestanden, 1994), 57.

13. WRR , *Allochtonenbeleid*. Rapporten aan de Regering 36 (Den Haag: SDU, 1989).

14. Frits Bolkenstein, *Address to the Liberal International Conference at Luzern* (Den Haag: VVD, 1991).

15. Brubaker, *Citizenship and Nationhood*, 81–82.

16. Kees J. Klop, "Religie of etniciteit als bindmiddel?" *Migrantenstudies* 4 (1999): 252.

17. Sunier, *Islam in Beweging*, 224.

10

Islam and Muslims in Europe:
A Silent Revolution toward Rediscovery

Tariq Ramadan

The impact of Muslims on Europe dates back to the Middle Ages, when Muslims created a thriving civilization in Spain that became the conduit of social, religious, and scientific knowledge to Europe. Thus, Muslims are proud of the fact that they have contributed tremendously to the formation of western, secular, and modern rational thought. The new Muslim presence on the European continent, however, dates back only some sixty or seventy years. In this context, Islam is still in the extremely early stages of establishing its identity and of interacting with other members of the host cultures in ways that will allow Muslims to feel at home and to acquire some of the rights guaranteed to the more longstanding citizens. While the influence of Islam and Muslims is increasingly being felt, tensions between Muslim culture and the established cultures of the host countries are far from resolved. In the 1980s, the new and fairly sudden visibility of Muslims in Europe evoked suspicion on the part of Europeans (often based on misconceptions) and, at times, mutual rejection. The resulting tensions, felt on both sides, were normal and logical. Given the anticipated temporary status of the Muslim immigrants and their unstable economic circumstances, it has been difficult to establish an atmosphere in which genuine dialogue can take place or close working relationships between the newcomers and the resident population can be sustained.

The first waves of Muslim immigrants were predominantly laborers from North Africa, Turkey, or Indo-Pakistan. They were a people of modest means who were under severe economic pressures. The new economic context in which they found themselves brought many hardships, some of which still continue for Muslim immigrants today: unemployment, rejection, alienation, violence. Their generally low educational standing, their tentative status in the European host countries, and their concern for the larger family unit at home made it very difficult for them to consider staying permanently in the new lands. All of these factors contributed to making the process of integration difficult and complex. It was left to the second and third generations to bring about changes in the mindset of these early laborers, who believed that their stay in Europe would only be temporary. The children and grandchildren of these early immigrants are now demonstrating that their presence in Europe is not only a reality but a permanent choice.

More recently, Muslim immigrants have had to face the backlash of a number of international events that have had a deep impact in shaping perceptions of Islam on the part of European citizens. Among the most influential have been the Iranian revolution of

1979, the Salman Rushdie affair, the "madness" of the Taliban in Afghanistan, intermittent violence in the Middle East, and the daily horror of Islamist repression in Algeria. It is difficult to estimate the degree to which these events have helped foster a negative perception of Islam among Europeans, but what we do know is that such a negative perspective is currently a widespread phenomenon that transcends particular national European borders. We also know that the scandals and events in the Middle East have fed the tensions stemming from the social crisis that has gripped much of Europe, manifested in its high levels of unemployment, exclusionary reactions, and recurring violence.

Seen as directly related to the immigration of foreigners into European society, these factors have made it very difficult, and sometimes virtually impossible, to engage in significant and creative debate over the issue of the Muslim presence in Europe. "Islamophobia," the title of a study commissioned in Great Britain by the Runnymede Trust in 1997,[1] may well symbolize the state of mind of many Europeans in response to Islam. Such attempts to demonize Muslims have made it very difficult for many people to engage in a really thoughtful evaluation of the changes that have been occurring in virtually all European communities. Were these events and attitudes the whole measure of European response to Islam, it would be easy to come to the conclusion that Islam is incompatible with European legislation or mindset and, by the same token, that it is impossible for Muslims to integrate. A true analysis both of the character of the Muslim identity and of its possibilities for integration into European society must also take into account the realities both of history and of everyday life, with its energy, fluctuation, and development.

The Pressures of the Second and Third Generations

It has been the second- and third-generation Muslims who have played the most active role in helping change the perspectives of many European Muslims toward the temporariness of the Muslim presence in Europe. Two reasons that at first blush may appear contradictory have been instrumental in the process. First is the fact that adherence to religious practice by many young Muslims has been somewhat weak, because for many integration within the society means total assimilation.[2] First-generation leaders of the mosques and associations have been forced to take this reality seriously, rethinking the framework they devised for Muslim life in Europe and for how their teachings are being implemented. Committed to an ideology that seeks to bring about Muslim governments, through militant means if necessary, they have learned to adapt both to the context in which these young people are living and to the language that they speak. They have redefined their religious doctrines and reoriented the way they carry out social and cultural activities.

The second reason is the resurgence of a young, practicing Muslim minority, which has been instrumental in creating a multitude of associations. Within fifteen years, the number of Muslim organizations has doubled or even tripled. Empowered, these young Muslims, born in Europe and educated in European universities, have become involved in an increasing number of activities. Their commitment represents a deep shift in mental attitude from that of the early immigrants, because they consider themselves at home in Europe and see themselves as having the right to make the most of their environment. Unlike the first-generation immigrants, these young people have moved openly to carve a place for themselves within the European intellectual and social spheres.

It is the second generation's involvement in European culture that has forced their parents' reassessment of the role and future of Islam and Muslims in Europe. Many of the parents who were exiled were former members of Islamic movements in North Africa, the Middle East, and Asia. For them, this is not a temporary or tentative adjustment but rather a complete reassessment of their previous way of functioning, as well as of their intellectual positioning in the context of the new environment in which they are now living. This phenomenon has fostered important debates within the Muslim communities and, in particular, among the Muslim scholars ('*ulama*). Consulted on matters such as Islamic law and jurisprudence, they have been compelled to reevaluate their own positions in light of new legal opinions adapted specifically to the western way of life. Associations in the United Kingdom, such as Young Muslims (YM) and Islamic Society of Britain (ISB), and in France, such as Jeunes Musulmans de France (JMF), Union des Jeunes Musulmans (UJM), Association des Étudiants Islamiques de France (AEIF), and many others across Europe have been asking for clarification of legal and theological issues. Accordingly, the '*ulama* have had to take their concerns into consideration.

These associations have been formed because many young Muslims in the 1980s and 1990s have seen the necessity of a resurgence of Islamic thought in the West. As Europeans, they have asked direct and indirect questions that require explicit answers. Should Europe (according to the terminology and geopolitical factors of the '*ulama* of the ninth century) be considered as a *dar al-harb* (an abode of war) or a *dar al-Islam* (a place where Muslims are the majority and live in security and according to the law)? In other words, is it possible according to Islamic law to live in Europe? If the answer is yes, then what should be the relationship of Muslims with regard to the legislation of the nation-state? Can a young Muslim acquire a European nationality and fully play his role as a citizen? Many of the questions being asked are ones that Muslim scholars have never addressed and to which they still are not always able to respond in a manner that is concrete, complete, and detailed.

In the 1990s, the changes that have taken place in the community and the development of new institutions multiplied the encounters. Generally, the subject matter has been theology and legal issues. The '*ulama* of the Muslim world, along with the groups of Imams and intellectuals who have settled in Europe, are taking part in these profound dialogues.[3] They have raised and discussed a number of very important points in regard to Islamic jurisprudence. After extensive study, reflection, and debate, both groups, namely the scholars of the Islamic world and members of the European Muslim communities,[4] have arrived at a consensus on many significant issues. The remainder of this essay summarizes some of their conclusions.

References and Principles

During the first few years of the Muslim presence in Europe, the feeling most widely shared by the immigrants and Muslim scholars ('*ulama*) was that they were in the midst of a transition. They harbored the hope that one day they would return to their countries of origin. Strengthened by a few legal opinions communicated as quickly as possible on such topics as *halal* meat, mosques, financial transactions, and the like, they did not feel the need to reflect carefully on what it means to be Muslim in a non-Muslim context. Satisfied with the answers widely applied to mundane concerns, they gave them no further thought. It is only with the emergence of the young Muslim generation that it has been deemed necessary to reanalyze the main Islamic sources (Qur'an and Sunnah) when it comes to interpreting legal issues (*fiqh*) in the European context. Many of these young people intend to stay permanently in a European country, and a large number have already received their citizenship. New forms of interpretation (known as *ijtihad*) have made it possible for the younger generation to practice their faith in a coherent manner in the new context. It is important to note that this has been a very recent phenomenon. Only within the past few years have Muslim scholars and intellectuals felt obliged to take a closer look at the European laws and, at the same time, to think about the changes that have been taking place within the diverse Muslim communities. To highlight all the multiple facets of this transformation is impossible in a brief essay. What should be mentioned, however, are the five main points that have been agreed upon by those working on the basis of the Islamic sources and by the great majority of Muslims living in Europe:

1. Muslims who are residents or citizens of a non-Islamic state should understand that they are under a moral and social contract with the country in which they reside. In other words, they should respect the laws of the country.
2. Both the spirit and the letter of the secular model permit Muslims to practice their faith without requiring a complete assimilation into the new culture and, thereby, partial disconnection from their Muslim identity.
3. The ancient division of the world into denominations of *dar al-harb* (abode of war) and *dar al-Islam* (abode of Islam), used by the jurists during a specific geopolitical context, namely the ninth-century Muslim world, is invalid and does not take into account the realities of modern life. Other concepts have been identified as exemplifying more positively the presence of Muslims in Europe.[5]
4. Muslims should consider themselves full citizens of the nations in which they reside and can participate with conscience in the organizational, economic, and political affairs of the country without compromising their own values.
5. With regard to the possibilities offered by European legislation, nothing stops Muslims, like any other citizens, from making choices that respond to the requirements of their own consciences and faith. If any obligations should be in contradiction to the Islamic principals (a situation that is quite rare), the specific case must be studied in order to identify the priorities and the possibility of adaptation (which should be developed at the national level).

To understand the significance of these five principles as presented, it is necessary to take with great seriousness the extensive reflection and efforts at adaptation that have gone into developing the various steps in the evolution of scholarly and intellectual Muslim thought. These efforts are important precisely because they illustrate the reality that Muslims have faced a great number of situations in the past for which they have had no answers. The five points mentioned here translate into the most essential principles. They provide a point of reference for Muslims today, offering specific examples of the ways in which opinions have been given on a variety of subjects in areas where Muslims were at a loss for a precedent, especially in matters that are marginally understood or inadequately interpreted. I now discuss three areas of specific contemporary concern.

Identity

The concept of Muslim identity has been widely discussed because it appeared to be a barrier to integration. It was therefore necessary to clarify the requirements, perspectives, and richness of Muslim identity, while also affirming that living in Europe is not an obstacle to its maintenance. Four elements can be identified as constituting that identity: (1) faith, spirituality, and practice; (2) a rational and intelligent understanding both of the Islamic sources and of the social, political, and cultural context of Europe; (3) education in and dissemination of the faith; and (4) action and participation in the social dynamics that lead to justice and a better way of life.

Every Muslim should be able to have a guarantee that these rights will be protected in whichever country he or she lives in. In other words, a Muslim must have the "right to identity" and to concrete ways in which to express freedom of conscience.[6] In Europe today, the legal system does protect and guarantee the manifestation of this identity. The current challenges that Muslims face are more related to a minimalist interpretation of Islamic jurisprudence that presents Islam as not yielding to new interpretation. A curtailed vision and understanding of the secular model, as well as the concern about possible prejudice against Islam and Muslims, constitute a large part of the discussion concerning Islam. In other words, perceived problems about living a true Islamic life in Europe often have more to do with the mental orientation of the believer than with any real legal incompatibility.

Community vs. Ghettoization

The practice of Islam, by its very nature, exemplifies the community. Whether it be through the practice of prayer or fasting, the payment of the social purificatory tax (*zakat*) or the pilgrimage to Mecca, it is the community dimension of the faith that, through brotherhood and solidarity, touches the very essence of a Muslim's being. Beyond his immediate family, the community is the first setting for a Muslim's social enlightenment. There are numerous Islamic teachings that guide the heart and spirit toward attaining one's own individual fulfilment, which has as its source the community, a place of faith and spirituality. In other words, if one refers to Islam, one automatically alludes to a community of beings, of faith, spirituality, and brotherhood. This is a fundamental basis for everyday religious practice. European state constitutions respect this and leave to the religions the responsibility of defining their own philosophies.

This being said, one should not confuse a community based on faith with an ambitious community whose sole purpose is to be isolated and to stand over against the social, political, and legislative framework. The whole notion of intellectual and physical segregation is alien to the very spirit of Islam. Practicing one's faith within a community is one thing; isolating oneself from the surrounding society is another. Legally and politically speaking, Muslims must be considered individuals who can exercise their consciences with regard to their rights and obligations as citizens. This, by definition, implies knowledge of laws and participation in the social, political, and economic climate. To put it simply, Muslims should have a genuine feeling of belonging within the European society. The mind-set that prevails among some second- and third-generation

Muslims that one should live isolated, ignoring the societal context without even having mastered the language, makes no sense. The community is the place for enlightenment of the spirit and should provide serenity and an intellectual vigor that permit the blossoming of the Muslim individual as a European citizen.[7]

Culture

For some Muslims, the idea of an "Islamic culture," similar to the concepts of identity and community, connotes the necessity of Muslim isolation from and rejection of European culture. Such an understanding suggests that Muslims are not genuine in their desire to integrate into the society in which they live. They play the citizenship card, while trying to maintain such cultural particularities as dress code, management of space when it comes to men and women, concern about music, and other issues. For them, real integration means becoming European in every aspect of one's character and behavior. This is, in fact, a very narrow vision of integration, almost resembling the notion of assimilation. One admits theoretically that Muslims have the right to practice their religion but revokes these rights when expression of their faith becomes too *visible*.

In actuality, the future of Muslim presence in Europe must entail a truly "European Islamic culture" disengaged from the cultures of North Africa, Turkey, and Indo-Pakistan, while naturally referring to them for inspiration. This new culture is just in the process of being born and molded. By giving careful consideration to everything from appropriate dress to the artistic and creative expression of Islam, Muslims are mobilizing a whole new culture. The formation of such a culture is a pioneering endeavor, making use of European energy while taking into account various national customs and simultaneously respecting Islamic values and guidelines. Far from being an isolated undertaking, it is a true acceptance of the realities of living in Europe, together with the promise of cultural enrichment. The mixing of ideas and initiatives among young Muslims is a sign of an interesting phase about to be set in motion.[8]

Which Muslim Presence?

One cannot say enough about the importance of taking into account the aspect of time when evaluating the integration process of Muslims in Europe. Behind the tensions and occasional violence experienced in certain areas, a new, profound, and unique energy is sweeping among the young generations of the Muslim communities. The period of the 1990s in this respect was a challenging one of transition and gestation, but also of rich promise. In less than ten years, a new consciousness has developed relationship to social, political, and economic concerns. More and more young Muslims of the second generation are acquiring confidence and a political maturity founded not only on the awareness of their own identity but also on thoughtful analysis of the legal, social, political, and economic parameters. They have achieved what their parents had not been able to achieve and have developed an attitude that is increasingly less frivolous and more participatory on both the local and the regional levels.

Protecting One's Faith and Remaining Muslim

Young Muslims active in certain associations for some time had been receiving the message that the price for toleration of their presence in Europe would have to be the renunciation of their religious practice. This rhetoric, articulated mainly by politicians and by people working in the media, seemed to be confirmed in practice. Faced with this challenge to their religious identity, these young Muslims concluded that it was better to be isolated. It is only very recently that they have become persuaded, after careful reassessment, analysis, and discussion, that nothing in the letter or the spirit of European legislation is in opposition to a peaceful and complete practice of the Muslim religion.[9] The laws do not accord with the intolerant interpretations of public officials, nor do they say what some would like to have them say. What practicing Muslims have always wanted is to be able to protect their faith and to be assured of their right to practice their religion. The recognition that these goals are possible both personally and legally, in effect that one can be fully Muslim and fully European, has led to the creation of a large network of Muslim associations and to open dialogue about issues of religious identity. This represents a significant break from the past, even ten years ago, when such discussions often were reactionary and aggressive. Such an achievement is of the utmost importance. It does not, however, mean that these associations are not constantly confronted by suspicion, fear, and the widespread misapprehension that if someone is actively practicing the faith it means he or she is "already" a fundamentalist.

Many, if not most, Muslim associations today are remarkable for the degree of consciousness, maturity, and energy that drives their members, who have been able to surmount many obstacles without compromising their religion as they have worked to be good and responsible citizens, aware of their obligations as well as their rights in the European setting. Frequent discussions with other social and political players on the local level are serving to strengthen relationships. Such initiatives are new, growing, and frequent, especially in France, England, Italy, Belgium, and Germany. An increasing number of Muslim associations are committed to instilling a sense of civic awareness in their members. Citizen training programs are in the process of being developed, both within the Muslim organizations themselves and in collaboration with certain institutions that specialize in this area. Thus far, these initiatives remain at the discussion stage.

The growth and maturity of these kinds of organizations are signs that Muslims are not only finding their voices but also moving toward political and financial independence. It is true that, for the moment, the organizational movement appears to be somewhat chaotic. This time is needed, however, as a transition from the old isolationist way of thinking to a new mode of participation. This has manifested itself in the adoption of a large number of new projects that respond to urgent needs and in the mobilization of the Muslim community at the regional level, for example, to finance new construction totally independent of a foreign power. Access to this kind of financial and political independence is crucial and pressing, for it is through this that Muslims will be able to fully and freely attend to the challenges that are waiting for them in Europe.

The future of the Islamic community in Europe requires that Muslims be respected for having made the fundamental choice to remain Muslim and give evidence of it. The changes that are now under way will help create a representative core leadership. In the time of transition and the building of awareness, more and more Muslims are showing stability. They recognize that the only reasonable road to follow is one that allows for a plurality of expression. One of the options may be a large council that can succeed in bringing together the diverse ways of thinking in response to the urgent need to make certain decisions. It is hoped that the various initiatives being undertaken will help foster leadership also at the local and regional levels. We are very far still from this reality. While it is clear that the Muslim community needs time to develop its voice on many issues, the European governments appear to be in a hurry.

We are, however, getting closer to the time when the diverse Muslim communities will be able to focus more clearly on their common concerns. The open and positive confirmation of the Muslim identity, as we have discovered, is a concrete reality, as is the de facto integration of the citizen. Far from the ghetto mentality, the majority of Muslims are now opting for an open public presence in which they will be able to demonstrate their understanding of what it means to be European and Muslim. Some go so far as to propose a "European Muslim Culture." An "intimate integration" into European society must be the final objective, as is the case in any pluralist society that respects the interplay of identity and difference.

One must not, however, hope for too much too soon. The obstacles are great, and explicit or subtle rejection and discrimination are everyday realities of many Muslims, who at times question the motivations behind the actions of some politicians and public figures, as well as of the European citizenry. They know that, in the eyes of some people, to be more European means that one by definition must be less Muslim. The many meetings, debates, and communal projects that have been taking place at the local level provide very important ways to move beyond mutual suspicion and mistrust. Some Muslims have found hope in the fact that these encounters have shown their fellow participants to be respectful, constructive, and ready to commit to an honest and coherent dialogue. Change truly does seem to be under way.

Such encounters provide the opportunity for many Muslims to see themselves in a different light. Some still deal with matters of assimilation by trying to make themselves as inconspicuous as possible, providing an "invisible presence" in the European context. Pressure has made them hide their religion as one hides an inferiority complex. Such an attitude does not promise social peace and harmony but rather can lead to an explosive situation. The present dynamics should be very helpful in transforming this kind of attitude. I believe that, in time, Muslims will understand that their presence deeply enriches European society. As the debates unfold and better understanding emerges in relation to such topics as values, education, and ethics, this presence will allow Europe to access and appreciate its religious diversity and its new and unique culture. Increasing participation in these debates is required of European Muslims, who must learn now to work together with their social, political, and economic partners. In this way, they will be full and responsible citizens, while at the same time maintaining their spiritual integrity.

Notes

1. Commissioned study of the Muslims of Britain, overseen by Professor Gordon Conway: *Islamophobia: Fact Not Fiction* (London: Runnymede Trust, 1997).

2. Sixty to 70 percent say they fast during Ramadan, but only 12 percent to 18 percent pray every day; 75 percent to 80 percent do not speak their mother tongue or speak it very badly. See Tariq Ramadan, *To Be a European Muslim* (Leicester: Islamic Foundation, 1999).

3. About a dozen 'ulama of the Muslim world met in July 1992 and in July 1994 at the European Institute of Social Sciences at Chateau Chinon to give an Islamic legal perspective on the Muslim presence in Europe. In Great Britain, the Islamic Foundation increased its efforts in this respect as of 1990. But London has also seen the creation, in March 1997, of the European Council to elaborate on judicial opinions and research. See the periodical *Sawt Uruba* (The voice of Europe), published by the Federation of Islamic Associations of Europe, Milan, May 1997.

4. Several groups, including At-Tahrir, Al-Muwahhidun, and Al-Muhajirun, aggressively call for a minimal implementation of the shari'a in Europe. Their efforts are very isolated, even though the media accord them great importance.

5. In *To Be a European Muslim* (Leicester: Islamic Foundation, 1999), I call attention to the discussion surrounding these concepts and propose, in the light of Islamic sources, the concept of *dar-ash-shahada*. This is a space where one gives witness to his or her belief in the oneness of God (*ash-shahada*), which makes a Muslim who he is (intimate dimension), and witness before others, which is an exemplification of his participatory presence in the society in which he lives (collective and social dimension).

6. One should note and repeat that each individual has the right to choose among the principles mentioned earlier, and to practice in his own way. The storehouse of essential principles is for those who want to simply practice their faith.

7. The contradiction perceived between Muslim and European is, according to this perspective, a false construct, since the two are neither from the same source nor of the same priority. To be a Muslim is to carry a concept, a meaning of life and death; to be French, English, or German is to play one's role as a citizen of a nation. There is no more contradiction between being Muslim and French or English and than in being a humanist and French or English. For example, the formulation "French humanist" shocks no one when it refers to a philosophic framework or refers to a political commitment. We should use the same argument when referring to Muslims.

8. Next to some simple musical imitations, which are sufficient enough to "Islamisize" the text, there are some very interesting and original experiments in the subject areas of song, theater, organization of celebrations, and clothing design. The fundamental idea is to harmonize the respected Islamic recommendations and the process of expression in a way that maintains the connection with societal roots and customs.

9. The question of integration does not apply to those men and women who have decided not to practice their faith.

Part II

Muslims in American Public Space

11

Muslims in American Public Life

Mohamed Nimer

The American Muslim community has experienced rapid growth over the past three decades. This is in part a result of the movement triggered by the decision of Warith Deen Mohammed to move the Nation of Islam to mainstream Islamic teachings. It also reflects the growing number of immigrants from Muslim-majority countries since the 1965 liberalization of immigration laws. Muslims have established more than 1,200 mosques and prayer halls in America, the largest numbers of which are found in California, New York, Michigan, Illinois, and Pennsylvania. In addition, 200 Islamic schools have been established to offer education to thousands of students, and dozens of social service and relief organizations have been organized to provide assistance to women, children, and the needy at home and abroad.

Several Muslim public affairs groups have emerged locally and nationally since the early 1990s, working to defend Muslims against discrimination and defamation, to give them a voice in the public arena, and to represent their needs before governmental and nongovernmental bodies. This chapter focuses on groups that identify themselves as Islamic and work to carve out a place for the Muslim community in the American mainstream and does not include the activities of ethnicity-based groups, whether religious or secular.

The Debate over American Muslim Involvement in Public Life

Most of the concerns raised by Muslims in the United States have centered on issues of religious belief and practice. Increasingly, there is also discussion and debate as to whether Muslims should take part in American political and social institutions. For the most part, this conversation is carried on through e-mail exchanges and oral encounters in local mosques and has not been addressed in articles in magazines or newspapers published by any of the major American Muslim groups.[1] Although the majority of those who engage in this debate favor involvement in American public life, there are still many who oppose any Muslim identification with the "American system."

Opponents of involvement maintain that Muslims should not lend legitimacy to institutions and processes that do not follow Islamic precepts. According to one interpretation, *wala wa-bara* means that Muslims should not assimilate into the institutions of the unbelievers (*kuffar*). In support of this position, they cite the following passage from the Qur'an, 5:49: "And this (He commands): Judge thou among them by what

Allah hath revealed. And follow not their vain desires, but beware of them lest they beguile thee from any of that (teaching) which Allah hath sent down to thee." Muslims who maintain such a view do not necessarily believe that all American values are contrary to Islamic principles or that the pursuit of individual happiness in this world (*al-dunya*) is not a permissible objective. Many of those who oppose involvement are successful professionals and small-business owners. Most of them put their children in Islamic or home schools, advocate the development of Muslim social, educational, and economic institutions, and limit interaction with non-Muslims to matters of absolute necessity. Some believe that involvement in American politics eventually will corrupt Muslims and make it harder for future Muslim generations to lead a moral life dedicated to following the commandments of God. The Tabligh Jama'at (Transmission of Faith Group) group favors this position.

A number of groups influence intercommunity debates. These include sympathizers with international Islamic movements, such as the Ikhwan Muslimun, or Muslim Brotherhood (founded in Egypt), who have immigrated to the United States. One such group is the Muslim American Society, headquartered in Virginia, which describes itself as part of the "worldwide Islamic movement."[2] Other groups that were established outside the United States but have U.S. sympathizers include the Islamic Call Group, or Tabligh Jama'at, which was founded in India; various Sufi orders, founded centuries ago in several parts of the Muslim world; Salafi groups (those following the model of the Prophet and his companions); and Hizbul Tahrir, or Liberation Party, which was founded in Jordan. Despite differences in the articulation of Islamic doctrine among these groups, they all grew as part of Islamic reawakening during the European colonial control of most of the Muslim world. They emphasize the need to preserve the individual Muslim character and the unity of the Muslim *ummah* (community of believers). Thus, they find a natural place in the functions of mosques, schools, youth groups, and other community activities.

The various Sufi orders in the United States stress spiritual issues and usually stay away from issues that involve politics. One exception to this tendency toward avoidance is Shaykh Hisham Qabbani's recently established Islamic Supreme Council of America, which fully endorses participation in the political process. There are two main Salafi groups: the Islamic Assembly of North America (IANA) and the Quran and Sunnah Society, both based in Michigan. These groups are preoccupied with issues of theology and sources of Islamic knowledge. The Tabligh Jama'at conducts Islamic call programs and has no record of addressing issues of political nature.

Other small groups, such as Hizbul Tahrir, hold the view that America is *dar al-kufr* (the abode of disbelief) and that Muslims should devote their energies to reestablishing the Islamic Caliphate state that was abolished by Mustafa Ataturk of Turkey in 1924. Advocating isolation from state institutions, leaders and members of this group think of their very presence in the United States as only a transient experience that will end once an Islamic state has been established. They also believe that the integrationist Muslims are naïve at best in believing that the *kuffar* (i.e., the western powers) will ever be truly fair in accommodating the concerns of Muslims. This isolationist position, however, does not mean that groups such as Hizbul Tahrir would shun interactions in the form of polemical debates over contemporary social and political affairs. Some supporters of the salafi perspective follow the late hadith scholar Nasser al-Din al-Albani, who advised against involvement in politics even in Muslim countries on the grounds that it would serve to corrupt Muslims.

Larger groups, such as the Islamic Circle of North America (ICNA), promote the notion of America as *dar al-da'wah* (abode of Islamic call).[3] ICNA leaders believe that Muslims should maintain their identification with the universal Islamic Ummah, or community, as a primary objective, but, as long as they can propagate Islam freely in America, they should engage society and government at any level where they think that they can make a positive contribution. ICNA leaders have taken more interest in social involvement, for example endorsing and organizing participation in the efforts of the African American Imam Siraj Wahaj to clean up the drug-infested neighborhood of Masjid al-Taqwa in the mid-1980s, and to establish soup kitchens to serve the poor. ICNA has so far refrained from taking any position on issues of political participation, leaving the matter to individual initiatives at the local level. ICNA members in New York, where the group is headquartered, voted with enthusiasm for the Muslim candidate Muhammad Mahdi (who won about 65,000 votes) for a seat in the U.S. Senate in 1996.

Other groups, such as the Islamic Society of North America (ISNA), based in Plainfield, Indiana, and Warith Deen Mohammed's Muslim American Society, based in Chicago, Illinois, take a more pragmatic line, promoting the idea that American Muslims are simultaneously part of the worldwide Muslim community of believers and of the pluralistic American society. The MAS website carries links to news articles about Islam and Muslims but does not generally address issues such as Muslim political participation in the United States. The group's secretary general, Shaker Elsayed, however, has delivered sermons at the Dar al-Hijrah Islamic Center, in Falls Church, Virginia, in which he called on Muslims to cast their votes in American local and national elections.[4]

Leaders of these major community development organizations stress the Islamic exhortation of enjoining what is good and avoiding what is bad. This position is rooted in the realization that the United States is a world power whose influence permeates sociopolitical interactions even in Muslim-majority countries. Thus, engaging the institutions of government is deemed desirable by Muslims who believe Islamic values offer guidance to humanity.[5]

Proponents of this view believe that those who oppose any political involvement not only lack appreciation of the American political system but also misunderstand Islamic law. According to scholars of Islamic jurisprudence, *ibadat* (acts of worship) are not acceptable unless they are supported by the Qur'an and Sunnah. Muslim Imams, for example, cannot decide to prescribe a daily prayer in addition to the five sanctioned by Qur'an and Sunnah. However, conduct regarding relations between Muslims and others fall in the *mua'malat* (human affairs) category of actions, which are deemed permissible according to Islamic law unless there is an injunction from the Qur'an and Sunnah against them.

Drawing on this understanding of Islamic law, the measuring stick for whether participation is consistent with Islamic law is the concept of *maslaha* (benefit), which legitimizes action in pursuit of the best collective interest of Muslims. Proponents believe it is in the best interest of American Muslims, who constitute a growing community with a distinct religious identity, to be fully involved. The Muslim absence in public debate has left the community vulnerable to scapegoating and alienation. From this standpoint, the survival of the community is seen to be dependent on its participation in forums where public policies are debated, formulated, and implemented. Proponents also maintain that Muslims should focus on how American legal and political institutions affect Muslim lives. Isolationism is an illusion because of compulsory taxation, intrusive state laws, regulations and policies, and the globalization of economic and political interactions. Events that take place in one part of the world affect the conditions of people in other parts of the globe. Even such simple acts as purchasing food from a supermarket or clothes from a department store means substantial participation in the American-dominated world market. On the basis of on this analysis of reality, proponents of participation believe that Muslims should be engaged to the degree that American institutions offer Muslims equal opportunity.

Proponents of involvement acknowledge that all people who earn income in this country are involved in public life because their tax dollars pay for government programs. These programs affect many aspects of the lives of American Muslims. The more influence Muslims have, the better equipped they are to push for the inclusion of Muslim values and ideas in the formulation and implementation of laws and programs. Thus, it is not only acceptable but necessary to use such means as voting, lobbying, and coalition building to gain this kind of influence. From this standpoint, the challenge before Muslims is to mobilize their community for effective representation of American Muslim viewpoints.

Muslims who hold a pro-involvement perspective look to the experiences of Muslim minorities in other parts of the world. In the South American country of Guyana, Muslim involvement in the government has led to official recognition of the need to accommodate Islamic holidays and dietary requirements. In India, despite the regular outbreak of violence between Muslims and Hindus and the intense conflict over self-determination for the state of Jamu and Kashmir, Muslims have been deeply involved in Indian political life. Among the religious freedoms they enjoy is the application of Islamic law in personal status matters. This is the case also in some African countries, such as Kenya, where the Muslim minority has its own Sharia court to oversee marriage, divorce, and inheritance matters.

Leading Muslim organizations have taken concrete steps toward involvement in the political process. Even groups that focus on the development of religious institutions are engaged in voter registration activities. ISNA and the Muslim American Society host voter registration booths in their annual conventions. Muslim public affairs groups, most of which have been established since 1990, have made strides in changing Muslim attitudes in favor of greater involvement in America's political and legal institutions. These groups include the American Muslim Council (AMC), the Council on American-Islamic Relations (CAIR), the American Muslim Alliance (AMA), the Muslim Public Affairs Council (MPAC), and Muslims for Good Government.

Discrimination and Religious Accommodation

A 1996 survey of members of the Islamic Society of North America asked, "Have you ever discussed with an employer or a teacher any matter that relates to the religious practices of yourself or any of your children?" Sixty-one percent of the respondents answered "Yes." Another question asked, "Can you describe any specific matter or request that you discussed with officials at work or school regarding religious practices?" Three-fourths of the responses had to do with accommodation to special needs of religious practice in schools and the workplace. Muslims want to be allowed to perform their prayers, to celebrate their holidays without penalty, to follow their dietary requirements, and to observe other religious requirements without fear of discrimination. The respondents also indicated the need for greater public awareness about Muslims and what their religion has contributed to human civilization.[6]

Some Muslims have taken their employers to court over issues of religious accommodation. In a number of cases, the courts have affirmed the right of Muslims to religious practices. On October 4, 1999, the Supreme Court rejected an appeal of a lower court ruling that allowed Muslim police officers in Newark, New Jersey, to wear beards, despite the Newark Police Department's no-beard policy. This handed the American Muslim community perhaps its most significant legal victory since the prisoners' rights movement in the 1960s.[7] In the earlier ruling issued by the U.S. Court of Appeals for the Third Circuit Court in *Fraternal Order of Police v. City of Newark*, the court opinion stated: "Because the Department makes exemptions from its policy for secular reasons and has not offered any substantial justification for refusing to provide similar treatment for officers who are required to wear beards for religious reasons, we conclude that the Department's policy violates the First Amendment."[8] This accommodation of an element in Islamic law within America's secular legal tradition may embolden Muslims to call for greater religious tolerance toward Islamic religious practices.

Still, many practicing Muslim employees often face the choice between job and religion. Although the Civil Rights Act of 1964 requires employers to provide reasonable accommodation of the religious practices of company employees, the law is not self-enforcing. Corporate personnel policy manuals often lack appreciation for the religious practices of company employees. Companies usually prefer to deal with issues of religious accommodation on a case-by-case basis but do not commit themselves to enacting procedures to prevent incidents of discrimination. As a result, Muslim women wearing the *hijab* (modest dress with head-covering worn by Muslim women) complain repeatedly that they are denied jobs because of their dress. Some have successfully used the agency of the Equal Employment Opportunity Commission to assert their right to their religious practices. Other Muslims have simply opted to be nonconfrontational, mainly because they are unfamiliar with the law or lack the financial resources to seek legal solutions.

Another area in which Muslims have started to raise concerns is the public school system. Although Islamic schools are increasing in number, the overwhelming majority of Muslim students attend public schools. Muslim students complain that these schools do not provide time and space to offer their prayers. School districts exercise discretionary powers in implementing religious accommodation policies. These regulations tend to reflect federal interventions, such as the Equal Access Act, which allows students in middle and high schools to establish extracurricular clubs. In some districts, this act has been used to win approval for Muslim high school students to organize Friday prayers. In other districts, however, time restrictions do not permit students to meet at the religiously appropriate time for the prayer. Other Muslim concerns include the lack of alternative food items when pork is offered in school lunches. Also, Muslims point out that social study textbooks often contain misrepresentation of Islam and Muslims.

At the national level, the Council on American-Islamic Relations (CAIR), which was established in June 1994, has defended Muslims who feel that they have been discriminated against in schools and in the workplace. CAIR has used moral persuasion and public pressure in resolving almost 100 cases of discrimination and lack of religious accommodation experienced by members of the Muslim community. Complementing this community service effort, CAIR has published educational material that explain Islamic religious practices to employees, educators, and healthcare professionals.[9] CAIR also challenges misrepresentation and defamation of Islam and Muslims by major corporations. Since 1996, CAIR has issued an annual report logging incidents of anti-Muslim discrimination and violence occasioned by such ethnic and religious features as beard, complexion, accent, name, birthplace, and national origin.[10] The CAIR 1999 report noted that, despite the persistence of discrimination, an increasing number of employees have eased their objection to Muslim women wearing *hijab*.[11]

While this monitoring at the national level has defined Muslim public issues, local Muslim activism has brought some changes in public religious accommodation. For example, the Newark-based Majlis Ash-Shura of New Jersey (Council of Mosques and Islamic Organizations) produced a handbook designed to educate New Jersey's 2,600 public schools about Islamic religious practices. The Department of Education in the state agreed to let the Muslim council distribute the booklet to public schools.[12] Later, the Paterson County School Board voted to close schools on the two major Muslim holidays. The Muslim Education Council in Fairfax County, Virginia, has successfully lobbied the county school board to mark pork items in school lunch listings, to offer Arabic classes, and to issue a directive allowing Muslim students to wear more modest clothing during gym classes. The leadership of Imam Ghayth Kashif led to a decision by the Prince George's County, Maryland, public schools to include the beginning of Ramadan (the month of fasting), *'Eid al-Fitr* (the celebration at the end of the period of fasting) and *'Eid al-Adha* (the holiday at the end of the Hajj or pilgrimage) on the school district's calender of religious holidays. Although most Muslim children attend public rather than Islamic schools, few other local communities have seriously addressed issues of religious accommodation in the school system.

Media Stereotyping

Many Muslims agree that anti-Muslim stereotyping is a serious challenge facing the community. Muslims reported a rash of attacks following the false accusations, promulgated in almost all the media, that Muslims bombed the Murrah Federal Building in Oklahoma City on April 19, 1995.[13] Following the crash of TWA flight 800, similar speculations about a radical Muslim involvement in the downing of the plane were also reported but did not occupy the main headlines. A search of the Nexis computer database of United Press International, Associated Press, and Reuters during the forty-eight hours following the TWA crash yielded 138 articles containing the words "Muslim" and "Arab" in connection with the tragedy.[14]

Concern about anti-Muslim defamation can be seen in local-level activism. For example, when the *Dallas Morning News* referred to Muslims who contribute to charities such as the Holy Land Foundation (HLF) as "useful idiots," the local Muslim community quickly formed Citizens for Equal Justice in the Middle East to challenge the alleged terrorist connection.[15] For three months, the group sustained a daily protest against the newspaper. Leaders of the protest developed a database of Muslim storeowners in Dallas and convinced more than 150 stores to boycott the newspaper until it apologized, published news articles on the contributions of Muslims to society, and offered internships for Muslim students interested in journalism. On September 10, 1996, the newspaper published an editorial acknowledging increased community efforts by Dallas-area Muslims, including weekend programs for Muslim youth, volunteer efforts in the distribution of food to low-income families in South Dallas, and open houses to invite residents of all faiths to visit local mosques.[16]

Grassroots activities in a number of instances have also targeted those who malign Muslims in general. In December 1998, Muslim activists across the country staged leaflet campaigns in front of movie theaters when *The Siege* was released. The film featured several scenes in which bombs go off in U.S. cities in connection with Muslim prayer rituals. Muslim activists distributed literature about Islam and invited moviegoers to open house activities in local Islamic centers. Similar protests took place following the release of *Executive Decision* in 1994, which featured a conspiracy of religiously motivated Arab radicals to bomb American targets. Muslims do not dispute the fact that Muslim radicals have attacked American targets and acted against Islamic teachings prohibiting the targeting of noncombatants. AMC and MPAC have condemned the World Trade Center bombing in New York in 1993 but believe that this and other incidents do not warrant the stereotypical depiction of Muslims as fanatics waging holy war against infidels. They also point out that, in their depictions of Muslims and Middle Easterners, the producers of American movies have focused almost exclusively on conflict and radical acivity.

Prejudice and various forms of attack impact the lives of all minority groups in America. For Muslims, their overly unsympathetic portrayal in the entertainment industry compounds the problem. As a result of these unflattering portrayals, a number of mosques have been subjected to attacks and threats in periods of crisis. Others have been attacked even in noncrisis times. The Islamic Center in Springfield, Illinois, suffered an arson attack in June 1995, causing an estimated $30,000 in fire and heat damage.[17] The Huntsville Islamic Center was broken into in July of the same year. Islamic religious texts were ripped, computers were damaged, and other equipment was stolen. The level of damage rendered the mosque unusable for the immediate future.[18] Masjid Al-Momineen, in Clarkston, Georgia, was vandalized in September 1995, resulting in broken windows, damaged light fixtures, and the discharge of fire extinguishers; Satanic symbols were burned into the mosque's carpet. Six days later police caught one suspect who admitted responsibility for the incident.[19] The Islamic Society of Greenville, South Carolina, was set ablaze by an arsonist in October of that year. The South Carolina Law Enforcement Division ruled the case as a suspected arson and estimated the damage at $50,000.[20] The same day, vandals spraypainted an obscene anti-Islamic message on the exterior of the Flint Islamic Center/Genesee Academy, in Flint, Michigan, with a vulgar sexual reference to God, using the word "Allah." Although the police said that there were no suspects in the incidents, the Genesee County Sheriff's Department promised Muslim community leaders that it would increase patrols in the area.[21]

In West Springfield, Massachusetts, bottles were thrown into the local mosque. The community claims that vandalism has increased ever since the minaret and the dome of the mosque were completed.[22] Good police work led to the capture of persons responsible for an attack on the Islamic Center in Fort Collins, Colorado, in January 1998, which was well covered in local television stations. A reward offer of $1,000 by the local Muslim community may have contributed to the arrest of two men, who were charged with vandalism and criminal mischief. In most other cases, however, no one has been caught or charged. In Austin, Texas, a ram's head was thrown into a mosque in May 1998; the Mosque of El Barrio, in New York, was broken into and robbed of a stereo in June, and vandals broke the windows of the mosque in Amarillo, Texas in July but were caught by the police.

Many attacks, however, go unreported. The Imam of Dar al-Huda, in Springfield, Virginia, for example, claims that the center has been subjected to half a dozen vandalism incidents since its establishment in 1996, including graffiti with hostile remarks. The words "terrorists" and "get out of here" were spraypainted on the center's walls and doors. In one summer incident, a car parked overnight on the mosque property was burned. The local fire department put out the fire and the police were notified of the incident, but it was not classified as a suspected arson attack. The local press did not cover the attack, and leaders of the mosque did not attempt to publicize it. The Imam reasoned that publicity would only bring attention to the mosque, which would invite more attacks.[23]

This passive attitude reflects fear and lack of connection to American public institutions, which remains prevalent in local communities. However, Muslim activism is beginning to change this state of affair. Following CAIR's lead, several local Islamic centers have started sending information each year to local newspapers and radio and television stations about Ramadan, Hajj, and the two major 'Eids, or Islamic holidays. The Internet has proven to be a very speedy, low-cost venue for Muslim groups to reach out to news outlets. Muslim groups have established websites and mailing lists accessible to journalists seeking information about the Muslim community. As a result, mainstream media coverage of American Muslim celebrations and experiences of discrimination have remarkably increased in recent years.

Government Relations

With the establishment of the American Muslim Council in June 1990, leaders of the organization resolved that it would be in the best interest of Muslims if a new atmosphere were to be created to help American Muslims feel welcome at government offices. To achieve such a goal, leaders of AMC worked to make sure that Muslim Imams, like rabbis and priests, are invited to offer the opening prayer before congressional deliberations. Six months later, with the help of Representative Nick Rahal, Imam Siraj Wahhaj, of New York, opened the 1991 Congress with a prayer.

Under the leadership of its executive director, Abdul Rahman al-Amoudi, the AMC decided to approach the Pentagon about issues concerning religious freedom for Muslims who serve in the military. The Council recognized that this would present a challenge but decided that it was time to consider the status of uniformed Muslims. Most

Muslims who serve in the armed forces volunteer because service provides a means to support their families. In the early 1990s, the U.S. military was the largest employer in the world. AMC intended to ensure that Muslims in the military would have access to Qur'ans and Islamic books and would be able to visit the holy places in Mecca at the time of the Hajj. The Pentagon informed an AMC delegation that Muslims in the military are in need of chaplains to lead their prayer and to offer spiritual and religious advice. The Islamic Society of North America had already applied, to no avail, for a Muslim chaplaincy program within the Department of Defense. Since then, the Department of Defense has been more forthcoming. It has appointed four Muslim chaplains and has dedicated a building as a mosque at the Norfolk Naval Station in Virginia.

After the Gulf War in 1991, the AMC complained that President George H. W. Bush recognized Muslims abroad in his address on the occasion of the 'Eid, but he did not address Muslims in this country. Six months later, with the help of chief of staff John Sununu, the Council received an 'Eid greeting message on videotape from the president. When Bill Clinton became president, he continued the practice of sending 'Eid greetings to Muslims in the United States and around the world. Still, the AMC pressed the White House to conduct a ceremonial celebration of the 'Eid, as it does for Christian and Jewish holidays, and in 1996 their efforts were rewarded. First Lady Hillary Clinton conducted the celebration and invited Muslim leaders and their families to attend. The first-ever Ramadan *Iftar* (breaking of the fast meal) party on Capitol Hill was held in 1996 and attended by congressional representatives, their Muslim aides, and AMC members.

The AMC also has coordinated regular town meetings between members of local Islamic centers and elected officials. With this visibility, AMC has participated in meetings at the White House and at various departments of government. The Council's call for increased government appointments of American Muslims prompted the Clinton administration to appoint Osman Siddiqui, in 1999, to be the first-ever Muslim ambassador to represent the United States in Fiji, Nauru, Tonga, and Tuvalu. Other recent appointments include Dr. Laila al-Marayati, who serves on the Commission on International Religious Freedom, and Dr. Ikram Khan, a member of the Board of Regents for the Uniformed Services University of the Health Sciences.

State and local Muslim involvement has resembled the work of national organizations that push for greater recognition and inclusion of the American Muslim community. In Michigan, the House of Representatives opened its first session after the 1999 summer recess with an invocation by Dr. R. M. Mukhtar Curtis, a spokesperson for the Islamic Center of Ann Arbor. Muslims in the Detroit–Ann Arbor metropolitan area constitute perhaps the largest single concentration of Muslim population in the United States. In Ohio, the Islamic Council of Ohio, with the cooperation of other Islamic centers, organizes an "Islamic Day in Ohio" event. The day is celebrated every year in a different city, allowing Muslims to meet with state and local officials, media representatives, and other members of the interfaith community.[24]

Despite these initiatives, Muslims are acutely aware that senior government officials often have failed to confront anti-Muslim speech in their own departments. In one incident aboard the aircraft carrier USS *Enterprise*, for example, the secretary of defense ignored a Muslim request for disciplinary action against a crew member who inscribed, on a missile designated for an attack on Iraq, "Here's a Ramadan present."[25] In another incident, an American Muslim requested that the Senate Republican Policy Committee rebuke the anti-Muslim policy analyst James Jatras, who suggested that the very presence of Muslims in America is a "population infiltration" and that NATO policy in the Balkans was foolish because it offered aid to Muslims. Senator Larry Craig, of Idaho, chairman of the committee, stood by his aide, claiming that his views are merely protected speech and that disagreement is only part of the democratic process. The National Republican Committee refused even to comment on the controversy. To Muslims who saw Jatras's remarks as an obvious expression of bigotry, the Republican responses reflected a lack of sensitivity toward non-Christians among senior party leaders.

Muslims have also been critical of some government initiatives that they believe have unfairly targeted members of their community. For example, Muslim and Middle Eastern travelers have reported that they have been singled out for extra scrutiny at airports. Most airport complaints were reported after the government's intrusive implementation of the Computerized Automated Passenger Screening (CAPS, known as passenger profiling), initiated by the White House Commission on Aviation Safety and Security after the crash of TWA flight 800. Although the use of passenger profiling diminished after authorities concluded that the TWA crash was due to mechanical failure rather than sabotage, the program can be reactivated at any time. Another discriminatory policy has become known as Secret Evidence; since the enactment of the 1996 Anti-Terrorism and Effective Death Penalty Act, several individuals of Arab and Muslim heritage have been detained on the basis of classified information they are not allowed to challenge in court.

Most recently, members of the Muslim community have organized fund-raising events to support the re-election campaigns of congresspersons who have endorsed the 1999 Secret Evidence Repeal Act. The Act is designed to retract powers authorized in the 1996 law that permit the government to deny rights to immigrants on the basis of classified information that is not subject to the legal process of cross-examination. The main sponsors of the act, David Bonior, of Michigan, and Tom Campbell, of California, received some $20,000 from Muslim donors through events held in Santa Clara, California, and Falls Church, Virginia, in June 1999.

Local issues, of course, are somewhat different. Contributions at the local level have focused on issues such as mosque zoning permits and the resolution of parking and traffic problems. For example, Bassam al-Estewani, the patron of Dar al-Hijrah in Falls Church, Virginia, has organized three fund-raising events since the 1992 elections in support of Jim Moran and Tom Davis, who were elected to the Virginia House of Representatives. The three events raised about $45,000. The two congressmen have written letters to Fairfax City officials opposing a motion by Falls Church residents to revoke the mosque's user permit. They have also supported Dar al-Hijrah's request that Fairfax County install a traffic light to facilitate street crossing in front of the mosque.[26]

Realizing that effectiveness in meeting local and national challenges requires collaboration, Muslim public affairs groups in 1998 established the American Muslim Political Coordination Council (AMPCC). One of the Council's first undertakings was to start a dialogue with the Council of Presidents of Arab-American Organizations. The issues that they agreed should have priority are importance of Jerusalem for Muslims, use of secret evidence, and voter registration. September was declared Arab and Muslim Voter Registration Month. In 1999, AMC distributed in a number of states a kit that included information on voter registration, tips on organizing voter registration activity, working with volunteers, material to be included in a voter registration table, and a request to file a report on activities, including a record of registered voters, with AMC.

Another action taken by the AMPCC was its endorsement of the creation of American Muslims for Jerusalem (AMJ) in July 1999. This followed a number of local and national activities aimed at highlighting the religious significance of Jerusalem in Islam. For example, a multiethnic Muslim coalition in California held a United for Al-Quds (Jerusalem) Conference in 1998. Muzammil Siddiqi, president of ISNA, published an article citing verses from the Qur'an and Hadith that illustrate the Muslim religious attachment to the city and its holy places.[27] AMJ maintains that it does not work for a nationalist agenda but stresses that government and nongovernment organizations must respect Muslim religious sensitivities on the issue.

Although Muslims are not represented in Congress, some Muslim candidates—all of African American descent—have won electoral seats at the state and local levels. In 1996 Larry Shaw became a state senator in North Carolina—the first Muslim ever to occupy such a position in any state. Several other Muslims have won city council seats, including Yusuf Abdus-Salaam, in Selma, Alabama; Lateefah Muhammad, in Tuskegee, Alabama; Yusuf Abdul-Hakeem, in Chattanooga, Tennessee; and Nasif Majid, in Charlotte, North Carolina. Two dozen members of the American Muslim Alliance, most in Texas, were elected to party conventions in 1966 at the precinct, county, state, and national levels, a reflection of the focus of the organization on educating Muslims about the American election and party systems. In New Jersey, Muslims first endorsed one senatorial candidate, then changed their endorsement to his opponent after the first candidate slighted Muslims. They were credited publicly by the winner, Robert Torricelli, for their contribution to his victory.[28]

Interactions with Other Groups

Institutions that affect Muslim life in America have their social roots in ethnic and religious communities. Muslims realize that they can not ignore the groups to which bosses, government officials, teachers, and law enforcement agents belong. Thus, Muslims have recognized the need to reach out to other groups in the attempt to foster greater understanding. In a number of Islamic centers, such moves have grown out of necessity, as churches, for example, have offered mosques the use of their parking lots to help compensate for the lack of parking space, especially at Friday prayer services. Many Islamic centers around the country are members of local and regional interfaith groups. These groups exchange speakers who introduce their faith to other groups and send delegations to attend religious celebrations of other faith communities.

One of the leading Muslim groups in the area of interfaith relations is the Muslim Public Affairs Council, headquartered in Southern California. Led by Maher Hathout, a physician with considerable Islamic knowledge, the center offers a forum for interfaith dialogue. Groups invited to speak at the forum include local and national Jewish organizations, the National Conference of Catholic Bishops, and the National Council of Churches of Christ. Still, a sense that the public is barraged with misinformation about Islam and Muslims in the media and in the discourse of leaders permeates the activities of MPAC. As its executive director, Salam Al-Marayati, put it, "We have to deal with issues that are given high profile by the public."[29] Thus, the council has issued statements on counterterrorism; Bosnia, with a focus on the use of rape as a weapon of ethnic cleansing; and the treatment of women under the Taliban, with a focus on separating the link between Islam and the Taliban's interpretation and implementation.

Most political interactions between Muslims and others have centered on issues of civil rights and freedom of speech. Muslim groups such as CAIR, AMC, and MPAC joined the American Civil Liberties Union (ACLU)–led coalition opposing the 1996 antiterrorism law, which contained the secret evidence provision that many groups believe violates the constitutional protections for the accused in the American legal system. Although the effort did not succeed, Muslim participation offered an opportunity for Muslim groups to experience firsthand the inner workings of lobbying and coalition building.

Immediately following the passage of the secret evidence law, the federal government detained a number of Muslim activists. The ACLU has accused the Immigration and Naturalization Service (INS) of illegally detaining Nasser Ahmad and seeking to deport him on the basis of classified information. Ahmad, who had been seeking political asylum in the United States, had worked as a paralegal in the defense of Omar Abdel Rahman during his trial in the World Trade Center bombing case but has never been charged or accused of any terrorist activity. The ACLU filed a lawsuit seeking his release and asked that the INS be prohibited from using classified information to deport immigrants.[30] A judge threw out the government case against Ahmad and ruled that he could not be deported on the basis of secret evidence.[31] Other cases involving secret evidence include those of Mazen al-Najjar, a Palestinian journal editor suspected of association with anti-Israel groups, and Anwar Haddam, an Algerian (who was elected to Parliament in the aborted 1992 elections) suspected of incitement to violence against the military government in his home country.

Muslims have confronted groups and leaders who have made anti-Muslim statements. For example, Pat Robertson, the founder of the Christian Coalition and host of the "700 Club" cable TV program, said, on October 27, 1997, that "to see Americans become followers of quote Islam is nothing short of insanity." This remark set off a campaign of protest by a wide spectrum of groups. Muslim organizations joined the Interfaith Conference of Metropolitan Washington and People for the American Way, a group that monitors Robertson and other politically active Christians, in denouncing Robertson's remarks.[32]

Contrary to the conduct of Robertson, who has exhibited clear anti-Muslim bias, officials of the Christian Coalition tried to court Muslims in the 1998 elections. On October 12, 1998, David Spady, executive director of the Christian Coalition of California, met with representatives of the United Muslims of America and officials of the Islamic Society of Orange County, asking them to distribute the Coalition's election literature to Muslim voters. Moreover, groups associated with the Christian Coalition in the past have joined Muslims in action. For example, Concerned Women for America has joined the International Association for Muslim Women and Children in coordinating a conservative response during the Beijing Women's Conference held in China in 1996. Other expressions of anti-Muslim sentiment by non-Muslim leaders have come from religiously conservative groups. An analyst with the Hoover Institution, a right-wing policy research group, for example, called immigrant Muslims a "security threat" to the United States.[33] Last year, Henry Jordan, a member of South Carolina Board of Education and a former Republican Party hopeful, remarked, in a public meeting, "Screw the Buddhists and kill the Muslims."[34]

Father Richard Neuhaus, editor of *First Things*, a journal dedicated to discussing the role of Christianity in public life, published a scathing anti-Muslim article in the October 1997 issue. The piece promoted the idea that Islam is the chief enemy of the West. Muslims responded rapidly with a flood of letters protesting this bellicose attitude. In the February 1998 issue of *First Things*, Neuhaus clarified that he thought dialogue with Muslims has become increasingly imperative. His only purpose, he said, was to make the point that Christianity is closer to Judaism than to Islam, because "Islam is not, as Judaism is, an integral part of the Christian understanding of the story of salvation."[35] But Neuhaus did not explain how this theological position translates into a warning against a Muslim bogeyman threatening Christianity and the West. Nevertheless, Muslims viewed his partial retreat as a signal that a coolheaded dialogue might still be possible.

In general, however, relations with the Catholic community have been increasingly conciliatory, perhaps reflecting a worldwide trend in Catholic-Muslim relations. The Vatican issued a policy statement, the Declaration on the Relations of the Church to Non-Christian Religions, in 1965. The document, which represents an attempt by the Vatican to recognize the legitimacy of other religions, states: "The Church has also a high regard for the Muslims. They worship God, who is one, living and subsistent, merciful and almighty, the Creator of heaven and earth. . . . For this reason they highly esteem an upright life and worship God, especially by way of prayer, alms-deeds and fasting . . . for the benefit of all men, let them together preserve and promote peace, liberty, social justice and moral values."[36]

Muslim groups have recognized a number of Catholic voices and have cooperated with them on common-ground issues. The Islamic Center of Long Island, one of the largest Muslim communities in New York, joined the Catholic League for Religious and Civil Rights, in October 1998, to protest *Corpus Christi*, a play that depicted a Jesus-like figure engaging in sexual acts with his disciples. The protest did not call for a ban on the play but tried to call attention to the fact that the denigration of religious values must be challenged. This shared concern emanates from a realization that secularism is no longer limited to the separation of church and state but has reached the point now where religious communities encounter hostility from those who oppose public expression of religion of any kind.[37]

The dialogue between CAIR and the General Board on Church and Society of the United Methodist Church started on February 2, 1998, when the two groups exchanged public speeches, published columns, and office visits. CAIR initiated the dialogue as part of a conscious effort to survey the political playing field. Some nine million strong, Methodists constitute the second-largest Protestant denomination in the United States. Its general conference has adopted resolutions in the past in favor of increased tolerance and religious accommodation of Muslims. In the public policy arena, the Methodist view of the natural world is concerned with the protection of the environment. The Muslim way of life is essentially conservationist. The Qur'an and the tradition of the Prophet Muhammad are replete with warnings against waste and overspending—moderation in consumption is a supreme value. On the drug crisis, the General Board on Church and Society advocates prevention and treatment. Across America, Muslims are actively involved in programs that include youth programs in inner cities, patroling of neighborhoods, and distribution of educational literature to prevent drug abuse. On the matter of prayer in public schools, both Muslims and Methodists believe in the right of students to initiate prayer activity but oppose the imposition of a generalized prayer in classrooms and in other school meetings.

Such contacts and coalition-building efforts with religious and secular groups have served the Muslim community on more than one occasion. Most recently, the General Board on Church and Society, along with the Catholic League for Religious and Civil Rights and the Interfaith Alliance, cosponsored a letter to Senate majority leader Trent Lott, asking him to take a stand on the issue.[38]

Relations with the Jewish community have been fractious, as issues of disagreement have overshadowed areas of collaboration. The American Muslim Council has endorsed a statement drafted by the American Jewish Congress and other groups on religion in public schools.[39] In another instance, the American Jewish Committee in Los Angeles joined the Women's Coalition against Ethnic Cleansing. Leading the effort to formulate this alliance was the Muslim Women's League. The group compiled information and testified in Congress on the rape of Muslim women during Serb attacks on Bosnian towns.[40]

Still, Israeli settlement activity in the occupied territories has caused sharp disagreements between American Muslim and Jewish groups. When AMJ threatened to boycott the fast-food restaurant Burger King because of its franchise in the Jewish settlement Maali Adomim, the Anti-Defamation League (ADL) called the boycott entirely inappropriate and contrary to the peace process. AMJ, which led the successful campaign to cancel the franchise, sees the ADL position as a reflection of a zealous Jewish solidarity that runs counter to the advancement of peace. The American-Israel Public Affairs Committee (AIPAC) has listed a host of American Muslim and Arab American groups as "Israel detractors." Many Muslims believe Jewish groups place the issue of Israel ahead of any common concerns in dealing with fellow American Muslim citizens.

Pro-Israel groups have used their influence to block American Muslim access to government. The Washington office of the ADL and the Zionist Organization of America (ZOA) opposed inviting CAIR and MPAC to participate in meetings of the State Department's newly established office on international religious freedom. Opposition from pro-Israel groups to Muslim involvement in public debate has extended to areas that bear no relation to the Palestinian-Israeli conflict. Daniel Pipes, head of the Middle East Forum, opposed the publication of an article describing anti-Muslim attacks that followed false accusations that Muslims bombed the Murrah Federal Building in Oklahoma City in 1995. The intended venue for that article was the *Muslim Politics Report*, published by the Council on Foreign Relations.

Accusing CAIR of giving support to "Hamas terrorism," a spokesman for the American Jewish Congress opposed the participation of CAIR in a panel organized in May 1998 by the U.S. Commission on Civil Rights on the religious rights of students and teachers in public schools. CAIR officials deny that they support Hamas and charge that pro-Israel Jewish groups in America are taking a belligerent stand toward Muslim groups because they are intimidated by the Zionist Organization of America, which regards the Islamic faith as an enemy.[41]

Most recently, major Jewish groups opposed the appointment of Laila al-Marayati, of the California-based Muslim Women League, to the Commission on International

Religious Freedom. They cited al-Marayati's weak stand on terrorism as the reason. Also, all major Jewish groups, including the Council of Presidents of Major Jewish Organizations, opposed the nomination of Salam al-Marayati, of MPAC, to the National Commission on Terrorism. Al-Marayati had expressed the view that Israeli repression of the Palestinian people has led to a violent reaction among the Palestinians. His condemnation of attacks against noncombatants was not seen by pro-Israel groups as sufficient evidence of his opposition to terrorism.

This action by the Washington-based Jewish groups, however, triggered dissent among Jewish leaders, especially after editorials in major national and California newspapers, including the *Washington Post* and the *Los Angeles Times*, criticized pro-Israel groups and House Representative Richard Gephart, who withdrew the nomination. Rabbi Alfred Wolf, of the Skirball Institute, which is administratively linked to the American Jewish Committee and whose national office opposed the nomination of Salam al-Marayati, along with three other local rabbis, disagreed with the view of the East Coast Jewish leaders. They argued that it is not in the best interest of the Jewish community to block the nomination. A dialogue initiative between Muslims and Jews in California that had started before this incident received further impetus. The dissenting West Coast rabbis are engaging local Muslim Imams and other leaders in a discussion of what they call "a code of ethics," which decries rumor mongering and prejudice and calls for a fact-based discourse.[42]

The main goal of American Muslim participation in mainstream politics is empowerment. The success of this effort, however, depends on the degree to which Muslim organizations can institutionalize their work and improve its management. In this respect, the course of development pursued by each Muslim public affairs groups seems uncertain. AMC, for example, aspires to become the main Muslim lobby in Washington, but it has suffered financial setbacks in the past two years. Its staff decreased from eighteen in 1997 to seven in 1999. MPAC has not defined a clear role for itself as an organization. Its leaders see their effort evolving along lines of public policy advocacy groups, but their resources are too restricted for this ambitious role. The organization has one office in Los Angeles and another in Washington, D.C., with two full-time directors and two part-time assistants. AMA largely depends on volunteer workers as it struggles to establish its office of operation. CAIR states that it is a grassroots organization, but it does not have bylaws that indicate the rights and duties of members. Local efforts, the backbone of any future success, are in worse shape than these national groups. Their activities are usually scant and ad hoc in nature. For example, Citizens for Equal Justice in the Middle East, in Dallas, Texas, ceased to exist after it successfully challenged the *Dallas Morning News*. AMPCC declared September national voter registration month for the Muslim community, but local communities did not heed the call in massive numbers.

Muslims also realize that the game of power in America is dependent on money and votes, which, because of the relatively small size of the Muslim community and its recent experience in political participation, means that Muslims are not likely to become a significant political force anytime soon. These challenges, however, must be seen as part of the normal experience of any new organizations. Still, Muslim public affairs groups have been able to make stereotyping of Muslims a matter of public debate, have been able to resolve many incidents of discrimination and defamation, and have demonstrated the ability to mobilize support for their concerns about the treatment of Muslims by government, media, and civic groups. There are also signs of limited improvement in the effort to register Muslim voters; AMC was able to mobilize only half a dozen Islamic centers in its 1996 voter registration drive, but that number increased to two dozen in the 1999 campaign.[43]

Moreover, efforts by Muslim public affairs groups, modest in strength though they may be, have sparked a debate over very signficant issues related to Muslim integration into a predominantly non-Muslim society. Increasingly visible relations with non-Muslim groups set off public exchanges among Muslims. Some argue that rapprochement with unbelievers is an exercise in futility; others stress that the Prophet Muhammad set the example of recognizing non-Muslim groups as social entities that have rights and duties and can be accepted as allies on matters of common good. Muslims have learned to appreciate the diversity of Protestant, Catholic, and Jewish voices. Thus, the perception of tensions between Muslims and non-Muslims is generally giving way to a more engaging vision that identifies actions and views with specific groups, rather than broad religious communities.

As a result of these encounters, Muslims have become better acquainted with the political process and have engaged some of its players, managing to initiate dialogue with diverse groups on issues of common interest. Whether the issue is Jerusalem, defamation, or discrimination, it is a sensitive matter related to Islamic beliefs and practices. Robert Fowler and Alan Hertzke, writers on religion and politics in America, predicted that Muslims may join like-minded groups in what is known as the Religious Right in opposing secular forces.[44] Evidence shows that Muslims have entered alliances on an issue-by-issue basis. It is too early to predict how and whether a Muslim consensus can be developed in favor of a strategic place for the community in the American body politic, as the main thrust of the American Muslim public discourse is still preoccupied with combating prejudice and ignorance.

Notes

1. One exception to this appears in the Internet magazine *iviews.com*, which includes a forum for debating American Muslim political participation.

2. Muslim American Society, n.d.

3. Interview with ICNA secretary general Zaheer al-Din, 30 Sept. 1999. One of ICNA's main programs is the mobilization of volunteers to distribute literature on Islamic concepts to the public at malls, on street corners, at airports, and on campuses. *The Message*, ICNA's monthly magazine, often features articles on social problems in America as seen from Muslim perspectives. For example, the cover story of the September 1999 issue discusses the problem of spousal abuse and how it impacts the Muslim community and the public at large.

4. On 27 Oct. 1999, Shaker Elsayed gave a talk during a Candidates' Night program organized by the Coalition of Muslim Organizations of Northern Virginia. He addressed the candidates, listing Muslim concerns in the Commonwealth of Virginia. He raised Muslim concerns about discrimination and lack of religious accommodation. MAS is different from the organization of the same name founded by W. D. Muhammad.

5. Imam Warith Deen Muhammad, "Our Duty and Pride as Muslims and American Citi-

zens," *Journal of Islamic Law* 4, no. 1 (Spring/Summer 1999): 3–10. Interview with Sayyid Sayeed, secretary general of ISNA, 5 Oct. 1999. ISNA's *Horizons Magazine* regularly features articles that stress the American Muslim identity. For the past three years, ISNA has held an annual conference on the position of Islam in America.

6. Findings of the survey paint a picture of the average ISNA member as a young, highly educated professional who lives in a middle-class, family-oriented, and possibly ethnically diverse household. However, only a small percentage of African American Muslims identify with the organization; ISNA draws its membership primarily from immigrant and practicing Muslim populations.

7. For more details on the prisoners' rights movement, see Kathleen Moore, *Al-Mughtaribun: American Law and the Transformation of Muslim Life in the United States* (Albany: State University of New York Press, 1996), 69–102.

8. *Fraternal Order of Police v. City of Newark*, App. No. 97-5542.

9. Council on American-Islamic Relations (CAIR), *An Employer's Guide to Islamic Religious Practices* (1997), *An Educator's Guide to Islamic Religious Practices* (1997), *A Health Care Provider's Guide to Islamic Religious Practices* (1999). Washington, D.C.: CAIR Research Center.

10. *The Status of Muslim Civil Rights in the United States* (Washington, D.C.: Council on American-Islamic Relations, 1998), 6–11.

11. *The Status of Muslim Civil Rights in the United States* (Washington, D.C.: Council on American-Islamic Relations, 1999), 2–10.

12. *The Record*, 15 Feb. 1999.

13. *A Rush to Judgment* (Washington, D.C.: Council on American-Islamic Relations, 1995), 9–20.

14. Mohamed Nimer, *The Usual Suspects: Media Coverage following the Crash of TWA Flight 800* (Washington, D.C.: Council on American-Islamic Relations, 1996), 4.

15. *Dallas Morning News*, 10 April 1996.

16. HLF is one of three dozen Muslim charity organizations around the country that provide assistance to the poor at home and abroad. Ironically, some of the efforts of these groups had been noted by the *Dallas Morning News*. For example, following the 1995 Oklahoma City bombing, HLF contributed $7,500 and blood to the relief effort and flew in fifty volunteers to help Feed the Children distribute food to families of the victims. *Dallas Morning News*, 24 April 1995.

17. *St. Louis Post-Dispatch*, 17 June 1995.

18. *Huntsville Times*, 16–17 July 1996.

19. *Atlanta Journal/Constitution*, 16 Sept. 1995.

20. *Greenville News*, 22 Oct. 1995.

21. *Flint Journal*, 23 Oct. 1995.

22. *Union News*, 25 Oct. 1996.

23. Interview with Imam Abdul Hameed, 17 Sept. 1999.

24. Interview with Andy Amid, secretary of the Islamic Council of Ohio, 18 Sept. 1999.

25. The Associated Press distributed a photo with the this inscription on 21 Dec. 1998.

26. Interview with Bassam El-Estewani, 28 Sept. 1999.

27. *Islamic Horizons* (July/August 1999).

28. *Washington Report on Middle East Affairs* (July/August 1998), 9–10.

29. Interview with Salam Al-Marayti, 15 Sept. 1999.

30. *New York Times*, 10 Sept. 1997.

31. *New York Times*, 11 Nov. 1999. The newspaper reports that, in the declassified testimony of an FBI official, the government argued against the release of Mr. Ahmad, fearing that he might gain respectability in the Arab and Muslim community.

32. *Washington Post*, 9 Nov. 1997.

33. James Philips, "Islamic Terrorists Pose a Threat," in *Urban Terrorism*, ed. A. E. Sadler and Paul Winters (San Diego: Greenhaven Press, 1996), 62–65.

34. Jonathan J. Goldberg, "Jewish Power: Inside the American Jewish Establishment" (Reading, Mass.: Addison-Wesley, 1996), 88, 197–226, 337–67.

35. *First Things*, February 1998, 64.

36. Vatican, "Declaration on the Relations of the Church to Non-Christian Religions," Proclaimed by His Holiness Pope Paul VI on 28 Oct. 1965. The Pontifical Council for Interreligious Dialogue (PCID) oversees relations with other faith groups. The PCID has a special commission for relations with Muslims that engages in studies on different aspects of Christian-Muslim relations. Since the reorganization of the PCID in 1988, the Pope has visited several Muslim countries and received delegations from various Muslim communities, including a visit by an American Muslim delegation in 1999.

37. Address of Kenneth Whitehead at CAIR panel, "Muslims and Catholics: Challenging Antireligious Bias," 14 Oct. 1998; "Religious Expression in the Public Schools," testimony by William Donohue, president of the Catholic League for Religious and Civil Rights, before the U.S. Civil Rights Commission, 20 May 1998, and published in *Catalyst* (July/August 1998): 8–9.

38. The letter was published as an advertisement in the *Washington Times* on 29 June 1999.

39. "*Religion in Public Schools: A Joint Statement of Current Law*" (Washington, D.C.: ACLU, n.d.).

40. Interview by the author with Laila al-Marayati, president of the Muslim Women League, on 16 May 1997. The league is affiliated with the Muslim Public Affairs Council.

41. Whitehead, "Muslims and Catholics."

42. Interviews with Rabbi Alfred Wolf and Salam al-Marayati, 30 Sept. 1999.

43. Interview with Manal Omar, of AMC, 25 Oct. 1999.

44. Robert Fowler and Alan Hertzke, *Religion and Politics in America: Faith, Culture, and Strategic Choices* (Boulder, Colo.: Westview Press, 1995), 190–94.

12

Representation of Islam in the Language of Law: Some Recent U.S. Cases

Kathleen M. Moore

The following exchange between a convicted defendant and a judge occurred at the culmination of the trial of Ramzi Yousef for his part in the 1993 bombing of the World Trade Center Building in New York and in the conspiracy to bomb American jetliners in the Far East. Speaking face-to-face in a federal courtroom in Manhattan on the day of sentencing, January 8, 1998, the condemned verbally sparred with the judge. Ramzi Yousef proclaimed,

> The Government in its summations and opening statement said I was a terrorist. Yes, I am a terrorist and I am proud of it. And I support terrorism so long as it was against the United States Government and against Israel, because you are more than terrorists; you are the one who invented terrorism and [are] using it every day. You are butchers, liars, and hypocrites. . . . You don't believe in human rights nor [sic] ethics nor [sic] anything. All that you believe in are your own interests and being bribed. That is what you worship, money. Money is your God, hypocrisy your courier. . . . You were the first one who killed innocent people and you are the first one who introduced this type of terrorism to . . . history . . . when you dropped an atomic bomb which killed tens of thousands of women and childrens [sic] in Japan and when you killed over a hundred thousand people, most of them civilians, in Tokyo with fire bombings. You killed them by burning them to death. And you killed civilians in Vietnam with chemicals as with the so-called orange agent. You killed civilians and innocent people, not soldiers, innocent people every single war you went [sic]. You went to wars more than any other country in this century and then you have the nerve to talk about killing innocent people. . . . And since this is the way you invented and since this is the means you have been using against other people, which you continue until this day to use in killing innocent people . . . it was necessary to use the same means against you because this is *the only language you understand*. (Emphasis added)[1]

At the same time, Judge Kevin Thomas Duffy, who had presided over the trials of all the World Trade Center defendants, chastised Yousef before sentencing him to life in prison:

> Ramzi Yousef, you claim to be an Islamic militant. . . . Ramzi Yousef, you are not fit to uphold Islam. Your God is death. Your God is not Allah. The Qur'an teaches in connection with the People of the Book, in Surah Al Imran, ayat [verse] 72-73: "Grace is surely in Allah's hand. He gives it to whom he pleases . . . he specially chooses for his mercy whom he pleases and Allah is the Lord of Mighty Grace." And again, the book teaches

in the Surah the Cave, ayat [verse] 29: "The truth is from your Lord; so let him who please believe, and let him who please disbelieve." Thus it can be seen that the *true* worship of Allah does not allow the compulsion which you sought to bring about. You weren't seeking conversions. The only thing you wanted to do was to cause death. Your God is not Allah. . . . What you have shown is your total disdain beyond doubt for the people whom Allah has made.[2]

The conviction of Yousef was expected. This exchange, however, is startling. Here, as in any courtroom, the language of the law predominates. Yet the words uttered raise questions about identity and meaning. On what authority do these two men speak? To which laws do they refer? For his part, Yousef adopts the language alternately of American criminal law and international human rights law. For the first time he admits to being a "terrorist"—an identity he had not claimed during the trial.[3] At his sentencing he assumed the label "terrorist" somewhat reluctantly, but with pride. Moreover, in a reflexive move, Yousef turns the appellation back onto his prosecutor and judge by accusing them of the same crime—"you" (i.e., the American government) are the quint-essential terrorists because "you" invented terrorism and were the first to terrorize inno-cent civilians. In invoking images of wartime atrocities—bombings of Hiroshima and Nagasaki, Tokyo, and Vietnam—the accused thinks he holds a mirror to the faces of his accusers. He presumes that his statement in the courtroom on the day of his sentencing will be intelligible because it contains some shared meaning. His acts of terrorism were "necessary" because this is "the only language you understand."

Again, none of this seems out of the ordinary or controversial, given the political na-ture of the crimes involved in this trial. There are a number of presuppositions that listen-ers would have to accept to make sense of Yousef's polemics. For instance, the message implied in Yousef's indictment of the United States—that attacks on American (and Is-raeli) targets are in fact defensible *counterattacks* against an imperialist power—relies on a set of presuppositions about the structural violence that results from American cultural and economic hegemony around the world, as well as the direct violence perpetrated by the United States and its allies against so-called third world interests. The images of war-time atrocities and the presuppositions upon which Yousef's statement rests must be understood in relation to the collage of images invoked by recent global events, namely by the end of the Cold War and the (re)emergence of Islam as the "new" global threat since the fall of the Communist "Other."[4] The very act for which Yousef is convicted, the bombing of the World Trade Center in New York, is often portrayed by the media and in many academic accounts as the opening salvo in the new post–Cold War era, needing what *Newsweek* has called in a headline "A New Kind of Containment."[5] "The global war between 'us' and 'them', previously scripted as that between capitalism and communism, is being reconstructed by such propagandists [e.g., *Newsweek*] as that between the Christian and Muslim societies."[6] Hence, the World Trade Center bombing is labeled as the kind of "fanatical violence" typical of the religion of the main villains in this new warfare, and Yousef's indictment of the United States can be readily dismissed as false propaganda from the enemy. Perhaps not surprisingly, "we" in the West might read ourselves in this indictment "as the others of our others."[7]

What is more surprising is that the judge, Kevin Thomas Duffy, made a rather dra-matic shift at the moment of sentencing Ramzi Yousef. While wearing the robes of the judge that signify his authority on the bench of an American court, Duffy assumed the mantle of Islam. Just before pronouncing the sentence, he indicted Yousef not in terms of what American criminal law requires, even though there is no absence of such law with which to convict. Rather, he chastised the defendant in terms of what he, Duffy, saw in the Qur'an as its ethical message. Judge Duffy said he knows the true nature of Islam (that it does not allow compulsion) and that the defendant was mistaken if he thought his actions were justified. Further, he claimed that the People of the Book (e.g., the Jews and Christians) must be treated with mercy ("Grace is surely in Allah's hands"). He cited chapter and verse from the Qur'an in support of both of these assertions. Thus, in what may seem an ironic twist, the convicted defendant spoke at his sentencing about his crimes exclusively in terms of positive law,[8] and the judge spoke in terms of the standards of morality contained in the Qur'an.

In decoding this critical moment in American justice, we could make various observations about the mixed sources of justice operative in the transaction between the condemned and the judge. Some might say that in that fleeting moment when two "incommensurable" world views stood face-to-face in the courtroom, two men tried to launch missiles across the chasm that separated them, each translating his message into the native tongue of the other. However, this argument would be essentializing identity, positing that the judge, a man of Irish-American descent who grew up in the Bronx,[9] and the defendant, a Middle Easterner of Islamic faith, were incapable of transcending their fixed "essences," hedged in by their respective cultures, as well as by their respective roles as judge and defendant. In this interpretation, the courtroom becomes the battlefield in which the two "warriors" may transgress their cultural boundedness only momentarily, for tactical gain. The instability of the transgressive moment serves only to reinforce the categorical opposition of the two men and their failure to share a vocabulary of tradition and legal convention.

An alternative interpretation might posit that the exchange between the condemned and the judge is full of signifying resources and illustrates the transformation of dominant meaning. According to this interpretation, the sentencing is the medium through which some meanings are privileged and others delegitimized. The judge chooses to speak of Islam and to provide his selective "proof texting" in order to tell the convicted defendant that his (the defendant's) understanding of Islam is wrong (e.g., "your God is not Allah" and "you are not fit to uphold Islam"). Thus, on the basis of his authority as an officer of the court, the judge substitutes his version of Islam, the putatively "correct" one, for that of the defendant. This is a question not necessarily of disparaging Islam but of subjecting it to a particular standpoint.[10] This privileging of a particular interpretation of Islam delimits possibilities by aligning a judicially sanctioned "Islam" with the power structures of the state.[11] Not that the judge's definition is in any way definitive. However partial or imperfect it is, though, the judicial demarcation of what constitutes "Islam" enters into the political environment to join other sources of "knowledge" about Islam (e.g., journalistic, academic, religious, and entertainment sources) to shape ideas about Islam and to give meaning to what Islam represents in the new world order. Islam, in effect, is reconstructed discursively through its encounter with the American judicial system into terms that make sense for the law's secular system of meaning.[12]

Legal Orientalism

What *are* the representations of Islam in American law? The British scholar John Strawson has written about the construction of Islamic law in English texts about law, such as Charles Hamilton's *The Hedayah, A Commentary on the Mussulman Law* (first edition, 1791, second edition, 1870). He writes about the role that law played in British colonial rule and how the Orientalist methodology of "making Islamic law understandable to the English lawyer or official" was mobilized for administrative purposes in the interests of consolidating colonial power.[13] Classical texts of Islamic law were turned into authoritative "positivist instrument[s] of colonial rule,"[14] which were pivotal in constituting the colonists' management of disputes within a particular cultural system of meaning. Following Strawson's suggestive lead, in this chapter I want to examine the role played by the primary "texts" of American law—judicial decisions—in reproducing what Strawson has called "legal Orientalism,"[15] although for a different historical context. My inquiry highlights the language of alterity in legal constructions of cultural and national identities framed in the post–Cold War era, and in particular its domestic implications. The picture I present is not meant to be comprehensive, for it is indeed hard to imagine how a comprehensive picture could be drawn, given the recent increase in the numbers and kinds of encounters Muslims are having with the American legal system.[16] Instead, I try to illustrate what the public understandings are of the one word "Islam" and how these can circumscribe the opportunities that exist in the American legal order for Muslims to seek legal protection for fundamental rights.[17] To show how representations are reproduced in the law, in the following sections I analyze briefly some recent encounters between Islam and the law in the United States. I want to emphasize at the outset, though, that law is only one of the several sources of meaning that are involved in the reproduction of representations of Islam. However, the close connection between the day-to-day, practical requirements of the government body and the representation of Islam promotes a certain kind of regulatory power within which the contemporary American national identity is constructed.

Expert Testimony

While Judge Duffy pronounced his understanding of Islam from the bench on the day of Ramzi Yousef's sentencing, most occasions in court are met with a great deal more circumspection. Judges often refrain from interpretation themselves, allowing "expert testimony" of witnesses to provide definitions of religious belief systems such as Islam for the court. For instance, in an appeals court case in New Jersey,[18] the court was asked to review the First Amendment claims brought by two Newark police officers who are Muslim and who wore beards in compliance with the requirements of Islam. Officers Faruq Abdul-Aziz and Shakoor Mustafa are both devout Sunni Muslims who assert that they believe they are under a religious obligation to grow their beards. The officers were sanctioned by the police department for violating the department's no-beard policy. They argued that, while the police department allowed exemptions from this policy for medical reasons, exemptions for religious reasons were not granted, and this violated the First Amendment's guarantees of free expression and free exercise of religion. While the appellate decision was limited to providing a review of religious exemption jurisprudence[19] and ruled in favor of the Muslim police officers on that basis, the record does include a Muslim cleric's testimony relating Islamic requirements for grooming. The decision reads, "according to the affidavit of an imam, it is an obligation for men who can grow a beard, to do so" and not to shave. The affidavit of the Imam continues:

> The Quran commands the wearing of a beard implicitly. The Sunnah is the detailed explanation of the general injunctions contained in the Quran. The Sunnah says in too many verses to recount[:] "Grow the beard, trim the mustache." . . . I teach as the Prophet Mohammed taught that the Sunnah must be followed as well as the Quran. This in the unequivocal teaching for the past 1,418 years, by the one billion living Sunni Muslims world wide. . . . The refusal by a Sunni Muslim male who can grow a beard, to wear one is a major sin. I teach based upon the way I was taught and it is understood in my faith that the non-wearing of a beard by the male who can, for any reason is as [serious] a sin as eating pork. . . . This is not a discretionary instruction; it is a commandment. A Sunni Muslim male will not be saved from this major sin because of an instruction of another, even an employer to shave his beard and the penalties will be meted out by Allah.[20]

The court relied on the expert testimony of one Muslim cleric to determine whether this was a matter of some external authority requiring facial hair. In effect, what the appellate decision attempts to do is to assess the strength and nature of the Muslim individual's religious obligation to grow a beard and to couch this language in terms of institutionalized "rights." In other words, the court searched for an Islamic law that requires men to grow beards and, significantly, for any legitimate reasons a man may be excused from this requirement. Given that the Muslim cleric said there were no legitimate exemptions, that refusing to grow a beard is a major sin even if done at the instruction of an employer, the majority of the appellate bench concluded that the Muslim officers' request for a religious exemption from the police department's "no-beard" policy was valid.

In reaching this decision, the court needed to represent Islam in a way that made it cognizable under the law. In other words, Islam was narrowed down to a set of obligations that set Muslims apart from everyone else. Once that was established, through the testimony of the Muslim cleric, the judicial task then became one of weighing the absoluteness of the Islamic requirement against the validity of the police department's policy. Through such a balancing test, the court recognized the police department's position that it had legitimate concerns about uniformity of appearance and a desire to convey the image of a "monolithic, highly disciplined force," while permitting beards for religious reasons would somehow "undermine the force's morale."[21] However, the court determined that these justifications for the refusal to allow religious exemptions from the "no-beard" policy were not enough to outweigh the Muslim officers' interest in wearing beards in compliance with their religion. Thus, the particular obligation of wearing a beard was given the status of a fundamental "right" protected by the First Amendment.

My point here is that an issue that started out as a matter of belief and obedience to God's will was translated through the judicial process into terms that made sense in the eyes of the law. For example, Officers Abdul-Aziz and Mustafa contended in their appeal that, since the Newark police department grants medical, but not religious, exemptions from its "no-beard" policy, the department "ha[d] unconstitutionally devalued their religious reasons for wearing beards by judging them to be of lesser importance than medical reasons."[22] In response, the department maintained that it gave medical exemptions in order to comply with a federal statute, the Americans with Disabilities Act (the ADA, adopted in 1994). In evaluating these claims, the court held them in tension. While it is true that the ADA requires employers to make "reasonable accommodations" for individuals with disabilities, the court noted, another federal statute, Title VII of the Civil Rights Act of 1964, also imposes the "reasonable accommodation" requirement on employers with respect to religion.[23] These parallel requirements in the law of reasonable accommodation reduce Islam to a series of rules. As an artifact of legal reasoning, Islam is regarded not as a transcendent belief system but as a set of ritual practices of traditional origin that applies to Muslims and not to others. As Michael King puts it, "Islam takes on an identity-in-law of 'legal religiosity', offering to its adherents an absolute or limited right to engage in prayer and ritual. . . . Muslims are accepted as different, but not so different that they cannot be brought within the ambit of the liberal state."[24] Once the transformation has been made and Islam is reconstituted as a set of rules and rights, it can take its "place in a legal world where [its] particular demands and obligations may be related to, compared with and placed in rank order with all other rights, obligations and demands."[25]

Another dimension of the court's influence in defining the "essence" of Islam in this case, allowing the one cleric to provide testimony to the effect that men are required to wear beards, presents only one Muslim standpoint. This suggests that Islam is monolithic and provides a representation of Islam that fails to reflect the considerable degree of diversity in the socioeconomic backgrounds, gender, political orientations, and religious practices among those who profess Islam. Yet this reduction to one standpoint is necessary for the law to be able to "reconstruct religion" as a set of rights, such as the right to wear beards, or headscarves, in ways that conform to certain religious obligations. If multiple versions of Islam were permitted to speak in court, a cacophony of voices would clash over what Islam requires, and then courts would have to evaluate the relative merits of each claim in order to assess the "true" representation.

"Culture" in Court

In the preceding section Islam was seen to be understood in the law as a set of essentialist practices (behavioral traits and customs) largely unaffected by history or a change of context. We saw how particular understandings of Islam became privileged in legal discourse, and how Islam has been reconstructed in terms of the secular meanings of the common law, narrowed from a religion to a specific set of social and moral obligations applicable to certain individuals and not to others. It became an external marker of a different system of meaning that had to be accommodated under the law. In this section we focus on constructions of "culture" that are connected to a specific sense of American national identity.[26] These constructions of "culture" as static, as a fixed and stable set of beliefs, values, and institutions, facilitate a certain capacity for positioning the United States in a superior location vis-à-vis its various Others (in this case, Islam), as a civilized nation now home to a host of "primitives" whose practices are portrayed as antithetical to the construct of American-ness. Through the language of alterity, an image of American selfhood is constructed within the broader context of cultural essentialism.[27] The examples discussed in this section provide a picture of American domesticity in an Aramco compound in the Saudi Arabian desert; U.S. prohibitions on female genital mutilation; an "incest" case in which the cultural meaning of family intimacy is contested; and the arranged marriage of two child brides.

A Rockwellian World

The child custody case described in this section does not involve Muslims directly but nevertheless involves the deployment of certain images of Islam in the judicial evaluation of a father's claims. In December 1997, Judge Eileen Bransten of the Supreme Court of New York rejected the efforts of Milo Lazarevic, the noncustodial parent of a six-and-a-half-year-old boy named Adrian, to stop Adrian's mother from relocating to Dhahran, Saudi Arabia, taking Adrian along with her as she settled into her new life in an Aramco compound with her husband and their two children.[28] The judge notes that Adrian's mother, Jan Fogelquist, has been Adrian's primary nurturer since birth and that the child has close emotional ties to his stepfather and his half-siblings. The consideration the judge says she has to make is whether granting Mr. Lazarevic's petition to prevent Ms. Fogelquist from leaving the United States with Adrian would be "in the best interest of the child." The construction of a particular (nuclear) vision of family life becomes apparent in the judge's evaluation of the child's best interests, and concepts of Islam as threatening, dark, and censorious play a subtle role in the construction of this idyllic vision.

Adrian's father, Mr. Lazarevic, is portrayed in the court record as an unemployed artist who has made no effort "to secure gainful employment" in order to support his son should Mr. Lazarevic gain custody. He lives in a rent-controlled apartment on Riverside Drive in New York, which he shares with several roommates, and is building a house in Coxsackie, New York, paid for by insurance money received after another house he had owned burned down. His financial worth is listed: $10,000 in assets and nearly $20,000 in debts. In contrast, Adrian's stepfather, who has been hired by Aramco as a civil engineer, is listed as earning $102,000 after taxes, and his new position will provide him and his family with subsidized housing, free education, medical insurance, and reimbursement of high school tuition. The judge notes that, while relocation to Saudi Arabia will result in a dramatic change in Adrian's life, the benefits (economic stability) outweigh the potential losses (emotional bond with father). In evaluating the child's best interests, the judge weighs the risks associated with the bohemian lifestyle of Adrian's father against the financial security offered by the boy's stepfather.

But the judge says that economic security is not the sole factor in determining the best interests of the boy. She continues by describing life in the Aramco compound in Dhahran in glowing terms, portraying the world of a Norman Rockwell painting, where the children run in the streets playing soccer, baseball, and football and families don't have to lock their doors at night. Judge Bransten also notes approvingly that Adrian's mother, Ms. Fogelquist, has chosen to leave a lucrative private practice as a psychiatrist in order to be a "stay-at-home" mother. The move out of New York City to Saudi Arabia will permit this nuclear family to remain intact, with the stepfather as civil engineer being the sole breadwinner. What draws our attention in this portrait is its patriarchal, familial character and how, in order to preserve a particular set of social relations associated with the American Family, these particular American citizens are physically displaced to an enclave in a foreign country. The larger this portrait becomes in the judicial consideration of "the child's best interest," the more it is assumed that Islam is, in the Derridean sense, the "constitutive outside" of the ideology of domesticity. As we will see, the court reasons that any barriers both Islam and physical distance from the United States may present to the maintenance of the privileges associated with being American can be surmounted.

For example, the fear of physical danger intrudes upon this scenario. Both Adrian's father and the law guardian representing Adrian's interests[29] argue that Adrian will be placed at risk of terrorist attack by the mere fact that he is in Saudi Arabia. The specter of the recent (June 1997) bombing of the Khobar towers in the nearby American military base in Dhahran, which killed nineteen American soldiers and nearly 400 other people, is raised at the court hearing. The father and law guardian deploy images of Islamic fundamentalism and fanatical violence in a general fashion, asserting that the Aramco compound and its residents are "sitting ducks in a volatile region already targeted and attacked by terrorists." Yet Judge Bransten addresses these images of danger when she writes,

> The court is deeply troubled by the prospect of sending Adrian to an area that might be a target for terrorism. Unfortunately, the court is also aware that there is no place in the world where a person is absolutely safe from a terrorist attack or, indeed, where a person is safe from an attack of random violence. After the recent assaults on American institutions, the World Trade Center, the Federal Building in Oklahoma City, and the nightly barrage of reports of children assaulted or killed by parents or by strangers, the court must conclude that it cannot insure Adrian's absolute safety anywhere in this turbulent world. It may be that Adrian might be as safe or even physically safer in the Aramco compound in Dhahran where Adrian will be in a secured environment protected not only by Aramco's security force but, if necessary, by the United States military which is stationed in close proximity to Dhahran.

The World Trade Center is the primary but not the *only* signifier of violence found in the judge's words. By imposing a broader perspective relating to security issues, suggesting that sometimes even parents pose the most dangerous threat to a child, the judge deflects the negative impact of the image raised in the courtroom of Islam as an inherently violent religion, although she does not suggest the concern is completely ill conceived. Rather, she relies on the presence of American troops, a physical reminder of the state's monopoly of force, to ensure the child's safety.

Adrian's father, Mr. Lazarevic, and the law guardian also deploy certain images of Islam and Muslims as being ignorant and censorious of art and information. They argue that Adrian will sacrifice the freedom of speech, freedom of assembly, and freedom of dress he would have enjoyed had he remained "here in America."[30] They argue that Adrian will suffer "deprivation of intellectual stimulation" and will not have access to the usual cultural outlets, such as museums and theaters. Finally, they argue that the schools Adrian will attend will not teach him about places and events that the Saudi government may feel threatened by, such as Israel and Judaism, and that the curriculum will place an emphasis on Muslim culture, while not offering instruction about topics that may offend Islamic values (e.g., European art). Judge Bransten states that, while much of this may be true, testimony at the court hearing shows that the American families already living in the compound deliberately vacation in places in Europe where there are museums and theaters so that they can "soak up culture" like a commodity or a nutrient in a well-balanced diet. She also asserts her faith in technology, in the capacity of the "virtual" to substitute for the "real," by suggesting that Adrian can gain access to "culture" through the use of computers, television, and videos. She writes that "the issue of cultural deprivation as a result of isolation is not as problematic as it may have been before the tools of modern life: Adrian will be able to share in the arts, theatre and music, if not necessarily in person, then through the use of modern communications." At another point she makes it a condition of the court's ruling in favor of Adrian's mother that, "before relocation is permitted," Adrian's mother and stepfather must "purchase and set up compatible computer systems" in Mr. Lazarevic's home and in their new home in Dhahran, with "dedicated phone lines in the child's bedroom" for the computer and a fax machine so that father and son can communicate.

The legal constructions in this case are complex and interesting. First, the judge relies not only on her faith in the power of computer technology and other electronics to stand in for "the real thing"—to substitute for the face-to-face communications that create family life, to bring "culture" into the home for personal consumption but also on the presence of "things American"' to assure her that the child's best interests are served in spite of the "Islamic threat" lurking in the shadows. Culture here is posited as a tangible object, something that can be partaken. This construction of the "child's best interest"—represented by information technology, economic security, physical safety, and western culture—takes questionable forms as it requires parallel ideas that construct Saudi Arabia as a cultural desert, as unenlightened, underdeveloped, uncivilized, and dangerous. The judge is assured the Aramco compound is an oasis in the desert, a sanctuary of domesticity in "a turbulent world," because of the presence of American troops nearby. She also resists the suggestion, raised by Adrian's father, that Islam is the only source of violence to be taken seriously; nevertheless, Islam remains in her view a credible threat. Second, concerns about Adrian's education are allayed in the judge's mind (and in the court record) by the fact that Aramco will pay the tuition for Adrian to attend a "first-class private school" in the United States or Europe when he is old enough to go to high school. The judge tacitly consents to the proposition that there is a connection between the word "Islam" and its associated meanings—forced ignorance and lack of intellectual stimulation.

The suggestion that Adrian's mother will be able to afford to remain at home as a full-time "stay-at-home" mom merits, in the judge's eyes, a thorough evaluation of the risks associated with the relocation from New York to Saudi Arabia. The traditional ideal of family, with its specific authority structure—the father earning an adequate family wage to keep a wife at home—is favored by the court and is (ironically) tied to the construction of an American national identity. The irony lies in the fact that this ideology of domesticity may have immured this particular middle-class American woman, and others situated like her, in the home within the corporate oasis of an Aramco compound located in Saudi Arabia, a society often discredited for oppressing women. This masculine-dominant, gender-normative discourse gives official U.S. sanction to constructions of home life that confine women to domestic roles as mothers and homemakers. Finally, finding that the potential "threats" presented by Islam—

terrorism, ignorance, and censorship—can be diminished by access to the familiar (such as American troops and secondary education in a western boarding school), the judge concludes that the child's interests are best served by relocation. The judge does not challenge the prevailing negative stereotypes about Islam that are marshaled in the father's custody claim. She merely weighs the alleged dangers against the measures taken to anticipate the threat Islam poses to an "American" way of life in an Aramco compound. The result is an American colonization of spaces for American nuclear families such as Adrian's to inhabit in what is argued to be a "turbulent" and "volatile" world.

A Cultural Defense

The path to judging other "cultures" is always a slippery slope. It requires the establishment of what Edward Said calls the superior location from which to evaluate selected characteristics and practices of the Other.[31] In the United States, "culture" has become an increasingly common defense in courtrooms in recent years, as defendants assert that a person's cultural background is a factor that must be considered in assessing penalties for criminal offenses. Most often the term "cultural defense"—a defense strategy that seeks the admission of cultural evidence to benefit the defendant—has been associated in the United States with practices that are patriarchal and harmful to women's interests and is affixed to immigrants.[32] For instance, in a Los Angeles suburb, in 1994, the attorney for a man who beat his wife to death raised the "cultural defense" by stating that the victim had violated the norms of their Iranian Jewish community by serving her husband a bologna sandwich on the eve of the Persian New Year, an occasion usually celebrated with a feast. Further evidence brought to light by the defense showed that the woman had constantly ridiculed her husband during their twenty-five year marriage, calling him "stupid" in front of relatives and friends and making him sleep on the floor—again, violating the norms of Jewish Persian culture, in which the man is dominant. In his opening argument, the defense attorney had promised the jurors that they would hear evidence "about a culture that is vastly different from yours and mine," one that is male dominated and religious.[33] Judge Kathryne Ann Stoltz dismissed the first-degree murder charges against the defendant in the death of his wife, finding no evidence that the killing was premeditated. The jury convicted the defendant on the lesser offense of voluntary manslaughter, and he was sentenced to the maximum prison term of eleven years.[34]

A very real danger of the so-called cultural defense is the chance that, when the defense strategy essentializes a particular cultural group by focusing on specific traits, such as the dominance of males in the story of the Iranian Jewish couple just related, the argument can be appropriated by the institutions of dominant society to make the subordinate culture seem even more exotic and inferior. It locates a pathology in a particular cultural group by choosing to concentrate on specific elements of "culture" that support inappropriate behavior, while simultaneously overlooking the presence of similar shortcomings in the dominant society. Male dominance is an important example of this double standard at work.

Female Genital Mutilation

The case of female circumcision has raised just such a selective discourse about Muslim "culture" in the United States.[35] In 1986, authorities in De Kalb County, Georgia, charged a Somali woman, whose profession was nursing, with child abuse for having cut her two-year-old niece's clitoris. In what was probably the first criminal case in the United States involving the practice of female circumcision (also known as "female genital mutilation"), the government lost its case.[36] However, subsequently, efforts to ban the practice in the United States bolstered a drive to get Congress to adopt a law that would make female genital mutilation illegal. Such efforts culminated in 1996 when, aided by much media attention to the plight of Fauziya Kassindja, a young woman from Togo who had fled to the United States to escape the practice, supporters of a federal ban succeeded in getting legislation through Congress.[37] Opponents of these efforts to criminalize the practice argue that it is a cultural rite no worse than the American procedures of liposuction, rhinoplasty, and breast augmentation, "morally on a par with practices of dieting and body shaping in American Culture."[38] For these cultural relativists, the criminalization of female genital mutilation is hypocritical, given both the obsessive focus on the ideal body image in American culture *and* the epidemic levels of violence against children in the United States. Before condemning the custom of female circumcision and "exoticizing" it, they argue, Americans must be prepared to be critical of comparable practices in American society and show greater commitment to safeguarding *all* children.[39]

Child Brides

Another case that caused a flurry of media attention arose in Nebraska in 1996, when the Iraqi father of two young girls, who were then thirteen and fourteen years old, was charged with child abuse because he arranged marriages for his daughters. Reported in the *New York Times*, the case of the "forced" marriages met with public consternation because the girls were married to two Iraqi immigrants "more than twice their age," who then took the "brides" home and "consummated the marriages."[40] The *Times* coverage highlighted the legal and cultural complexity of cases, such as this one, that pose the dilemma about how to prosecute "when religious traditions become criminal offenses." The accused were charged with and convicted of statutory rape and child abuse. At sentencing, the defendants argued that they had conformed to the norms of Islamic "culture" and therefore deserved leniency. Nine months after the arrests, the *New York Times* followed up the initial story by reporting that the two men "who married girls half their age in a ceremony arranged by the youngsters' Iraqi-born father" were sentenced to serve four to six years in prison for the crime of sexual assault of a child.[41] These news accounts consistently eroticized and exoticized the incident by emphasizing the difference in ages of the brides and bridegrooms and the "arranged" nature of the marriages, as well as the fact that the ceremony was presided over by a Muslim cleric. As in the case of female genital mutilation, the practices depicted here are without question a detriment to women's rights. Female genital mutilation and forced marriages position gender and religious tradition in tension. However, the generalizations about the "culture" with which these practices are associated are hegemonic in that they represent the deficits as culturally specific, rather than as the product of gender and class power relations experienced by women across cultural boundaries. Media coverage of such occasions arouse the suspicions of many Muslims in the United States about American hypocrisy because of the selective attention paid to "Muslim" crimes that victimize women and children. As readily available as statistics are about sexual violence against women as well as children in the United States, most Americans still maintain that domestic abuse has social and psychological roots—except when it happens within the confines of an inferior "culture" such as Islam, when it is viewed as being congenital or culturally based.

Incest

In 1989 an Albanian Muslim-American named Sadri Krasniqi was arrested for allegedly molesting his four-year-old daughter in front of hundreds of people in a crowded gymnasium in suburban Dallas, Texas. Krasniqi admitted to having placed his daughter on his lap and reaching under her skirt to "fondle" her through her underpants as they watched Krasniqi's son compete in a martial arts tournament.[42] Horrified onlookers who watched the father caress his daughter alerted security officers, who in turn called the police. In his turn, Krasniqi was horrified upon his arrest to learn of the nature of the charges against him and that his two children were being removed from their family home and placed in foster care. The case against Krasniqi proceeded in two stages: a criminal trial and a civil trial. The civil trial to determine the custody of the two children resolved much earlier than the criminal trial. In April 1990, a jury ruled that Mr. and Mrs. Krasniqi's parental rights would be terminated and that the children, ages five and eleven, would be adopted by Christian parents.[43] Mr. Krasniqi was acquitted of criminal charges in February 1994. Witnesses at the criminal trial, including medical doctors, psychologists, and an anthropologist, testified that there was no physical evidence of sexual abuse of Krasniqi's daughter and that the case was one of cultural and religious misunderstanding. The "cultural defense" in this case argued that, while adult touching of children is considered suspect in the United States, where pedophilia is criminalized, it is common in Albania, where sexual molestation of children is "unthinkable." The assumptions are that Albanian cultural norms do not constitute "touching" of children as a sexual or inappropriate practice and that "touching" does not lead to other acts that are constituted as molestation. While successful in winning an acquittal in the criminal trial, none of this kind of testimony was raised in the earlier civil trial in juvenile court.

Upon his acquittal, Krasniqi fully expected to get his children back, but the termination of his parental rights and the adoption of his children were final and irreversible. Many Muslims in Texas and nationwide were angered by the adoption of Krasniqi's children by a Christian couple. In September 1995, Muslim protesters rallied on the steps of the juvenile court, demanding a reversal of the civil court decision and an apology from Judge Hal Gaither, the judge who had presided over the children's case. In a letter to the editor, published in the Dallas Morning News, Judge Gaither said that he could not apologize for what had happened in his courtroom, that no legal authority can overturn a jury verdict, and that Krasniqi's defense was based on the offensive assertion that "molesting young girls is acceptable in Muslim culture."[44] In effect, the juvenile court judge had understood—and rejected as relativistic—the defendant's argument that sexual crimes are cultural and relativistic. Moreover, the defense strategy of trying to mitigate Krasniqi's culpability generalized from the specific case of one man of Albanian birth to allow for the possibility that Albanian culture generically allows for the sexual abuse of children. Finally, in his letter to the editor, the judge characterized the defense as an argument that summed up the idiosyncrasy not of one man nor of Albanian "culture" but of the entire Muslim world. The legal defense implied generalizations about the world's substantial Muslim population (estimated at one billion) on the basis the actions of one man precisely because the dominant discourses about Islam make such an account seem credible. The generalizations validate core images of Islam and Muslims already structured by law.

In summarizing the process in which legal Orientalism is reproduced in judicial decisions, I want to return to the privileging of particular constructions of Islam with which I began. When Judge Duffy attempted to extract and salvage the "true" meaning of Islam from the motivations of the criminal suspects in the World Trade Center bombing, he quite possibly felt he was only doing what was expected of him as a fair and impartial officer of the court. Yet when a particular interpretation of "culture" is associated with the authority of the state, what is the excess? Or, to put it slightly differently, as Dennis Porter asks, "What happens when [a jurist] encodes atomized features of an alien culture into the linguistic codes and conventions of narrative forms of a culture of reference?"[45] Are there social impacts of these textual representations of Islam? The jurist cannot step outside the discursive formation in which she or he has encoded that, for instance, compulsion in the name of religion is never permitted by the "true" worship of Allah or that the Qur'an requires men to wear facial hair.

Yet the hegemony of the law is never complete. Like most languages, the law is an open-textured system of communication, amenable to differences in interpretation. People can disagree over its meaning in given contexts; thus, the law becomes an arena of ideological contest. People grasp the vocabulary of this system of communication and sometimes wield it as a means of resistance, either rejecting the ideology of law completely or overtly challenging it.[46] Moreover, if we assume, as critical discourse analysts would have it, that texts have the power to constrain readers' interpretations because words are not neutral, then it is crucial that we try to understand the social meanings of texts.[47] My goal here has been to provide a description and critique of the textual strategies used to make representations of Islam in American law appear to be common-sense, apolitical statements, to be "taken-for-granted as the natural and received shape of the world."[48] In sum, the law provides both resources and constraints in terms of constructing narratives about Islam. The connection between the texts analyzed here and the politics of Muslim-American communities lies in the ways the law constitutes social relations, how it generates signs and symbols with which differences between the dominant society and minority groups within society are constructed and given meaning. Legal discourses are central to the hegemonic processes of governance, but they can also be a crucial resource in the construction of resistance, otherwise known as "counterhegemonic" discourses.[49]

A certain ambivalence toward Islam exists in judicial decisions and can be seen in an apparent willingness to credit Muslims with the moral high ground in some cases, but not in others. This raises doubts about the law's utility in the minds of many Muslims, and yet the rate of legal activism among Muslim communities continues to rise. Organizations such as the Council on American-Islamic Relations (CAIR) and the American Muslim Council (AMC) have been especially dedicated to documenting acts of discrimination, violence, and harassment against Muslims in the United States, and they devote some of their resources toward litigation. In 1997, a group of young Muslim lawyers in Chicago established a local, citywide Muslim Bar Association, which they say helps to serve the needs of their community and to promote the participation of Muslims in the American legal field. These organizations, with the exception of the Muslim Bar Association, tend not to view litigation as an exclusive means of promoting their goals. They are committed to other political tactics as well, such as lobbying Congress, holding press conferences, and enhancing public education about Muslims' presence, practices, and beliefs in the United States.

There is a connection between the emergence of legal strategies and key changes in demographics among Muslim communities in the United States. Muslims engaged in organizing advocacy groups, as well as those who are encouraged to file formal complaints of religious discrimination, tend to be young, often native-born Muslim Americans whose parents arrived in the United States from the late 1960s onward. This younger generation has been raised in a "civil rights" society and, while not entirely persuaded by the "myth of rights," demands more of the institutions of a democratic government than their parents' generation did. Rights are seen as more than mere abstractions; they are embedded within the social practices and relationships of the current generation. Groups such as CAIR, AMC, and others enact provisional closures around public representations of Islam and either counteract or elaborate them in order to project an identity politics beyond the reactive mode.

Liberal legalism posits that the law is central in establishing a liberal society organized so that each individual has a wide area of freedom in which to decide how to live. It presents an idealized understanding of American law in part by suggesting that political change is possible through litigation and by upholding those moments in which "law offers leverage to the relatively powerless" in society.[50] The framework of liberal legalism presents itself as the mechanism whereby certain values (e.g., equality under the law and the protection of life, liberty, and property) will be implemented. The representations of Islam that are found in judicial decisions may either become constraints on the promise of gaining positive rulings for Muslim litigants or be of sufficient complexity to present openings for a counterhegemonic discourse to develop. Perhaps more important, these representations being reproduced in the law may serve as a basis for challenge and contestation, leading us to reform the dichotomous structure of how we view Muslims' place in the new world order.

Notes

I am grateful to Professor Cynthia Lee, director, Women's Law Project, Mills College, and to John Strawson, a law lecturer at the University of East London, for their comments on an earlier draft of this essay. All mistakes are my own.

1. Excerpts from transcript of sentencing in *U.S. v. Ramzi Ahmed Yousef*, S12 93 CR 180 (KTD), 9, 12–14, and 18.

2. Ibid., 21–22, 23.

3. Yousef did not testify in his own defense. However, he did issue one statement to the press during his trial and granted an interview to an Arab newspaper in which he attacked American and Israeli policies and endorsed terrorism against the United States and Israel. However, he never claimed responsibility for the attacks for which he was prosecuted until his sentencing. See Benjamin Weiser, "Mastermind Gets Life for Bombing of Trade Center," *New York Times*, 9 Jan. 1998, sec. A, p. 1.

4. I emphasize the re-emergence of Islam as enemy because historically Islam played the same role in the formation of western (i.e., European) identity. Karim H. Karim ("The Historical Resilience of Primary Stereotypes: Core Images of the Muslim Other," in *The Language and Politics of Exclusion: Others in Discourse*, ed. Stephen Harold Riggins [Thousand Oaks, Calif.: Sage, 1997], 160) writes, "The *Reconquista* against Muslims who had occupied Spain, southern Italy, and Sicily, which required making common cause against the infidel Saracen, sharpened the sense of a European identity. The very consolidation of Western Christendom under the Holy Roman Empire and the papacy seems to have contributed to the rise of the Muslim as the primary Other."

5. Karim, "Historical Resilience of Primary Stereotypes," 166.

6. Ibid., 165.

7. Dennis Porter, "Orientalism and Its Problems," in *Colonial Discourse and Post-Colonial Theory: A Reader*, ed. Patrick Williams and Laura Chrisman (New York: Harvester Wheatsheaf, 1994), 150–61 (citation at 150).

8. Positive law consists of the legal *rule* laid down by the state and backed by state power, which may or may not have any connection with a moral or political foundation. "The essential feature of positivism is the view that there is no necessary connection between legal validity and moral defensibility." Mark J. Osiel, "Dialogue with Dictators: Judicial Resistance in Argentina and Brazil," *Law and Social Inquiry* 20, no. 2 (1995): 481–560, citation at 491.

9. National Public Radio coverage sensationalized the personalities of the judge and defendants in the World Trade Center trials, portraying the event as a series of skirmishes of global importance. NPR coverage represented Judge Duffy as a colorful, Pattonesque character, "irreverent, unpredictable, and not one to mince words," who had faced off with members of the Black Liberation Army and the Gambino crime family in previous trials ("All Things Considered," 20 Feb. 1998, Transcript # 98022013-212). NPR reported that, during his hour-long commute between his home and his office every day, the judge read books, including the Qur'an, from which he selected his text for Yousef's formal sentencing. In juxtaposition, the World Trade Center defendants remained all but nameless, unknown, and shadowy, menacing figures. Ramzi Yousef was repeatedly called the "mastermind," a word with a sinister connotation. The juxtaposition of the irascible but likeable figure of Duffy against the menacing bombers almost resembles a Hollywood script of a World War II movie.

10. For a similar point with regard to law use in the history of British colonialism, see John Strawson, "Islamic Law and English Texts," in *Law and Critique* 7 (1995): 21–38.

11. John Brigham shows that legal language is full of symbols generated by courts that influence how things get done. He writes, "by interpreting the authoritative concepts governing politics, the courts exert their greatest influence. By refining the language of politics they contribute to the association of what is possible with the authority of the state." *The Cult of the Court* (Philadelphia: Temple University Press, 1987), 196.

12. Michael King makes a similar point about representations of Islam in English cases in his essay, "The Muslim Identity in a Secular World," in *God's Law versus State Law: The Construction of an Islamic Identity in Western Europe*, ed. Michael King (London: Grey Seal, 1995), 91–114.

13. Strawson, "Islamic Law," 22.

14. Ibid., 28.

15. Ibid. See also John Strawson, Note, "Interpreting Oriental Cases: The Law of Alterity

in the Colonial Courtroom," *Harvard Law Review* 107 (1994): 1711–30. For an alternative point of view, see *Islam and Human Rights* (Boulder, Colo.: Westview Press, 1991), 10, where Professor Ann Mayer asserts that Edward Said's *Orientalism* "is not a concept developed for application to the field of law" (cited in Strawson, "Islamic Law and Legal Texts," 21). Rather, Mayer argues, this form of analysis is applicable only to literature, philosophy, and anthropology.

16. The Council on American-Islamic Relations (CAIR) monitors discrimination against Muslim Americans and annually publishes a report (e.g., *The Status of Muslim Civil Rights in the United States: Unveiling Prejudice* [Washington, D.C.: Council on American-Islamic Relations, 1997]) on efforts to defend Muslims' rights through legal activism. CAIR claims that the level of legal activism among Muslims in the United States is rising. See also Irshad Abdal-Haqq and Qadir Abdal-Haqq, "Community-Based Arbitration as a Vehicle for Implementing Islamic Law in the United States," *Journal of Islamic Law* (Spring/Summer 1996): 61–88.

17. Fundamental rights here are understood to be binding statements of duties to individuals, implied or explicit in the United States Constitution.

18. *Fraternal Order of Police* (FOP) *Newark v. City of Newark* (3rd Cir., No. 97-5542, decided 3 March 1999).

19. For exemption jurisprudence, see *Sherbert v. Verner*, 374 U.S. 398 (1963); *Wisconsin v. Yoder*, 406 U.S. 205 (1972); *Thomas v. Review Bd. Of Indiana Employment Div.*, 450 U.S. 708 (1981); *Bowen v. Roy*, 476 U.S. 693 (1986); and *Employment Div., Dep't. of Human Resources of Oregon v. Smith*, 494 U.S. 872 (1990). The *Smith* decision changed the legal landscape dramatically because the majority of the Court refused to apply the "strict scrutiny" standard in a case of free exercise of religion. ("The right to free exercise does not relieve an individual of the obligation to comply with a valid and neutral law of general applicability on the ground that the law proscribes [or prescribes] conduct that his religion prescribes [or proscribes]." *Smith*, 494 U.S. at 879.) However, the *Smith* holding does not apply in this case because the Newark police department already makes a secular exemption from the "no-beard" policy for medical reasons. The appellate court concludes that the officers are entitled to a religious exemption because the department already makes secular exemptions.

20. *Fraternal Order of Police* (FOP) *Newark v. City of Newark*, 3–4.

21. Ibid., 24 and 25.

22. Ibid., 19.

23. Ibid, 20.

24. King, "The Muslim Identity in a Secular World," 111.

25. Ibid., 108.

26. The word "culture" is bracketed in scare quotes in this text to highlight how contentious the word has become over the past decade. Once constructed in anthropological literature—and then disseminated at a more popular level by the print and electronic media—as a set of ahistorical and collective behavioral, moral, and aesthetic traits that represented a group of people that was integrated, stable, consensual, bounded, and distinctive, the concept of "culture" has been critically reinvented (Sally Engle Merry, "Law, Culture, and Cultural Appropriation," *Yale Journal of Law and the Humanities* 10 [1998]: 575–603). Cultures are now seen to represent "flexible repertoire[s] of practices and discourses created through historical processes of contestation over signs and meanings" (Merry 1998: 577). Particularly influential in leading this intense scrutiny of cultural forms and practices are the anthropologists James Clifford (*The Predicament of Culture* [Cambridge, Mass.: Harvard University Press, 1988]), and John Comaroff and Jean Comaroff (*From Revelation to Revolution* [Chicago: University of Chicago Press, 1991]). See also Steven Vertovec, "Multiculturalism, Culturalism and Public Incorporation," *Ethnic and Racial Studies* 19, 1 (Jan. 1996): 49–70.

27. Uma Narayan defines cultural essentialism as the problem of conflating the socially dominant norms held by dominant groups with the actual values and practices of a "culture." It

"equates the values, worldviews, and practices of some socially dominant groups with those of 'all members of the culture.'" ("Essence of Culture and a Sense of History: A Feminist Critique of Cultural Essentialism," *Hypatia* 13 [Spring 1998]: 87–106; citation at 89).

28. The case of Milo Lazarevic, Petitioner, v. Jan Fogelquist, Respondent. Supreme Court of New York, New York County, 175 Misc. 2d 343; 668 N.Y.S2d 320; 1997 N.Y. Misc. LEXIS 640 (decided 12 Dec. 1997). All quotes in the following are taken from this case.

29. In New York persons under the age of majority are afforded a guardian *ad litem*, or legal guardian, in judicial proceedings to represent their interests, which may differ or even be in direct conflict with the legal interests of their parents.

30. These liberties are founded on a social contract and codified law, as opposed to status and custom, the stuff of "primitive" modes of government, including Saudi Arabia's. For a discussion of this in relation to the colonization of South Africa, see John Comaroff, "The Discourse of Rights in Colonial South Africa: Subjectivity, Sovereignty, Modernity," in *Identities, Politics, and Rights*, ed. A. Sarat and T. R. Kearns (Ann Arbor: University of Michigan Press, 1998), 193–236. The court here is appealed to as the guarantor of individual liberties, and the question implied by Mr. Lazarevic's argument about sacrificing these constitutionally protected liberties is this: once the rights-bearing citizen moves outside the nation-state's jurisdiction, do these rights continue to exist?

31. Edward Said, *Orientalism* (Harmondsworth: Penguin, 1978).

32. The cultural defense holds that people who are socialized in a minority or foreign culture, who conduct themselves in compliance with their own cultural norms, ought *not* to be held fully legally accountable for conduct that conforms to the proscriptions and prescriptions of their own culture. There is a tension between the demands placed on the legal system by the increasing diversity of the American population for greater sensitivity to "multiculturalism" on the one hand and the "core American values" of protecting the liberty interests of women and children on the other. See Leti Volpp, "'(Mis)Identifying Culture: Asian Women and the 'Cultural Defense'" *Harvard Women's Law Journal* 17, no. 57 (1994), in which she argues that cultural evidence is often used in ways that harm women; and Doriane Lambelet Coleman's response to and critique of Volpp's article, in "Individualizing Justice through Multiculturalism: The Liberals' Dilemma," *Columbia Law Review* 96 (1996): 1093–67 (citation at 1093).

33. Cited in Thom Mrozek, "Manslaughter Verdict Sought in Slaying; Courts: Judge Reduces Murder Charges against Iranian Immigrant in Wife's Death." *Los Angeles Times*, 10 March 1994, Metro section, Part B, p. 5. The promise of a tale of a "vastly different" culture exoticizes the defendant's world through legal argumentation and cultural evidence.

34. The point of a "cultural defense" strategy is to have the sentence reduced, as happened here, not necessarily to get the criminal defendant acquitted of his crime. The defense is a legal strategy raised by defendants to mitigate their responsibility for criminal behavior on the basis of an impaired mental state. For information about this case, see Thom Mrozek, "Manslaughter Verdict Sought in Slaying"; and Mrozek, "Husband Gets 11-Year Term for Killing Wife," *Los Angeles Times*, 30 April 1994, Metro, Part B, p. 4. See also Margot Slade, "At the Bar," *New York Times*, 20 May 1994, sec. B, p. 20.

35. Although the practice of female circumcision is most prevalent among Muslims in Africa, it is important to note that it is not the practice of a single culture or group. It is also practiced by some Christians and by followers of traditional African religions. The origins are not entirely known, but scholars believe female circumcision to have started "in Egypt or the Horn of Africa more then 2,000 years ago, before the advent of Christianity or Islam." Celia W. Dugger, "Rite of Anguish: A Special Report; Genital Ritual Is Unyielding in Africa," *New York Times*, 5 Oct. 1996, sec. 1, p. 1.

36. According to an article in the *Atlanta Journal and Constitution*, the ritual cutting of female genitals has been a time-honored custom in more than twenty central African countries, Yemen, and Oman and among Muslim populations in Malaysia and Indonesia. Some persons argue that

progress in getting the practice banned in the United States is slow because of the intensely personal and private nature of the custom. "Many immigrants reject what they see as Western interference in a highly private matter." There is no consensus that the practice is prescribed by Islam. In the *Atlanta Journal and Constitution* article, a Somali woman is quoted as saying that she would not have her five-year-old daughter cut because "she learned that Islam did not require it." All quotes from Jane Hansen and Deborah Scroggins, "Female Circumcision: U.S., Georgia Forced to Face Medical, Legal Issues," *Atlanta Journal and Constitution*, 15 Nov. 1992, sec. A, p. 1.

37. A federal ban on female genital mutilation passed on September 30, 1996. The law requires that federal authorities inform new immigrants from countries where female genital mutilation is commonly practiced that *parents* who arrange the excision of their daughters, as well as those who perform the excision in the United States, face a penalty of up to five years in prison. Additionally, the law requires U.S. representatives to the World Bank and other financial institutions to oppose loans to governments in African countries where the practice of genital mutilation persists, unless these governments can prove they have instituted educational programs designed to eradicate the practice. See Celia W. Dugger, "New Law Bans Genital Cutting in the United States," *New York Times*, 12 Oct. 1996 sec. 1, p. 1.

38. Martha C. Nussbaum, *Sex and Social Justice* (New York: Oxford University Press, 1999), 121. Nussbaum is critical of the cultural pluralists' position, and suggests that American feminists have devoted "considerably more attention to these problems [of dieting and body shaping] than to genital mutilation" (122).

39. Hansen and Scroggins, "Female Circumcision: U.S., Georgia Forced to Face Medical, Legal Issues."

40. Don Terry, "Cultural Tradition and Law Collide in Middle America," *New York Times*, 2 Dec. 1996, p. 17.

41. "National News Briefs: Prison Terms for 2 Men in Marrying Young Girls," *New York Times*, 24 Sept. 1997, sec. 2, p. 14.

42. Jim Schultze, "Albanian Cleared of Crime But Loses Kids Anyway; Clash of Culture Catches Couple," *Houston Chronicle*, 17 Sept. 1995, p. 1. All information and quotes in this paragraph are taken from this article.

43. According to Mrs. Krasniqi, after they were removed from her custody the children began to wear crucifixes around their necks and T-shirts with sayings about Jesus on the front, and they ate pork, a meat forbidden in Islam.

44. Judge Hal Gaither, "I Cannot Apologize but Others Should," Letter to the Editor, *Dallas Morning News*, 21 Sept. 1995, cited in Farah Sultana Brelvi, "'News of the Weird': Specious Normativity and the Problem of the Cultural Defense," *Columbia Human Rights Law Review* 28, no. 3 (Spring 1997): 657.

45. Porter, "Orientalism and its Problems," 150.

46. Susan M. Olson and Christina Batjer, "Competing Narratives in a Judicial Retention Election: Feminism versus Judicial Independence," *Law and Society Review* 33 (1999): 123–60; citation at 125.

47. Stephen Harold Riggins, "The Rhetoric of Othering," in *The Language and Politics of Exclusion: Others in Discourse*, ed. Stephen Harold Riggins (Thousand Oaks, Calif.: Sage, 1997), 3.

48. Patricia Ewick and Susan Silbey, "Subversive Stories and Hegemonic Tales: Toward a Sociology of Narrative," *Law and Society Review* 29, no. 10 (1995): 195–226; citation at 212.

49. See Sally Engle Merry, "Law, Culture and Cultural Appropriation," 578, where she writes, "[c]ultural forms construct hegemonic understandings as well as the counterhegemonies that challenge these understandings." See also Comaroff and Comaroff, *From Revelation to Revolution*.

50. Richard Abel, "Speaking Law to Power: Occasions for Cause Lawyering," in *Cause Lawyering: Political Commitments and Professional Responsibilities*, ed. Austin Sarat and Stuart Scheingold (New York: Oxford University Press, 1998), 69.

13

Interface between Community and State: U.S. Policy toward the Islamists

Mamoun Fandy

United States policy toward Islamists cannot be seen in isolation. It is part of a larger U.S. foreign policy in relation to the Middle East. In the past, the cornerstone of this policy was the need to protect the flow of oil from the Middle East at a reasonable price, to ensure the security of Israel, and to fight communism. In a world dominated by the mediated images of CNN, Muslims all over the globe are informed not only by what they themselves write but by what is written about them. In this interactive global moment, U.S. policy toward the Islamists abroad and the reaction to that policy shape Muslim views in the West and about the West. The issues are not defined in a unidirectional relationship. Muslims abroad define issues at home, and issues in the Muslim world define the attitudes of Muslims in the West. Thus, it is no longer useful analytically, except for manageability of research, to make a clearcut demarcation between Muslims in the West and Muslims in *Darul Islam* (the house of Islam) locally defined. With the collapse of the communist bloc, the priorities of U.S. policy in the region shifted; while oil issues and Israeli security remain central concerns of American policymakers, fears of Soviet expansion have been replaced by a preoccupation with other sources of global threat and regional instability. In an effort to counter these new threats and to safe-guard American interests, the U.S. administration has promoted various regional ini-tiatives. As delineated by Robert Pelletreau, former Assistant Secretary for Near Eastern Affairs, these include "a just and lasting peace between Israel and its Arab neighbors, Israel's security and well-being, a security framework in the Gulf that assures access to its energy resources upon which we and other industrial nations continue to be depen-dent, non-proliferation of weapons of mass destruction, control of destabilizing arms transfers, promotion of political participation, and respect for basic human rights, end-ing state-supported and other forms of terrorism, promotion of economic and social development through privatization and market economies, [and] encouragement of American business and investment opportunities."[1] Although this exhaustive list ap-pears to encompass a justifiable if ambitious set of initiatives, the way in which they are prioritized and implemented bears significantly on their true implications for the peoples and governments of the Middle East.

Considered within the context of policy implementation, the principles embodied in these initiatives are not uniformly applied. The United States identifies certain state and nonstate actors in the region as partners and friends, while singling out others as threats or potential threats to American interests. Although Israel enjoys a unique and unconditional position at the top of the "friends and partners" list, Arab governments in the conservative Gulf monarchies, Jordan, and Egypt are likewise considered American allies or at least regional moderates. Regional actors classified as threats or potential threats include not only the governments of Iraq, Iran, Libya, the Sudan, and Syria but also nonstate actors, particularly those linked to a phenomenon Pelletreau labels "resurgent political Islam." As an overview of past and present U.S. policy reveals, this classification system is used to "frame" policymakers' understanding of regional realities and to guide the prioritization and implementation of initiatives. American policy toward Islamists must thus be viewed in light of U.S. interests in the region, the initiatives promoted to advance these interests, and the system of classification or "framing" used to determine and justify how initiatives are prioritized and applied.

The "Framing" of U.S. Policy in the Region

Regardless of the particular political unit in question or the particular geographical and historical context in which it is situated, leaders adopt and construct frameworks to guide internal and external relations. These "frameworks" are neither static nor uncontested; rather, they represent a *process* of ongoing identity construction, negotiation, and projection. In today's world, where the "nation-state" occupies a hegemonic position in political and analytical discourse, discussions of foreign policy usually center on interactions between the leaders of these states and other states or regions. Obviously, these leaders' foreign policy choices are based upon multiple factors, including perceived political, economic, and strategic interests within domestic, regional, and global arenas. The way in which these interests are *framed*, however, plays a crucial role in determining how a nation-state's power is projected. Leaders adopt and construct specific understandings of Arab reality and communicate these understandings to multiple audiences at home and abroad. These "understandings" or "versions" of reality serve various functions. In addition to providing a guide or framework for policy formulation and implementation, they imbue particular policy paths with authoritative and normative meanings. These authoritative and normative meanings play a central role in determining or justifying how and when material power is used. In the process, particular understandings of reality often assume a power of their own, as policymakers accept them as given and unchanging.

When divorced from reality, these "understandings" can thus preempt an ongoing and critical examination of the policy prescriptions they inspire. These policy prescriptions have real-world implications, particularly when followed by a nation that possesses extraordinary capacity to project coercive, political, and economic power. Because the U.S. is currently the archetypical example of such a nation, the way in which its policymakers frame their understandings of regional and global realities has serious ramifications both at home and abroad. At present, these policymakers are particularly preoccupied with an ideologically, ethnically, and geographically diverse group of individuals lumped together under the term "Islamists."

For decades, the script of U.S. foreign policy rarely diverged from the underlying Cold War story line. Upon the collapse of the Soviet Union and the eastern bloc, however, policymakers had no alternative but to drastically revise their understandings of regional and global realities. New enemies surfaced as old ones faded, and the Unnited States sought to stake out new normative ground in a changing world. While this process of identity adjustment and revision is a continual, contested, and interactive process, the U.S. government's emerging understanding of reality was most clearly articulated during and after the Gulf War. Visions of a "new world order" in which the United States would strive to protect national sovereignty and democracy within a family of nation-states served as the backdrop for American policy and action.[2] States, groups, and individuals who refused to abide by family rules (as defined by the United States) would be isolated and punished (at the U.S. government's discretion). International bodies such as the United Nations and NATO would be championed as symbols of global democracy and collective action, even as the United States used its coercive and economic power to maintain its dominant position in a hierarchical (and nondemocratic) world system.

"Framing" the Islamists

Within this context of ideological posturing, U.S. policy toward Islamists evolved and assumed a prominent place in the realm of discourse and action. As articulated in various speeches given by Pelletreau, this policy is intricately linked to fears that an Islamist regime similar to that of Iran will emerge in the Arab world, that Islamist activities will disrupt the political status quo in the region, and that Islamist terrorist activities will pose a mounting threat within and outside U.S. borders. These fears are imbued with a sense of growing urgency, as indicated in an address Pelletreau gave to the Council on Foreign Relations in May 1996. He reported that terrorist activities and Islamic militancy, which he views as virtually synonymous, are on the rise, stating, "When I asked our informal internal group on militant Islam whether its appeal is still growing, most replied affirmatively." In light of the alleged link between violent Islamist groups and the 1998 bombings of U.S. embassies in Kenya and Tanzania, this sense of alarm and urgency has assumed even greater momentum. Pointing to the Saudi dissident Usama bin Laden as the embodiment of Islamist evil, the Clinton administration launched an aggressive initiative against what is perceived to be a unified, global movement that targets American citizens and interests.

As articulated by Pelletreau, U.S. policy sees Islam in terms of two ends of a spectrum: "One end is represented by the faith of Islam . . . at the other end of the spectrum are a cluster of extremist groups . . . that practice violence and terrorism." The policy is designed to isolate these "extreme" groups as a way of protecting U.S. interests in the region. These interests center around Israel, oil, and safeguarding the stability of "friendly" regimes threatened by internal opposition. Even a cursory overview of groups labeled as "Islamist," however, reveals a wide disjuncture between reality and the simplified, dichotomous version of reality posited by Pelletreau. Because interpretations of "Islam" vary widely, an accurate analytical framework must account for numerous "Islams" rather than merely distinguish between acts of "faith" and "terrorism." These many "Islams" are indeed more than abstract religious doctrines, since they also serve as the basis for diverse social and cultural texts incorporated into the lives of individuals and groups. Even when articulated in religious language, these texts are linked to local variables and vary widely among different individuals, groups, cultures, etc. Grouping these numerous "Islams" into two distinct categories creates a model that is far too simplistic to be of any analytical or practical use.[3]

Even among groups readily identified as "extremist," the boundaries between terrorism and other religious and social texts are not clearly defined. By way of example, the Palestinian Islamist group Hamas is infamous for its violent attacks against Israel. To simply place Hamas in the "extremist" box and consider the matter closed, however, is to ignore local context and a more nuanced understanding of social and political realities. Hamas itself is divided into political and military wings and includes within its ranks leaders who disagree as to the appropriate role of violent action. Even more significant, the organization's extensive religious and humanitarian activities discredit dichotomous oppositions between "the faith of Islam" and the "practice of violence and terrorism." In addition to controlling numerous mosques, Hamas provides welfare and educational services to many Palestinians whose needs are not met by the Palestinian National Authority. Because the beneficiaries of these services have a vested interest in Hamas's survival, the group's human resource base extends beyond the ranks of its official membership. Thus, simply isolating "extreme" groups in the name of American (or Israeli or Palestinian) interests is not the straightforward task enjoined by U.S. policy prescriptions. Ignoring the complications of reality can create local instability, intensify existing hostilities, and serve the cause of polarization rather than peace—effects that are clearly detrimental to U.S. interests. This is not to imply that the violent activities of Hamas or other Islamist groups should be condoned but rather to argue that closer attention to local context would contribute to more realistic (and ultimately more effective) U.S. policy.

Carrying the isolation of extremists to the level of nation-states, U.S. policymakers have embraced dual containment of Iran and Iraq as central to American strategy in the Middle East. Iran, particularly in conjunction with its connections to Islamist groups such as Hezbollah, Hamas, and the Armed Islamic Group, is seen as a threat to the peace process and to the security of Israel. The United States has responded to this threat by attempting to alienate Iran politically and economically, while also taking measures to thwart Iran's weapons development and procurement efforts. President Clinton issued an executive order in 1995 prohibiting all commerce between the United States and Iran, citing Iranian support for international terrorist organizations and Iranian opposition to the Israeli-Palestinian peace process. Although Iran's current president, Mohammed Khatemi, has expressed interest in improving the level of understanding and communication between Americans and Iranians, the United States remains critical of the nation's conservative religious establishment and continued links to Islamist groups. In response to Iranian requests for permission to purchase more than $500 million in American agricultural products, the U.S. administration expressed reservations.[4] Despite indications that the request was intended as a goodwill gesture designed to promote warmer relations, senior officials insist that Iran is still supporting Islamist terrorism and taking other actions detrimental to U.S. interests. These officials remain too focused on Iran's conservative religious establishment and too preoccupied with potential Islamist threats to fully explore constructive channels for advancing cooperation and encouraging moderation.

In terms of Iraq, notions of containment go beyond political, economic, and military isolation of the current Iraqi regime. Whereas the term "containment" seems to connote a situation in which efforts are taken from *without* to halt the spread of a threatening force, the United States has assumed a much more direct role from *within* Iraq in an attempt to undermine Saddam Hussein's hold on power. This direct role is exemplified by the United States's and Britain's enforcement of "no-fly" zones as well as by U.S. financial and logistical support for Iraqi opposition groups. After launching its latest military operation against Iraq in December 1998, the Clinton administration made no pretense about its ultimate objective of bringing an end to Saddam's regime.

Although the rhetorical and military conflict between the United States and Iraq would seem to distract from a simple adversarial framework that pits American interests against a unified, easily identifiable Islamist threat, concepts such as "dual containment" are conducive to ideological conflation. Just as Iran and Iraq are lumped together as sources of instability that must be controlled through a policy of coordinated though differentiated containment, the various "enemies" of the region tend to acquire an aggregate identity and to assume mythical proportions in American discourse. As noted by Fred Halliday, "the composite Arab-Palestinian-Muslim terrorist" took shape during the 1970s and 1980s and persisted into the 1990s.[5] Indeed, the U.S. administration continues to situate the "villains" of the region in one evil camp. The contest in the Middle East, as outlined by President Clinton in a speech to the Jordanian Parliament in 1994, becomes one between "tyranny and freedom, terror and security, bigotry and tolerance, isolation and openness." By implication, both the Iraqi regime and Islamic activism are identified with the negative choice, and "friendly" regimes and Western-style secularism are identified with the positive choice. When reflected in policy agendas, this aggregation of "enemies" has dangerous implications. It not only perpetuates distorted versions of reality that have negative ramifications for many Muslims and Arabs in the Middle East and world but also leads policymakers to misread actual threats to stability, peace, and American interests.

The tendency of U.S. policymakers to vilify Islamists and to create an aggregate image of Arab and Muslim enemies has implications for domestic as well as international relations. There are at least four to six million Muslims living in the United States today (more than in certain Arab states), and Islam is American's fastest growing religion.[6] By espousing simplistic foreign policy agendas framed in stark, adversarial language, the U.S. government alienates many of these Muslim-Americans and indirectly reinforces anti-Arab and anti-Muslim sentiments and actions. Policymakers' aggressive rhetoric against an aggregate collection of foreign "Islamists" places certain domestic Muslim groups on the defensive and influences their agendas and discourse. If these groups feel threatened on the level of rhetoric or action, they are more likely to become a dissonance variable within American society. The confrontational tone and insensitivity of U.S. foreign policy toward Islamists thus perpetuates cycles of polarization, misunderstanding, and hostility at home, as well as abroad.

The Islamic "movement," "resurgence," or "revival" envisioned in U.S. discourse actually consists of many different movements, groups, and forms of social, religious, and political action. The very notion of a *return* to Islam is in itself misleading, since Islamist groups and Muslim governments are responding and contributing to change in the modern and postmodern world, rather than simply reviving traditional modes of thought and practice. Diverse groups with diverse agendas draw on the language of Islam as they react to and influence local, regional, and global conditions. Whether Islam is embraced as a means of maintaining the status quo or as a path toward reform and change, contextual variables are central to understanding the meaning of religious and political language and action. International links between Islamist opposition groups and between state-supported religious establishments do exist; the former includes networks such as that headed by the Saudi dissident Usama bin Laden, and the latter includes official bodies such as the Islamic Conference Organization, founded in 1972 and based in Jiddah, Saudi Arabia.[7] Despite the existence of transnational and international ties, however, Islamist groups, as well as Muslim states, pursue diverse agendas linked to their own particular interests. There is thus a clear disconnect between reality and constructed images of a grand battle that pits the world's Islamists against the United States and other western nations.

Counterframing and the Manipulation of the U.S. Policy Script

The use of foreign policy as an instrument for "framing" U.S. interests and regional realities does not exist in isolation. Rather, it is part of an interactive process wherein the discourse and actions of one system actor set off counterreactions and counterframing in the discourse and actions of other actors. The way in which the United States frames "Islamist resurgence," "rogue states," or other perceived sources of threat and instability are manipulated and recast through the counterframing efforts of various states and nonstate groups. Those who are adversely affected by American discourse and actions in the region take advantage of U.S. policymakers' confrontational, simplified versions of reality, as well as the contradictions between American principles and their selective application. They legitimize and promote opposition to the United States by drawing on the very dichotomous models that American policy scripts perpetuate, pitting the Arab world and Islam against the Western world and secularism. As a result, U.S. efforts to "frame" a particular version of the Middle East and Islamists reduce the effectiveness of policy initiatives and have negative ramifications for American interests.

For a recent example of efforts to manipulate and "counterframe" the U.S. policy script and take advantage of its contradictions, one need only review the discourse and actions of Saddam Hussein.[8] Since the beginning of the Gulf War, Saddam has sought to recast his confrontation with the United States in religious and pan-Arab terms. Deliberately conflating his own struggle against American forces with imagined civilizational and ideological clashes, he casts himself as a regional defender of Arab and Muslim interests. These interests, according to Saddam, are threatened by an aggressive, imperialistic western power intent on weakening Iraq as part of a grand strategy to dominate the Arab and Muslim worlds and to advance American and Israeli interests. As evidence that this grand strategy exists, he points to the pro-Israeli bias in U.S. foreign policy, the repeated failures of American peace initiatives, the continued suffering and suppression of the Palestinian people, and the devastating impact of U.S. policy on Iraqi civilians. Above all, he emphasizes that the victims of this strategy are Arabs and Muslims who are subject to unjust treatment at the hands of non-Arab and non-Muslim perpetrators. This simplified, confrontational version of reality draws strength from the simplified, confrontational images found in American discourse. By lumping Islamists together in one group and perpetuating an aggregate image of the West's Middle Eastern enemies, U.S. foreign policy bolsters the ideological credit of those who claim to defend all Arab or all Muslim interests in the face of a unified foreign threat.

Despite widespread fear and animosity toward the Iraqi regime in the region, the Arab public, as well as Arabs and Muslims in the United States, identify with the causes that Saddam purports to defend, resent the double standards that characterize U.S. foreign policy, are frustrated by stalled progress in the peace process, and sympathize with Iraqis who suffer under the weight of economic sanctions and military operations. For Arab governments to simply condemn Iraq is thus to risk weighing in on the wrong side of intense political, cultural, and religious debates. In an effort to safeguard their own popular legitimacy, Arab and Muslim leaders must contend with the terms of the discourse dictated by Saddam. Many choose to carefully position themselves in opposition to the actions of his regime, while supporting the greater political, cultural, and religious causes he claims to defend. The precarious political position of these leaders becomes particularly acute during times of regional crisis (i.e., whenever the United States launches military strikes against Iraq). In the face of the specter of a western, secular power attacking an Arab, Muslim nation, the boundaries between government and Islamist discourse are increasingly blurred. Despite American assertions that their quarrel is with the Iraqi regime, rather than with the Iraqi people, the fact remains that non-Muslims are taking violent measures against a Muslim population. Political leaders such as Saddam as well as the leaders of various Islamist groups, frame this spectacle in the language of religious struggle—language that Arab governments can not simply dismiss without risking a loss of legitimacy or even political power. On a practical level, this translates into an erosion of regional support for American initiatives and a decline in the credibility and effectiveness of U.S. policy in the Middle East.

Beyond Saddam Hussein's efforts to manipulate and recast U.S. discourse, numerous other state and nonstate actors employ "counterframing" techniques to advance their own local, regional, or global agendas. Militant Islamist groups such as Hamas, as well as nonmilitant Islamist groups such as the Committee for the Defense of Legitimate Rights (CDLR), a Saudi Arabian Islamist group that emerged after the Gulf War, draw attention to American double standards and espouse dichotomous, confrontational versions of global relations in order to advance their own local objectives. In the case of Hamas, these objectives include actively resisting Israeli occupation and exposing the failings of the Palestinian National Authority; in the case of the CDLR, they include reforming the Saudi state and exposing the failings of the Saudi royal family. While these groups' central aims are grounded in local, rather than international, relations, they coopt global discourse in order to bolster their legitimacy and garner popular support. By highlighting pro-Israeli and anti-Islamic biases in U.S. policy and echoing American discourse that pits Islamists against the West, leaders of Hamas and the CDLR give voice to widespread feelings of resentment and perceptions of unfair treatment. Like Saddam Hussein, they are thus able to manipulate the U.S. policy script in order to mobilize support and lend credence to their cause.

Just as U.S. policy "framed" by adversarial images of Arab and Islamist enemies has negative ramifications within the Arab-American and Muslim-American communities, so, too, do the "counterframing" efforts of political and religious leaders in the Middle East. By manipulating and reinforcing the simplified, confrontational versions of reality posited by American policymakers, leaders such as Saddam Hussein and groups such as Hamas exacerbate anti-Arab and anti-Muslim sentiments within the United States and contribute to the polarization of political and religious discourse in the domestic arena. The effects of counterframing thus transcend the realm of international relations to have an impact much closer to home.

Problems with the Current Policy

The problems with U.S. policy toward the Islamists are both conceptual and operational. At the conceptual level, policymakers continue to think in state-based, Cold War terms, disregarding differences between Islamist groups, as well as transnational economic, political, and technological changes. At the operational level, these skewed perceptions precipitate misguided, contradictory, and ineffectual initiatives.

Conceptually, the current U.S. policy fails to distinguish between Islam as a religion and Islamist activism, as well as between Islamism aimed at changing internal situations within countries and that aimed at the United States. The United States identifies all political activism that uses Islamic symbols as a means of mobilization as "terrorism" aimed at undermining the U.S. grand strategy in the Middle East. It fails to acknowledge that a multitude of Islamic and Islamist discourses and programs of action exist. Rather than attempt to differentiate between numerous "islams," U.S. policymakers seem content to make a much simpler (and contrived) distinction between the Islamic religion and Islamist violence. Although the United States fervently claims it has "no quarrel with Islam" but only with "terrorism," it is clear that vast populations in the Middle East and elsewhere do not believe this to be the case. The U.S. list of countries that sponsor terrorism is dominated by Muslim states: Libya, Iran, Sudan, Syria, and Iraq. It appears to Muslims that the United States looks at Islam only in the context of terrorist threats.

Even when policymakers attempt to distinguish between Islam as a religion and "political Islam," they tend to ignore the many forms of "political Islam" that exist. U.S. policy draws attention to Islamist efforts to instigate violent change by attacking "friendly" regimes and American interests, yet downplays Islamist efforts to create peaceful change from *within* systems of governance and civil society. In countries where Islamists are permitted to participate in national parliaments, such as Turkey, Kuwait, Jordan, and Yemen, groups have some space to promote their agendas and communicate their messages within a legalized, pluralistic framework. Kuwaiti Islamists, while not a monolithic group, play an active role in their country's parliamentary process and were particularly successful in the postwar elections of 1992, when they won sixteen seats (30 percent of the total) and were appointed to three cabinet positions.[9] Even when Islamists' access to parliamentary participation is limited through informal or formal means, many have sought alternative channels of peaceful change and political power. By way of example, Egyptian Islamists have conducted extremely successful campaigns in professional syndicate elections. While the Egyptian government has taken some measures to curtail Islamists' influence in the syndicates, their presence as an active force in civil society indicates a willingness to pursue peaceful change. By taking a stand against "political Islam" as a whole, U.S. policy ignores these and other examples of nonviolent Islamist activity.

This failure to differentiate between Islamists and "Islams" is compounded by inattention to recent change. In a world where time and space have been compressed by dramatic advances in communication and transportation, Islamist movements can not be understood simply as localized phenomena existing within "traditional" and non-western societies. While local context and indigenous issues remain central to Islamist messages and agendas, it is impossible to separate "the local" from "the global" and tradition from modernity. Increasingly, Islamist groups are not only projecting multiple messages to multiple audiences at home and abroad but also conveying these messages through new technological means. Cassette tapes, fax machines, radio and television broadcasts, and the Internet provide communication channels that transcend national boundaries and create new, hybrid spaces between "the local" and "the global" and tradition and modernity. The imagined lines dividing East and West are more and more difficult to discern, as people and ideas move in and out of distant and diverse spaces.

It is significant, for instance, that almost all websites concerning Islamic activism in Egypt, Saudi Arabia, Algeria, or Bahrain are operated from Denmark, London, and the United States. By way of these websites, Islamists have greater freedom to formulate messages of dissent against particular regimes and to project these messages back to their local populations, as well as to international audiences. Islamists who have been exiled from their homelands can thus remain in touch with local constituents and even acquire heightened status as they magnify their local and global presence via modern technology. The Committee for the Defense of Legitimate Rights (CDLR), a Saudi Arabian Islamist group that emerged after the Gulf War, provides but one example. Under the direction of Muhammad Mas'ari and other Sunni religious leaders, the group provided an organized forum for voicing widespread criticisms of the Saudi royal family's extravagance, reliance on western military forces, coopting of the official religious establishment, and failure to carry through with promised political reforms. Although the Saudi government banned the CDLR and exiled its leaders, the group continued to carry on its activities from London. From its new headquarters in the West, the CDLR projected its message back to Saudi audiences via fax machines and an Internet home page. Interestingly, other Islamist groups operating out of London influenced the CDLR's agenda and message, which gradually shifted away from an exclusively Saudi focus to encompass wider regional and international issues. Clearly, this case demonstrates the need for an understanding of the ways in which Islamists are utilizing new media in order to circumvent domestic interference, magnify their presence, and transcend nation-state structures—an understanding missing from a U.S. foreign policy discourse based on highly simplified assumptions about Islamist movements.

In order to bring the conceptual component of U.S. policy toward Islamists in line with reality, policymakers must address new developments in a world characterized by hypercommunication. Conventional understandings of resistance, political or religious opposition, and revolutionary or reform movements are often inadequate in light of modern changes. In order to understand and differentiate between Islamist groups, it is necessary to pay closer attention to the multiple spaces that they utilize to formulate and project their messages. These spaces are no longer confined to geographical locations; they also exist in the world of global technology, communication, and finance. Failure to account for this widening and diversification of political, religious, and economic space results in a skewed understanding of Islamist groups and misguided, ineffective U.S. policy.

On an operational level, the U.S. approach to the rise of violent Islamist organizations has been limited to militarily opposing terrorism and militarily protecting the stability of pro-US regimes. U.S. policy has failed to distinguish, for example, those groups that can clearly be characterized as terrorist but that do not target U.S. interests. In addition to being divorced from local and geographical context, the U.S. view seems devoid of historical awareness. The current policy fails to take into account either a long-term view of Islamism or a long-range view of U.S. interests in the region. Islam as a system of thought goes through historical cycles. In the past, when Muslim identity, culture, and modes of life were disrupted by outside forces such as European (and Ottoman) colonialism and western-backed Christian missionary activity, movements that claimed the mantle of defending Islam arose. The current rise of political Islam is in part a response to a perceived threat against Islamic values by western popular culture and by American military and political domination of the region. This perceived threat is increasingly acute in light of the United States's unprecedented deployment of forces during the Gulf War and continued military intervention in Iraq. Moreover, the constructed and confrontational images espoused by U.S. policymakers toward Islamists perpetuate and intensify Islamist groups' sense of threat, thereby contributing to the spread of polarized and hostile discourse.

Furthermore, contradictions in the implementation of American policy principles exacerbate existing tensions and misunderstandings. The U.S. backing of an inequitable peace between Israel and the Palestinians and between the rich and poor of the Arab world has led to heightened anti-American sentiments in the region, as well as to Islamist attacks on U.S. targets. American policy is generally perceived by Arab and Muslim Americans, as well as by people in the Middle East, as one of double standards. It condemns any Muslim or Arab transgression, yet fails to criticize Israel's blatant violations of human rights and its neighbors' borders. Whereas the U.S. government avidly denounces Arab and Islamic terrorism, as it did at the 1996 Doha Conference, it refuses to take a strong stand against Israeli practices that target Palestinians, such as collective punishment, settlement activity, home demolitions, and torture.[10] Even when there has been a clearcut aggression on the part of Israel, such as the April 1996 attack against civilians in Qana, Lebanon, the United States rejected the UN report that suggested that Israel might be accountable. In this case and others, events that do not conform to U.S. policymakers' constructed version of reality and dichotomous view of struggle are downplayed, ignored, or recast in more acceptable terms. To the consternation of Arabs and Muslims in the United States, the consequent double-sided nature of U.S. foreign policy is perpetuated at official levels and informally reinforced by selective reporting in the mainstream American press.

Muslims are puzzled by the fact that the United States has more economic and strategic interests in the Arab world than in Israel, yet somehow chooses Israeli rights over Arab or Muslim rights and even seems indifferent to human rights abuses inflicted on Christians and Muslims in the area. The only explanations accepted by Muslims in the United States and in the region are that (1) the United States is a racist and intolerant country that despises Arabs and Muslims, (2) the United States is not willing to deal with Arabs in terms of cooperation but prefers domination, and (3) Israel is the instrument by which to assert U.S. control over Arab destiny. None of these answers helps create friendly, collaborative relationships between the United States and the people of the Middle East. None of these help Muslims feel at home in America.

What Should the United States Do?

It is obvious from the foregoing discussion that American policy on Islamism lacks sensitivity and coherence. In the minds of Muslims, there is only one Islam, which makes American condemnation of political Islam while paying lip service to Islam as a great religion very offensive to Muslims. If the concern is still oil, Israel, and the stability of regimes friendly to the United States, then this terminology is enough to characterize some of the forces that threaten these interests without involving language that is offensive to both secular and religious Muslims. The lack of coherence comes from the way American policy is being applied on the ground. While there is respect for human rights in the policy, the application of this notion is selective. American policymakers should condemn Israel and other "friendly" regimes whenever they abuse human rights.

If the United States is interested in promoting a liberal and tolerant version of popular Islam in the Middle East, it has to deal with the root causes that make people turn to religion as a last refuge. Individuals and groups that have limited access to formal political participation and/or are experiencing rapid cultural transformation and economic hardship often seek alternative channels of expression and reform. In the Middle East, the available channels include societal groups that subscribe to discourses and agendas characterized by an Islamic consciousness. Thus, it is important to work with civil society organizations to promote specific programs of sociopolitical progress without imposing a non-Muslim ideology (e.g., secularism, consumerism, materialism, and disrespect for local mores and ethics) on the region as necessary means to modernization. The effort and money spent on military and covert "counterterrorism" activities to suppress Islamist violence would be better spent addressing the root causes of these problems in Muslim countries: poverty, government corruption, and lack of legitimate means of political participation for the majority of citizens.

It is also very important that the United States conduct a direct dialogue with American and foreign Muslim intellectuals at various level, instead of relying on third-party accounts about Islamists and their agendas. Such a dialogue would reveal a great deal to policymakers about the actual beliefs and intentions of the Islamists. This dialogue could be conducted, for example, by hosting Muslim intellectuals at American educational institutions. So far, America's relations with the Middle East lack a cultural cover. American policy has been implemented with what is perceived as contempt and by means of force. It is important that Americans show a greater sensitivity to and respect for the culture of the Middle East and Arab and Muslim contributions to human civilization. There is also another America, beyond the vulgar American popular culture so widely promulgated in the Middle East for commercial purposes. Middle Easterners need to see this other America. Interaction between American and Muslim intellectuals could assist in illustrating the humane and humanistic side of secularism—the nonviolent, nonsexual high culture of American society—as practiced in the West.

The United States should also get some distance on its apparent obsession with the Iranian model of governance. Islamists in other places, such as Jordan, Turkey Lebanon, Yemen, and Egypt, have participated in parliaments and have shown a great deal of responsibility. In Yemen, Islamists are partners to the army in governance, and no radical changes have occurred. The United States should study these models carefully and encourage what deserves encouragement and discourage only those who are genuinely hostile to U.S. interests.

It is important that the United States be wary of the manipulation of local regimes that attempt to justify American aid to them by claiming that they are defending U.S. interests against fundamentalism. Saddam Hussein claimed this and later showed his true colors. This shortsighted policy of supporting whoever claims to be against Islamism is destructive in the long run. The policy should be that the United States is willing to work with whoever is representing the will of the people of a particular country. It did not change a thing that the United States refused for decades to acknowledge that the PLO was the representative of the Palestinian people. In spite of this denial, the United States had to deal with the reality and later negotiated with the PLO. It now tries to protect the PLO from threats by other segments of Palestinian society. Fighting "Islamism" now (as well as insistence on a term redolent of religious bigotry) will only create greater problems for the future. The United States should respect the desire of other nations to choose whichever governments they want.

American policymakers should make clear to the American media that the target is not Islam. Disrespectful and bigoted reporting on Islam in the American press is certainly complicating the U.S. task of building cultural bridges in the Middle East and alienating American Muslims. In addition, through its intellectuals, the United States must make its case to the Arab people in the Arab media, not merely try to force the compliance of Arab rulers. Finally, to show that it cares about the human rights of Muslims, the American government must publicize the State Department's human rights reports of violations against Islamists, as well as against religious minorities. While these conceptual and operational changes in the American position toward Islamists and the Middle East can not automatically reverse years of official bias and selectively applied principles, they can provide a starting point in the search for more just and effective U.S. foreign policy that has a direct impact on the well-being of its Arab and Muslim citizens.

This is in no way an external issue, for Muslims in the United States now constitute a very sizeable minority that made its presence felt in the 2000 presidential elections. To be aware of the linkages between issues that connect American Muslims to other Islamic communities and states outside the U.S. borders and of the feedback loop connecting them is to avoid what policymakers call "the blowback effect." The connection between the Muslims in the United States and the Muslim world outside is very real and should be taken into account in formulating policies toward things Islamic.

Notes

1. Robert Pelletreau, Jr., Daniel Pipes, and John Esposito, "Symposium: Resurgent Islam in the Middle East," *Middle East Policy* 3, no. 2 (1994): 1.

2. President George H. W. Bush, "Transcript of His Address to the Annual Convention of National Religious Broadcasters on January 28, 1991," in *Just War and the Gulf War*, ed. James Turner Johnson and George Weigel (Washington, D.C.: Ethics and Public Policy Center, 1991), 142–45.

3. Mamoun Fandy, *Saudi Arabia and the Politics of Dissent* (New York: St. Martin's, 1999), 22.

4. Thomas W. Lippman and David B. Ottaway, "Iran Requests $500 Million in Food Items; U.S. Weighs Whether Deal Would Aid Ties or Be Unearned Reward," *Washington Post*, 19 Jan. 1999, p. A13.

5. Fred Halliday, *Islam and the Myth of Confrontation: Religion and Politics in the Middle East* (London: Tauris, 1996), 183.

6. John L. Esposito, *Islam: The Straight Path*, 3d ed. (New York: Oxford University Press, 1998), 208.

7. *The Middle East* (Washington, D.C.: Congressional Quarterly Inc., 1994), 188.

8. Mamoun Fandy, "Is Saddam a Threat to Middle East Security? Not a Military Threat," *World & I* (September 1998): 70–71.

9. Mamoun Fandy and Roy P. Mottahedeh, "The Islamic Movement: The Case for Democratic Inclusion," in *The Persian Gulf at the Millennium: Essays in Politics, Economy, Security, and Religion*, ed. Gary Sick and Lawrence Potter (New York: St. Martin's Press, 1997), 305.

10. Fandy, "Is Saddam a Threat to Middle East Security?" 70–71.

14

Multiple Identities in a Pluralistic World: Shi'ism in America

Liyakat Takim

Most discussions on Islam in America have focused on Sunni Muslims, thereby neglecting the experience of Shi'i Muslims.[1] As a matter of fact, it is correct to state that, even in academic discourses, most studies seem to equate Islam in America with Sunnism in America. This monolithic view has obscured the proper recognition and understanding of the religious experience of a significant religious minority in America.[2] This chapter examines the early history and contemporary religious, social, and political experience of Shi'i Muslims in America. Given the dearth of literature on Shi'ism in America, much of this information comes from personal interviews that I conducted with representative of the American Shi'i community.

The Early Shi'is in America

Studies show that voluntary migration to America by members of the Muslim community began between 1875 and 1912.[3] Among those who emigrated in the 1880s were Shi'is from what was then called Greater Syria, many of whom settled in Michigan.[4] At about the same time, some Shi'is also began to arrive from other parts of the Muslim world, including India and Iran.[5]

Between 1900 and 1914, several hundred settlers with diverse religious backgrounds migrated from the Middle East.[6] Many of these immigrants were Lebanese Shi'is who settled in Detroit to work at the Ford Motor Company. Immigrants from the Lebanese community continued to come from 1918 to 1922.[7] By the 1940s, some 200 Sunni and Shi'i families had settled in Detroit.[8] Khalil Alwan, a member of the Dearborn Shi'i community in Michigan, was born in America in 1930. He recalls that his father came from Lebanon in 1914 to work for the railroads in Cedar Rapids, Iowa, and in Sioux Falls, South Dakota. By the time Khalil's father moved to Detroit in the 1920s, many Shi'is had settled in that area. Hajjia Marium 'Uthman, who came to Dearborn in 1949, also remembers that there was a steady influx of her Lebanese neighbors and friends after she and her family migrated to Dearborn.[9] By the 1950s, the Shi'i community was dispersed in different parts of America.

The influx of these Lebanese immigrants led to the establishment of Shi'i institutions and centers of worship in America. Throughout the 1930s, Sunni and Shi'i communities arranged joint gatherings. This continued until the late 1930s, when the Hashimite Club was established.[10] Along with some of his friends, Khalil Alwan established an Islamic Sunday school in the mid-1940s. He recalls that, during this period, there were more social than religious activities. Around this time, Shi'is in Detroit would rent a hall to mark religious and social events. The Hashimite Club, as it was then called, served the Shi'i community until the early 1960s, when a permanent mosque was built. The first Shi'i mosque in America was the Islamic Center of America, which opened its doors in Dearborn, Michigan, in 1963. Shaykh Muhammad Jawad Chirri, who had relocated to America in 1949, served as the Imam of the center. With a population of about 35,000 Lebanese immigrants, Dearborn presently has one of the largest Shi'i communities in America.

While most of the Shi'is in America during the early part of the twentieth century were Lebanese, the present American Shi'i community is composed of highly diverse ethnic and cultural groups, most of whom have come in large numbers since the 1970s. Various factors have influenced their emigration, including the revolution in Islamic Iran,[11] the civil war in Lebanon, the civil strife and breakup of Pakistan, the exodus of East African Asians[12] during the regime of Idi Amin in Uganda, the Russian invasion and the ensuing civil war in Afghanistan, and the sociopolitical conditions in Iraq. During the Gulf War, many Iraqi soldiers escaped to Saudi Arabia from Kuwait. After spending some time in camps in Saudi Arabia, they sought and were granted asylum in America. Today, Iraqi refugees, who are predominantly Shi'is, are located in different parts of America. They come from Iran, Iraq, Lebanon, the Indian subcontinent, the Gulf states, East Africa, and parts of North Africa. In addition, a growing number of African Americans are converting to Shi'ism, having initially converted to Sunni Islam or to the Nation of Islam. There are no reliable statistics about the number of Shi'is in America; estimates vary broadly.

Lois Gottesman's contention that there are no more than 300,000 Shi'is in North America is palpably outdated.[13] M'roueh, in contrast, claims that, of the 9.6 million Muslims in America in 1995, two million were Shi'is. He further maintains that there are 256 Shi'i mosques in America, a figure that appears highly exaggerated.[14] Yasin al-Jibouri's estimate that the Shi'i community in the United States forms between 15 percent and 20 percent of the total population of six to seven million Muslims in America appears more tenable.[15] In the absence of accurate statistical data, it is impossible to verify the figures cited.

Larry Poston's view that Shi'is are confined to certain coastal areas can also be challenged.[16] A survey that I conducted in 1996 indicates that Shi'i communities are located in virtually all the major cities of North America.[17] The Shi'i community in America is relatively young in age. My survey indicates that the mean years of existence of Shi'i institutions in North America is 10.28. This suggests that the community is at an embryonic stage, seeking to establish itself in America.

The Role of the *Marja'* in the Establishment of Shi'i Centers

The influx of Shi'i immigrants to America necessitated the establishment of centers and places of worship to meet the needs of the community. As previously noted, the first

Shi'i center was founded in Detroit, Michigan, in 1963. Subsequently, isolated associations and groups were established to serve the needs of the growing community. In 1973, Yasin al-Jibouri founded the Islamic Society of Georgia and began publishing a newsletter called *Islamic Affairs*, which was, in the view of the author, "the most powerful advocate for Shi'ism in the country."[18] In 1976, the most prominent Shi'i spiritual leader of the time, Ayatollah al-Khu'i (d. 1992), sent a representative, Shaykh Muhammad Sarwar, from Quetta, Pakistan, to establish the Khu'i Foundation in America.[19] This marked the beginning of an epoch in which the Shi'i religious leadership actively engaged in furnishing religious guidance to its followers in the West. Eleven years later, al-Khu'i asked al-Sayyid Fadhil Milani to establish a similar center in London, England. Subsequently, more centers were established throughout America. Whereas the Ayatollahs have financed some centers in America, many Iranian-run centers have been financed by the Alawi Foundation. This foundation, through which Iranian politicoreligious ideologies and teachings are disseminated, has a major say in the overall direction of the centers. The World Federation of Khoja Shi'a Ithna 'Ashari communities, based in England, has also financed many Khoja centers in America. I have collected addresses of more than 150 Shi'i centers and mosques in the United States and Canada, a figure that is continuously increasing.

The Shi'i experience in America is different from that of the Sunnis because of the influence exerted by the Shi'i scholars and the institution of *marja'iyya*. A *marja'* (pl. *maraji'*) is the most learned juridical authority in the Shi'i community, whose rulings on the Shari'a (Islamic moral-legal law) are followed by those who acknowledge him as such and commit themselves to base their religious practices on his juridical edicts. In the absence of the twelfth Shi'i Imam,[20] the *marja'* is seen by the Shi'is as legitimately invested with the authority to make binding decisions for the public interest in the Shi'i community. He is also responsible for reinterpreting the relevance of Islamic norms for the modern era, which enables him to influence the religious and social lives of his followers. The process of following the juridical rulings of the most learned jurist (*a'lam*) is called *taqlid* (literally, imitation). It is the *taqlid* factor that has acted as the main catalyst for unity of the Shi'is, fostering ties between different Shi'i centers and establishments that often have been divided by cultural, ethnic, and linguistic considerations. Because of this, Shi'is are allied to the *maraji'*, rather than to any foreign government.

A corollary to the institution of *taqlid* is the practice of giving a fifth (*khums*) of one's net savings as a tithe to a *marja'* or his representative. The revenue generated from *khums* has enabled the Shi'i *maraji'* to finance the running of Islamic centers and the salaries of religious preachers. Traditionally, *khums* has made the Shi'i centers independent of government control, empowering their religious leaders to address any issue they deem appropriate. In the American context, the *khums* factor has enabled the religious leaders, although residing abroad, to direct the religious and socioeconomic lives of the Shi'is in America.

The *maraji'* are represented by their agents (*wukala'*), whom they send to guide their followers and to administer the running of the centers. The appointment by the *maraji'* of financial and religious deputies to act as their representatives has enabled the community members to engage in major projects to provide facilities for religious education for the Shi'i community in America. Major cities like New York, Los Angeles, Washington, D.C., and Detroit have sizeable Shi'i populations. It is in these cities that the centers have daily religious-secular schools, in addition to places of worship. At present, there are fewer than ten such schools within the Shi'i community in America. Shi'i religious schools differ from their Sunni counterparts in that the religious content of the courses offered is structured on the hermeneutic model provided by the Shi'i Imams.

The institutionalization of different centers under the leadership of the *wukala'* has also resulted in competition for *khums* money that flows into the centers. As noted, the earliest Shi'i center in New York was founded by the prominent *marja'* Ayatollah al-Khu'i. Besides providing basic religious services, it has a daily Islamic school where both religious and secular subjects are taught. After the death of Ayatollah al-Khu'i in 1992, al-Khu'i Foundation chose to ally itself with Ayatollah Seestani, who was regarded by many as the most learned (*a'lam*) after al-Khu'i.

Located quite close to al-Khu'i Foundation is the Iranian-based Imam 'Ali Center, which runs a daily Islamic school and offers services similar to those provided by al-Khu'i Foundation. Although the Imam 'Ali Center caters mainly to the Iranian community, there is frequent competition between the two institutions. Moreover, al-Husseini *madrasa*, run by the Khoja community, is also located in the vicinity. A similar situation obtains in Dearborn, Michigan, where seven Shi'i centers compete to render similar services to the local community. Shi'i institutions in America have become a source of dissension among followers of the different *maraji'*, duplicating services and competing for public attention and *khums* dues. When questioned through my survey about what they see to be the contemporary challenges confronting the Shi'i community in America, one center responded: "To get different nationalities to work together and to communicate with other Shi'i groups."

The religious centers generally affiliate themselves with different *maraji'*. Khoja, Pakistani, and Iraqi centers generally follow the rulings of Ayatollah Seestani, whereas Iranian centers follow the *taqlid* of Ayatollah Khamenei or Iran. Lebanese Shi'is tend to follow either Ayatollah Fadlallah, of Lebanon, or Seestani. Traditional differences generated abroad between the camps of the Ayatollahs have resurfaced in America, engendering further fragmentation within the Shi'i community. This was clearly evident when both Khomeini and al-Khu'i were alive. Followers of the two leaders frequently accused each other of abandoning the ideals of the Imams. Al-Khu'i, in particular, was criticized by the followers of Khomeini for being too passive and for not supporting Khomeini's notion of *wilayat al-faqih* (the comprehensive authority of the jurist in conducting the affairs of the community). Similarly, Lebanese Shi'is in Dearborn replicate the divisions that obtain in Lebanon and are frequently divided over the positions adopted by Ayatollahs Fadlallah and Mahdi Shams al-Din.[21]

In addition to differences generated by *taqlid*, political allegiances adopted abroad also impact the stances adopted by some Shi'i centers in America. The Islamic Center of America (Jami') in Dearborn is sympathetic to the cause of the Lebanese-based Harakat Amal, whereas Dearborn's Majma' is more closely linked to the politically active Hizb Allah movement.[22] Hizb al-Da'wa, a politicoreligious movement opposed to the Iraqi regime, has recently purchased a mosque in Dearborn. This center (called the Islamic Cultural Center) has been partially financed by Ayatollah Fadlallah. His call for active resistance to injustices is propagated in such centers.[23] The Majlis, which is also based in Dearborn, is Iranian influenced. It maintains a very strict dress code, adopts a more rigorous interpretation of Islam, and reflects views ascribed to Iran.[24] Centers run by the Khoja community in America traditionally maintain a politically quiescent posture. Hence, they do not reflect the political ideals of any Islamic country.

The preceding discussion suggests that, apart from the *taqlid* factor, differences among centers arise due to differing political alliances engendered in the Middle East. Although *taqlid* has united different ethnic groups under the leadership of a *marja'*, the fact that institutions are affiliated to different *maraji'* has often precipitated differences among Islamic centers. This is most evident at the time of celebrating the 'Eid holiday, when, depending on their affiliations, different centers often commemorate the beginning or end of Ramadan on different days.

Leadership within the American Context: The Shi'i *Ulama*

In an effort to unite the diverse ethnic groups that comprise the American Shi'i community, an indigenous council of Shi'i *ulama* was formed in 1993. Composed of seventy American *ulama*, the Council of Shi'a Muslim Scholars in North America meets annually to discuss issues germane to the community. Among the stated aims of the Council is to support the American Shi'i community by strengthening unity and cooperation among the Shi'a *ulama*.[25] In addition, the Council seeks to deal with issues that require the collective efforts of *ulama* and to defend Islam in general and the *madhab* (school of law) of the *ahl al-bayt* (the progeny of the Prophet) in particular. It further seeks to unite all Muslims by bringing various Muslim schools of thought closer to one another.

At the head of the central committee of the Council is an executive committee that manages the activities and affairs of the Council of Shi'i *Ulama* of North America. Although it has been in existence for seven years, the Council has yet to produce a body that resembles the Sunni-based Fiqh Council of North America. This is a body of *fiqh* councilors that seeks to "confront the many legal issues facing Muslims in North America."[26] The Fiqh Council further seeks to extract juridical rulings from the revealed texts and rational sources by employing methodologies of *usul al-fiqh* (principles for deriving juridical rulings). It may even depart from rulings stated by classical jurists.

The Council of Shi'i *ulama*, on the other hand, has not provided a comparable viable hermeneutic of the Shari'a. The Council has also failed to formulate any definitive direction for the Shi'i community or to bridge the chasm that has divided different ethnic groups within the community. A comment heard from many Council members is that they are too preoccupied with activities of their own centers to be concerned with the Council of *Ulama*. The fact that leadership of the Council is centered on a single individual and that it does not rotate among different Council members has made the Council inert and created general apathy among its members. The Council of *Ulama* also suffers from a dearth of financial and administrative resources. There is thus an absence of the strong leadership needed to direct the social, economic, and political activities of the Shi'i community in America. Many Shi'is are not even aware of the existence of the Council of Shi'a *Ulama* or of its objectives and mandates. As Yasin al-Jibouri, a prominent member of the Shi'i community, candidly admits, "Shi'is in America are neither organized nor united. The institution created by the *ulama* has so far failed to unite the community or provide it with any direction."[27]

As with other Muslim groups, there is a paucity of Shi'i *'ulama'* who understand the socioreligious challenges that confront Shi'i Muslims in North America. Few *'ulama'* in the West are conversant with issues relating to the local community or fully instructed in Islamic tradition to give an authentic Islamic solution to the problems faced by community members. *'Ulama'* imported from India, Pakistan, or the Middle East have little understanding of western culture or the pressures encountered by modern youth. Frequently, these scholars are not able to converse in English, and the contents of their sermons are deemed by many to be irrelevant to modern-day issues.[28] While the traditional *'ulama'* have not been able to address issues posed by the younger generation, Muslim intellectuals and leaders who have become a significant part of the American academic scene have been able to provide an interpretation of Islam relevant to life in America, as well as to the modern world. Shi'i scholars like Mahmoud Ayoub, Abdulaziz Sachedina, Seyyid Hossein Nasr, and Abdolkarim Soroush have been able to capture the imagination of many Shi'is living in America and abroad. In recent years, statements made by these scholars as a result of their academic researches have differed with views traditionally enunciated by the *'ulama'*, thus challenging their authority as the sole interpreters of the teachings of the *ahl al-bayt* (family of the Prophet). In particular, there is much debate in the Shi'i community on topics like religious pluralism, apostasy, slavery, the testimony and inheritance rights of women, and the correct mode of dressing for women. Views of Shi'i scholars trained in both the traditional centers of Islamic learning and the universities differ appreciably from those propounded by the *'ulama'*.

The community is becoming aware of the need for Islamically trained but indigenous American religious leadership. The range of activities that Imams have to perform in America has widened considerably. Besides catering to basic religious services, they are also required to provide pastoral care, counsel members of their congregation, visit the sick and needy, adjudicate disputes between members of the mosque, participate in interfaith dialogue, and promote a positive understanding of Islam.[29]

To produce indigenous scholars who can provide an authentic Islamic solution to the challenges of living in the West, some members of the Shi'i community established an Islamic seminary (*hawda*) in Medina, New York, in the 1980s. After completing four years of studies, many students trained at Medina are sent to Iran for further studies. Others choose to serve local Shi'i communities. However, the courses taught at the Medina seminary closely resemble the subjects offered in Qum (Iran) and Najaf (Iraq). Since these courses do not relate to issues pertaining to Muslims in the West, students who have graduated from the seminary have yet to make a significant impact on the religious lives of Shi'is in America.

A comparison with the Sunni experience in America indicates that Sunnis are influenced by mass movements from the Indian subcontinent and the Middle East that try to permeate mainstream Muslim life, using mosques as bases for their activities. The main objective of movements such as the Tablighis is to preach to Muslims, urging them to return to the *sunna* (teaching/practice) of the Prophet and early companions.[30] The Shi'i experience is quite different in that it is the religious guides residing abroad who exert much influence by sending their representatives to establish centers and to guide their followers. However, leaders are seldom equipped to direct the social, economic, and political activities of the Shi'i community in America.

Cultural and Ethnic Diversity within the Shiʿite Community

In America, the smaller, ethnically oriented, communally based Islamic groups appear to have more validity and appeal than the notion of a universal Islam that unites its constituents. The increasing number of ethnic immigrants has led to the fragmentation of the Shiʿi community. Instead of forming religious organizations based exclusively on Islamic provenance, other characteristics, such as ethnic, cultural, and even national identity, have prevailed. The process of ethnicization, involving linking a specific population to distinctive cultural characteristics,[31] is important to many communities, as it unites communal members and perpetuates customs imported from the home country. Thus, mosques have tended to fragment along ethnic lines, and leadership has remained tied to customs followed in home states. In the processes of cultural negotiations, involving redefinitions and reappropriation of a different culture, members of the Shiʿi community have tried out different ways to adapt to the American milieu.

The immigrant adult population prefers to cleave to the imported ancestral traditions and cultural practices, rather than cede to the demands of modernity or western culture. The younger generation, on the other hand, has appropriated a distinctly American culture, which has engendered a great deal of friction within the centers. A new culture appears to be spreading among Muslim youths—the American culture. As one youth states: "We are less likely to identify with the homesick mosque culture and more likely to assert a very active political role for the Islamic center, and to do it as an American Muslim community—not as an Egyptian, Pakistani, or Malaysian Expatriates [sic], but as Americans."[32]

The Shiʿi community in America is increasingly shaped by identification with specific cultural and sectarian convictions, defining itself as a sociocultural or ethnic entity that assumes a common regional and linguistic background. The linguistic and cultural bias of programs held at the centers also means that Shiʿi communities often experience Islam in a culturally conditioned form, marginalizing them from other Shiʿi communities. Many centers hold programs in languages that reflect the countries of origins of their members (Urdu, Persian, or Arabic), which serves to alienate Shiʿis from different cultural or linguistic backgrounds. The predominance of ethnic centers has also meant that integration within the Shiʿi community is confined to those members who share the dominant ethnic backgrounds. There are few interethnic marriages, and few Shiʿis have friends outside their own ethnic groups. African American converts often complain that, having converted to Shiʿism, they face discrimination by both Sunnis and their fellow Shiʿis. Ethnicity and rituals endemic to a particular community have become the main categories of identification in America.

Diversity has made it difficult for Shiʿi centers to create a common agenda to direct the lives of community members. In large cities like New York and Los Angeles, Iranian, Pakistani, Iraqi, Lebanese, and Khoja mosques exist with little interaction between them. It is only in smaller Shiʿi communities that pluralistic centers can be found. In Indianapolis, Seattle, and Austin, for example, the ethnic divide is almost nonexistent, as different ethnic Shiʿi groups coalesce under the common banner of the ahl al- bayt. Others may even hold joint religious programs with local Sunni communities.

It is important to bear in mind that the ethnic factor is more accentuated in Shiʿism than in Sunnism. Whereas Sunni religious events generally are confined to prayers in which Muslims from different ethnic backgrounds in the diaspora congregate, the Shi'i calendar is punctuated with events that mark the birth and death dates of Imams.[33] These events are commemorated differently by the various Shi'i communities. Thus, Pakistani Shi'is who congregate at the *Husayniyya*[34] mark occasions like the martyrdom of Husayn ibn 'Ali, the grandson of the Prophet, differently from Iraqi or Iranian Shi'is. Shi'is from the Indian subcontinent and from East Africa reenact the events in Kerbala with their own culturally generated symbols and modes of expression. These include representations of the flag of 'Abbas[35] (*'alam*) and the cradle of Husayn's six-month-old child. These symbolic representations of events in Kerbala are alien to Arab and Iranian Shi'is. Acts of kissing and expressions of reverence to these symbols are often rejected by Shi'is from the Middle East, who view them as subtle forms of idolatry.

To unite the different Shi'i ethnic entities, the *ahl al-bayt* assembly of America was formed in 1996. The stated aim of the assembly is to promote Islamic teachings according to the Qur'an and *Sunnah* as interpreted by the household of the Prophet. The assembly's mandate also requires it to introduce Islamic education, to produce and distribute Islamic literature, and to communicate with the media to provide an Islamic perspective on news items that affect the Muslim world. Since its founding, the *ahl al-bayt* assembly has serviced the needs of the Shi'i community in Washington, D.C. However, it has failed to realize its goal of uniting the Shi'i community in America. The attempted unification of different ethnic centers under an eclectic and centralized institute that would provide strong leadership for the American Shi'i community still remains a distant dream.

Shi'i Interaction with Non-Muslim Communities: Interfaith Dialogue

The challenge for American Shi'is is twofold: to ensure that the younger generation within the community does not get assimilated with the West and to ensure that it is not influenced by anti-Shi'i propaganda instigated by Wahhabis. In America, Shi'is have been more concerned with maintaining their distinct communal and sectarian identity than with engaging in dialogue with other faith groups. Moreover, since they form a small percentage of the wider Muslim community in America, the primary focus of the Shi'i community has been the preservation rather than the extension of its spiritual boundaries. This assertion is supported by responses to a question posed in my survey. Few Shi'i centers are involved in any extensive dialogue with other Muslim or non-Muslim communities. Instead, they stress the provision of basic religious services to members, thus accentuating the distinct beliefs and rituals of Shi'i Islam. It should be noted that, since Shi'is do not engage in interfaith dialogue in their own countries of origins, they have not been able to construct an effective medium of dialogue with non-Muslims in America. In their own countries, many Shi'is have been trained to vindicate the preponderance of Shi'i faith and liturgical practices over corresponding Sunni praxis. The emphasis on sectarian polemics in their own countries has limited the exposure that Shi'is have to other monotheistic religions.

The focus on preservation rather than on extension of boundaries is further corroborated by my survey, which indicates that most converts from the African American community convert to Shi'ism as a result of their own research, rather than due to extensive proselytization activities from the Shi'i community. Shi'i missionary outreach has been limited to a few poorly funded organizations that are not properly structured for extensive *da'wa* (proselytization).[36] Thus, unlike the Sunni experience, Shi'i discourse in the American public square is extremely limited. It is correct to state that American Shi'is are introverted, rather than outwardly directed. The activities of most centers are directed to providing basic religious services like prayers, weddings, and funerals for community members.

Because of the negative western view of Islam in general and Shi'ism in particular, some Shi'i centers have initiated dialogue with local communities to promote a more tolerant understanding of their faith. The Islamic Education Council of Maryland, for example, organizes annual interfaith events that discuss topics that affect other faith groups in America. Issues like marriage and the importance of inculcating proper values in young people have been discussed with local Christian and Jewish communities. The Khu'i Foundation of New York also participates in a number of national and international interfaith and intrafaith initiatives. The Islamic House of Wisdom (IHW), in Dearborn, is more open to interfaith dialogue and adopts a more liberal view of American society since the Imam of the center, Imam Elahi, is considered to be "liberal" and "open-minded." Accommodation to American society or refusal to compromise with the West vary with the origins and outlook of the Imams who serve a center. IHW's community newsletter of December 1998, called *Salaam*, proudly states: "With the spirit of giving thanks to God for all His blessings, the Islamic House of Wisdom opened its doors to metro Detroit's premier interfaith event: the Interfaith Family Celebration of Thanksgiving on Wednesday evening, November 25 [1998]." It goes on to quote Imam Elahi as saying: "Islam is the most misunderstood religion in this country and hopefully by showing our openness, respect and love for our guests, we will have an opportunity to remove some of this misinformation about our faith."

Areas that have a sizeable Shi'i community engage in more dialogue with other communities. Institutions like the Islamic House of Wisdom in Detroit broadcast lectures on television. In Los Angeles, Christians and Jews have been invited to mosques to participate in interfaith dialogue.

Shi'i Political Discourse in America

In the classical period of Islam, Shi'i jurists, like their Sunni counterparts, divided the world into the realms of belief (*dar al-Islam*) and unbelief (*dar al-kufr*). It was assumed that Muslims would live in *dar al-Islam*, and, if they ventured into *dar al-kufr*, it would be on a temporary basis for specific purposes. A Muslim residing permanently in *dar al-kufr* seemed to be an anomaly.[37]

In the contemporary period, adverse social, political, and economic conditions in their country of origins have forced Shi'is to settle in the West on a permanent basis. As a matter of fact, since there is nothing in the revealed texts that explicitly forbids Shi'is from living in non-Muslim states, the *maraji'* have not prohibited their followers from becoming citizens of non-Muslim countries. On the contrary, they have urged their followers to become law-abiding citizens of the country in which they choose to live.[38]

Thus, there is little discussion in Shi'i circles in America as to whether it is legally permissible to become a citizens of a non-Muslim country. Most have used the legal system to apply for citizenship.

The question of political participation by the American Shi'i community is premised on two important considerations. Traditionally, Shi'is have eschewed political involvement, because Shi'i political theory is based on a hermeneutical structure that deems all governments in the prolonged absence of the twelfth Imam to be illegitimate.[39] Because of this, even in their own countries, most Shi'is have remained politically inactive. Lack of Shi'i involvement in the American political process can also be explained by the relatively young age of the centers. Since most Shi'i centers in America have been established since 1985,[40] Shi'is have used their limited financial resources to build and consolidate their centers, rather than to engage in projects outside the community.

Traditional Shi'i aversion to American politics can be seen in the following anecdote. In 1996, there was a major discussion on the Shi'i-based Internet discussion group called the Ahl al-Bayt Discussion Group (ABDG) as to whether Shi'is should support candidates running for federal elections. The majority felt that, since they were living in a non-Muslim country, Shi'is should eschew all political involvement. Others even argued that, given American support of Israel, voting for a candidate would be tantamount to supporting the Israeli cause. Therefore, they decreed that it was *haram* (religiously prohibited) to support or vote for a political candidate. A small minority disagreed, arguing that voting for a candidate of their choice might help the Shi'i cause in America and perhaps influence American foreign policy.

According to al-Sayyid Mustafa al-Qazwini, an Imam of a Shi'i center in Orange County, California, few if any Shi'i mosques have considered engaging in interfaith dialogue or involvement in the American political discourse on a regular basis.[41] In a few isolated cases, some Shi'is have nominated themselves to run for Congress by seeking votes from local Shi'i and Sunni communities. However, most of these candidates run independently and are not directly supported by any Shi'i institute. An example of such a candidate is Habib M. Habib, a Shi'i from East Africa. He was appointed to the Washington State Commission on Asian-Pacific American Affairs by the state governor, Gary Lock. The group started as an advisory council to the governor, and the legislature made it a statutory body to address state policy issues that involve Asia. It is in this capacity that Habib also deals with matters that affect Muslim interests. Habib aims to be involved in the political system as a Muslim legislator, for it is in the legislature, rather than in the executive branch, that Muslims can fight for equal rights, education, and fair immigration laws, while opposing unjust and morally indefensible laws. As Habib says: "As legislators and politicians, Muslims will be able to effectively define themselves and their values. This will prevent others, who have agendas of their own, from defining Muslims."[42] Habib frequently lectures to the Muslim community, seeking its support in his political activities.

Shi'i political aspirations in America have yet to crystallize into a concrete body with a properly formulated political agenda. In the absence of such political institutes, political activism manifests itself in public discourse on moral and social issues that impact the Muslim community. In Dearborn, an advertisement in the November 1998 issue of the newsletter of the Islamic Center of America (ICA), called *Islamic Insights*, urged its readers to go to the polls to vote against a proposal that seeks to legalize assisted suicides. "As Muslims we have a responsibility to the society in which we live. . . . Go to the polls on November 3."

Like many other Imams in Dearborn, Imam al-Hasan al-Qazwini, of ICA, encourages the community to be more politically active, especially in local elections. When the local school board planned an expansion project that was against the interests of the Muslim community, local Sunni and Shi'i communities rallied together to defeat the scheme. Gradually, Muslims are gaining influence over policies adopted by local school boards.

Participation by local mosques and centers in the American political process is not restricted to lobbying. Some mosques are fostering closer ties with local political figures so that their particular concerns are addressed. The October 1999 edition of the newsletter of the Islamic House of Wisdom (IHW), entitled *Salaam*, contains a letter from Senator Spencer Abraham, of Michigan. The senator states that he is "sponsoring the first congressional resolution regarding tolerance towards Islam that is aimed at expressing Congress' view of religious tolerance in America today." The resolution further calls on Congress to take the lead in condemning anti-Muslim tolerance and discrimination and recognizes the contributions of Islam. The fact that Senator Abraham informed the Muslim community in Detroit of his pro-Muslim political stance is indicative of the closer ties being fostered by some centers with local politicians. Increasingly, American politicians are acknowledging the need to rely on Muslim support in their constituencies. The March 1999 issue of the Islamic Center of America journal *Islamic Insights* carried 'Eid greetings from the state representative to the local Muslim community. 'Eid greetings were also sent by Governor John Engler, of Michigan. The governor had initially sought support from the Michigan Muslim community in running for his post. He attributed his victory in part to the support he received from the local Muslim community.

The Islamic Center of America of Dearborn also tried to build relations with candidates running for nomination in the 2000 election. George W. Bush was invited by Imam al-Hasan al-Qazwini to visit the Islamic center in Detroit. When Vice President Al Gore wanted to meet representatives of the Muslim community in Michigan, he was introduced to Imam al-Hasan Qazwini. The Imam encouraged him to include more Arabs and Muslims in his administration. The encounter with the vice president led to the Imam's being invited to a breakfast meeting arranged for religious leaders at the White House. The Imam was the first Shi'i leader to receive such an invitation. President Bill Clinton affirmed his support for Islam and Muslims and encouraged Muslims to participate in the political process.[43]

Increasing political activism in the Detroit community is apparent from the fact that many community members are politically engaged with Arab organizations. The Arab American Political Committee (APAC), in Detroit, has lobbied for certain political issues. Although most APAC members are Shi'is, they prefer to identify themselves as an Arab, rather than as an Islamic, political entity. In all probability, this is to avoid stereotypical images associated with Islamic organizations.

In some areas of America, Shi'i political activity has taken the form of establishing eclectic bodies that transgress sectarian boundaries, cooperating with Sunnis to create a unified and effective challenge for local posts. Shi'i institutions like the al-Khu'i Foundation, in New York, have persuaded its members that their votes and involvement in political processes can make a difference to their lives in America. Thus, some Shi'is cooperate with Sunnis to provide Muslim candidates for school boards and municipal posts and work for the election of Muslim mayors and state legislators. The intent is to get Shi'is to vote for fellow Muslim candidates, planning for an eventual Muslim presence in Congress or the Senate. As a political commentator said: "The onus of repositioning Islam as an element of American national interest and not a threat to it lies with the American Muslims."[44]

Some Shi'is have also allied themselves with the Sunni-based American Muslim Council (AMC). Dr. Ahmad Hashim, a Shi'i proselyte living in Maryland, recalls how he used the offices of AMC to write to senators who made statements deemed offensive by Muslims. Like Dr. Hashim, many Shi'is have subscribed to the mailing list of the Council on American-Islamic Relations (CAIR) and have taken positive steps to defend Muslim interests, condemning the initial indifference of the United Nations to the Bosnian crisis.[45] They have even taken CAIR's advise to seek out "Muslim-friendly" candidates in the election years. However, due to financial and administrative constraints, Shi'i political exertions have yet to concretize into independent political bodies or lobby groups that represent their political aspirations in America.

A key consideration in Shi'i politically motivated activities is the desire to influence American foreign policy, especially as it impacts Muslim countries. Shi'is have often felt the need to voice their concerns about American foreign policies, especially those that pertain to Iraq. While Shi'is do not support Saddam Hussein, they also do not condone American policy in support of economic sanctions that continue to impoverish the Iraqi people. Such instances have forced Shi'is to abandon their traditional ambivalent stance toward political intervention.

Shi'i encroachment in the political arena in order to safeguard the interests of Muslim countries is evidenced in the fact that al-Khu'i Foundation of New York enjoys Non Government Organization (NGO) status with the United Nations. In 1997, the Foundation applied for General (Category 1) Consultative Status at the Economic and Social Council of the United Nations (ECOSOC) at UN headquarters in New York. In 1998, Sayyed Nadeem Kazmi was appointed as the Foundation's representative to ECOSOC. Since it enjoys a general consultative status, the Foundation is allowed to observe UN proceedings and to make submissions on important issues. When the Taliban government in Afghanistan turned against the Hazara Shi'i community in North Afghanistan, the Foundation's NGO representative was quick to alert member states in the United Nations Council about the religious discrimination endured by the Shi'is in Afghanistan. The Foundation's representative also connects with ECOSOC and other UN bodies, identifying UN priorities and themes and linking those with the Foundation's own agenda and program of activities. These include combating racism and HIV/AIDS, creating mutual understanding between different cultures, ethnicities, and religions, and working for equality of access to education and the eradication of poverty. Existing projects of the Foundation also provide humanitarian services, foster adult literacy, distribute aid, and support education to help reduce "Islamophobia" in the media. In addition, al-Khu'i Foundation also provides other humanitarian services through its affiliation with Amnesty International Religious Bodies Liaison Panel. In December 1997, the Foundation hosted United Nations Human Rights Day.[46]

The past decade has witnessed the immigration of diverse Shi'i communities to America. The major challenge that the community has faced is in translating a majority religion to an area in which it is a nascent minority.

As a community that exists as a distinct minority within the minority Muslim community in America, Shi'is experience a heightened sense of alienation as the identity of its members is hyphenated and broken into many components. The identity of a Shi'i from Pakistan, for example, is Pakistani-Shi'i-Muslim-American. As has been illustrated, the problem of identity that confronts Shi'is in America is greater than that facing the Sunnis, because the Shi'is seek not only to assert their Islamic identity in the West but also to maintain their own distinct Shi'i identity. It is therefore correct to say that Shi'is are in a double (and sometimes even triple) minority status.

The preceding discussion indicates that, like the rest of the Muslim community, the Shi'i community is characterized more by diversity than by homogeneity. The community includes immigrants who cleave to the tradition and culture of their ancestors and those who are willing to adopt some western ways. Differences in culture and ways of responding to the Islamic message arise not only within centers but also among them. The ethnic divide within the Shi'i community is most obvious in cities that have large Shi'i populations. Instead of integrated religious gatherings, it is the racial-ethnic identity that is accentuated in Shi'i mosques in America.

The struggle of American Shi'is to define themselves, to give meaning to their new identity as American Muslims, and to acknowledge the new sociopolitical context of their existence is manifesting itself in tensions between traditional and modern, intellectual and conservative, indigenous and immigrant, and young and old, as well as between Sunni and Shi'i Muslims. The community is also composed of youths and African American converts who identify with an American culture. Indigenous conflicts have arisen as the immigrant community has had to come to terms with an alien culture. Discussion on whether to assimilate into or to try to remain isolated from western culture has created much dissension between the older and younger generations within the community.

Notes

1. In this chapter, the term Shi'i is used to refer to Twelver Shi'is only. Therefore it excludes other Shi'i groups like the Zaydis, the Bohra, and the Agha Khani Isma'ilis.

2. Among the few studies on the Shi'i experience in America are Linda Walbridge, *Without Forgetting the Imam: Lebanese Shi'ism in an American Community* (Detroit: Wayne State University Press, 1997); and Abdulaziz Sachedina, "A Minority within a Minority: The Case of the Shi'a in North America," in *Muslim Communities in North America*, ed. Yvonne Yazbeck Haddad and Jane I. Smith (Albany: State University of New York Press, 1991), 3–14. See also Vernon Schubel, "Karbala as Sacred Space among North American Shi'a: Every Day Is Ashura, Everywhere Is Karbala," in *Making Muslim Space in North America and Europe*, ed. Barbara Metcalf (Berkeley: University of California Press, 1996), and "The Muharram Majlis: The Role of a Ritual in the Preservation of Shi'a Identity," in *Muslim Families in North America*, ed. E. Waugh, S. M. Abu-Laban, and R. Qureshi (Edmonton: University of Alberta Press, 1991).

3. Yvonne Yazbeck Haddad, ed., *The Muslims of America* (New York: Oxford University Press, 1991), 11; Larry Poston, *Islamic Da'wah in the West* (New York: Oxford University Press, 1992), 27; Yvonne Yazbeck Haddad and Adair Lummis, *Islamic Values in the United States: A Comparative Study* (New York: Oxford University Press, 1987), 13–15. The first identifiable Muslim in America is said to be Estevan, a black Muslim guide and interpreter who came to Florida from Spain in 1527 with Panfilo de Narvaez's expedition. Richard B. Turner, *Islam in the African-American Experience* (Indianapolis: Indiana University Press, 1997), 11.

4. Yvonne Yazbeck Haddad and Jane I. Smith, *Mission to America: Five Islamic Sectarian Communities in North America* (Gainesville: University Press of Florida, 1993), 19. This was confirmed to me in a recent interview I conducted with an informant in Dearborn, Michigan. She is sixty-seven years old, and her mother was born in Michigan at the turn of the century.

5. Youssef M'roueh, "Shi'a Population in North America," in *Ahlul Bayt Assembly of North America: Abstract of Proceedings of 1996* (Beltsville, Md.: International Graphics, 1997), 44.

6. Walbridge, *Without Forgetting the Imam,* 16–17.

7. Ibid., 17–18.

8. Ibid., 42. Some Lebanese migrants settled in Alberta, Canada, in the early part of the twentieth century. Coming from La-la in the Baka Valley, Ali Hamilton took up the fur trade and settled in Lac La Biche, north of Edmonton, Canada. He also served as president of the Lac La Biche Chamber of Commerce. See *al-Ilmu Noorun,* Edmonton, Alberta (June 1995): 4. Subsequently, other Lebanese migrants settled in Lac La Biche.

9. Conveyed in a personal interview conducted in December 1999.

10. Conveyed in a personal interview conducted in 1996.

11. According to some estimates, there are approximately one million Iranians in America. They include Shi'is, Jews, Armenians, Zoroastrians, and Baha'is.

12. Most of these Asians are Khojas, a term that refers to an Indian caste that initially converted from Hinduism to Nizari Isma'ilism. Today, there are Isma'ili, Sunni, and Twelver Shi'i Khojas living in parts of India, East Africa, and the West.

13. Poston, *Islamic Da'wah,* 30.

14. Yosef M'roueh, "Shi'a Population in North America," 57. The author does not cite the source of his figures.

15. Yasin al-Jibouri, "A Glance at Shi'a Communities in the U.S.," in *Islamic Insights,* Virginia (October 1993): 1. See also Jane I. Smith, *Islam in America* (New York: Columbia University Press, 1999), 61.

16. Poston, *Islamic Da'wah,* 30.

17. I would like to thank my research assistant, Carl Gabrielsen, for his help in sending out various questionnaires and collating the results. I would also like to thank the Islamic Education Center of Potomac, Maryland, for sharing its survey results with me.

18. Poston, *Islamic Da'wah,* 108. Later on, Yasin al-Jibouri relocated to Virginia, where he founded the Islamic society of Virginia Inc.

19. This was achieved with the considerable help from Yasin al-Jibouri. See Poston, *Islamic Da'wah,* 109.

20. Twelver Shi'is believe that before his death, Muhammad appointed 'Ali to be his successor. They also believe that 'Ali was succeeded by a series of divinely guided Imams, the last of whom, the twelfth Imam, went into an occultation when he was four years old in 874 C.E. He is the messiah whose reappearance is expected at the end of time.

21. See the discussion on this in Walbridge, *Without Forgetting,* 79–81.

22. Ibid., 53.

23. On the transformation from a politically quietist to an activity oriented Shi'i movement, see Abdulaziz Sachedina, "Activist Shi'ism in Iran, Iraq and Lebanon," in *Fundamentalisms Observed,* ed. M. Marty and R. Appleby (Chicago: University of Chicago Press, 1991), 403–56.

24. Walbridge, *Without Forgetting,* 54–55.

25. I am grateful to Shaykh Fadhil Sahlani, chairman of the Council of Shi'a Muslim Scholars of North America, for sharing the Council's constitution with me.

26. Yusuf Talal DeLorenzo, "The Fiqh Councilor in North America," in *Muslims on the Americanization Path?* ed. Yvonne Yazbeck Haddad and John L. Esposito (Atlanta: Scholars Press, 1998), 83.

27. Stated in an interview conducted in November 1999.

28. See also Haddad and Lummis, *Islamic Values*, 63.

29. On the increased role of Imams in America, see ibid., 59.

30. On the mass movements in Sunni mosques in America see Barbara Metcalf, "New Medinas: The Tablighi Jama'at in America and Europe," in *Making Muslim Space*, ed. Barbara Metcalf (Berkeley: University of California Press, 1996), 113.

31. Rachel Bloul, "Engendering Muslim Identities: Deterritorialization and the Ethnicization Process in France" in *Making Muslim Space*, ed. Barbara Metcalf (Berkeley: University of California Press, 1996), 234.

32. Steven Barboza, *American Jihad: Islam after Malcolm X* (New York: Doubleday, 1994), 58.

33. See also Vernon Schubel, *Religious Performance in Contemporary Islam: Shi'i Devotional Rituals in South Asia* (Columbia: University of South Carolina Press, 1993), 71.

34. *Husayniyya* refers to a place where Shi'is congregate to commemorate the death and birthdays of the Imams. It is distinguished from a mosque in that rules governing ritual purity of mosques are not applied.

35. 'Abbas ibn 'Ali was the half-brother of Husayn. He was also killed in Kerbala.

36. I am grateful to Dr. Ahmad Hashim, a Shi'i proselyte who lives in Maryland, for sharing this observation with me.

37. Poston, *Islamic Da'wah*, 32. See also Karen Armstrong, *Holy War: The Crusades and Their Impact on Today's World* (New York: Doubleday, 1991), 41.

38. Ayatollah al-Sayyid 'Ali al-Husayni al-Seestani, *Contemporary Legal Rulings in Shi'i Law*, tr. Hamid Mavani (Montreal: Organization for the Advancement of Islamic Knowledge and Humanitarian Services, 1996), 74.

39. Said Arjomand, *The Shadow of God and the Hidden Imam: Religion, Political Order and Societal Change in Iran from the beginning to 1890* (Chicago: University of Chicago Press, 1986), 36–38.

40. According to my survey, the average age of the centers is 10.28 years.

41. Related in a personal interview conducted in December 1999.

42. See "Muslims in Politics," *Living Islam* (Summer 1998): 34.

43. I am grateful to Imam al-Qazwini for sharing his political experiences with me.

44. Smith, *Islam in America*, 186.

45. I am grateful to Dr. Hashim for sharing his political experiences with me in an interview.

46. Nadeem Kazmi, NGO representative of al-Khu'i Foundation to the United Nations, was kind enough to share this information with me.

15

South Asian Leadership of American Muslims

Karen Leonard

Muslims are an increasingly important part of the sociopolitical landscape in the United States. The number of African American Muslims has always been substantial and the number of Euro-American converts is growing, but the growth of Islam in America is mainly a result of the rapid influx of immigrants and their relatively high birthrate.[1] American Muslims come from a range of backgrounds, but, I argue here, South Asian Muslims (primarily from Pakistan and India) have increasingly come to the fore as their intellectual and political leaders. I also want to argue that second-generation South Asian Muslim Americans, because of a dissolving of diasporic identities in the future,[2] will become a less distinct part of an evolving leadership group of young American Muslims in the increasingly transglobal movement toward a "modern" and meaningful *ummah*.

Muslims in the United States

It might seem easier to argue for South Asian leadership of Islam in Great Britain, where Muslims can be viewed as a fairly homogeneous diasporic community, with a clear majority of Pakistani and Indian immigrants who have a shared past and similar Islamic beliefs and practices. In the United States, the situation is quite different, for South Asian Muslims are relative newcomers, and many other Muslim immigrants preceded them. Furthermore, African Americans constitute some 30 percent to 43 percent of the American Muslim community.[3] Not only are indigenous Muslims the single largest group, but also immigrant Muslims come from many and very different diasporas.[4] Nevertheless, at the present time, first-generation South Asian Muslim Americans are taking a conspicuous lead in the formulation of an American Islam and the political mobilization of American Muslims.

Despite the notion that diasporas can actively work across and/or against nation-states,[5] the projects of nation-states clearly shape immigrant culture and politics. Furthermore, while anthropologists no longer see cultures as discrete and bounded entities, it is possible to discern core concepts, distinctive patterns of beliefs and practices, that can be located and labeled.[6] Some immigrant Muslims had hoped to avoid an "Americanization" of Islam,[7] but this process has already occurred among earlier immigrant populations[8] and is now being analyzed among contemporary Muslim Americans.[9] American versions of Islam, developed and based in the United States, are inevitable.

American Islam is being shaped by both national policies and the particular groups that constitute the U.S. Muslim population. The U.S. white-dominated version of cultural pluralism extends equal rights to immigrants as citizens and to ethnic communities without expecting them to give up their "difference."[10] Yet, unlike Canada, which has explicit multicultural policies that support the maintenance of ethnic cultures, the United States has a laissez-faire approach and a strong emphasis on individualism. People must mobilize themselves, and here "identity entrepreneurs"[11] can help create and police ethnic or communal boundaries. Such policing can be both internally motivated and at the insistence of the ruling majority.[12] "All identity is constructed across difference,"[13] and the configurations of sameness and difference in the United States have important implications for American Islam. Racial and linguistic fault lines stem from the American heritage of racism based on slavery and its substantial black population and "frontier society" violence against Native Americans, Asians, and Latinos. Strikingly, most indigenous converts to Islam have been African Americans, and conversions among Latinos are increasing.[14]

The construction of the category of Muslim in the United States is relatively new. The first Muslim immigrants to the United States[15] were from Lebanon and other Arabic-speaking countries; they were part of an Arab immigrant group that was, in fact, largely Christian in the early decades. Not only were Christian and Muslim Arabs viewed as a single category, as "Arabs," but also it was a category largely unremarked by the larger society.[16] Early scholarly writing either followed this "Arab" categorization or focused on national-origin groups (e.g., the Lebanese, the Syrian-Lebanese),[17] and only in the 1980s did scholars really begin to focus on "Muslims" as they became the majority among Arab immigrants and as more Muslims came from countries all around the world.

In the periodization proposed for Muslim immigration in the mid-1980s, only the fourth and fifth waves included South Asians. In this scheme, the first wave occurred between 1875 and 1912 and consisted mostly of uneducated young Arab men. The second wave, from 1918 to 1922, consisted mostly of the relatives of the first wave, although there were some urban people. The third wave, from 1930 to 1938, consisted primarily of relatives of previous immigrants. The fourth wave, from 1947 to 1960, included Muslims not only from the Middle East but also from South Asia, the Soviet Union, eastern Europe, and other places. Many in this fourth wave were urban elites who were seeking higher education and better opportunities, and many were refugees. The fifth wave, from 1967 to the present, includes highly educated professionals, as well as skilled and semiskilled workers.[18]

South Asian Muslims in the United States

The United States began getting immigrants from British India around 1900, mostly Sikhs from the Punjab,[19] but large numbers of Indian and Pakistani immigrants began arriving only after major changes in U.S. immigration policy in 1965. Immigration statistics and the census show the increasing numbers from India and Pakistan, and, after 1970–1971, Bangladesh.[20] In studies done in the 1970s and 1980s, the emphasis was still on Arabic-speaking Muslims based on the East Coast and the Midwest. However, an important group of highly educated Pakistanis in upstate New York loomed large in one important study, which found them to be the most "conservative" in beliefs and practices.[21] The demographic shift in sources and numbers of Muslim immigrants, then, seemed at first to signal an interruption in a pattern of fairly unproblemetic Muslim "assimilation" or adaptation to American society.

In the context of the U.S. population and its Muslim population, South Asian Muslims now hold a significant place. Attempts to count and categorize Muslim Americans offer varying results. One breakdown puts African Americans at 42 percent, South Asians at 24.4 percent, Arabs at 12.4 percent, Africans at 6.2 percent, Iranians at 3.6 percent, Southeast Asians at 2 percent, European Americans at 1.6 percent, and "other" at 5.4 percent. Another breakdown puts "Americans" at 30 percent, Arabs at 33 percent, and South Asians at 29 percent.[22] Either way, Arab and South Asian Muslims are the largest immigrant groups. The Arabs are far more diverse in terms of national histories (and colonial pasts), coming from Lebanon, Egypt, Syria, Palestine, Iraq, Jordan, or Morocco (and, in smaller numbers, from Tunisia, Algeria, Libya, Saudi Arabia, Kuwait, Bahrein, Yemen, or other Persian Gulf states). South Asian Muslims are almost all from one of three countries, India, Pakistan, and Bangladesh, with a largely shared subcontinental history of successive Hindu, Indo-Muslim, and then British colonial rule.

Almost all of the immigrants to the United States from Pakistan and Bangladesh are Muslims, while perhaps 12 percent of those coming from India are Muslims.[23] One might view these immigrant groups as three separate communities, given the recent divisions among them, but I see South Asian immigrants in North America as a single diasporic population. In fact, the United States, along with other overseas diasporic sites, is an important site of reconnections among Indians, Pakistanis, and Bangladeshis, not least in Muslim American arenas. These immigrants share cultural presents and "remembered" pasts. They constitute a diasporic aesthetic community, drawing on languages and cultural traditions that cross current political borders. They also bring "memories" of British colonialism, the 1947 partition of India and Pakistan, and the 1971 breakaway of Bangladesh (East Pakistan) from (West) Pakistan. Thus, these immigrants are marked by "peculiar allegiances and alienations"[24] that stem from these shared, if differently interpreted, historical events.[25] It is true that the ease of transnational travel and communications gives Pakistani, Indian, and Bangladeshi immigrants little chance to "forget" homeland politics, politics that can divide them. However, the immigrants often work together, particularly with respect to American Muslim discourse and politics.[26]

Although they are diverse in terms of languages, religions,[27] and national backgrounds, the new South Asian immigrants are still relatively homogeneous in terms of socioeconomic class. In the 1990 U.S. census, the immigrants from India had the highest median household income, family income, and per capita income of any foreign-born group, and they also had the highest percentage of persons with a bachelor's degree or higher and the highest percentage of persons working in managerial and professional fields.[28] While appropriate nationwide statistics are not readily available, a careful study of southern California ethnic groups shows Indians and Pakistanis ahead of "Arabs" with respect to education, occupational level, and household income.[29]

It is not surprising that these new Indian and Pakistani Muslim immigrants should be conspicuous and powerful in Muslim American discourse and politics. As we have seen, they are a particularly privileged group,[30] giving them "the powers of diaspora," as one theorist has put it.[31] Their command of the English languages is quite impressive: most of the post-1965 immigrants have been educated in that language since childhood. Indian Muslims are accustomed to being in the minority. Indian Muslims, Pakistanis, and Bangladeshis share a heritage of political struggle with white or colonial rulers; they also, to different degrees, come to the United States with experience in democratic politics, particularly student politics (in contrast to Muslims from many Middle Eastern countries, who have less experience with democratic processes).

Also quite importantly, South Asians in the United States are often classified as white, and the construction of racial categories is a key component of U.S. society and politics. There is disagreement about this, with many South Asians claiming nonwhite status or claiming that others consider them as nonwhite, yet it is undeniable that they are often classified as white.[32] Perhaps, as Jonathan and Daniel Boyarin argue for Jews, it is the persistence of racism and the presence of African Americans that has promoted this classification for many South Asians.[33] South Asian Americans are probably even more often classified as Asian American, itself an increasingly important category and one commonly perceived as a "model minority" in America. Asian Americans are a rapidly rising proportion of the U.S. total population (they will constitute 8 percent of the population by 2020), and Asian Indians are the third largest Asian American group (after Chinese and Filipinos).[34]

Finally, South Asian Muslims are better positioned than Arab Muslims with respect to the American media and the general public. While American historical connections to the various countries that send Muslim immigrants to the United States vary tremendously, historical connections to South Asia and Muslims from there are fairly weak and unproblematic. At the least, one can say that American foreign relations with South Asia are certainly not as politically charged as those with the Middle East and its Muslims.[35] Thus, some of the prejudice suffered by Arab Americans[36] is less easily triggered by South Asian Muslim leadership.

This overall position of privilege gives South Asian Muslims leadership potential in religion, as well as in other arenas.[37] This is a difficult arena for assessment, because Islam has no centralized clergy, and mosques operate independent of one another. Furthermore, since mosque attenders are only 10 percent to 20 percent of American Muslims,[38] religious developments should not be equated with what is going on in the mosques. Yet one can generalize that, while Arabic speakers tend to have greater proficiency in Arabic and in *fiqh* and *shari'a* (jurisprudence and Islamic law), enabling them to dominate in many mosque functions and in teaching the young (Arabic lessons, the first reading of the Qur'an), it is the recent South Asian professional immigrants who have been fuelling both the building of local mosques and the regional and national mobilization of Muslims on religious and political issues.[39] In the leadership of many mosques, too, South Asians are also becoming prominent.[40]

The gradual shift from Arabic-speaking to South Asian leadership of Muslim Americans is apparent from a survey of institutions and organizations developed by American Muslims over the decades.[41] Table 15.1 rather arbitrarily sorts major organizations[42] into three groups, partly on the basis of their constituent populations and partly on the basis of chronology. (These are not mutually exclusive groups by any means; there are many cross-cutting ties.) "African American Islam" in its many manifestations developed first, without benefit of major or strong links to the historical Islamic world; it is

Table 15.1. Muslim American organizations

Name	Founding Date and Information	Initial Location
	I. African American Islam	
Moorish Science Temple	1913, Noble Drew Ali	East Coast, Midwest
Ahmadiyyas	1920, Missionaries from Indian (later Pakistani) sect; published first English-language Muslim newspaper in United States, 1921; members predominantly African American until 1970s, then Pakistani	East Coast, Midwest
Nation of Islam	1930, Wallace Fard Muhammad, Elijah Muhammad; 1975, leadership assumed by Warith Deen Muhammad, son of Elijah Muhammad	Detroit, Chicago
American Muslim Mission	renamed 1980s, led by W. D. Muhammad into mainstream Sunni Islam	
Muslim American Community	renamed 1990s, W. D. Muhammad; 1981, Louis Farrakhan splits off, NOA; 2000, reconciled with MAC	
Darul Islam	1962–83, by African American Sunnis; 1983 became Fuqra through influence of a South Asian Sufi	New York
	II. Islam in America	
FIA: Federation of Islamic Associations	1953, by Lebanese immigrants	Midwest, Canada
MSA: Muslim Students' Association	1963, by Muslim students in the U.S.	
ISNA: Islamic Society of North America	1982, grew out of MSA	Plainfield, Indiana
ICNA: Islamic Circle of North America	1971, Pakistani Jamaati Islami party ties	New York
	III. American Muslims	
AMA: American Muslim Alliance	1989, by political scientist Agha Saeed	Fremont, California
AMC: American Muslim Council	1990	Washington, D.C.
MPAC: Muslim Public Affairs Council	1990s, by Islamic Center of Southern California	Los Angeles
CAIR: Council on American-Islamic Relations	1990s	Washington, D.C.
AMPCC: American Muslim Political Coordinating Council: the four above.		Youngstown, Ohio

still the largest group if taken as a whole. Then comes an "Islam in America" category, drawing chiefly on immigrants and emphasizing religious beliefs and practices. Priorities for this category are religious education, spiritual regeneration, and *da'wa* (conversion, or outreach) activities, although there are important links to the next category. Finally, I call the last group "American Muslims," to emphasize its focus on political activities, rather than religious doctrine. This category again draws chiefly on immigrants but advocates the participation of Muslims in American electoral politics. This last group is the most broad based, able to draw on both of the first two groups and also on the 80 percent to 90 percent of "unmosqued" Muslims in the United States.

While African American Islamic movements had early input from South Asian Muslim missionaries to America, most significantly from the Ahmadis,[43] most early efforts at Islamic coalition building were led by Arab Muslims. The Federation of Islamic Associations (FIA), founded in 1953, and the Muslim Students' Association of the United States and Canada (MSA), founded in 1963, emphasized religious activities and were led mainly by Arabic-speaking Muslims.[44] Gradually the FIA was superseded by the growth of, and differentiation within, the MSA, which became the Islamic Society of North America (ISNA) in 1982.[45] ISNA is a multipurpose umbrella organization, but its chief focus is on religious issues and activities. Its current head is from India, as is the secretary general and chairman of the editorial board (for its influential bimonthly journal, *Islamic Horizons*).[46] The Islamic Circle of North America (ICNA) focuses strongly on religious issues and activities. Closely linked to Pakistan's Jamaat-i-Islami party, it is led by a Pakistani American physician.[47]

There are now four "American Muslim" groups that emphasize participation in mainstream American politics, a shift of emphasis within the American Muslim community that has occurred since the mid-1980s. Earlier, more national leaders opposed such participation or gave only qualified support to it; in 1986, Dr. Muzammil Siddiqi advocated residing only temporarily in Dar ul-Kufr, or the place of unbelievers (the United States). But, by the end of that same year, ISNA, the leading North American Muslim activist association, took a position favoring citizenship and political participation for Muslims in the United States.[48] Internal conflicts reported among and within developing Muslim organizations in the United States revolved around issues animated by politics outside the United States, such as Sunni-Shi'i differences heightened by the Iranian revolution of 1979 and the Iran-Iraq war or Salafiyyah-Ikhwan ul Muslimeen differences (that is, between the Saudi and Gulf-based orthodox movement and the Egyptian-based Muslim Brotherhood movement).[49] In the 1980s, American Muslim organizations did begin establishing national offices with professional staffs, instituting bureaucratic procedures, and moving toward electoral and mass, rather than elite, politics.

These four groups of American Muslims focused on U.S. politics are the AMA, the AMC, MPAC, and CAIR; together, they form AMPCC, the American Muslim Political Coordinating Council. They engage in political lobbying and encourage Muslims to run for electoral office. The AMA and the AMC are (in early 2000) led by South Asian American Muslims, while MPAC and CAIR are led by Arabic-speaking American Muslims; AMPCC's leader is the AMA's leader, a Pakistani American academic. Another (smaller) organization, the NCIA (National Council on Islamic Affairs, based in New York and founded by an Arab Muslim activist) has just, in early 2000, been merged into the AMA. The current head of AMA (and AMPCC) remarked that the merger marked "the beginning of a new phase of American Muslim politics, a phase of convergence and consolidation of organizations with similar agendas, and reflects the growing maturity of our community."[50] An historic event in early 2000 involved the venerable ADC (American-Arab Anti-Discrimination Committee): it brought together the four major Arab American and the five largest Muslim American organizations in Washington, D.C., to coordinate work on the future of Jerusalem, civil and human rights, participation in the electoral process, and inclusion in political structures.[51]

Another way of measuring national leadership among American Muslims is by looking at the four leading journals.[52] One, *Islamic Horizons*, published by ISNA, has already been mentioned. Another is *The Muslim Journal*, published by the Ministry of Imam W. D. Muhammad, of the Muslim American Community, chief body of African American Muslims today. Another is the *Message International*, published by ICNA (which also maintains a popular website, Soundvision). Finally, there is *The Minaret*, published monthly by the Islamic Center of Southern California and edited by Dr. Aslam Abdullah, an Indian American academic and journalist. Three of these four most influential Muslim American journals are edited by or closely linked to South Asian American Muslim leaders. The Islamic Center of Southern California, which initiated MPAC and publishes *The Minaret*, is one of the most successful interethnic Islamic congregations in the United States, and it has made a very self-conscious effort to formulate and represent an American Islam.[53]

This infusion of new leadership or shift in American Muslim leadership has been accompanied by a shift in the goals and audience of national Muslim organizations. The early efforts were focused inward, in contrast to current efforts. The credo of the FIA was "Hold fast to the rope of God all together and do not disperse," while the credo of ISNA, the organization which in effect superseded it by 1982, is "You are the best community raised up for humanity, enjoining what is right and forbidding what is wrong." Kathleen Moore points to this major change in perceptions of the appropriate role of Muslims in America.[54]

The focus on a wider audience is reflected in the ways in which American Muslims deal with the widespread ignorance of Islam among Americans as they energetically enter the political sphere. One way to counter this ignorance is to talk about Islam's closeness to Christianity and Judaism, and particularly to the majority community, Christianity. The discourse of immigrant Muslim American leaders frequently asserts that Christianity and Islam are monotheistic "religions of the book," with shared origins, prophets, and values. American Muslims also write about the compatibility between Islam and democracy. Leading American Muslim political organizations had good contacts with the Clinton administration, which made conspicuous efforts to bring Muslims into U.S. public life.[55] One young Indian American Muslim political scientist writes somewhat euphorically, "But internally, it [the U.S.] is the most Islamic state that has been operational in the last three hundred years. Internally, it is genuinely seeking to aspire to its ideals and the growing cultural, material and religious health of American Muslims is the best testimony to my claim. This debate, the existence of a Muslim public sphere where Muslims can think freely to revive and practice Islam is its gift to Muslims. Something unavailable in most of the Muslim world."[56]

The privileged position of South Asian Muslims lies behind this aggressively optimistic stance, I argue. It is primarily South Asians who have spearheaded drives to build new mosques in city after city, broadening rights for Muslims and building on the legal victories achieved by African American Muslims.[57] And it is they who have more reasons to put their political energies in the new, rather than the old, homeland. South Asian American Muslims do contribute to educational and other efforts in Pakistan, India, and Bangladesh, but it is hard to assess the extent of their diasporic engagement with the mother countries. In the 1980s, Indian Muslim attention remained firmly focused on India; a book published about them was oriented almost exclusively toward the homeland. Pakistan too has generated much activity on its behalf in the United States over the decades.[58] Yet, for many *muhajirs* (refugees from India), Pakistan did not quite become a homeland, and for many Indian Muslims, India has become less of a homeland. In both these cases, South Asian Muslims may be reluctantly relinquishing homelands where ideological reinterpretations of the past marginalize or exclude them from cultural and political power.[59] Arabic-speaking American Muslims, largely from Muslim-majority homelands, are more heavily invested in diasporic politics. The Israeli-Palestinian problem compels their engagement and often sets them directly in conflict with current U.S. policies.[60]

Beyond American electoral politics and diasporic politics, American Muslim activist discourse and practice[61] are constructing an international Islamic community, or universal *ummah*. All the American Muslim newspapers, journals, and media give news regularly about Muslim countries and issues that involve Islam or Muslims. Envisioned communities of suffering embodied in acts of giving and lobbying across national boundaries[62] unify North American Muslims as they address problem areas such as Palestine, Bosnia, Kashmir, and Kosovo. Strongly voiced public stances on problems overseas help override differences among Muslims in the United States, differences that are unavoidable, since American Muslims come from many countries and include, along with the dominant Sunnis, Shias, Sufis, Ahmadis, Druze, Zaidis, Imamis, and many other sects.[63]

The rise to prominence of South Asian immigrant Muslim leaders has been remarked with mixed feelings by some scholars and probably has contributed to a sense of "competing visions of Islam" among American Muslims themselves.[64] Yvonne Haddad and Adair Lummis, among the first to document differences between Muslim "liberals" and "conservatives" in the United States in their 1980s study, say, "More highly educated on the average than any other national group in our survey, the Pakistanis nonetheless tend to believe that God is the determiner of everything in life. Aside from this group, those in the Muslim community with higher education, especially those who have received such education in the United States, generally understand that God allows humans a significant measure of free will in determining their lives and their destinies."[65]

Aminah Beverly McCloud, an eloquent scholar and spokesperson for African American Muslims, notes many tensions between them and recent immigrant Muslims, and others make similar points. The indigenous, predominantly African American "new Muslims" jostle uneasily alongside the immigrant "new Americans." Historically shaped by American race and class struggles, African American Muslims saw Islam as a way to develop a separate and non-Christian identity in the United States.[66] *Asabiyah*, or group identity, must be given priority over the *ummah*, or the universal Muslim community, at this stage in African American Muslim life, African American Muslims argue, and they do not accept the customs or authority of immigrant Muslims.[67] There have been attempts to bridge this gulf—Imam W. D. Mohammed was on ISNA's Shura Council, for example—

but even the long-standing partnership between African Americans and Ahmadiyyas has experienced major strains now that Pakistanis are the well-off majority.[68]

Young American Muslims

My final point concerns the probable consolidation of American Islam or Islams by the younger generations, descendants of both South Asians and Arabic-speakers, and perhaps of both indigenous and immigrant Muslims. Although the centrality and future dominance of the young American Muslims in America and beyond it is being predicted, their religious ideas and practices are just beginning to be studied. They may or may not take over the leadership of existing institutions and organizations—so far, there is a continuing influx of new immigrants, of first-generation leaders to replace earlier first-generation leaders.[69]

Yet, clear generational differences, particularly among the immigrants, are emerging. Issues of language arise, as members of the second and subsequent generations lose competence in the languages of the homelands, and Arabic-speaking Muslims assume centrality in mosque affairs and private tutorials. Sometimes, issues of integration in the dominant American culture, of fusion or crossover culture, divide parents and children. And there are gender issues: since the use of public space is heavily influenced by dominant culture practices, immigrant Muslim women are often more visible in public spaces in America than in their homelands, even if (and perhaps because) they take to wearing the *hijab*, or headscarf. These gendered and generational changes may cause tensions within Muslim immigrant families, but they probably augur well for the future of American Islam, since the youngsters are converging, forming American Muslim identities more alike than different.

"The jury is still out," one man told me, about the youth of the community. Some will be lost to Islam, and some are "returning" to mainstream Arabic Islam through their study of the Qur'an and the Hadith. Certainly, many are moving from ethnic or national origin identities to a religious identity, and their formulations of Islam may be "grassroots," rather than guided by ISNA or the MSA.[70] Islam is taught to the young people in the United States not through everyday immersion in Arab or South Asian contexts but primarily through texts and texts taught in an American societal context.[71] On the one hand, this can result in greater standardization and "orthodoxy" as the non-Muslim-majority societal context reduces diversity among American Muslims, especially among young people. Yet, many of the "texts" are new ones, as young American Muslims rely heavily on books, cassettes, videos, and Internet materials produced in the United States.[72]

Among young American Muslims, there is great enthusiasm for Islamic messages and mediums not necessarily deemed orthodox by their elders. Islamic doctrine and discourse are being presented in "accessible, vernacular terms," as Dale Eickelman and Jon Anderson put it.[73] The Internet is the most obvious example of this. Another is the great popularity among Muslim young people of speakers like Shaykh Hamza Yusuf and Warith Deen Mohammed, the former a white American convert with Sufi leanings, the latter the leader of the Muslim American Community, or the African American Muslims. These men are "like rock stars," their talks avidly attended, recorded, and widely distributed on cassettes. Then there is "Muslim rap," a hybrid music integral to the politics of young African American Muslims, if incomprehensible to older immigrant Muslims, and Sufi qawwali, sung in South Asia in devotional settings but performed in North American public settings for largely non-Muslim audiences more accustomed to rock and roll. Most recently, Arab music was recognized by inclusion in the mainstream television Grammy Awards in 2000.[74] Another significant development is an "Islamic American English," being produced together by young and old indigenous and immigrant American Muslims.[75] This "dialect" incorporates Arabic phrases and Muslim terms of address into everyday speech, not only among Muslims but also, increasingly, with non-Muslims. Thus, some American Muslims or their answering machines now answer the phone with "Asalam aleikum" and expect to be understood by any caller.

American Muslim "identity entrepreneurs" and ordinary members of all generations confront the problem of connecting to others in the U.S. national context. A South Asian American Muslim has choices, to join with Middle Easterners, other American Muslims, Asian Americans, or people of color, and the U.S. context encourages different kinds of coalitions in different conditions. The lead seems to come from campuses—more than 60 percent of American high schoolers go on to some kind of college or university, and the proportions among Asian Americans and American Muslims are probably higher.[76] Thanks to the pioneering work of African Americans, Chicano/Latinos, and earlier Asian Americans, South Asian Muslim college students can work with others of Asian descent under the Asian American banner.[77] Another possibility is working with other American Muslims, reaching out to the majority African American Muslim communities in an effort to achieve social justice in America.

The Asian American and Muslim American identities and campus groups appear to be competing ones so far, and, in both broader coalitions, there is a tension between the "diasporic perspective" and "claiming America," best delineated by Sau Ling Wong. The "claiming America" view derives from the struggles of the early Asian (Chinese, Japanese, Korean, and Asian Indian) immigrants, and the "diasporic" view better reflects the large numbers of post-1965 immigrants from Vietnam, Korea, the Philippines, Thailand, and other countries in South and Southeast Asia.[78] For young American Muslims, the future, more than the (diasporic) past, shapes efforts to define and defend an Islamic world well beyond America, and "claiming America" might mean, for some among the upwardly mobile and confident new Americans, to redeem it through conversion to Islam. These phrases come from and better fit the Asian American arena, but they can easily be adapted to the Muslim American arena: they might translate as "Islamicizing America" or "Americanizing Islam," the former suggesting a retention of an "original" Islam and the latter an assimilation or adaptation to American conditions. The tension is there, as immigrants accept the phrase "American Muslim" but still express reservations about "American Islam."

The sociopolitical experiences that have shaped "memories" and their transmission for young American Muslims decisively position them in the histories, cultures, and languages of the United States. These young Muslims are engaged in the construction of new identities, ethnicities, and coalitions in the United States. Between the first and later generation Muslim immigrants, there are slippages and ruptures that change the coalitions envisioned to achieve religious and political goals. This claiming of differently constituted old and new homelands helps explain the weakening diasporic nature of both the South

Asian and the Arabic-speaking American Muslims in the United States. As younger American Muslim leaders emerge, we can expect creative new versions of Islam in America; the challenge will be to bring existing versions closer together.

Notes

I thank Garbi Schmidt, C. M. Naim, Hakan Yavuz, Omar Khalidi, Zahid Bukhari, Syed Ali, Riaz Hassan, and Nadine Naber for their extremely helpful comments on the draft of this chapter.

1. Islam is poised to displace Judaism and will be second to Christianity in the number of its adherents in the United States. Estimates of the number of Muslims in the United States ranged from 1.2 to 4.6 million in about 1990; in 1992 the American Muslim Council put the number between five and eight million: Fareed H. Nu'man, *The Muslim Population in the United States* (Washington, D.C.: American Muslim Council, 1992), 13. Not all Muslim immigrants have high birthrates—that of the Iranians is low, for example.

2. See Karen Isaksen Leonard, "State, Culture, and Religion: Political Action and Representation among South Asians in North America," *Diaspora* 9, 1 (Spring 2000): 21–38, where I argue that both Asian American and Muslim American politics lead to a dissolving, rather than a perpetuation, of the diasporic nature of these communities.

3. Nu'man, *Muslim Population*, puts African Americans at 42 percent and European Americans (some may be immigrants) at 1.6 percent; Ilyas Ba-Yunus and M. Moin Siddiqui, *A Report on the Muslim Population in the United States* (New York: CAMRI, 1999), put "Americans" at 30 percent.

4. I am using "diaspora" in the current, rather loose, fashion to refer to emigrant transnational populations. See William Safran, "Diasporas in Modern Societies: Myths of Homeland and Return," *Diaspora* 1, no. 1 (1991): 83–99; and Steven Vertovec, "Three Meanings of 'Diaspora,' Exemplified among South Asian Religions," *Diaspora* 6, no. 3 (1997): 277–99.

5. While people in diaspora are partially defined by the local, the new site, that site is in interaction with the "homeland" or with other diaspora sites; thus, the concept of diaspora is a resource to be used in rethinkings of the nation-state system: Jonathan Boyarin, "Powers of Diaspora," forthcoming in Jonathan Boyarin and Daniel Boyarin, *Powers of Diaspora* (Minneapolis: University of Minnesota Press); Khachig Tololyan also emphasizes the "statelessness" of diasporas: "Rethinking Diaspora(s): Stateless Power in the Transnational Moment," *Diaspora* 5, no. 1 (1996): 3–36.

6. James Ferguson and Akhil Gupta, eds., *Culture, Power, Place: Explorations in Critical Anthropology* (Durham, N.C.: Duke University Press, 1997), for the introductory discussion of cultural unboundedness; and, for an illustrative attempt to analyze distinctive features of Indian Hindu, Japanese, and Moroccan Muslim cultures, see McKim Marriott, "Alternative Social Sciences," in *General Education in the Social Sciences: Centennial Reflections*, ed. John MacAloon (Chicago: University of Chicago Press, 1992), 262–78.

7. Omar Afzal, "An Overview of Asian-Indian Muslims in the United States," in *Indian Muslims in North America*, ed. Omar Khalidi (Watertown, Mass.: South Asia Press, 1991), 11–12; in the same volume, Raymond Williams argues for an evolving American Islam, "Asian-Indian Muslims in the United States," 17–26.

8. See discussions of generational differences, in, most recently, Barbara C. Aswad and Barbara Bilge, *Family and Gender among American Muslims: Issues Facing Middle Eastern Immigrants and Their Descendants* (Philadelphia: Temple University Press, 1996); Earle H. Waugh, Sharon McIrvin, Baha Abu-Laban, and Regula Burckhardt-Qureshi, eds., *Muslim Families in North America*

(Edmonton: University of Alberta Press, 1991); Yvonne Yazbeck Haddad and Jane Idleman Smith, eds., *Muslim Communities in North America* (Albany: State University of New York Press, 1994); and Mehdi Bozorgmehr and Alison Feldman, eds., *Middle Eastern Diaspora Communities in America* (New York: Hagop Kevorkian Center for Near Eastern Studies at New York University, 1996).

9. See especially the *Islamic Horizons* (March/April 1998) special issue on Islam in America; Yvonne Yazbeck Haddad and John L. Esposito, *Muslims on the Americanization Path?* (Atlanta: Scholars Press, 1998); Jane I. Smith, *Islam in America* (New York: Columbia University Press, 1999).

10. One can, of course, critique this, showing that cultural differences (food, clothing, art) may be celebrated while inequalities of economic and political power are unrecognized.

11. Barbara Lal theorizes the concept of identity entrepreneurs, "Ethnic Identity Entrepreneurs: Their Role in Transracial and Intercountry Adoptions," *Asian and Pacific Migration Journal* 6, no. 3-4 (1997): 396-400; see also Yen Le Espiritu, *Asian American Panethnicity: Bridging Institutions and Identities* (Philadelphia: Temple University Press, 1992), for an optimistic view of the potential for political mobilization of Asian American panethnicity. See Linda Vo, *Constructing Identity, Community, and Organization: Asian American Mobilization in San Diego* (Philadelphia: Temple University Press, forthcoming), for indications of its limitations.

12. Khachig Tololyan discusses the policing of boundaries, "Rethinking Diaspora(s)," 14.

13. Stuart Hall, "Minimal Selves," in *Identity*, ed. Homi Bhabha (London: Institute of Contemporary Arts, 1987), 45.

14. Stephen Castles, "How Nation-States Respond to Immigration and Ethnic Diversity," *New Community* 21, no. 3 (1995): 301-2. For comments on Latino converts, see Smith, *Islam in America*, 66-67 (and, on Native American converts, 68), and Hisham Aidi, "Ole to Allah: New York's Latino Muslims," http://www.belief.net/story/9/story_996_l.html (the last source thanks to Hakan Yavuz).

15. African Muslim slaves, some 10 percent of African slaves brought to America, preceded these immigrants: Allan D. Austin, *African Muslims in Antebellum America: A Sourcebook* (New York: Garland, 1984).

16. Nadine Naber, "Ambiguous Insiders: An Investigation of Arab American Invisibility," *Ethnic and Racial Studies* 23, no. 1 (2000): 37-61. This article's title makes the point very well, and she shows the multiple and conflicting categories that have accounted for this relative "invisibility" of Arab Americans.

17. For example, Sameer Y. Abraham and Nabeel Abraham, eds., *Arabs in the New World: Studies on Arab-American Communities* (Detroit: Wayne State University, 1983), and Alixa Naff, *Becoming American: The Early Arab Immigrant Experience* (Carbondale: Southern Illinois University Press, 1985).

18. Yvonne Yazbeck Haddad and Adair T. Lummis, *Islamic Values in the United States: A Comparative Study* (New York: Oxford University Press, 1987), 13-14. The African Muslim slaves are not included, probably because, as Sulayman Nyang remarks, "there is no evidence of any African Muslim slave family that survived slavery and maintained Islam as a way of life": "Islam in America: A Historical Perspective," *American Muslim Quarterly* 2, no. 1 (Spring 1998): 10-11.

19. See Karen Isaksen Leonard, *Making Ethnic Choices: California Punjabi Mexican Americans* (Philadelphia: Temple University Press, 1992).

20. See Appendices I and II in Karen Isaksen Leonard, *The South Asian Americans* (Westport, Conn.: Greenwood Press, 1997), 171-73. India and Pakistan became independent in 1947, and Bangladesh, formerly East Pakistan, became independent in 1971. In 1980, there were 387,233 Indians, 15,792 Pakistanis, and 1,314 Bangladeshis; in 1990, there were 815,447 Indians, 81,371 Pakistanis, and 11,838 Bangladeshis.

21. Haddad and Lummis, *Islamic Values*, point to this conservatism in numerous places, for example, 30-33, 123-24, 127 (they also see considerable adaptation among earlier immigrants).

22. Estimates of U.S. Muslims range from three to eight million. For the first breakdown, see Nu'man, *Muslim Population*, 13; for the second, Ba-Yunus and Siddiqui, *Report on the Muslim Population*.

23. India's population is about 12 percent Muslim. Indians Muslims may constitute a smaller proportion of emigrants from India, since their socioeconomic resources are on average lower than those of Hindus, or they may be a higher proportion, since they are more urbanized and experience communal pressures. If they constitute 12 percent of emigrants to the United States, Indian Muslims would approximately equal in number Pakistani Muslims in the United States (see note 21).

24. James Clifford, "Notes on Theory and Travel," in *Traveling Theory Traveling Theorists*, ed. James Clifford and Vivek Dhareshwar (Santa Cruz: Center for Cultural Studies, 1989), 185, emphasizing here two aspects of his characterization of migrants as people "changed by their travel but marked by places of origin, by peculiar allegiances and alienations."

25. The past, as Stuart Hall cautions, is "always constructed through memory, fantasy, narrative, and myth. . . . Cultural identities are the points of identification, the unstable points of identification or suture, which are made within the discourses of history and culture." Stuart Hall, "Cultural Identity and Cinematic Representation," *Framework* 36 (1989): 71–72.

26. Conversely, some political issues may seem to link them through Islam—Pakistanis and some other Muslims may view the Kashmir problem as fundamentally a religious issue. But, in my experience, most Indian Muslims do not agree with the Pakistani position on Kashmir.

27. In terms of religion, the three main groups are Hindus, Muslims, and Sikhs. In the United States, Hindus are the most numerous South Asian religious group; Muslims are second, and Sikhs third. But in the United States as a whole, it is Muslims who are most numerous.

28. Among Indian immigrants in the 1990 census, 10 percent were medical doctors and 17 percent were engineers. Leonard, *South Asian Americans*, 77–78. (Omar Khalidi, referring to the 1999–2000 directory of physicians of Indian origin in the United States, says these figures are too high.) Such statistics are not available for Indian and Pakistani Muslim immigrants, but physicians loom large among activist Muslim leaders. A second wave of immigrants shows a slightly different distribution of occupations and socioeconomic measures, as family reunification policies bring less-qualified people; the second generation also has a leveling effect: ibid., 81–83. The very small number of Bangladeshis, many of them undocumented, do not fit this profile.

29. James P. Allen and Eugene Turner, *The Ethnic Quilt: Population Diversity in Southern California* (Northridge: California State University Press, 1997), 57, 71, 135, 136.

30. Iranian Muslims, also highly educated and sharing many of the attributes outlined for South Asians, are overwhelmingly secular in their orientation: see Mehdi Bozorgmehr, "Internal Ethnicity: Iranians in Los Angeles," in *Sociological Perspectives* 40, no. 3 (1997): 387–408, particularly the chart on 398, where only 5 percent are religiously observant "always and often" and 95 percent are so "occasionally and never." Also, Iranians are Shi'i, the minority sect within Islam, and within American Islam as well.

31. Boyarin, "Powers of Diaspora," meaning that they have some agency with respect to assimilation, repatriation, or the perpetuation of diasporic community; he, too, sees "linguistic adaptability" and the high levels of competence in English as major reasons for this.

32. Claiming minority status for preferential purposes was controversial within the community: Robert J. Fornaro, "Asian Indians in America: Acculturation and Minority Status," *Migration Today* 12 (1984): 28–32. Also, Asian Indians are the least residentially clustered (or segregated from whites) in several studies, for example, Allen and Turner, *Ethnic Quilt*, 231. For views embracing minority or nonwhite status, see the *Amerasia* issue on South Asian politics: 25, 3 (1999–2000).

33. Jonathan Boyarin and Daniel Boyarin, eds., *Jews and Other Differences: The New Jewish Cultural Studies* (Minneapolis: University of Minnesota Press, 1997), xi.

34. Karen Isaksen Leonard, *The South Asian Americans*, 68–69. Eighty percent of South Asians in the United States are from India and Pakistan.

35. Until the 1990s, U.S. policy was consistently favorable to Pakistan, although this may be changing as paranoia about Islamic terrorism rises.

36. Edward Said, *Covering Islam* (New York: Pantheon, 1981; 2d ed. New York: Vintage, 1997).

37. Their prominence is clear in academia and in mainstream cultural arenas such as literature, film, and music, too: see Leonard, "State, Culture, and Religion."

38. Haddad and Lummis, *Islamic Values*, 8, for the estimate.

39. I am not discussing here clearly political efforts (such as funding candidates for political office according to their stances on Kashmir) or efforts aimed at disaster relief or development in the homelands, although these are important and numerous among South Asian Muslims.

40. Yvonne Yazbeck Haddad, "At Home in the Hijra: South Asian Muslims in the United States," in *The South Asian Religious Diaspora in Britain, Canada, and the United States*, ed. Howard Coward, John R. Hinnells, and Raymond Brady Williams (New York: State University of New York Press, 2000), 239–58 mentions a Pakistani woman elected president of a New York mosque organization: 245. Imams (clerics) from South Asia are less well trained, most think, than those from Arab countries, some of the latter having been driven out by persecution at home.

41. Speaking as an outside observer of Islam and Muslim politics in America, I am not clear about the extent to which members of Muslim American groups themselves perceive this shifting leadership at the national level or, if they do, find it desirable to point it out.

42. The many smaller organizations range from the Muslim Students' Association-Persian Speaking Group (MSA-PSG), which Iranian Shi'is formed after 1979, to the Hizb-ul-Tahrir, which publishes the journal *Khalifornia* and rejects participation in *kafir* (unbeliever) politics.

43. See Aminah Beverly McCloud, *African American Islam* (New York: Routledge, 1995), 18–21, 24–26, 57–58. There are other links: a Pakistani immigrant began the Hanafi Madhhab movement among African Americans (Kareem Abdul-Jabbar is a Hanafi member); a Sunni African American group, the Darul Islam Movement, in the 1970s the largest black Muslim Sunni group in the United States, was transformed by its leader's devotion to a South Asian Sufi *shaykh* of the Qadirayya Order into a Sufi movement by 1980: Smith, *Islam in America*, 97–98.

44. Haddad and Lummis, *Islamic Values*, 5; Akbar Muhammad, "Muslims in the United States: An Overview of Organizations, Doctrines, and Problems," in *The Islamic Impact*, ed. Yvonne Yazbeck Haddad, Byron Haines, and Ellison Findly (Syracuse: Syracuse University Press, 1984), 195–218. Muhammad also indicates that Arabic-speaking countries such as Arab and Persian Gulf states were the leading supporters of Islamic activity in America, although American Muslims are not "dependent on external aid or . . . controlled by their foreign donors" (213).

45. ISNA has many affiliated organizations and institutions: MSA, or Muslim Students Associations; IMA, or Islamic Medical Association; AMSE, or American Muslim Engineers and Scientists, founded in 1969; AMSS, or American Muslim Social Scientists, founded in 1972; and others. See Nyang, "Islam in America," 7–38; Smith, *Islam in America*, 167–71; Gutbi Mahdi Ahmed, "Muslim Organizations in the United States," in *The Muslims of America*, ed. Yvonne Yazbeck Haddad (New York: Oxford University Press, 1991), 11–24.

46. These are Dr. Muzammil H. Siddiqi, Orange County, California, and Sayyid M. Sayeed (a Kashmiri), Plainfield, Indiana (ISNA headquarters), respectively.

47. Dr. Mohammed Yunus, a physician from Pakistan who now lives in Florida, is the longtime leader of ICNA, but in 1999 twenty professionals who had been organizational leaders resigned, dissatisfied with the heavy influence of Pakistan's Jamaat-i-Islami party ("Twenty

Resign from ICNA in Protest," *Pakistan Link*, 8 Oct. 1999, 45). That party, one informant said, was "not in tune with modern or postmodern conditions in the United States."

48. Larry Poston, *Islamic Da'wah in the West* (New York: Oxford University Press, 1992), 32, citing an *Islamic Horizons* (May–June 1986) article by Dr. Siddiqi, "Muslims in a Non-Muslim Society," 22; for ISNA's initiative, see Steve A. Johnson, "Political Activity of Muslims in America," in Yvonne Yazbeck Haddad, *The Muslims of America* (New York: Oxford University Press, 1991), 111. However, by 1999–2000, Dr. Siddiqi had changed his view and was president of ISNA.

49. Johnson, "Political Activity," 111–24.

50. Dr. Agha Saeed, a political scientist of Pakistani origin who now teaches at California State University, Hayward, in northern California, leads not only the now-enlarged AMA ("National Council on Islamic Affairs Announces Merger with American Muslim Alliance," *Pakistan Link*, 25 Feb. 2000, 20) but also AMPCC. Dr. Nazir Khaja, a physician of Indo-Pakistani origin now from southern California, heads AMC; Dr. Maher Hathout, a physician of Egyptian origin, and Salam Al-Marayati, of Palestinian ancestry, now of southern California, head MPAC; and Nihad Awad, a Palestinian now of Washington, D.C., heads CAIR. After this chapter was written, Dr. Khaja resigned as president of AMC, and several other South Asians also resigned after a no-confidence vote "more or less on ethnic lines": Aslam Abdullah, "Turmoil at AMC," *Pakistan Link*, 17 March 2000, 14.

51. "Landmark Meeting of Arab and Muslim American Organizations," *Pakistan Link*, 5 Feb. 1999, 39. The Muslim groups were the AMA, AMC, CAIR, MPAC, and CFGG (the Coalition for Good Government), and the Arab ones were the ADC (American-Arab Anti-Discrimination Committee), AAI (Arab American Institute), AAUG (Arab American University Graduates), and the NAAA (National Association of Arab Americans). Another blurring of the lines proposed in the chart is the effort by AMA, AMC, CAIR, MPAC, ICNA, ISNA, ADC, AAI (Arab-American Institute), AMGPJ (American Muslims for Global Peace and Justice), LIFE (Life for Relief and Development), and MAS (Muslim American Society) against the sanctions imposed on Iraq. ADC and CAIR both protested the State Department's overemphasis on the Middle East and South Asia in its "Patterns of Global Terrorism, 1999," released 1 May 2000, which implied a link between Islam and terrorism.

52. Sulayman Nyang mentions these four as the leading ones: "Islam in America," 29. There are many others, some in Urdu on the East Coast, and the *Pakistan Link* has a section entitled "Muslim Link."

53. Juan E. Campo, "Islam in California: Views from 'The Minaret,'" *Muslim World* 136, 3–4 (1996): 294–312. This pioneering study takes what is probably an exceptional case—we need more studies of American Muslim discourse and politics, orthodoxy and orthopraxy, in particular institutions and places.

54. Kathleen M. Moore, *Al-Mughtaribun: American Law and the Transformation of Muslim Life in the United States* (Albany: State University of New York Press, 1995), 105–6.

55. Dr. Laila Al-Marayati, of the Islamic Center of Southern California and its Muslim Women's League, was the one woman from California picked for the U.S. delegation, led by Hillary Clinton, to the 1995 International Women's Conference in Beijing. In 1998, beginning a new tradition, the White House hosted a celebration of 'Eid al-Fitr, the end of the holy month of fasting, with the help of the Muslim Women's League and MPAC (*Los Angeles Times*, 28 Jan. 1998, pp. B1, B8).

56. Mohommed A. Muqtedar Khan, "Muslims and American Politics: Refuting the Isolationist Arguments," *American Muslim Quarterly* 2, no. 1–2 (1998): 68. Similarly, a physician from Pakistan writes that "Muslims believe in the same values for which this country [the U.S.] was founded. . . . they feel closer to the founding fathers than what America has become. . . ." Shahid Athar, *Reflections of an American Muslim* (Chicago: KAZI, 1994), 7.

57. Moore, *Al-Mughtaribun*, argues that political and legal institutions in the United States have combined with values of religious liberty and tolerance to shape distinctively American Muslim identities and to broaden religious and cultural pluralism in America. Both of her mosque-building case studies are of Pakistani-led efforts, in Rochester, New York, and Fremont, California, where she shows the broadening of municipal land use decision-making processes to include non-Christian places of worship. Gulzar Haider, a Pakistani Canadian architect, testifies to the assertion of Muslim identity through mosque architecture in "Muslim Space and the Practice of Architecture," in *Making Muslim Space in North America and Europe*, ed. Barbara Daly Metcalf (Berkeley: University of California Press, 1996), 31–45; see also Omar Khalidi, "Approaches to Mosque Design in North America," slightly different versions published in *Islamic Horizons* (January/February 1998), 23–28, and in Haddad and Esposito, *Muslims on the Americanization Path?* 399–424.

58. Khalidi, *Indian Muslims*. Strong groups include IMRC (Indian Muslim Relief Committee) and AFMI (American Federation of Muslims from India), PAK-PAC (Pakistani Political Action Committee), and APPNA (Association of Pakistani Physicians in North America).

59. See Karen Isaksen Leonard, "Hyderabadis in Pakistan: Changing Nations," in *Community, Empire, and Migration: South Asians in Diaspora*, ed. Crispin Bates (London: Macmillan, 2001), 224–44. Pakistan's recurring crises and frequent requests for dollars from abroad inspire decreasing enthusiasm; loyalty is displayed in the company of Indians, but a consensus may be emerging that Pakistan is a "failed" homeland. Indian Muslims are increasingly distressed by the communalism, or anti-Muslim feelings and actions, now rising in India.

60. Sally Howell, "Aesthetic Interventions: Arab (American) Artists between Ethnicity and Transnationalism," in *Diaspora* 9, no. 1 (Spring 2000), 59–82; Yvonne Yazbeck Haddad, "American Foreign Policy in the Middle East and Its Impact on the Identity of Arab Muslims in the United States," in *The Muslims of America*, ed. Yvonne Yazbeck (New York: Oxford University Press, 1991), 217–235.

61. See Karen Leonard, "American Muslim Discourse and Practice," in *Islamic Modernities*, ed. Paul Lubeck (forthcoming), for an exploration of key issues.

62. Werbner discusses the constitution of such materially-grounded moral or religious transnational communities in Pnina Werbner, "Essentialising Essentialism, Essentialising Silence: Ambivalence and Multiplicity in the Construction of Racism and Ethnicity," in *Debating Cultural Hybridity: Multi-Cultural Identities and the Politics of Anti-Racism*, ed. Pnina Werbner and Tariq Modood (New Jersey: Zed Books, 1997), 238–40.

63. Yvonne Yazbeck Haddad and Jane I. Smith, *Mission to America: Five Islamic Sectarian Communities in North America* (Gainesville: University Press of Florida, 1993); Marcia K. Hermansen, "Hybrid Identity Formations in Muslim America: The Case of American Sufi Movements," *Muslim World* 90, nos. 1–2 (2000): 158–97; Poston, *Islamic Da'wah*.

64. This is the title of a recent book by Kambiz Ghanea Bassiri, *Competing Visions of Islam in the United States: A Study of Los Angeles* (Westport, Conn.: Greenwood Press, 1997).

65. Haddad and Lummis, *Islamic Values*, 32.

66. Some leaders within the African American Muslim community interpreted Islam as not only anti-Christian but antiwhite, these include Louis Farrakhan, whose Nation of Islam constituted some 4 percent of African American Muslims. Having long promised to join the Sunni mainstream, in February 2000 Farrakhan did "reconcile" with W. D. Muhammad's American Muslim Community (but what exactly this means is still unclear).

67. McCloud, *African American Islam*, particularly the conclusion and 4–5. Robert Dannin argues that African American "new Muslims" are engaged in self-definition, rather than accepting religious authority and customs as defined by immigrant "new Americans" (in Bozorgmehr and Feldman, *Middle Eastern Diaspora Communities*, 159, 169). Richard Brent Turner outlines and stresses differences from immigrant Muslims: *Islam in the African-American Experience*

(Bloomington: Indiana University, 1997) and "Mainstream Islam in the African-American Experience," *ISIM Newsletter* (March 1999): 37.

68. Linda Walbridge and Fatimah Haneef, "Inter-Ethnic Relations within the Ahmadiyya Muslim Community in the United States," in *The Expanding Landscape: South Asians and the Diaspora*, ed. Carla Petievich (Delhi: Manohar, 1999), 144-68, details some of the problems.

69. Garbi Schmidt, *American Medina: A Study of the Sunni Muslim Immigrant Communities in Chicago* (Lund, Sweden: University of Lund, 1998), 242-44; and see forthcoming dissertations by Nadine Naber, University of California at Davis, on young Arab Americans, and by Syed Faiz Ali, "Re-membering Selves: From Nobility and Caste to Ethnnicity and Class in an Indian City," University of Virginia, 2001, on Muslim identities in New York and India.

70. I draw here on comments from Zahid Bukhari, Nadine Naber, and Syed Ali.

71. John Bowen, for example, talks about the movement of texts across societal boundaries and the movement of believers between sacred texts and legal, moral, and social applications: *Muslims through Discourse: Religion and Ritual in Gayo Society* (Princeton, N.J.: Princeton University Press, 1993), 8.

72. Garbi Schmidt, "I Created You as Nations and Tribes: Muslim Social Activism, a Transnational and American Phenomenon," in *Muslim Identities in North America*, ed. Karen Leonard (forthcoming), discusses the impact of these American materials in Europe.

73. Dale F. Eickelman and Jon W. Anderson, eds., *New Media in the Muslim World. The Emerging Public Sphere* (Bloomington: Indiana University Press, 1999), particularly their own ch. 1, "Redefining Muslim Publics," 1-18; the quote is on 12.

74. Hamza Yusuf lives in northern California, W. D. Mohammed in Chicago. For Muslim rap, Ted Swedenborg, "Transnational Islamic Rap," paper for the American Anthropological Association, (1996); personal communication, Lorraine Sakata, Los Angeles, May 1999; and Mattias Gardell, *In the Name of Elijah Muhammad: Louis Farrakhan and the Nation of Islam* (Durham, N.C.: Duke University Press, 1996), 293-300; for Sufi *qawwali*, see Regula Burckhardt-Qureshi, *Sufi Music of India and Pakistan: Sound, Context and Meaning in Qawwali* (Chicago: University of Chicago Press, 1995); for Arab music's inclusion in the television Grammy Awards in 2000 (the Algerian singer Cheb Mami, with Simon Shaheen leading an all-Arab violin group, Jihad Racy and Ensemble, with Sting), e-mail received 23 Feb. 2000, from Nadine Naber.

75. The phrase "Islamic American English" comes from Schmidt (a Dane), *American Medina*, 252-55, although Metcalf earlier discussed "Islamic English" in her edited volume, *Making Muslim Space*, xv-xix; both Schmidt and Metcalf credit Isma'il Raji 'al Faruqi, a Palestinian immigrant who published a pamphlet on the subject in 1986 (and who founded AMSS and the Institute of Islamic Thought, in Virginia). Whether this is really "American" or a broader development (used by religious English-speaking Muslims in many countries, as C. M. Naim suggested) remains to be seen; it may be wishful thinking.

76. While affirmative action programs in American universities set not quotas but goals and were meant to be transitional, and while neither Asian Americans nor Muslim Americans were usually included in the goal setting at either the student or the faculty level, these programs have had an undeniable effect in helping to legitimize curricular and structural focuses on Asian American, African American, Chicano/Latino, Native American, and women's studies. Muslims, like Jews, do not fit easily into these boxes. Religious studies, rising in popularity among students, may not gain (or regain) a foothold on campuses.

77. Mitchell J. Chang, "Expansion and Its Discontents: The Formation of Asian American Studies Programs in the 1990s," *Journal of Asian American Studies* 2, no. 23 (1999): 181-206.

78. Sau Ling Wong, "Denationalization Reconsidered: Asian American Cultural Criticism at a Theoretical Crossroads," *Amerasia Journal* 21, no. 1-2 (1995): 1-27.

16

Continental African Muslim Immigrants in the United States: A Historical and Sociological Perspective

Sulayman S. Nyang

Since the beginning of the twentieth century, Africans have immigrated into the United States as free men and women. Unlike their predecessors, who had come to America in chains after having gone through the Middle Passage, these Africans came to this country voluntarily and with differing motivations. While there are no reliable data to confirm why these men and women left their homes, whether in search of education, fortune, or romance, one can theoretically postulate four categories of Africans who have come to America as free persons and for one reason or another decided to settle.

The first are the students who arrived in the late nineteenth century. They were supported and aided by American missionaries who hoped that they would later return to collaborate with like-minded Christians in establishing missions and extending the message of Christ to their fellow Africans. These students went primarily to historically black colleges and universities. Many of them were from West and southern Africa, with a few from eastern Africa. The second group comprises the African students who arrived throughout the twentieth century to pursue their education. For one reason or the other, often because of conjugal entanglements with white American and African American women, many of them decided to stay permanently in the country. The third group consists of seamen and stowaways who found their way to American seaports such as New York City and New Orleans. Many of these men who sailed with American or foreign ships settled in the New York/New Jersey area. The fourth groups of Africans who have become part of the growing African immigrant community are the political refugees, most of whom are victims of civil wars fought either for a superpower in the Cold War or for their ethnic group. African Muslims belong to all these categories.

The intention of this chapter is to address the challenges and opportunities that face the African immigrant community and the African immigrant family, with special emphasis on the African Muslims. In this task we have four main objectives: (1) to identify the building blocks that go into the making of the African immigrant community in the United States of America; (2) to explain how changing times, conditions, and circumstances have combined to define the nature of the relationship between the African immigrant and the larger American society; (3) to identify the main issues facing the leaders and their followers in the African immigrant communities around the United States; and (4) to provide a synthetic conclusion based on my assessment of the evidence gathered while investigating this subject matter. Recognizing that the African immigrant community is not monolithic and that cultural background can serve as a negative or a positive influence for these immigrants, I argue that the assimilation process for African immigrants depends on critical variables, such as the inherited colonial language, social class, and the sociocultural origins of the immigrant.

The Muslim Factor in the Making of the African Immigrant Community

African immigrants started coming to the United States not long after the Civil War and the abolition of slavery. During the first thirty years after the war, the number of free Africans who ventured to this part of the world was very small, although there are some accounts of Africans from various places in the continent who visited the United States in that period. Many of these men and women were West Africans from Liberia or other points along the coast. The African Americans who settled in Liberia established linkages between the African peoples and African Americans, opening up opportunities for many continental Africans who had previously not dared to come to this part of the Atlantic while the slave trade was still going on.[1] One African immigrant whose activities form a chapter in the history of Pan Africanism and in the history of African immigration to the United States was a man named Chief Sam, from Ghana. Professor Jabez Ayodele Langley's wonderful book on the Pan African movement in West Africa tells the story of how Chief Sam came to the United States in the late nineteenth century and settled in New York. His business ventures enabled him to prosper and to establish a network of friends among African Americans. In the early part of this century, when race relations between blacks and whites in the United States began to sour and many incidents of lynching took place in Oklahoma and Kansas, Chief Sam offered his services to black families who wished to emigrate from the United States to the African continent. His efforts failed not because of his inability to organize and lead his followers into the "promised land" but because the colonial authorities conspired to stymie his efforts. They saw this massive migration of New World blacks into their newly pacified colonies as a real and present danger.[2]

Though we do not know much about the lives and times of African contemporaries of Chief Sam in New York or in other places within the United States, there is circumstantial evidence from the writings of others that points to an African immigrant presence in Harlem during the first three decades of the twentieth century. Writing in the 1960s, Ras Makonen, a Trinidadian who was actively involved in the global Pan African movement, reported in his *Pan Africanism from Within* that there were some Africans living in New York during the period between the world wars.[3] We now know that many of these men were Somalis who reached this part of the United States either as seamen or stowaways. Many of these Muslim seamen settled in Harlem and started new lives. In my investigation of Islam among the African Americans, I have come across data from my interviews with some of the earliest Muslim activists in Harlem that suggests some Moroccan, Somali, and West African presence among the blacks settling in New York. Farther to the west, we have records of the appearance in Pittsburgh of Muhammad Majid, a Sudanese who came to the United States to work with African

American converts to Islam. According to FBI records obtained under the Freedom of Information Act by Professor Robert Hill, of UCLA, the editor of the Marcus Garvey papers, this man from Sudan attracted the attention of the authorities, who saw him as part of a Japanese propaganda campaign against the United States. He left the United States in 1928. Details about Muhammad Majid and his activities will soon be presented to the scholarly community by Professor John Hunwick and a Sudanese colleague. The two researchers stumbled upon a scholarly gold mine when they located a box of files relating to the life and times of this Sudanese immigrant who had settled in Pittsburgh some seventy years earlier.

Another revealing story is that of Duse Muhammad Ali, a Sudano-Egyptian journalist, playwright, and activist who came to the United States in the 1920s. He settled for some time in Detroit before relocating in West Africa, where he founded newspapers and contributed to the Pan African discourse. Prior to his appearance in the United States, Duse Muhammad Ali was the editor and publisher of the *African Times and Orient Review*. Because of the nature of this publication and the manner in which it dealt with the events of the times, one can make the case that Duse was the doyen of Afro-Asian journalism in England.[4] One of his protégés, who would later enter history as a great Pan Africanist, was the Jamaican immigrant Marcus Garvey. Garvey, too, crossed paths with many Africans in Europe and in the United States.

One can begin to sense the complexity of the many elements that went into the making of the African immigrant community over the past century. Besides the figures who made history, there have been many other African immigrants who played their own roles in the process of adapting to their new country. Their stories are often parts of anecdotes told by individual family members, as was the case of Kunta Kinteh and the Haley family.[5] These modern families can reconstruct their past with the aid of official documents because their African ancestors came to the United States without going through the degrading and humiliating experiences of the Middle Passage.

The African immigrant community changed its complexion in the 1930s and 1940s, when a growing body of African students started to come to the United States for higher education. Many of these men and (later) women were breaking with tradition in the sense that they chose American schools over British ones. The vast majority of these students of the interwar period returned to Africa. Some of them became known nationally and internationally; others simply faded into the mist of African history. We learn certain things from the autobiographies of several of the men who wrote about their experiences in the United States. In many respects, they portrayed a picture of life in the United States common to the experiences of all continental Africans.

One early account came from the pen of Nnamdi Azikiwe, of Nigeria, who studied at Lincoln University. While some of his contemporaries from West Africa who came to America chose to stay in this country, Azikiwi returned home and later became his country's first president.[6] We also have the story of Dr. K. W. Aggrey of Ghana, part of the first generation of African professors in America, whose activities in the United States are legendary.[7] One of the first generation of African professors in America, this educator from Ghana was destined to return home and teach at Achimota. Aggrey also left an American legacy. His children by his African American wife, his grandchildren, and his great grandchildren are now a part of the African American community. His son Rudolph rose to the rank of U.S. ambassador in the State Department and served as the director of the Howard University Press in Washington, D.C., for many years. The Africans we know about in the earlier period of immigration were predominantly Christians. Currently we do not have enough information to know if they had Muslim counterparts. More research on continental African Muslim students in American colleges and universities needs to be done.

In the 1930s, the generation of Kwame Nkrumah followed the first wave of Africans who came to the United States in this century. Some of the students who came with Nkrumah later decided for one reason or the other to stay permanently in America.[8] Their descendants are now part of the heart of black America. In the postcolonial period, the composition of the African immigrant population was determined primarily by two specific factors. The arrival of political independence in the African continent opened the floodgates of "Americanism" in Africa; many African peoples saw this as a rare opportunity to go and see for themselves the wonders of American civilization. An overwhelming majority of those who reached American shores belonged to a category that I have identified elsewhere as "the Children of the Cold War."[9] In other words, they were the beneficiaries of the ideological rivalry between the Soviet Union and the West. These two contending powers offered generous scholarships to young Africans who wished to receive higher education. Chosen purposely to serve as ideological proxies in the Cold War, most returned home to obtain lucrative jobs in their countries of origin. However, for one reason or the other a tiny fraction decided to remain in America. This body of Africans gradually became a significant building block in the emerging Muslim community in America.

The second factor that must be considered in looking at the gradual but significant development of an African immigrant community in America is the state of African governance in the postcolonial period. Though the arrival of political freedom in Africa spelled success for many of those with western education, the political battles for a piece of the African pie soon led to instability and bloodshed. Because of this, many Africans found their homelands transformed into killing fields and their careers wasted by political breakdowns and chaos in their countries. Frightened because of the bloodshed from political disorder and civil wars, many of these men and women fled back to the West, where they had originally come for their education. There they hoped to find shelter and succor, which most of them did. As a result of this influx, the African immigrant population in America became diversified, and those who had stayed in this country for marriage and family reasons saw their numbers increased by refugees seeking political asylum.

The first waves of African Muslim refugees who came to the United States were North African in origin and disposition. Some victims of Nasserism in Egypt fled to the United States, while most went to other Arab lands, especially the Gulf states. The ideological struggle between Nasser and the House of Saud made these political refugees useful allies of King Saud and his half-brother and successor, King Faisal Ibn Abdul Aziz. Many of these Egyptian refugees who had fled to the Gulf states later emigrated to the United States. Today, Egyptian American families often can trace their settlement in America to those days. Some of these families have now become prominent among Arab Americans living on the West and the East Coasts of the United States.

Besides the Egyptians, there were also many Maghrebians who left Morocco and Algeria to settle in America. For the most part, the Algerians came with U.S. scholarships to study in American colleges and universities. Most of these men and women went back home to assume positions in their government, but, because of changing times and circumstances, many later returned to the United States. Bilingual and increasingly "Anglo-Saxonized," they were very clear that their futures were better served by staying in the United States. This was certainly the case among the small but soon growing numbers of Algerians who opposed the National Liberation Front (FLN) government. They found that in America one could be both modern and religious without being politically persecuted for it. Many of the Algerian students accepted some form of the Muslim Brotherhood philosophy. Like Sayyid Qutb, of Egypt, they came to America and drank from its foundation of knowledge without getting drunk on the wine of secularism. Inspired by either Ben Badis or Malik Bennabi, of North Africa, these Maghrebian Muslim students on American college campuses became active members of the Muslim Student Association.

The diversity of the African immigrant community has been manifested not only in terms of regional variation but also by gender. Until the postcolonial era, African immigrants were overwhelmingly male and single. This distribution pattern changed with political independence. By the time African countries received their political freedom, a large and growing body of women had gotten western-style education. They were beginning to compete with their male counterparts for opportunities to study in colleges and universities abroad. Like the men, some of these women returned home after time overseas. Others married African men who decided to stay on in the United States. A small percentage became the wives of American men, often Peace Corps volunteers who had spent time in African countries. A tiny fraction of these women came from Muslim backgrounds. Marriages between Peace Corps volunteers and African women in tropical Africa were rare, and clearly the exception to the Corps rule against nonconjugal entanglements. Some African Muslim women married American men, black or white, who came to their countries to study Arabic and Islam. Such cases, however, were more frequent north of the Sahara. Some such couples have become leaders among the Muslim academics in the United States of America.[10]

The coming of political independence to many African countries was a very important factor in the diversification of the African immigrant population. Up to the early 1960s, these men and women were mainly from English-speaking areas of the continent. They had some degree of command of the English language and for this and other related reasons were able to navigate the stormy waters of American society. The postindependence period opened up many opportunities for Africans from other colonial territories. As a result, the African immigrant community now embraces permanent residents from virtually every country on the continent, from Algeria to Zambia. Naturally, the numbers vary greatly from country to country. Economic as well as political conditions play a major role in emigration. Those exceptional African states that have witnessed stable political regimes since the early 1960s and that are economically well off by African standards are less likely to have many émigrés in the United States. The largest concentrations of Africans in America are from Nigeria, Ethiopia, Ghana, Sierra Leone, Liberia, South Africa, Somalia, Senegal, and Kenya. There are also significant numbers from Zaire, Sudan, Egypt, Eritrea, Uganda, Cameroon, Algeria, Morocco, Libya, Mali, and Cape Verde. The African immigrant population also counts among its numbers immigrants from smaller states like the Gambia, Togo, Mauritius, and Lesotho.

Many of these are students who ostensibly came to study but, due to certain circumstances, have decided to stay on in the United States. Some African immigrants at one point returned home to take lucrative jobs but, because of changes in the political fortunes of their country, felt they no longer could live in their original homelands.[11] Among the countries I have listed with largest numbers of African immigrants in the United States, Cape Verde, Cameroon, Zaire, Liberia, and Ghana have the smallest percentages of Muslims in their aggregates.

The most recent and significant additions to the growing list of African immigrants are the Somalis and the Rwandans. The collapse of the Somali state and the highly televised bloodletting that followed the crisis attracted the attention of many Americans. Because of Operation Restore Hope, organized by the George H. W. Bush administration and sanctioned by the United Nations, the United States authorities became involved in the humanitarian operations in Somalia. Thousands of Somalis now live in the United States, scattered in various parts of the country. Some are in the greater Washington, D.C. area, especially in northern Virginia; according to figures from the Immigration and Naturalization Services (INS), three thousand Somalis took up residence in the northern Virginia region. Many of these are women and children waiting for a reunion with their husbands and fathers.[12] Others are on the West Coast, particularly in San Diego, California; still others are in the Midwest, especially in Minnesota and parts of Illinois.

It is important to distinguish between those Somalis who came to the United States for higher education and other reasons before the eruption of civil war and those who arrived after the fall of the country's former military dictator, Siad Barre. Somalis have visited this country since the beginning of the past century. The few who had come in the interwar years were following in the footsteps of their Yemeni neighbors. Taking full advantage of the opportunities created by the opening of the Suez Canal, they became either seamen or stowaways on board vessels bound for the Americas. Some of these early Somalis found their way to Harlem, where they constituted a tiny fraction of the foreign blacks living among a community of African Americans who had migrated from the south.

The Somali presence in the United States more recently is simply part of a larger phenomenon of twentieth-century Somali dispersal in western societies. Somalis are found in large numbers in Canada, where they form a significant segment of the ethnic and religious tapestry of Toronto. Even in the cold climate of a country like Norway, one can find Somali women walking in their national garb in the parks and public places. The Somali diaspora in the West has grown dramatically, and because of the Islamic orientation of some, Somalis may be influential in helping shape the direction of European and American Islam.

The Rwandan crisis has triggered a series of migrations outside the country. Most Hutus fleeing their troubled homeland relocated in African territories. A very small number of Rwandans are in the United States, unable to benefit from U.S. immigration as have other refugees from Africa. The Rwandans who were in the United States at the time of the slaughter received Uncle Sam's bureaucratic wink to stay on until matters get better in their home country. This was the same response given to the Ugandans and Liberians when their societies were going through turmoil. To the best of this researcher's knowledge, not many Rwandans currently living as political refugees in America are Muslims.

Challenges to and Opportunities for the African Immigrant Family

Several issues confront the investigator studying the African immigrant family in the United States. Most of these problems are not peculiar to Africans but are faced by all immigrants living outside their homelands. The first issue is that of identity and self-definition. How have African immigrants fared thus far in a white and Christian-majority society? The answer to this question is not conclusive—the jury is still out. There is a need for more research on individual African groups, although studies have been done on the Nigerians, the Ethiopians, and the Senegalese who live in various parts of the United States. Muslims are present within all these three major continental African groups, especially among the Senegalese communities. The Folklife unit of the Smithsonian Institute has been studying these continental African communities in the greater Washington, D.C., area. Though their research does not give a statistical breakdown along religious lines, it does take into account the Muslim elements among them. The writings of Diana Ndiaye, at the Folklife unit of the Smithsonian, and Sylvaine Diouf, in New York City, help paint a revealing picture of these Senegalese immigrants along the eastern seaboard.[13]

What we learn from these studies is that the new immigrants are juggling with multiple identities. Their American experience has forced them to take a hard look at conditions in American society and at their circumstances within them. In a society where people define themselves racially, ethnically, economically, and linguistically, African family members begin to realize that they have multiple identities and that each of these identities is meaningful, depending on the context in which they find themselves. On one level, one is a black person in a sea of whiteness. On another level, one is a Christian or Muslim, as opposed to a Jew or an atheist. The same African may be in one instance the only restaurant owner at the Parents/Teachers Association meeting and in another instance the parent from Ethiopia, as opposed to Gambia or Ghana. Within the smaller universe of continental Africans, the immigrant may be one out of thousands of Nigerians, Sierra Leoneans, South Africans, or Kenyans living within a given city.

Under these conditions, the African immigrant may find that the splintering of the original African community in that city has turned into what I have called elsewhere the "islandization" process. That is, the immigrant now witnesses the clustering effects of culture and language and the increase in the number of "homeboys" and "homegirls." This process of islandization leads to the rediscovery of one's ethnic, subethnic, and African high school identities. There are many African organizations whose creation is the result of such kinds of self-definition among African immigrants. The process can also take on a religious character. In their study of the Ethiopian communities in the United States, for example, the husband- and-wife team Getachew Metaferria and Maiginet Shifferew demonstrate how the Ethiopian Coptic Church now plays an important role in the adjustment of Ethiopian immigrants in American society.[14] The Nigerian, Ghanaian, Sierra Leonean, and Liberian Christian churches are playing similar roles in their communities. The Nigerian Catholics are among the most organized within the African Christian communities in the United States; in some areas, they now offer religious services in Ibo, largely because the Ibo constitute a significant portion of the Nigerian community in the United States, and a sizeable number of them are Catholic.[15]

The Protestant groups are also organizing. The Africanized Christian churches have taken the lead in helping African families adjust to the challenges of American life and culture. The Brotherhood of the Cross, founded by Olumba Olumba Olu (OOO), now has branches in several American localities. With about two million followers world-wide, this religious group caters to its African flocks in those U.S. cities where sizeable numbers of Nigerians live. The Cherubim and Seraphim Church, International House of Prayer for All People, founded by the Reverend (Dr.) Fred O. Ogunfiditimi, has a chapter in Washington, D.C., with followers also outside the area. According to the research findings of Chike Anigboh, the church has staked a claim for itself in the realm of healing and spirituality for Nigerians and other members. With the ever-growing challenges of daily stress and pain, the African immigrants, especially those with limited financial and emotional means, find themselves drawn to these churches. They serve as socializing agencies, addressing the material and spiritual needs of immigrants who are trying to cope with city life. The Reverend (Dr.) Ogunfiditimi's church, for example, "provides an immediate place of abode for stranded Nigerians and Nigerians who are coming to the United States for the first time, and to enable them to sort out their problems. These stranded Nigerians could stay at the church for two months."[16]

African immigrants of the Islamic faith have also embraced their religion to provide succor and meaning to their life in this new environment. There are Senegambian, Sierra Leonean, Ghanaian, Nigerian, Ethiopian, Somali, Sudanese, and other North African Muslim organizations in America. The Islamic groups among the African immigrants are inspired by the traditional Sufi orders back home or by the Islamic revivalism that presently holds sway in certain circles of the Muslim world. From a recent essay by Sylvaine Diouf-Kamara on Senegalese immigrants living in the United States, especially those in New York City,[17] we learn that the women are increasingly becoming independent, largely because of the changes in gender relations that occur in their new environment. The need for a double income and the struggle for daily survival in an industrial society have made it difficult for one man to take care of himself and his family. Such circumstances are serving to change attitudes and perceptions in the mental and social landscapes of the African Muslim immigrant. According to Diouf-Kamara's study, the number of highly educated women emigrating from Senegal to the United States has increased in recent years. These changes and the manner in which they are received and perceived by the African Muslim population has serious consequences for the shaping of family values among African immigrant Muslims.

Another issue that confronts the African immigrant is the "myth of return." All immigrants entertain the notion of coming here, striking it rich, and then returning home. More often than not, this does not happen. The single immigrant instead often marries a local woman and ends up fathering a child or two, staying at least long enough to see those children start their own families. The perpetuation of this myth of return among the African immigrants creates a serious gap between ideals and realities. Most of these immigrants have grand ideas about how their homelands should be transformed. Because of their procrastination and ambivalence, they focus on the homelands, while neglecting the proper socialization of their children for the return journey home. Many immigrants do not bother to teach their children any African language, resulting in a growing body of young Africans who have no knowledge of their fathers' or mothers' tongues. Many have thought that these languages would be acquired, as if by osmosis, through the child's interaction with members of the family. This is the point where it is appropriate to raise the question of socialization and the need for social and moral agencies in the education of African immigrant children. There is a serious gap between the ideals of the first generation and the needs of the second. The research data are still very limited, and there is serious need for more intensive study of this phenomenon.[18]

Besides the myth of return, there is the issue of sending remittances to relatives back home. African immigrant families cannot think in terms of nuclear family arrangements but must consider the extended family system in Africa. The average African immigrant comes from a large family, with many siblings and cousins. Many of those who have close social and familial ties to continental Africans follow a monthly ritual of going to American banks or African-managed foreign exchange bureaus to send money home or of giving money to returning compatriots to deposit for their relatives in Africa. A study written by two Nigerian researchers has shown why the Nigerian banking system has not profited from the large sums of monies sent by Nigerians abroad. The main problem, in their view, lies in the almost complete lack of faith in the banking system. This problem deserves serious study; researchers should begin to examine how African governments, in collaboration with émigré organizations, can begin to tap this source of foreign exchange. This issue of foreign exchange and the role African immigrants can play leads to the discussion of the role and place of African diplomatic missions in the United States. It is not an exaggeration to say that most African immigrants have little or no contact with their embassies, visiting them only when their passports are near expiration. On all other occasions, they try to keep the embassies out of their personal business.

There are several reasons for this state of ambivalent relationship. The first is that the political conditions in the country of the immigrant may be such that he or she does not want to get too close to those who rule the homeland. Often these immigrants belong to a losing party and for this and other related reasons decided to come to the United States. Another possible reason is that the African immigrant may feel that the embassy does not have much to contribute to his welfare because the officers running it are from a different part of his country and do not share his views of things. These ethnic or regional biases often have poisoned the waters of African solidarity abroad.

The problems of immigrant living have led to certain types of adjustment for continental African Muslims. I like to class these into three groups of response, which I label the grasshopper, the oyster, and the owl modes of adjustment. The "grasshopper" Muslim of African background usually becomes highly secularized to the point of identifying in many respects with American culture, especially those aspects that are clearly associated with African American pop culture. Such persons may be " 'Eid Muslims," participating in Islamic activities only by attending the festival occasions, or they may simply be cultural Muslims who go about their business in American society, using Anglicized forms of their Muslim names. If they decide not to change their names, they may find themselves in the awkward position of defending Islam and Muslims in non-Muslim circles and fighting with fellow Muslims over the purity of the faith and the seriousness of their commitment to the *Din* (religion).

Those African Muslims I call "oysters" favor living in isolation, as in a shell. They are rare in the case of immigrants from south of the Sahara and are more likely to be found among North Africans. This results from the historical patterns in the development of Islam in the two zones of Africa. These Muslims, who live isolated lives, are also found among Sudanese and Libyans. They are generally identified with the Muslim Brotherhood, the Salafi, the Wahabi, and the Sudanese National Islamic Front activists among the continental African Muslims. The tendency to avoid mixing with the dominant culture can also be found among the conservative Somali families in the United States. This is evident both in their mode of dress and in the greater restriction of movement they impose on women.

The "Muslim owl" is someone who tries hard to strike a balance between the radical assimilationist and the Muslim fundamentalist. This type of Muslim strives to wisely navigate the stormy waters of secular humanism in the United States. The thoroughgoing assimilationist family may lose its cultural identity, and the oyster Muslims may also suffer the fate of a social dinosaur.

Another issue that is increasingly affecting African immigrant families is the spread of "American problems" into the African immigrant community. These negative forms of Americanization have manifested themselves in such ways as participation in the drug culture by some Africans, the emergence of some cases of homelessness, and the rise of criminal activities among some elements of the African immigrant community. The invasion of drugs into immigrant African life must be seen in historical context. Those Africans who do venture into this dangerous domain are generally persons who have some familiarity with this lifestyle before their arrival in the United States. There are many gaps in our knowledge about this phenomenon. As in other areas mentioned, new research needs to be done. The generation of data on the African immigrant in the United States could also influence and change public policies both in the United States and in Africa. However, even with our limited data, we know that the acquisitiveness of the African drug pushers and their desire to engage in mass consumption has propelled them into the arms of their local counterparts. Many an African immigrant is now incarcerated in a U.S. prison because of his or her involvement in the narcotic trade.

Related to but not necessarily caused by the drug culture is the new phenomenon of homelessness among some African immigrants. Thus far it is very limited and generally applies to those Africans who have become seriously dislocated after having settled in the new country. There is very little information about this phenomenon, and the need for new constructive research is urgent. The generation of data on the African immigrant in the United States has the potential to influence and even change public policies both in this country and in Africa.

Five points are worth remembering about the new waves of African immigrants in the United States. There is first the fact that Africans have now decided to settle in the United States voluntarily, almost one hundred years after the Civil War and the end of the slave trade. This is a historical watershed in the sense that the diversity of Africa that characterized the first waves underwent transformation in the colonial era. Whereas the first wave of Africans came as "tribesmen" and speakers of individual languages of Africa, their brethren who came here during the past one hundred years arrived with passports of nations that did not exist in 1619 or 1865.

The second point to remember is that the new Africans carry multiple identities, and this set of identities will affect their relationships with African Americans, with white Americans, with other non-European Americans, with fellow African immigrants, and with persons living in the home country. This is a part of the new reality of globalization. Those African immigrants who can successfully juggle these multiple identities are qualified to call themselves "glocals," men and women who are not only comfortable in their culture of origin but have mastered the global environment and are able to operate in it meaningfully and effectively.

The third point is the reality that the African immigrant family faces the same difficulties that other immigrants have faced in the past and will continue to face. The problem of identity and self-definition will remain an issue, but each person and each community must addresss this issue individually. The fourth point deals with the role and place of religion in the lives of the African immigrants. With respect to this question, we can say that religion will continue to greatly affect many Africans. The African tendency to hedge one's metaphysical bets is most evident in the embrace of an Abrahamic faith, while simultaneously pouring libations at weddings, baby showers, public events, and funeral rites.

The final point to remember is that African immigrants are now a part of the American experience, and their children and grandchildren will be as driven by the quest for the "American Dream" as are others in the society. It remains to be seen, of course, what kinds of contributions these Africans will be able to make to their newly adopted land, as well as to the societies from which they have come.

Notes

1. For discussion of the founding of Liberia and the postbellum relations that exist between Africans and African Americans, see Edward Wilmot Blyden, *Christianity, Islam and the Negro Race* (London: Whittingham, 1887), which has been republished several times. See also D. Elwood Dunn and Svend E. Holsoe, *Historical Dictionary of Liberia* (Metuchen, N.J.: Scarecrow, 1985); and Dunn and S. Byron Tarr, *Liberia: A National Polity in Transition* (Metuchen, N.J.: Scarecrow, 1988).

2. The story of Chief Sam is available in Jabez Ayodele Langley's *Pan-Africanism and Nationalism in Africa 1900–45* (New York: Oxford University Press, 1973), 41–58.

3. Ahmed I. Abu Shouk, John O. Hunwick, and R. X. O'Fahey, "A Sudanese Missionary to the United States: Satti Majid, Shaykh al-Islam in North America and His Encounter with Noble Drew Ali, Prophet of the Moorish Science Temple Movement," *Sudanic Africa, a Journal of Historical Sources* 8 (1997): 137–91.

4. For more information on Duse Mohamed Ali, see Ian Duffield's unpublished dissertation on this African journalist and activist, "Duse Mohamed Ali," University of Edinburgh, 1981.

5. For Alex Haley's fictionalized version of Kunta Kinteh's life, see *Roots* (New York: Dell, 1976).

6. For some continental views on American society and culture, see Nnamdi Azikiwe, *My Odyssey: An Autobiography* (New York: Praeger, 1970).

7. For discussion on Kwegyir W. Aggrey, see Kenneth King, "James E. K. Aggrey: Collaborator, Nationalist, Pan African," *Canadian Journal of African Studies* 3, no. 4 (Fall 1970): 511–30.

8. Kwame Nkrumah gives some interesting accounts of his experiences in American society. See *The Autobiography of Kwame Nkrumah* (Edinburgh: Nelson, 1957); Basil Davidson, *Black Star: A View of the Life and Times of Kwame Nkrumah* (London: Allen Lane, 1973), 29–40;

Imanuel Geist, *The Pan African Movement: A History of Pan-Africanism in America, Europe, and Africa* (New York: Africana, 1968), 363–84.

9. Sulayman S. Nyang, "Islam in America: A Historical Perspective," *American Muslim Quarterly* 2, no. 1 (Spring 1998): 17; Nyang, *Islam in the United States of America* (Chicago: ABC International, 1999), 18.

10. For some discussion on African students and immigrants in the West, especially in the United States, see Joseph Takougang, "Recent African Immigrants in the United States: An Historical Perspective," *Western Journal of Black Studies* 19, no. 2 (Spring 1995): 50–57; Anonymous, "Africans in America," *Ebony Magazine* 44, 2 (December 1988): 46.

11. For U.S. Immigration and Naturalization Services statistics on African immigration since the late 1950s, see INS Statistical Abstracts for the 1945–1999 period. These databases do not give figures that match the claims of the respective nationalities representing different parts of Africa.

12. For some discussion on the Somali presence in these three areas of the United States since the fall of the former dictator Said Barre, see the entries on the Bell & Howard Index for the *Washington Post*, the *Los Angeles Times*, and the *New York Times*.

13. For Diana Ndiaye's work with the folk life of the Smithsonian Institute, see the folk life website: www.si.edu/folklife. Sylvian Diouf-Kamara, "Senegalese in New York: A Model Minority," *Black Renaissance* 1, 2 (Summer/Fall 1997): 92–115.

14. Getachew Metaferria and Maiginet Shiffrew, *Ethiopian Immigrants in the United States* (Buffalo, N.Y.: Edwin Mellon, 1992).

15. For details on this subject, see Chike Anigboh, "The African Neo-Diaspora: Dynamics and Prospects for Afro-Centrism and Counterpenetration—A Case Study of the Nigerian Community in the United States," Ph.D. diss., Howard University, 1994.

16. See Anigboh, "The African Neo-Diaspora."

17. Diouf-Kamara, "Senegalese in New York."

18. There are limited studies on African immigrants regarding language maintenance. For discussion of the African Muslim immigrant situation, see Sulayman Nyang, "African Muslims," in *American Immigrant Cultures: Builders of a Nation*, ed. David Lecincon and Melvin Ember, vol. 1 (New York: Macmillan, 1997), 20–31.

17

Crescent Dawn in the Great White North: Muslim Participation in the Canadian Public Sphere

Karim H. Karim

A Muslim presence is increasingly visible in Canada, where the cityscapes are dotted with the distinctive architecture of the occasional *masjid, jamatkhana,* and *imambara.* Traditional male Muslim garments may be spotted only in certain areas, but the headscarves worn by numbers of Muslim women are to be seen in city center streets, shops, offices, and parks. M. G. Vassanji, a prize-winning Muslim author whose novels have captured the experiences of a fictional diasporic Muslim community,[1] has been recognized by the Canadian literary elite. An increasing number of broadcast programs supported by Muslim groups are appearing on what Charles Husband calls "the multi-ethnic public sphere";[2] apart from crisis coverage about Muslims, however, mainstream Canadian television still shies away from including images of Islam in its day-to-day programming.

The population of Muslims in Canada rose by 153 percent in the period between the national censuses of 1981 and 1991. This spectacular growth, mainly through immigration, brought Canadian public life into firsthand contact with large numbers of people who had recently arrived from Muslim societies in Asia and Africa. Differences in cultural and religious outlook between mainstream Canadian society and the burgeoning Muslim community were highlighted by dramatic events in some of the home countries of Muslims and their diasporic communities. These included the resurgence of Islamic piety, violence carried out in the name of Islam, the institution of *hudud* punishments by governments, the strong reaction of many Muslims to *The Satanic Verses,* the Gulf War, and the conflicts in countries like Afghanistan and the former Yugoslavia. The 1980s and the 1990s also saw the increasing institutionalization of multiculturalism in Canada, the country that claims to have invented this contemporary social policy. The rapid growth of the Canadian *ummah* has posed challenges to the nation's institutions, some of which have attempted to adapt to the country's evolving demographic reality. It has also given some opponents of change what they view as evidence of the destruction of the integrity of Canadian society.

Even though the rapid growth of the Canadian *ummah* has made Islam the religion with the second-largest following in the country after Christianity, effective access to the corridors of political power remains largely elusive for Muslims. Apart from external barriers, certain internal tendencies may also be the causes for this situation. A significant number of immigrant Muslims have not yet settled into the Canadian scheme of things. Rather than deal with issues such as political and social participation on Canadian terms or engage intellectually with issues of modernity, they tend to look to their home countries for solutions to their current problems, whether they have to do with religious architecture[3] or the generation gap. However, indications are that Muslims born and raised in Canada are more willing than their immigrant parents to interact with the larger society of the only home they have known.

Muslims in the Canadian Public Sphere

Recorded history indicates a Muslim presence in Canada since the mid-nineteenth century. Daood Hamdani's study of an archival document suggests the birth of a child in 1854 to an immigrant Muslim couple living in Ontario.[4] The earliest official record of Muslims in Canada is from 1871, when the national census counted thirteen Muslim residents. The numbers of those arriving remained fairly small until the end of the Second World War. The remnants of race-based immigration restrictions were lifted in the 1960s, and the past three decades have seen substantial growth in the quantity and the diversity of immigrants' origins (see table 17.1). Whereas the early arrivals were mainly of Arab and Turkic origins, the more recent immigrant Muslims come from many other parts of the world. The most recent census data (1991) on religious affiliation put the number of Canadian Muslims at 253,260, or just under 1 percent of the country's population. Hamdani, a government statistician, has estimated the number to have been around 450,000 in 1996; he projects that the figure will rise to 650,000 by 2001.[5] (Most immigrants from non-European countries tend to adopt Canadian citizenship, which they can normally apply for after three years of residence in the country.)

Whereas the majority of Muslims in Canada are Sunnis, there are substantial Shi'i communities of Isma'ilis and Ithna Ash'aris in almost all major centers. Ahmadis are also present in significant numbers, and there are some Druze in various cities. Sufi tariqas are also part of the Canadian *ummah*. Although the current Canadian Muslim

Table 17.1. Growth of the Muslim population in Canada

Year	Population
1871	13
1901	47
1911	797
1921	478[a]
1931	645
1951	1,800
1961	5,800
1971	33,430
1981	98,160
1991	253,260

Source: Compiled from Hamdani (1984) and Multiculturalism and Citizenship Canada, 1983.

[a]A large number of Turks left Canada during World War I because they were considered enemy aliens. Zohra Husaini, *Muslims in the Canadian Mosaic* (Edmonton: Muslim Research Foundation, 1990), 20.

population comes from around the world, the bulk is of South Asian and Arab descent.[6] The Council of Muslim Community of Canada (CMCC, formerly the Council of Muslim Communities of Canada), the Canadian Council of Muslim Women, the Ismailia Council for Canada, the Islamic Society of North America, the Islamic Circle of North America, and the Ahmadiyya Movement in Islam are among the bodies with a presence across the country. Virtually all Canadian universities and many high schools have associations of Muslim students. There are many other Muslim associations that have a religious or ethnic focus, some of which have been in existence for decades and others that are transitory. The proliferation of associations indicates that there is no monolithic voice that speaks for all Muslims; different issues are championed by specific organizations, as is made evident in this chapter. Whereas embassy officials from Muslim-majority countries interact with sections of the local community, the heterogeneity of organizations in the Canadian *ummah* tends to limit their influence.

The earlier immigrant Muslims were mostly men with little education or capital; many of them worked either as unskilled laborers or as itinerant peddlers.[7] In contrast, contemporary Canadian Muslim men and women tend to be highly educated. Analyzing the 1981 census figures, Zohra Husaini notes that "It is particularly significant that at the university level, the percentage of Muslims is twice as high as that of other immigrants and close to three times as high as the total Canadian population."[8] The preference of the Canadian immigration system for applicants with high educational qualifications appears to be a factor in the educational discrepancy between native-born and immigrant residents. A third of the Muslim adult male population was in each of the occupational categories of professional, white-collar, and blue-collar jobs; however, women have been found mainly in white-collar positions.[9] Certain Muslim individuals have been successful in Canadian business, including high-technology ventures. Sunera Thobani, who is Muslim, is the former head of the National Action Committee on the Status of Women, the largest umbrella group of Canadian women's organizations.

There are a number of Muslims working at various positions in federal and provincial governments, with the highest-ranking a woman, Nurjehan Mawani, who is the chairperson of the Immigration and Refugee Board of Canada. A Muslim development organization seeking to influence Canadian foreign policy making lamented that, despite having "a powerful group of Muslim senior civil servants in the municipal, provincial and federal governments,"[10] community groups were not seeking their advice on the mechanics of lobbying officialdom.[11] However, apart from the relatively low hiring rates of minorities by the Canadian public service, there is also resistance to permitting certain kinds of postings for Muslims. In a meeting with the Islamic Coordinating Council, the minister for the foreign affairs department said that he would not appoint a Muslim diplomat to a Canadian mission in a Muslim country.[12]

Muslim men have been elected to provincial parliaments in the past, with one holding a cabinet portfolio in Alberta. An outspoken "Muslim feminist," Fatima Houda-Pépin, holds office as a member of the assembly in Quebec, and Rahim Jaffer, a young Albertan who belongs to a right-wing party, is the first Muslim elected to the federal parliament. However, Muslims have far less strength in Canadian politics than members of the Jewish community, whose population numbers they have recently overtaken, or the even smaller Sikh community, which has ministerial presence in the federal and the British Columbia cabinets. Even Lebanese Muslims, who have had some political success, are largely outstripped by Lebanese Christian politicians, one of whom rose to be premier of the province of Prince Edward Island. Daood Hamdani notes that

> Muslim participation in nearly all phases of the political process—exercising the franchise, campaigning for candidates and running for office—is discouraging, partly reflecting the lack of exposure to such processes in their native countries and partly the belief that they are numerically too small to count. A Political Action Committee came into existence just before the 1979 federal general elections but it failed either to mobilize the Muslim voters or to impress upon the political parties that it had any clout with the community.[13]

In February 1997, Al-Shura, a coalition of forty-nine Toronto-area Muslim groups that seeks to ensure Muslim political representation in Canada, met in Ottawa to discuss strategy. Delegates recognized that the failure to elect substantial numbers from the community may be a result of the differences in origin and in religious views as well as the "anti-democratic, anti-West and pro-terrorist" image of Muslims among the Canadian public.[14] However, the election of several Muslims to the leadership of Canadian university organizations across the country seems to indicate the emergence of a more politically engaged generation. Javeed Sukhera, a Muslim high school student, was chosen as the "student premier of Ontario" in 1998.

There is also Muslim presence in Canadian ethnic media, including print, radio, and television outlets, as well as on-line media. A half-hour Muslim program called "The Muslim Chronicle" runs on the national religious channel, Vision TV; Islamic religious and ethical content is also carried on a variety of ethnic programs produced by Muslims. Muslim periodicals include the *Muslim Tribune, The Ismaili, Canada,* and *The Right Path;* the more successful newspapers largely serve ethnic groups such as Pakistanis and Arabs. A few members of the community have also managed to gain senior positions in the mass media. Muslims have served on the staff and editorial boards of major urban dailies, but they have had less success in the broadcast media. Apart from news stories, there are regular features in newspapers about Ramadan and Islamic celebrations in metropolitan dailies. When a newspaper publishes what may be viewed as inaccurate or derogatory material on Islam, Muslims usually respond with letters to the editor. However, Haroon Siddiqui, editorial page editor of the *Toronto Star,* has lamented that members of the community generally do not seem to understand that the media would like to carry out a dialogue with minorities. "Muslims have not approached me. They are simply absent from the newsmaking process, unlike other communities. The exception among the Muslims are the Ismailis, followers of the Aga Khan; they are miles ahead of other Muslim groups in their sophisticated media skills."[15] The problem, according to the editor, is that many immigrant Muslims have been unable to consider themselves part of the North American milieu and have consequently not developed the skills to deal with the institutions of industrial society.

The level of success achieved in the Canadian public sphere by (Nizari) Ismailis seems partially to be the result of centralized leadership that resides in a tight institutional infrastructure.[16] The Aga Khan Development Network, which is transnational in scope, is made up of religious, social, cultural, sports, health, educational, humanitarian, and economic institutions that are operated largely in the Ismaili diaspora. Female education is encouraged, and leadership positions are held by women in community institutions. Estimates of the size of the community in Canada run between 60,000 and 70,000, making it a significant portion of the entire Muslim presence in the country. The Ismailia Council for Canada and its regional bodies govern community affairs and coordinate participation in charity events in the larger Canadian society. The Council has been able to develop links with governmental institutions, leading to initiatives like an innovative joint agreement to resettle Afghani refugees in Canada.[17] Similarly, the Aga Khan Foundation Canada, an organization that designs and manages development projects in African and Asian countries,[18] has signed a major accord with the Canadian International Development Agency. The Aga Khan Development Network Centre, in Ottawa, and the prominently situated *jamatkhanas* serve to give the community a significant profile. It is noteworthy that the public figures I have mentioned—the member of the federal parliament, the most senior Muslim public servant, the former head of the national women's organization, and the prize-winning writer—all have Ismaili backgrounds. The current president of the Ismailia Council for Canada, Firoz Rasul, runs a successful high-technology company.

Other Muslims who have gained prominence in the Canadian public sphere have also been those engaged in the larger issues of society. Fatima Houda-Pépin, the Moroccan-born Muslim member of Quebec's legislature and the founding president of Le Centre Maghrébin de Recherche et d'Information, has been recognized in Quebec society for her efforts in promoting the French language. She has also publicly commented on issues that touch the Muslim community from both positions. Houda-Pépin espouses a modernist view of Islam that often pits her against the more conservative leaders. Nevertheless, she has formed alliances with several Muslim and non-Muslim organizations and has often defended the rights of other minority groups. Houda-Pépin made her research center into a forum for public discussions on the rights of Muslim women, the Rushdie crisis, and the Gulf War, as well as other issues that affect minorities, such as their rights in Quebec's educational system. The media, which has called her a "Muslim feminist,"[19] regularly seeks her out for comment on issues that affect the community in Quebec. Aziz Khaki, the Vancouver-based head of an antiracism organization, has similarly been active in public affairs. His prominence as a community activist and a respected participant in interfaith fora has led to his appointment to several government advisory bodies.

The general tendency among the Muslim leadership in Canada is to search for social justice within the Canadian environment, rather than to adopt an isolationist attitude. Conferences organized by Muslim organizations sometimes include speakers from outside the *ummah*. Agendas also frequently include discussion of youth issues, with young members of the community participating in the panels. Dating and intermarriage with non-Muslims are usually looked at unfavorably, and views on the role of Muslim women in the community tend to lean towards conservatism. However, several Muslim men and women are asking for a reassessment of the place of women. As Ibrahim Hayani states, "No self-respecting society can afford to ignore or under-utilize its scarce resources, especially its human resources, and be they men or women. Of all the topics or issues related to Islam in Canada, the role of women in the collective life of the Canadian Muslim community is probably one of the most critical, if not the most critical, issue that needs to be discussed and debated rationally, constructively, and courageously."[20]

The Canadian Council of Muslim Women is a leading organization in bringing such issues to the fore. However, the conservatism of many newly arrived Muslims in Canada and that of some Imams seems to slow the pace of change in this area.

Muslim Symbols and Spaces in the Public Square

Muslims have engaged in a series of public debates about the place of their religious symbols in the Canadian public square. Edmonton's Al Rashid Mosque, which was built in 1938 and is the oldest in North America, was the subject of a controversy in the late 1980s.[21] When the municipal council decided to establish the Fort Edmonton Park for the preservation of the city's heritage, it agreed on a master plan for the park that did not specify a particular historical period. Subsequently, a request was made to include Al Rashid Mosque, which had been recognized by the provincial government as a heritage building in the park. The Friends of Al Rashid Mosque, an organization that had already received a substantial provincial grant, was willing to bear the cost of relocation and maintenance.

But the Fort Edmonton Foundation added a cutoff date of 1929 in a revised master plan, which was submitted at the same meeting during which the Al Rashid request was to be discussed. The reason given for the date, which would disqualify the historic mosque from automatic inclusion, was ostensibly a desire to keep the park authentic. However, the revised plan did state that exceptions could be made for meritorious projects. A polarized debate was waged in the *Edmonton Sun*, which has a right-wing stance, and the *Edmonton Journal*, which leans toward the left, about whether the mosque should be included in the heritage park. This was an example of the competing discourses on the inclusion of diversity in the officially multicultural public sphere of Canada.[22] The *Sun* fiercely opposed the presence of "other people's cultures" in a park that "is a unique expression of our history." Such discourses tend to be based on the image of Canada as a white, Christian country. The alternative discourse of the *Journal* cited the role that Edmonton's Muslim community played in the history of the city and the contributions that Christians and Jews also made to the construction of the mosque. Following a long-running discussion, the city council and the park foundation ultimately agreed to place the mosque in the heritage park.

Plans to build new Muslim places of worship frequently meet with opposition from residents of the neighborhood for which the building is proposed. They usually cite concerns about noise and traffic congestion that would result from meetings at a congregational center. Some occasionally express the fear of being swamped by adherents of an alien religion. Consequently, Muslim religious and social centers are often located in industrial and other nonresidential zones. Sometimes their construction is opposed even at such sites, as was the case in 1990, when it was proposed to build a mosque in a Calgary industrial park. Some Muslims said that the opposition seemed to be motivated by racism: "Kazi Ahmed, acting chairman of the East Calgary Islamic Centre, said people always cite potential traffic problems when there is a proposal for a temple [sic] or cultural center. 'But when other cultural centers are built, like the Austrian Canadian Club, there doesn't seem to be as many problems,' Ahmed said."[23] An alternate site to build the mosque was eventually agreed upon by the city council and the Muslim community. Obtaining reserved space in cemeteries has also been problematic. The allocation of preestablished burial plots to Muslims frequently does not allow the custom of placing the head of the deceased in the direction of Mecca. Certain Islamic burial rituals also cannot be performed under some of the existing work routines of cemetery staff.

The headscarves that some Muslim women and girls choose to wear as an expression of their Islamic beliefs has been the subject of much public controversy in France; Quebec has had minor versions of "l'affaires des foulards." A judge expelled a Muslim woman wearing a *hijab* from the courtroom, saying, "When one goes to Rome, one lives like the Romans."[24] In another incident, the principal of a public school sent home a Muslim student who was wearing a scarf. Conversely, a Muslim school in the city requires that all female teachers, including those who are non-Muslim, wear a headscarf. Fatima Houda-Pépin, the sole Muslim member of the provincial parliament, opposed the requirement, saying that it contravenes the Canadian Charter of Rights and Freedoms; in its defense, the school invoked the Quebec Charter of Rights and the Universal Declaration of Human Rights.[25]

Canadian Multiculturalism

Canada was the first country to institute an official policy of multiculturalism and is the only one to have a law recognizing the cultural diversity of its population.[26] The roots of Canadian multiculturalism are to be found in the long-standing policy of biculturalism. Since the nineteenth century the demands of the francophone population for linguistic rights led the government of the former British dominion to forgo the model of a unicultural state. This eventually paved the way for recognition of the significance of groups of other origins that had contributed substantially to the development of Canada. The federal government announced the adoption of the multiculturalism policy in 1971,[27] which led to the emergence of programs for the implementation of the policy and eventually to a full-fledged multiculturalism act in 1988.

The goal of the legislation is to preserve and enhance multiculturalism in the country. It recognizes the diversity of Canadians with regard to race, national or ethnic origin, color, and religion as a fundamental characteristic of Canadian society. The act supports the promotion of the diverse cultures of the population and commits the multiculturalism minister to take measures to encourage and assist individuals, organizations, and institutions to project the multicultural character of Canada in their domestic and foreign activities. It specifically cites the obligations of federal institutions to enhance the ability of all Canadians to contribute to the growth of the country.[28] Ottawa's lead was followed by provincial governments, some of which also passed multiculturalism legislation and devoted resources to programs that support cultural diversity.

Various federal institutions have advisory groups that include representatives of minority groups, including Muslims. During the Gulf War, the federal minister for multiculturalism formed an advisory committee that included Arab, Muslim, and Jewish leaders. Individual Muslims had significant roles in key public consultation exercises such as the Citizens' Forum on Canada's Future (Azhar Ali Khan as senior adviser) and the British Columbia Task Force on Family Violence (Mobina Jaffer as chairperson). Hanny Hassan (later president of CMCC) served as president of the Ontario Advisory Council on Multiculturalism and Citizenship. Organizations like CMCC and the Canadian Society of Muslims were asked by the education ministry of the province to participate in developing suggestions for authors and publishers involved in producing materials for schools.[29] However, in recent years, opportunities for such participation at the provincial level have been reduced for minorities in places like Ontario and Alberta, whose governments have drastically reduced the administrative infrastructure devoted to cultural pluralism. While the federal multiculturalism program has also become a shadow of its former self, the legislation still stands.

Even though a given act may mention religion as a factor in the diversity of Canadians, the administration of the policy usually avoids religious issues. This tendency is influenced by the separation of church and state in western liberal states. Projects centered on religious activities are not funded; nevertheless, the bureaucracy does recognize that it cannot completely disregard minority organizations that define their identity in religious terms. Muslim activities supported by the federal multiculturalism program have included organizational development, conferences, citizenship enhancement, youth leadership development, exhibitions, teacher training, and the teaching of minority languages, including Urdu, Arabic, and Farsi.

Nöel Kinsella, a senior public servant who headed the multiculturalism department during the early 1990s, was particularly interested in promoting religious equality in the country. He recognized that, despite the nominal separation of church and state in Canada, religion does play an important symbolic function in the state ceremonial. One initiative during his tenure involved the amendment of the official table of precedence, which determines the presence and sequence of appearance of individuals during important state events. A certain category in the table refers to religious officials, which at that time allowed for the presence only of Christian and Jewish representatives. This category was expanded to include all religious groups. The senior official also worked in conjunction with Abdul Lodhi, a Muslim academic at St. Thomas University, in New Brunswick, to draft a proposal for a national code of conduct that would foster religious harmony.

The political climate created by official multiculturalism allows politicians and government officials to speak up for ethnic and religious minorities, especially when they are overtly maligned. This is especially significant in cases where the offending party belongs to a university or media outlet, institutions that enjoy considerable freedom of expression. For example, when Peter St. John, a University of Manitoba professor, organized a conference titled "Islamic Terrorism in the 1990s and the Threat to North America," Mark Assad, a member of parliament of Lebanese Christian background, asserted in the assembly that the theme of the conference was offensive to Muslims in Canada. The minister of multiculturalism, Gerry Weiner, who is Jewish, expressed dismay at the manner in which the conference linked terrorism to the religion. Murad Velshi, a Muslim member of the Ontario legislature, also spoke out. As a result of these statements and pressure from the Muslim community, the format of the conference was changed, and Muslim speakers were added to the program. In another instance, the chief commissioner of the Ontario Human Rights Commission wrote to the *Globe and Mail*, the elite newspaper in the country, criticizing the publication of an editorial cartoon that was viewed as being derogatory to Islam.

During the Gulf War, the multiculturalism minister affirmed the place of Arab and Muslim Canadians as "equal citizens of this country,"[30] even as security forces were questioning some members of these communities (discussed later). The opposition party member responsible for multiculturalism proposed an all-party motion expressing the confidence of the parliament in the loyalty of Canadian Arabs and Muslims. Several mayors of Canadian cities took the initiative to bring together leaders of Muslim, Jewish, Christian, and other religious organizations to discuss how to avoid tensions during the war. The Multiculturalism Act is limited to promoting cultural community harmony, but it does not provide enforcement powers. Minorities have to turn to other legislation to seek recourse for their particular circumstances.

Muslims and the Canadian Legal System

The Canadian Muslim Society circulated a brief in the early 1990s that proposed changes to the Canadian legal system that would allow Muslims to administer and pay for their own system of family and personal law. It cited examples from India, Greece, and the former Yugoslavia.[31] The brief argued that, even though the country's constitution cited the supremacy of God, Canadians were not permitted to attain their spiritual ideals in the primarily secular society.

It criticized the favoring of Roman Catholics, whose school system receives public funding, above all other religious communities in Ontario, even though educational taxes are collected from all real estate owners. (Education is within provincial jurisdiction and is therefore not covered by federal legislation.) With the vast majority of Muslim students attending public schools, a number of Muslim schools across the country are running deficits. According to the Canadian Muslim Society, these problems would be resolved if all religions had equal standing in Canada. However, the organization has failed to gain support for its proposals from other Muslim groups.

Muslims have used a variety of existing legal instruments in the effort to extend their rights in Canada. Human rights legislation has enabled members of the community to make some gains regarding time off for religious practice from places of employment. Muslims and members of other minority religions have filed a string of complaints with the federal and provincial human rights commissions, which have been instrumental in resolving some such issues. Hamdani gives the following example:

> In one case, a Muslim working for a business firm wanted time off for Friday prayers. His dispute over this with his employer led to the termination of his employment. The Canadian Human Rights Commission took up his case and this Muslim was reinstated in his job with retroactive pay and fringe benefits and is now allowed to take 1 ½ hours per week as leave without pay to go to Friday prayers.[32]

However, time off from the workplace for nonstatutory religious holidays tends to be arranged on an individual, unofficial basis. (The only statutory religious holidays are Christmas and Easter.) Under the Ontario human rights code, companies must attempt to accommodate the religious observances of employees so long as this does not cause the employers undue hardship. A grievance by two Jewish workers in the Ontario public service led the provincial government to introduce a religious holidays policy that gives its employees two paid days off for nonstatutory religious holidays. The list of these holidays (which included the 'Eid al-Adha and 'Eid al-Fitr) was compiled in consultation with leaders of some twenty religious organizations. However, attempts by minority-faith groups to have school calendars amended to accommodate their holidays have been less successful.

Individual Muslims charged with certain crimes have occasionally presented arguments ostensibly based on Islam to explain their actions. The lawyer of a Winnipeg man, who pleaded guilty to a charge of assault causing bodily harm to his nine-year-old son, stated that he was "raised in a very strict Moslem household and . . . in a value system where severe physical punishment of children is not only accepted, but also a means of showing care and affection."[33] Other members of the Muslim community in the city, including the president of the Manitoba Islamic Association, were indignant at the presentation of such a defense. They told the media that the man was attempting to blame his own shortcomings on Islam. The case ended with the judge rejecting the accused man's explanation. But a Quebec court accepted a convoluted religious defense presented by the lawyer of another Muslim. The man was tried for sodomizing his daughter; he asked for a mitigated sentence because he had avoided vaginal intercourse out of respect for the emphasis in his religion on safeguarding virginity before marriage. This defense was denounced by local Muslim organizations.[34] Another Winnipeg Muslim was prevented by a judge from carrying out the marriage of his fourteen-year-old daughter to a twenty-seven-year-old man. A person had to be sixteen years old to obtain a marriage license under Canadian law of the day. The father, who grew up in Lebanon, stated that, even though his daughter was born in Canada, "she still follows Muslim beliefs that allow a daughter having reached puberty to marry if she wishes, with the consent of her father."[35] While the judge acknowledged that Canada is a pluralistic society, he ruled that the common values and standards take precedence: "Their aim is to protect all citizens and to provide the foundation upon which our successful Canadian democratic system is based. From time to time they may conflict with specific religious, moral or cultural practices and beliefs. Subject to reasonable compromise, any such conflict must be resolved in favor of that general public interest."[36] Such judicial decisions are setting the limits of cultural pluralism in the public sphere of this officially multicultural country.

The few Muslim immigrants who were in polygamous marriages in their countries of origin find themselves in a difficult situation under Canadian legal and social welfare systems, since polygamy is banned in Canada. Although the Law Reform Commission of Canada recommended the removal of the law against polygamy from the criminal code in order to permit religious accommodation, little action has been taken in this direction.[37] The National Federation of Pakistani Canadians has championed the challenge against yet another aspect of law affecting family life.[38] Immigration regulations have specified that for a Canadian to adopt a child from abroad, the child must be registered with an adoption agency or child welfare organization in the foreign country. However, the Federation has maintained that Muslim countries do not have such institutions, since the Qur'an places the responsibility for the guardianship of orphans on the extended family, rather than on governments. (Practice in this area varies among Canadian Muslims of different sectarian and ethnic backgrounds, who do not have monolithic interpretations of Scripture.[39]) One Ottawa-area family successfully challenged immigration regulations in a guardianship case by citing the equality section of the Charter of Rights and Freedoms. Another family, from Montreal, was able to obtain an appeals court decision that allowed it to bring over a child from a non-Muslim country by indicating that this would eventually lead to an adoption.

Canadian hate law prohibits the incitement of hatred against identifiable groups. However, despite the periodic vilification of Muslims by various kinds of publications,[40]

Canadian discourses on hate propaganda do not generally include them in the list of victims (who are generally identified as Jews and people of African origins).[41] At the height of controversy over the publication of Salman Rushdie's *The Satanic Verses*, which many Muslims deemed blasphemous to the Prophet Muhammad, the prime minister's office ordered that importation of the book into Canada be suspended in response to a complaint by the Islamic Circle of North America.[42] This move was strongly criticized by several writers' groups in Canada. Officials of the Prohibited Importations section of the revenue department studied the book (which is replete with cultural and religious allusions drawn from the Muslim and South Asian diasporas) and ruled that it did not constitute hate propaganda. The Islamic Action Committee, representing mosques and Muslim organizations in the Toronto area, called on Ottawa to set up a judicial review that would involve experts in Islam and Muslim culture to study the book.[43] However, this suggestion was not accepted by the government, which lifted its restrictions on the publication. The lack of understanding of Muslim sensitivities by government officials and the limitations of the hate propaganda law resulted in a failed effort to address the concerns raised by several Muslim groups.

Perceptions of Muslims as Threats to Public Security

The call for *jihad* by the president of Iraq during the war against the United Nations coalition forces in 1991, combined with the expressions of concern by Canadian Muslims that ranged from mild opposition to Canada's participation in the war to the highly publicized bluster of a few about enlisting in the Iraqi army, served to raise suspicions against the community. (Some Muslims, particularly certain Iraqi exiles, supported the actions of the UN coalition.) Prevalent images of Islam and terrorism did not ameliorate these perceptions. The federal security agency that monitors terrorism had a number of outspoken Muslims and Arabs under surveillance and carried out interrogations. Despite the statements of support from politicians affirming the status of Canadian Arabs and Muslims as full-fledged citizens, the government insisted that it had to investigate what it considered to be legitimate threats. The lack of sufficient knowledge of minority groups among the federal security agency's personnel led to the traumatizing of many who came under their scrutiny.[44]

The official actions against members of Arab and Muslim communities appear also to have encouraged public suspicion against them, which in certain cases led to harassment and even assault. This included name calling on the telephone, in the streets, in schoolyards, and in graffiti on public buildings such as post offices. A number of incidents of physical abuse were also reported in various parts of the country; women wearing *hijabs* were particularly targeted for verbal and physical attacks.[45] This affected the willingness of Muslims to participate in public demonstrations. The psychological effect of the abuse has been long lasting, especially for the young members of the communities who have considered Canada their only home.[46]

A particularly poignant case was that of Riad Majeed, an Edmonton resident who had come from Iraq in 1973. He was a member of the local chapter of the federal party in power and had built up strong connections in political circles, which he had used to help other Muslims and Iraqis. He felt very comfortable about his place as a Canadian citizen and party loyalist. When Iraq invaded Kuwait, he was interviewed by a journalist who was seeking a response from an Iraqi Canadian. Majeed told him he thought that "there was a coup in Kuwait and the Iraqi army was invited there."[47] When the article appeared, he started receiving a series of abusive and threatening phone calls. This was followed by the discovery of a pipe bomb outside his house, which was defused by the police. Majeed's sons were attacked by other boys while they were walking home from school. He sold his house at a considerable loss and changed his telephone number. As the attacks by the UN coalition began on Iraqi targets, violent incidents against Canadian Arabs and Muslims multiplied.

One day, Majeed himself received an unexpected call from the federal security agency on his unlisted number. He was asked to report to the intelligence service's offices, where he was interrogated.[48] Among other questions, he was asked for his opinion on Saddam Hussein and about the presence of Christian and Jewish troops near the Muslim holy places in Saudi Arabia and whether this inflamed him to the point of violence.[49] Majeed, who considered himself to be a well-placed Canadian, felt deeply insulted to be treated as a potential terrorist. All his connections in powerful places seemed to melt away, and it did not appear to matter that he had served on multicultural advisory bodies and that he currently held an important appointment in a federal agency. It seemed that during the time of national crisis, no opposition could be brooked against the government—especially not from a member of a minority that had a terrorist image. The security agency did not appear to consider it material that the members of that very minority were being terrorized by other citizens.

Discussion

The place of Muslims under Canadian multiculturalism, despite the intention of the policy to foster mutual respect and inclusion in the public square, remains uncertain. Notwithstanding the official discourses about enhancing diversity, practice at the state and the cultural levels does not facilitate a friction-free existence for minorities. Whereas the criticism that posits multiculturalism as creating a form of apartheid[50] is grossly misplaced, contemporary notions about the management of cultural pluralism within the state have largely failed to account for the complex identities of human beings. Debates on hyphenated Canadianism do not even begin to scratch the surface of the multiple identifications that individuals carry in their minds and souls. One person can be Canadian, Ottawan, Kenyan, South Asian, Indian, Pakistani, Muslim, Shi'i, Gujarati-speaking, and Anglophone all at the same time and feel passionately about various aspects of one's national, regional, ethnic, cultural, religious, and linguistic identity. The pressure exerted on nationals of a country to assert an exclusive loyalty to it does not correspond with human reality, especially in light of the strength of diasporic links that people have across borders.

Despite government rhetoric about globalization, real boundaries remain between the imagined territories of nation-states. Crossing borders, especially for the disadvantaged peoples of the southern hemisphere, inspires simultaneous feelings of courage and terror. Once in the new country, the newcomer is faced with a hierarchy of power, even in the countries that consider themselves champions of democracy, human rights, and cultural pluralism. The most recent immigrants to a country have the least claim on its public sphere.[51] Those who are perceived as being alien and threatening in their cultural and religious habits are usually on the bottom rung of society.

Nevertheless, the western liberal state does offer its minorities significantly more access to the public domain than is granted by many contemporary nonwestern jurisdictions. The network of human rights and citizenship legislation, together with the social climate fostered by multiculturalism, provide the political possibilities for minorities to claim space in the public square. However, it is up to minority communities themselves to take concrete steps in this direction. Steven Vertovec[52] gives the example of Muslims in the English city of Leicester, who have built bridges within and outside the community to develop an institutional structure that interacts effectively with various levels of society. The Islamic Centre, Surati Muslim Khalifa Society, Ismaili Jamaat, Dawoodi Bohras Jamaat, Ahmadiyya Muslim Association, Gujarati Muslim Association, and Rawal Community Association are among the members of Leicester's Federation of Muslim Organisations, which speaks to city and county authorities with a common voice. The federation has managed to secure a favorable decision regarding provision of *halal* meat in public institutions, permission to broadcast the *adhan* from mosque loudspeakers, and support to build Europe's only intentional *janazgah* in a public cemetery.

Muslims in Leicester, who like Canadian Muslims tend to be generally well educated, are represented at the highest levels of public institutional structures. They are present in the city council, the police department, and the educational system, as well as in other public fora such as political parties, unions, housing associations, women's organizations, youth groups, parent-teacher associations, and minority cultural organizations. Their reactions to *The Satanic Verses* and other controversies, in contrast to that of their coreligionists in other parts of the United Kingdom, have been made in peaceful, articulate, and efficient ways through well-controlled demonstrations and thoughtful statements to the media. The lessons for Canadian Muslims are clear in Leicester's model of multicultural incorporation—unity and coordination within the various parts of the Muslim community and participation in public institutions and in associations of civil society. Effective creation of Muslim spaces in the public sphere of a western country is possible when Muslim groups are willing to set aside differences among themselves and to build lateral links with the larger community.

The particular challenge that Muslims in Canada, as well as those in other western countries, face is the perception of essential difference from other groups. Even though Islam is part of the Abrahamic tradition that has many philosophical similarities with Christianity and Judaism, it is largely viewed in the West as an alien religion. Many conservative Muslims also insist on emphasizing differences with contemporary western society. Unlike the American Muslim leader Warith D. Mohammed, who has attempted to reconcile Islam with the American experience, there is no prominent leader or organization in Canada who has mounted a sustained effort to come to terms with the broader realities of the *ummah*'s existence. Whether it is architecture, intercommunity relations, or political participation, the predominant instincts are generally either to adhere to the past or to compartmentalize one's secular and religious lives. Despite the high level of education among Canadian Muslims, there has been a limited effort to engage intellectually with the philosophical bases of modernity from Islamic perspectives. Nevertheless, in addition to some progressive older Muslims, younger men and women from the community are beginning to tackle contemporary life within frameworks that combine Islamic outlooks with methodologies derived from the western humanities and social sciences. This, along with their growing participation in the politics of public institutions, is pointing to a more active future for the *ummah* in the Canadian public sphere.

Notes

1. *The Gunny Sack* (Oxford: Heinemann International, 1989); *The Book of Secrets* (Toronto: McClelland & Stewart, 1994); *No New Land* (Toronto: McClelland & Stewart, 1991); *Uhuru Street* (Toronto: McClelland & Stewart, 1992).

2. Charles Husband, "Differentiated Citizenship and the Multi-Ethnic Public Sphere," *Journal of International Communication* 5, no. 1 (June/December 1998): 134–48.

3. Gulzar Haider, "'Brother in Islam, Please Draw Us a Mosque': Muslims in the West: A Personal Account," in *Expressions of Islam in Buildings*, ed. Hayat Salam (Geneva: Aga Khan Trust for Culture), 155–66.

4. Daood Hassan Hamdani, "Muslims in the Canadian Mosaic," *Journal Institute of Muslim Minority Affairs* 5, no. 1 (January 1984): 8.

5. Daood Hassan Hamdani, "The Canadian Muslims on the Eve of the Twenty-first Century," *Journal Institute of Muslim Minority Affairs* 19, no. 2 (October 1999): 197–210.

6. Hamdani, "Muslims in the Canadian Mosaic," 10.

7. Baha Abu-Laban, "The Canadian Muslim Community: The Need for a New Survival Strategy," in *The Muslim Community in North America*, ed. Earle H. Waugh, Baha Abu-Laban, and Regula B. Qureshi (Edmonton: University of Alberta Press, 1983), 75–92.

8. Zohra Husaini, *Muslims in the Canadian Mosaic* (Edmonton: Muslim Research Foundation, 1990), 10, 25.

9. Ibid., 26.

10. International Development and Refugee Fund (IDRF), "Canadian External Policy and Muslim Community Response: Discussion Paper by IDRF" (unpublished).

11. Some groups have been successful in lobbying politicians to support their respective causes. For example, in 1989 the Ahmadiyya Movement in Canada convinced forty-six members of Parliament and senators to urge the prime minister to speak at an international conference about the issue of human rights in relation to the treatment of Ahmadis in Pakistan. William Walker, "MPs Increase Pressure on Pakistan Rights Issue," *Toronto Star*, 11 Oct. 1989, p. A27.

12. Frank Howard, "Muslims Seek More Diplomatic Postings," *Ottawa Citizen*, 7 March 1991, p. A7. Baha Abu-Laban comments on the contradiction between the western liberal state's avowed equality for all citizens and the denial of equality in practice. Baha Abu-Laban, "Muslims' Participation in Western Social and Political Structures: Problems and Prospects," paper presented at the Symposium of the Organization of Islamic Conference, "Islam and the West—Toward Dialogue and Understanding," Toronto, October 1996.

13. Hamdani, "Muslims in the Canadian Mosaic," 13.

14. Bob Harvey, "Canadian Muslims Try to Marshal Their Political Power," *Ottawa Citizen*, 15 Feb. 1997, p. C7. Such fears are not misplaced; a national survey that inquired into the comfort level of respondents with various groups in Canada ranked Muslim, Arabs, and Indo-Pakistanis almost at the bottom of the list. Angus Reid. *Multiculturalism and Canadians: Attitude Study 1991–National Survey Report* (Ottawa: Multiculturalism and Citizenship, 1991), 51.

15. Haroon Siddiqui, "Perceptions and Misrepresentations of Islam and Muslims by the Media," *Islam in America* 3, no. 3 (Fall 1996): 41.

16. Azim Nanji, "The Nizari Ismaili Muslim Community in North America," in The Muslim Community in North America, ed. Earle A. Waugh, Baha Abu-Laban, and Regula B. Qureshi (Edmonton: University of Alberta Press, 1983).

17. Citizenship and Immigration Canada, "Marchi and Canadian-Ismaili Community Sign New Resettlement Agreement," news release, 3 May 1994.

18. Other major Muslim organizations involved in development abroad are the International Development and Refugee Fund and Human Concern International.

19. Harvey Shepherd, "Muslim Feminist Dislikes Veiled and Submissive Stereotype," Montreal Gazette, 20 Feb. 1998, p. J8.

20. Ibrahim Hayani, "Textbooks Perpetuate Arab Stereotypes: Cultures and Religion Usually Portrayed in Unflattering Ways." Toronto Star, 18 Jan. 1994, pp. A16-17.

21. "Park Is Right for City's Mosque," Edmonton Journal (editorial), 19 June 1989, p. A4; "West Waiver Wrong," Edmonton Sun (editorial), 16 June 1989, p. 10.

22. Karim H. Karim, "Reconstructing the Multicultural Community: Discursive Strategies of Inclusion and Exclusion." International Journal of Politics, Culture, and Society 7, no. 2 (1993): 189-207.

23. Bob Beaty, "Muslims Say Racism behind Temple Furore," Calgary Herald, 9 Sept. 1990, p. B1.

24. "Judge's Lawyer Challenges Convictions of Muslim Expelled from Courtroom," Ottawa Citizen, 8 June 1994, p. A5.

25. Bellemare, Andre, "Fatima Houda-Pépin denonce l'obligation du part du Hijab faite a des enseignantes," La Presse, 24 Oct. 1994, p. A5.

26. Karim H. Karim, "Multiculturalism in Australia, US, and the UK," in The Battle over Multiculturalism, ed. Andrew Cardozo and Louis Musto (Ottawa: Pearson-Shoyama Institute, 1997).

27. The Canadian Charter of Rights and Freedoms, which is part of the national constitution adopted in 1982, recognizes the multicultural characteristic of the country.

28. Canadian Multiculturalism Act (Ottawa: Supply and Services Canada, 1988).

29. However, the success of this publication was brought into question by the continued inaccuracies about Muslims in Ontario textbooks. Hayani, "Textbooks," A17. See Karim, "Reconstructing," for a discussion on the systematic exclusion of minorities in dominant discourses.

30. "According to Weiner: Arab-Canadians Must Be Assured of Equality," Times Transcript (Moncton, New Brunswick), 28 Feb. 1991, p. 5.

31. Bob Harvey, "Muslims Propose Their Own Set of Laws," Ottawa Citizen, 15 June 1991, p. F6.

32. Hamdani, "Muslims in the Canadian Mosaic," 11. As the result of another complaint, the commission asked the federal government to amend the tariff regulations, which allow certain objects of religious significance to be brought into Canada free of duty, to cover all religions and not merely Christianity and Islam.

33. Judy Fosty, "Dad Jailed for Beating: Throws Out Cultural Defence," Winnipeg Sun, 20 May 1990, p. 10.

34. Le Centre Maghrebin de Recherche et d'Information,. "Non, Mme. La Juge Verreault, l'islam ne permet pas le viol et l'abus des enfrants," Communiqué de presse, 14 Jan. 1994. Muslim leaders have also condemned clitoridectomy, which is reportedly practiced by some immigrants from Africa and the Arabian peninsula.

35. Kevin Rollason, "Judge Says Girl Can't Marry: Muslim Man to Appeal after Court Says Daughter, 14, Too Young," Winnipeg Free Press, 21 Sept. 1993, p. A1. There is a broad range of views on marriage among Muslims in Canada.

36. Ibid.

37. Andreas Currie and George Kiefl, *Ethnocultural Groups and the Justice System in Canada: A Review of the Issues* (Ottawa: Department of Justice, 1994), 28.

38. Bob Harvey, "Adoption Rules Violate Charter, Muslims Say: Extended Family Can Not Bring in Orphaned Relatives," *Ottawa Citizen*, 17 July 1992; Anwar Islam, "Adoption of Guardianship," *Manitoba Multicultural Resources Centre Magazine* 1, no. 2 (Spring/Summer 1992): 8-9.

39. There is a tendency among spokespersons for Muslim organizations to claim to be speaking for all Muslims in Canada, belying the considerable diversity in the various Muslim communities in the country; see Mohammed Azhar Ali Khan, "False Assumptions: Media Wrong to Suggest Religious Group has Single, Authorized Viewpoint," *Ottawa Citizen*, 3 May 1994, p. A9.

40. Karim H. Karim, "The Historical Resilience of Primary Stereotypes: Core Images of the Muslim Other," in *The Language and Politics of Exclusion: Others in Discourse*, ed. Stephen Harold Riggins (Thousand Oaks, Calif.: Sage, 1997).

41. Even as it cited hate motivated violence during the Gulf War, a report for the federal Department of Justice referred only to incidents involving Jewish victims. Glen A. Gilmour, *Hate-Motivated Violence* (Ottawa: Department of Justice, 1994), 10. This overlooked overwhelming evidence of hate-motivated violence against Muslims and Arabs during the war. Zuhair Kashmeri, *The Gulf Within: Canadian Arabs, Racism and the Gulf War* (Toronto: James Lorimer, 1991); Baha Abu-Laban and Sharon McIrvin Abu-Laban, "The Gulf War and Its Impact on Canadians of Arab and Muslim Descent," in *Beyond the Gulf War: Muslims, Arabs and the West*, ed. Baha Abu-Laban and M. Ibrahim Alladin (Edmonton: Muslim Research Foundation, 1991), 119-42.

42. "Judge's Lawyer Challenges Convictions of Muslim Expelled from Courtroom," *Ottawa Citizen*, 7 June 1989.

43. Maureen Murray, "Judicial Review Urged of Rushdie's Book," *Toronto Star*, 25 Feb. 1989, p. A10.

44. Kashmiri, *Gulf Within*.

45. Service de documentation du CMRI. *The Impact of the Gulf War on Muslim Communities: Press Clippings* (Montreal: Centre Maghrebin de Recherche et d'Information, 1991); Kashmeri, *Gulf Within*; Abu-Laban and Abu-Laban, "Gulf War."

46. Hani Hassan, Conference presentation, Media and Ethnicity Conference, Mississauga, Ontario, April 1995.

47. Kashmeri, *Gulf Within*, 20.

48. A number of people of Arab origin who had made statements against the war, particularly Iraqis and Palestinians, were questioned by authorities. The Canadian Arab Federation was the most vocal organization objecting to such treatment of Canadian citizens.

49. Kashmeri, *Gulf Within*, 27.

50. Neil Bissoondath, *Selling Illusions: The Cult of Multiculturalism in Canada* (Toronto: Penguin, 1994).

51. See Will Kymlica, *Multicultural Citizenship: A Liberal Theory of Minority Rights* (Oxford: Clarendon Press, 1995).

52. Steven Vertovec, "Multiculturalism, Culturalism and Public Incorporation," *Ethnic and Racial Studies* 19, no. 1 (January 1996): 49-69.

18

Mexican Muslims in the Twentieth Century: Challenging Stereotypes and Negotiating Space

Theresa Alfaro Velcamp

Over a decade ago, M. Ali Kettani reported that "the Muslims of Mexico can be estimated at about fifteen thousand.[1] They are in majority of Syrian origin and spread out across the country. They are, however, not organized. Unless they do so soon, they are doomed to be absorbed religiously in the total population."[2] Kettani correctly pointed out that the Muslims, in order to survive and flourish, must negotiate a religious space for themselves in a predominantly Catholic society. However, the fact that they are scattered throughout Mexico may not be quite as threatening as Kettani thought. While presenting certain challenges, their dispersal illustrates both the cultural diversity of Mexico and the long-term viability of Islam in Mexican society. There is space for Muslims in Mexico, but how they negotiate this space is critical.

The first Muslim immigrants began this process of negotiation with Mexican society once they decided to settle and become part of the Mexican nation. Questions remain, however, about who really were the first Muslims. Some authors have suggested the first Spanish conquerors included some Muslims; however, little has been found to substantiate this claim.[3] Most scholars indicate that the first Muslims were Arabs who came at the end of the nineteenth century from the Ottoman Empire, generally from the area of Greater Syria.[4] According to my analysis of 8,240 Arab immigrants who came to Mexico between 1878 and 1951, 343 were Muslim. Fifty-six percent of the Muslim immigrants arrived between 1922 and 1927.[5] More recently, the constituency of the Muslim community has changed with the influx of Muslim immigrants from other areas of the Muslim world. Also contributing to the heterogeneity of Islam in Mexico is the presence of Muslim diplomats from various Muslim countries on temporary assignment in the country, as well as a small group of converts. Thus, Mexican Islam is not monolithic, nor is it isolated from the larger Islamic world.

How Mexican Muslims negotiate their religious space is directly linked to what is perhaps their biggest challenge, namely the "turco" stereotype that is associated with Muslims throughout Latin America. In a recent episode of a popular Mexican telenovela (soap opera), for example, the heroine whispers to her friends, as they leave an Arab merchant's apartment, "The Turk is cheap."[6] The Arab merchant has a large hooked nose and sports a comical bushy mustache with the ends twisted up. While this character is not particularly important to the story line, he does make an appearance, with his stereotypical features, trying to swindle these Mexican women.

Many Mexicans associate Arabs with this kind of stereotyped *turco*.[7] The construction of Arab identity, which is inextricably linked to the issue of Muslim identity, can be understood in terms of its historical development and the place of Arabs and Muslims in the national discourse. Some analysts believe that the business practices of some Arabs, in particular Lebanese and Palestinian, have helped the Mexican economy significantly. Others, critical of what have been depicted as unethical business practices, have suggested that the Arabs made their fortunes at the expense of Mexicans. There are at least four groups of Mexican Muslims: descendants of the first Shi'ite immigrants, recent Sunni and Shi'ite immigrants, Sunni and Shi'ite Muslim diplomats living in Mexico, and converts to Islam. All of these groups must face the prevalent stereotypes of Islam and Muslims in Mexico, while simultaneously seeking a place within Mexican society in which to practice their faith.

The Arab Muslim Immigrant Experience

Since the Spanish conquest of the sixteenth and seventeenth centuries, Mexicans have struggled to integrate their own indigenous religious beliefs into the teachings of the Catholic Church.[8] This has resulted in a kind of "folk Catholicism," which appears in distinct forms in various regions in Mexico. The beliefs of the Zapotecs in Oaxaca, for example, are different from those of the Yaquis in Sonora. Regardless of these divergent religious variations, however, Mexicans tend to identify themselves as Catholic. Yet there are clearly spaces for "others."

Scholars have recently begun to suggest that there is more religious freedom[9] in the northern states of Mexico—Chihuahua, Sonora, Nuevo Leon, Coahuila, and Durango—than in other regions. Some of these states share a border with the United States, which could partially explain the relative degree of religious tolerance. A more likely explanation is that the northern areas have traditionally been more isolated and therefore more open to foreign "colonists,"[10] including immigrant populations of Chinese, Japanese, Spanish, French, and Arabs. The north of Mexico has been at the center of significant foreign migration since Spanish colonization, and this tradition continued throughout the twentieth century.

Preliminary research shows that the majority of Muslim immigrants settled in northern Mexico, in particular in the Laguna area of the states of Coahuila and Durango, probably because of the region's religious toleration[11] and the social networks of the north. Families and friends from southern Lebanon started settling in this northern region in the late 1890s, thus facilitating family migration in the early twentieth century. Muslim immigration was also encouraged by government policies both at home and abroad, by economic incentives, and by war.

The Porfiriato (1876–1910)

Arab immigrants began arriving in Veracruz and other Mexican ports around 1878, during the regime of Porfirio Díaz (1876–1910), and continued to arrive throughout the twentieth century. Díaz sought to stimulate the Mexican economy by giving prefer-

ences to foreigners, both as investors and as settlers. He believed that the natural inferiority of the local *mestizo* stock[12] and the superiority of the Europeans and North
Americans warranted an "open door" immigration policy. In order to make Mexico
more attractive to foreign investors, Díaz and his *cientifico* ministers created an economic
climate attractive to investors by granting concessions to investors who planned to build
railroads. The foreign investors saw their greatest potential for profit in financing routes
that facilitated the transportation of products to ports or to the northern border.

Railroads facilitated the quick distribution of goods throughout Mexico and allowed
for the transportation of manual laborers to industrializing areas. In turn, this created
a demand for small markets to sell a wide variety of easily transportable articles. These
circumstances favored itinerant trade, which was quickly taken up by the Arab immigrants.[13] Since much of the railroad construction took place in Coahuila and Durango,
many Lebanese flocked to these northern states. Moisés González Navarro notes that
the first Lebanese who arrived in 1895 helped to construct the towns of Gómez Palacio
and Torreón in the state of Coahuila.[14]

For several reasons, however, it is difficult to know exactly how many Arabs and
Muslims came to Mexico in those early years. During the same period in the Middle
East, the Ottoman Empire forbade Muslim emigration. Yet, as Kemal Karpat points
out, "the available Ottoman documents indicate that, in fact, the number of Muslim
immigrants was substantial."[15] He suggests that the departure of Muslims from the
Ottoman state was necessarily clandestine, since they had been forbidden to emigrate
even before general restrictions were imposed.[16] This level of secrecy probably skewed
many of the early immigration records of the Arabs who arrived in Mexico and other
American cities because Ottoman Muslims were afraid to admit their religion and risk
being deported. Thus, scholars are forced to speculate about this early immigrant group
and to be cautious in using records on Arab immigration.

Late-nineteenth-century Mexican immigration policy further obscures our knowledge
about Muslim immigration. The Immigration and Naturalization Law of 1886, instituted
during the regime of Porfirio Díaz, conferred Mexican citizenship on certain foreigners
almost by default. Foreigners who owned property were considered to be Mexican citizens
if they did not express their determination—before the proper authorities—to maintain their
former nationality.[17] Porfirian policy was based on the idea that immigrants become necessary laborers and/or helped "whiten" and therefore "improve" Mexico. In short, Porfirian
Mexico, for the most part, welcomed its immigrants as symbols of progress.

The Mexican Revolution (1910–1920)

After Porfirio Díaz's long reign of favoring foreigners, peasants, working classes, and
disgruntled middle-class Mexicans rallied behind the anti-reelection campaign of Fran-
cisco Madero. As a result Porfirio Díaz had to flee Mexico in 1911. From 1910 to 1920,
revolutionary leaders[18] fought for power and sought widespread changes in Mexican
landholding patterns. By 1920, most of the revolutionary violence had ceased, and many
of the changes that had been fought for were embodied in the Constitution of 1917.
Foreigners and immigrants, once the symbols of progress, became the scapegoats of the
Mexican Revolution.

In 1893 Mexico and China had signed a Treaty of Amity and Commerce that contained a "most favored nation" clause welcoming Chinese immigrants to Mexico. They were joined by Chinese workers from the United States after the Exclusion Act of 1882. When revolutionary troops entered Torreón in May 1911, however, soldiers and civilians turned their wrath on the Chinese in a systematic attempt to wipe out the entire community. As William Meyers puts it, "in the next few hours, the rampaging mob indiscriminately murdered over three hundred defenseless Chinese and five Japanese, "owing to the similarity of features.'"[19] Alan Knight has explained the pogrom as a part of "competitive racism," or racism based on a socioeconomic rationale.[20] Many Mexicans apparently saw Chinese commercial activities as threatening their livelihood and felt a strong prejudice against them. Whether this resentment was manifested also against Arabs has yet to be explored.

Despite the violent nature of the Mexican Revolution at this time, Arab migration continued. Some Arabs played significant roles in bringing food and arms to revolutionary troops.[21] Many of the Arab merchants traveled throughout the country, coming into contact with all of the sectors participating in the armed conflict.[22] Others participated in the Mexican Revolution as revolutionaries and obtained military rank. Although it appears that the Arabs survived and perhaps even profited from the Mexican Revolution, in its aftermath they began to feel insecure in their sojourner status. This insecurity can be explained in part by the antiforeign backlash that came as a result of the revolution. Muslims were also affected by events outside Mexico, such as the increasingly more restrictive U.S. immigration policies, as well as events taking place in the Middle East.

After the Ottoman Empire surrendered to the Allies in 1918, much of its territory was occupied by Allied military forces. In 1920, Mustafa Kemal organized a nationalist Turkish movement to radically secularize the Turkish state. This exclusion of Muslim law, combined with Christian Allied occupation, clearly left many Muslims feeling dislocated. Meanwhile, in response to pleas from many Lebanese Maronite Christians, the French began dividing Syria and Lebanon into what would be four new nation-states that augmented the size of the former Mount Lebanon. Christians began to exert political and economic control over traditionally Muslim areas. These profound changes to Greater Syria left many people, especially Muslims in Lebanon, displaced socially, economically, and politically. Migration became an appealing option, although in reality many of the Muslim immigrants did not find a welcoming host country.

Postrevolutionary Aftershocks

In an effort to stabilize Mexican society in the postrevolutionary chaos, and to appease its northern neighbor, Mexican presidential administrations in the 1920s began to implement tougher immigration laws. Their policies largely followed those of the United States. From 1921 to 1929 discrimination against "otherness" increased in Mexico; during this time U.S. immigration laws brought immigration to a virtual halt.[23] In 1922, the Mexican government began imposing a fee structure on immigrants. On October 10, 1922, the United States consulate in Veracruz reported that "all immigrants [to Mexico] must have on their person the sum of 50.00 pesos ($25) or the equivalent in other money, besides passage money to cover expenses to their destination in Mexico. Chinese and Negroes are compelled, however, to have the sum of 500.00 pesos ($250.00)."[24]

On March 13, 1926, a Mexican immigration law was passed that expanded the list of medical reasons for which immigrants could be refused entry. Immigrants had to present official documents upon entering or leaving Mexico and had to demonstrate that they possessed the funds [a sum of 10,000 pesos] required to satisfy their basic needs.[25] In response to the protests of Mexican workers that the unfair competitive practices of foreign merchants were undermining Mexican economic interests,[26] the state in 1927 prohibited Armenians, Syrians, and other Arabs from entering Mexico. These prohibitions were not strictly enforced, but in 1929 entrance into the country was temporarily suspended for all workers.[27] The following year, the Interior Ministry decided to accept only immigrants from cultures similar to the Mexican culture, meaning persons with Latin roots.[28] Again taking its cue from the United States, Mexico made its immigration policy more restrictive. Its laws did not explicitly address Arab Muslims, but they clearly had an impact on whether Arab immigrants could enter the country and on how they could earn their living once there.

In 1932, the Mexican government decreed that all foreigners had to appear before the proper authorities and show their personal identification papers.[29] My research shows that 4.2 percent of all the Arab immigrants then in Mexico were Muslims. Of the Muslim immigrants, 88 percent were men and 12 percent women.[30] Many of the Muslim immigrants intended to return to Lebanon[31] rather than settle permanently in Mexico and become citizens. However, with the antiforeign backlash and the increasingly restrictive immigration policies, many changed their minds and registered with the Mexican Migration Department. This in effect "legalized" them and began the process of naturalization.

Zidane Zeraoui estimates that 73.9 percent of the Muslim immigrants in this period engaged in commerce, and 14.5 percent were nonprofessional, including housewives. Many sources have suggested that the Arab immigrants were farmers in the Middle East and that they became peddlers once they arrived in the Americas. Yet the data show that they declared themselves overwhelmingly to be merchants, *comerciantes*. Although most of the Lebanese Muslims migrated before the Cárdenas administration (1934–1940), it was during his presidency that many of the Arab immigrants sought Mexican citizenship.

Cárdenas (1934–1940) and the Post–World War II Period

The popular administration of Lázaro Cárdenas can be described as implementing the ideals of the Mexican Revolution. Cárdenas executed many of the revolutionary promises that had remained unfulfilled, such as land distribution and nationalization of the oil industry, yet scholars debate the degree to which he challenged foreign investors and immigrant populations. While he did impose restrictionist immigration policies, he also allowed Spanish refugees from the Spanish Civil War to emigrate to Mexico.

In 1936, a population law was passed to try to resolve the country's fundamental demographic problems by establishing and maintaining records on the immigration and repatriation of foreigners. This law prohibited the entrance of alcoholics, drug addicts, prostitutes, anarchists, and salaried foreign workers. It also prohibited the exercise of commercial activities to foreigners, except in those cases in which the activity was deemed necessary.[32] While the law did not explicitly mention Arabs or Muslims, it served in effect as a means of restricting the activities of Arab merchants. The law represents the general atmosphere of the time, which sought to regain "Mexico for Mexicans." Consequently, Cárdenas's reconstructed Mexico became increasingly more nationalistic and antiforeign, which explains in part why many Arabs began seeking naturalization.

Mexican antiforeign sentiment began to change after World War II. In 1947, a second population law was passed, which tried to resolve the discrepancies in the number of foreigners in the census data. The Mexican government, under the leadership of Miguel Alemán, saw the question of immigration as both a form of international collaboration and a mechanism of national development. Alemán offered hospitality to foreign populations displaced by the war, in particular Jews. As had been the case earlier, however, those admitted had to be able to "ethnically fuse with national groups."[33] This clause in the law gave Mexican policymakers latitude to interpret which ethnic groups would be most useful to the nation.

Despite these various legal restrictions, Arabs continued to migrate to Mexico. Statistical information, however, is somewhat unreliable. Muslim immigrants may not have been comfortable identifying their faith in an overwhelmingly Catholic country. Illegal immigration of Muslims, of course, is not recorded. For these reasons, the statistics on Muslim immigration are estimates at best. Arab immigration into Mexico continues to the present, although little research has been done on the topic.

The paucity of data leaves a number of questions unanswered, such as what happened to the Muslim immigrants who did not declare themselves to be Muslim. They may have called themselves Catholics for expediency, while continuing to practice their Muslim faith in private. We can only speculate about their numbers and their activities. If we can even assume that such a group of "unidentified" Muslims did exist, what happened to them? How did they integrate into Mexican society? Were they different from their self-identified Muslim brothers and sisters? Did they continue their Islamic faith or formally convert to Catholicism? How did they interact with Christian Arabs? Such questions are clearly the topic of further research.

We do know that, while initially Arab immigrants worked together to help one another, the conflicts in the Middle East combined with the economic success of the predominantly Christian (Maronite and Orthodox) Lebanese led to the distancing of Christian Arabs from Muslim Arabs, particularly in Mexico City. Lebanese Christians there have constructed their Lebanese history as predominantly one of Christians. Such distancing seems to be less the case in other areas of Mexico; in Torreón, Coahuila, where the majority of Muslims settled, for example, there appears to be more interaction between Muslim and Christian Arabs.

Recent scholarship on Mexican identity and culture rarely mentions the Mexican immigrant tradition. The discourse tends to focus on the *mestizo* paradigm, focusing on persons of indigenous and/or Spanish descent to the exclusion of "others." It is within this *mestizo* construct that the *turco* stereotype is perpetuated. It is difficult to challenge a stereotype when the majority of society believes that the population is composed of only two ethnic groups. The aim of this chapter is not to deconstruct the *mestizo* paradigm and to find the discourse of the Muslim Arabs but to show that Muslims do indeed exist in Mexico. Their exact numbers and impact on Mexican society have yet to be fully explored. Through a series of interviews, I have attempted to bridge the gap between the Arab immigrants who arrived at the early part of the century and their descendants in Mexico today.

The Children of Muslim Immigrants in Torreón, Coahuila

Records show that Shi'ite Muslim families tended to emigrate from places such as Nabatiyeh, Braachit, Damascus, Tripoli and Aramta, in Syria and Lebanon to Torreón, in northern Mexico, for a variety of reasons.[34] In interviews with members of the first generation of Mexican-born Muslims, I found that they attributed the emigration of their parents to Turkish oppression and the attempt to avoid conscription into the Ottoman army.[35] This pattern of avoiding military service is apparent in the growth in the numbers of young people who emigrated to Torreón between 1906 and 1908, during the Ottoman wars in the Balkans. One first-generation Muslim indicated that his father did not want to fight in a war and risk his life for the Turks. His father therefore fled Lebanon and spent six months in France before arriving in Mexico.

Others left Lebanon because of economic incentives and a desire to improve the standard of living of their family. One interviewee said that her mother was not permitted into the United States in 1923 because she had trachoma, so her parents moved to Tampico, Mexico. After twenty years in Tampico and the marriage of a daughter to a *paisano* (compatriot) from the United States, they decided to move to Torreón, a place known to have other Muslim *paisanos*. In both these interviews, the first-generation Muslims discussed the strong ties they had to the Shi'ite community in Detroit, Michigan; both have siblings who settled in Detroit. Personally, however, they prefer to live in Mexico.

Members of the first generation of Muslims appear to have retained many elements of their Lebanese culture, as well as their Islamic faith. Most of those interviewed reported that they had married Muslim compatriots. In some cases, the custom of marrying first cousins persisted. However, by the second generation, the trend of endogamy appears to have shifted. Even for those who married outside the faith, however, it was important to have a Muslim wedding, as a second-generation Lebanese Muslim told me. In addition, he did not want a wife who was "too" Catholic and inflexible. He married a Mexican woman (of Spanish descent) in a Muslim ceremony. Currently there is a small, informal community of Muslims in Torreón who participate in worship at the recently built mosque (discussed later). Before the mosque was built, according to one of the interviewees, Muslims would gather at a house on Morelos Street in Torreón to pray and celebrate holidays. Some today still prefer to pray at home. Most of the first generation of Muslims know Arabic and can read the Qur'an, a skill that has been lost, for the most part, with the second generation. Most members of the community, however, are familiar with the Qur'an in translation. All still prepare and eat Arabic food at least once a week. None of those interviewed eat pork or drink alcohol.

Despite their Muslim Lebanese backgrounds, most of the children of the immigrants (referred to as second-generation Muslims, the first to be born in Mexico) identify themselves as "Mexican." They are clearly proud of their Lebanese heritage, but their homes and hearts are in Mexico. The fact that one second-generation Muslim described himself as feeling more "Arab" than Mexican or Muslim can perhaps be explained by the more recent politicization of the Arab world. The Muslims in Torreón can not be described as *fanáticos* (fundamentalists); rather, they see themselves as spiritual people who accept interfaith marriages and are open to the changes taking place in their community. This community illustrates how Mexican Muslims negotiate a space within Mexican society in which to practice their faith, at the same time that they are accommodating to Mexican culture by assuming a Mexican identity. This fusion of culture and identity makes the Mexican Muslim experience unique.

The Suraya Mosque

Currently, the only mosque in Mexico is located at 1007 Guadalajara Street in the Colonia of Nueva Los Angeles in Torreón, Coahuila. When the wealthy merchant and jeweler Elias Serhán Selim and his wife, Suraya Mansur Serhán, lost their daughter Suraya in a car accident, they decided to donate money to build a mosque in her memory. With the help of the architect Hassan Zain Chamut, who designed it and donated his time, the mosque was completed in November 1989. In 1993, it received official status from the Mexican government as a religious association.[36] Chamut was adamant that the mosque be built completely by Mexicans.[37] In my conversations with them, Serhán and Chamut referred to the mosque as "a house of God and a place to give thanks to God."

An article by Dr. Mohammad Alí Anzaldúa-Morales describes the architecture of the mosque as Andalucian and Maghribi. From the outside, the building clearly stands out from typical Mexican architecture. It features a tower and dome over the main prayer room on the first floor. There is also a reception area, a suite of offices, an interior fountain, and a room to wash the deceased. The bathrooms are designed for *wudu'* (ablution). Classrooms, a large meeting room, and a small kitchen are found on the first floor.[38] Some of those interviewed expressed disappointment that the facility is not fully used. They said that, while on some days up to ten people pray at the mosque, other days no one shows up.

The mosque does provide literature to educate Mexicans about Islam, but it is not widely disseminated. It is not easy to be Muslim in a predominantly Catholic country, as illustrated in a comprehensive article by Hassan Zain Chamut that is available through the mosque. This piece describes both the internal and the external challenges that face Muslims in Mexico as they try to maintain their faith. Struggling to pass down their religion to often resistant children, they also have to cope with the reality that some members of the community are trying to reinterpret the faith to make it relevant to their circumstances in Mexico.

Among the publications distributed by the Suraya Mosque are the following: *Los fundamentos de la doctrina I* (published by Muslims in Iran and the United States), *El islam de un vistazo*, and *Que es islam*.[39] These publications, which are designed to encourage the conversion of non-Muslims, do not correspond to the attitudes of the Shi'ite Muslims in Torreón, who do not appear to be actively reaching out to the Torreón/Laguna community. The Islamic Cultural Center in Mexico also distributes the following materials: *El islam: prinicipios y islámica libro i caracteristicas*, a Spanish translation of the Qur'an, and a pamphlet entitled *Entiendo al islam y a los musulmanes*, published by an organization in Washington, D.C., which focuses on working with Spanish-speaking Muslims.[40] Meanwhile, the Shi'ites in Torreón appear quite complacent in their lack of proselytizing projects when compared with some of their Muslim counterparts. Some observers have suggested that many of the Shi'ite Muslims in the north do not truly understand the differences between the Sunnis and the Shi'ites. Rather, they are first-generation Muslims with an inherited version of Shi'ite Islam that they learned from their parents.

Muslim Immigrants and Diplomats in Mexico and Mexican Converts

It is reported that at the beginning of the twentieth century a small mosque in downtown Mexico City was regularly frequented by the Turks. However, with the breakup of the Ottoman Empire, the mosque apparently went out of use. Today the building houses a discotheque called *Deseo* in the Colonia Mixcoac.[41] The current Muslim population in Mexico City congregates at the Islamic Cultural Center (ICC).[42] The ICC is very interested in proselytizing for Islam and functions as an umbrella organization for Muslims throughout Mexico, and in particular in Mexico City.

A few Muslim immigrants have affiliated with the ICC, such as the Lebanese Palestinian whom I had the opportunity to interview.[43] For the purposes of this discussion, I will call him "Mustafa." Mustafa reported that he came to Mexico because he married a Catholic Mexican woman whom he had met in Canada. He had no problem getting into Mexico in 1985, although Mexican immigration policy at the time did not permit citizens from Lebanon to enter the country. When I asked how he felt about marrying a Catholic and living in a Christian country, Mustafa responded that religion became more important to him when he came to Mexico because he wanted to be able to explain his faith. In reexamining his Islamic beliefs, he has come to think that some of the Catholic practices are illogical, especially in Mexico. For example, he wondered why the priests do not memorize the Bible as Muslims do the Qur'an, and why so many Mexicans pray to the Virgin of Guadalupe in place of God. Mustafa reported that he is exposing his children to both Islam and Christianity, even though as children they cannot commit to a religion right now. He stressed that it is important to set a good example at home because children imitate their parents. Asked whether he considered himself Sunni or Shi'ite, he responded, "I am a Muslim," because all Muslims submit to one God. As a Muslim he prays five times a day, joins the Friday prayer at the ICC, and refrains from eating pork or drinking alcohol. He has not affiliated with other countrymen.

The prayer service in the large rented home in Polanco, Mexico City, that serves as the ICC's prayer hall is more traditional than that at Torreón. The former facility that functioned as a prayer hall was in the Colonia de Valle in Mexico City, which also served as the base of Mexico City's Islamic Cultural Center. The Saudi Arabian embassy supports the Sunni community by renting this house in Polanco.[44] The prayer service is clearly male dominated, with some eighty to one hundred men of all nationalities attending. Employees of the embassies of Algeria, Egypt, Indonesia, Iran, Iraq,

Malaysia, Morocco, Pakistan, Palestine, Tunis, Turkey, and Saudi Arabia in Mexico work with the ICC on various occasions. In contrast, Shi'ite social life in Mexico City revolves around an active Iranian embassy, which every year sponsors a book exhibition and supports the Shi'ite community by holding conferences on Islam.

Mexican Converts

The ICC, as noted, is very active in the propagation of Islam to the general Mexican population. It has developed a creative program to reach out to both Muslims and non-Muslims, and lists ten objectives for Muslim Mexicans: to establish daily prayers and invite the Muslims to prayer; to teach Muslims and non-Muslims the fundamentals of their creed and religious practices; to teach Arabic; to organize Islamic courses for children; to unite Muslims by organizing social gatherings; to provide scholarships for the study of Islam at the University of Medina; to translate and publish Islamic books for distribution; to buy more Islamic literature from other publishers from around the world; to establish small *musallahs* (prayer halls) in other major cities that can replicate its mission; and to raise funds to help them reach their objectives.[45]

The ICC has established the five prayers on a daily basis, and its leader reports that attendance is increasing. They hosted a two-hour radio program for two months in which they discussed Islam. The ICC has also set up bookstands at international book fairs in Mexico City and has published thirteen books. According to its records, twenty Mexicans have accepted Islam since the Center opened. I found these converts to be bright young men, speaking some words of Arabic and English and seemingly eager to share their experiences. Two Mexican Muslims have gone to the University of Medina, in Saudi Arabia, and another will be going to Egypt to study at the University of Al-Azhar to learn more about the *din* (religion).

According to its director, Mark (Omar) Weston, there is some coordination of *da'wa* (the call to Islam) activities between the Sunnis in Mexico City and the Shi'ites in Torreón. The ICC website states that "although Islam in Mexico is virtually non-existent consisting basically of about 100 . . . Muslims, by the mercy of Allah a small group of new Muslims and a few immigrants have managed to establish a small Musallah and a registered center for propagating Islam."[46]

The ICC has developed creative means of propagating the faith that are designed to reach the public. These means are identified as the seven "pillars" of their *da'wa* project. The Center promotes "car" *da'wa*, which consists of handing out selected brochures and pamphlets to passing cars on major streets. "Subway" *da'wa* means riding the subway and giving selected speeches between stations. Three Muslims participate in this kind of activity; one gives a short speech on *tawhid*, while the other two distribute the same speech in a written form. The ICC also promotes "park" *da'wa*, in which a large number of Muslims go to a crowded park to pray *duhr* or *asr*. According to the Center, people approach them "in dozens"; they offer a short speech about *tawhid* and distribute selected material.

"Book store" *da'wa* consists of renting a store in downtown Mexico City and exhibiting Islamic books, although the high cost of maintaining such bookstores demands that the ICC consider alternatives such as stalls in a flea market. "Flash" *da'wa* familiarizes people with Islam by "flashing" them with small and concise words, such as hanging an announcement saying "Islam" in a crowded stadium, which is then be televised to millions of people. ICC also posts bumper stickers that say "I love Islam." Another way to proselytize is called "expedition" *da'wa*, which means going to different towns and cities around Mexico and contacting Muslims, as well as preaching to the non-Muslims. ICC leaders indicate that is important to keep in touch with these new brothers. The last component of the ICC's *da'wa* program is to establish *musallahs* in key cities.[47] More recently, the ICC has been offering lectures to friends of Muslims on Saturdays to help foster a better understanding of Islam.

It is apparent that the Muslim community in Mexico City is striving to reach out to Mexicans and to inform society about Islam—to "demystify" many of the stereotypes imposed on anyone of Arab descent and of Muslim faith.

Mexican Converts to Other Muslim groups

In addition to Sunni and Shi'ite Muslims, Mexico is also home to groups of Sufis and Qadiyanis, in addition to some members of the Baha'i religion. Each group publishes and distributes its own books and pamphlets that identify their particular understanding of their faith. Consequently, Mexicans are exposed to a wide range of interpretations of Islam and religions that claim affiliation with Islam.

Sufis from the Halveti-Jerrahi Order of Dervishes have their mosque in Colonia Roma, in Mexico City. About twenty-five to thirty members attend their meetings. At the one I attended, the majority were European-looking women. The service began at around eight in the evening and lasted until midnight, with breaks to eat and smoke cigarettes. The group differed from the ICC membership not only in its predominantly female constituency but in what seemed to be its much more tolerant interpretation of Islam. As would be expected, its prayer service had a more mystical feel than the Sunni service I attended, which was more structured and formal.

There are a few other small groupings of Mexican Muslims outside Mexico City. Some medical students live in Guadalajara, Jalisco, and, in the north of Mexico, an active Shi'ite community in the state of Chihuahua helps the Iranian embassy by translating its literature into Spanish. The ICC also notes that there are some Muslims who live in Zacatecas. In Monterrey, Nuevo Leon, a small group of Sunnis are active in another Muslim center. Muslim immigrant children, Muslim converts, and members of the Muslim diplomatic community are optimistic about the future of Islam in Mexico. Whether the converts will be Sunni or Shi'ites or will follow another Muslim sect remains to be seen.

Arab Muslim immigrants first came as sojourners at the end of the nineteenth century and only later sought Mexican citizenship; many of their children inherited their parents' Islamic faith. But the Mexican Muslim community now extends beyond its immigrant tradition to include diplomats from a variety of Muslim nations, as well as Mexican converts. Most of the descendants of Muslim immigrants as well as the employees of the Iranian embassy, are Shi'ite, while converts and the majority of Muslim diplomats in Mexico tend to be Sunni. Given its diversity of backgrounds and interests, the

Muslim community does not operate as a unified entity. Yet it must cope with the negative stereotypes of all Muslims. By challenging Arab and Muslim stereotypes and negotiating with Mexicans for a religious space in which to practice their faith, the Muslims in Mexico are constructing a unique Mexican Muslim identity. As with most constructed identities, Mexican Islam is neither monolithic nor unconnected to the larger Islamic world.

In April 1999, the Shiʿites in Torreón and the Sunnis in Mexico City were working together to raise money and gather goods for their Muslim brothers displaced by the war in Kosovo. Although this effort could be attributed to the communication revolution, education, and international awareness, it also demonstrates the identification of Mexican Muslims with the larger Islamic world. This may be a beginning of a more pan-American Muslim consciousness that indeed challenges the *turco* stereotype and creates more religious space in a predominantly Christian Latin America.

Notes

The author would like to thank Yvonne Haddad, John Voll, Kathryn Coughlin, Michael Socolow, Mark (Omar) Weston, Hassan Zain Chamut, Osama Osmond, Rosa María Montes Rojas, and Alvaro Santana Saldaña for their valuable insights and assistance in this project.

1. Others have estimated that there are 500 Muslims in Mexico City and a total of 1,000 Muslims in all of Mexico.

2. M. Ali Kettani, *Muslim Minorities in the World Today* (London: Mansell, 1986), 209.

3. A recent NEH Seminar held at Georgetown University brought this issue to my attention. Although I have not come across any sources to document this claim, it is possible. However, the actions of the first Spaniards in Latin America tended to be more economically driven, making it extremely difficult to find cases of practicing Muslims.

4. Very little has been written about the Arab migration to Mexico. Several Mexican scholars in the past ten years have begun to discuss the role of various immigrants in Mexican society. (See María Elena Ota Mishima, *Destino México: un estudio de las migraciones asiáticas a México, siglos XIX y XX* [Mexico: El Colegio de Mexico, 1997], and Guillermo Bonfil Battala, comp., *Simbiosis de culturas: los inmigrantes y su cultura en México* [Mexico: Fondo de Cultura Economica, 1993].) This discourse challenges the traditional *mestizaje* ethnic paradigm that Mexican intellectuals have long sustained. The *mestizo* ethnic scheme consists of Spanish, indigenous, and *mestizo*, the mixture of the two. Obviously, this ethnic construction does not leave much room for those outside this paradigm. This narrowly defined construction of Mexican society left scholars and researchers perplexed as to how to address immigrant populations outside the Mexican mainstream. We therefore find it difficult to find secondary sources, in either Spanish or English, that discuss the role of Arab migration in Mexican history. In the 1980s, Mexican scholars, such as Luz María Martínez Montiel ("Lebanese Immigration to Mexico," in *Asiatic Migrations in Latin America*, Thirtieth International Congress of Human Sciences in Asia and Africa, 1976 [Mexico: El Colegio de Mexico, 1981], 147-61), and Carmen Mercedes Páez Oropeza (*Los Libaneses en México: asimilación de un grupo étnico* [Mexico: Instituto Nacional de Antropología, 1984]), wrote about the Lebanese in Mexico as overwhelming Christian and generally assimilating into Mexican society by the second and third generations. These pioneering works argued that the Lebanese were hard workers and brought economic benefits to Mexican society through their commercial activities. In the 1990s, Mexican authors such as Martha Díaz de Kuri

and Lourdes Macluf, *De Líbano a México: crónica de un pueblo emigrante* (Mexico: Gráfica, Creatividad y Diseño, S.A. de C.V., 1995); Jorge Nacif Mina, *Crónicas de un inmigrante libanés en México* (Mexico: Edición de Jorge Nacif Mina en colaboración con el Instituto Cultural Mexicano Libanés, A.C., 1995); and Roberto Marin Guzman, "Los inmigrantes árabes en México en los siglos XIX y XX: un estudio de historia social," in *El mundo arabe y américa latina* (Madrid: Ediciones UNESCO, 1997), continue this argument providing more anecdotal evidence. Zidane Zeraoui, "Los árabes en México: el perfil de la migración," in *Destino México: un estudio de las migraciones asiáticas a México, siglos XIX y XX*," ed. María Elena Ota Mishima (Mexico: El Colegio de México, 1997), 257–93, and Doris Musalem Rahal, "La migración palestina a México, 1893–1949," in *Destino México*, 305–64, diverge from this traditional historiography on Lebanese Christians and begin to describe the diversity within the Arab migration to Mexico. Zidane Zeraoui provides detailed statistical analyses of the Arab immigrants and compares his findings with other primary sources, such as Mexican census data. Doris Musalem's innovative research combines oral interviews and statistical data from the National Registry of Foreigners to develop a Palestinian-Mexican profile. All of these Mexican scholars are leading the way to create a new discourse in Mexican thinking about who constitutes Mexican society.

5. National Registry of Foreigners, Migration (1926–1950), Gallery 2, Archivo General de la Nación (AGN), Mexico City, Mexico.

6. *El privilegio de amar*, TV Azteca (September 1998–February 26, 1999).

7. Ignacio Klich and Jeffrey Lesser point out that the term *turco* is an imposed rather than a self-constructed label. The use of *turco* refers to the area of the former Ottoman Empire. Despite its historical orientation, the term does have negative connotations. Ignacio Klich and Jeffrey Lesser, "Introduction: '*Turco*' Immigrants in Latin America," *The Americas* 53, no. 1 (July 1996): 5.

8. See Nancy M. Farriss, *Maya Society under Colonial Rule: The Collective Enterprise of Survival* (Princeton, N.J.: Princeton University Press, 1984), and John M. Ingham, *Mary, Michael, and Lucifer, Folk Catholicism in Central Mexico* (Austin: University of Texas Press, 1986).

9. Paul Vanderwood, *The Power of God against the Guns of Government* (Stanford: Stanford University Press, 1998). Comments made at an AHA panel, January 1999.

10. Mark Wasserman notes, "the Catholic church, a pillar of Conservatism, was weak in the North [of Mexico] because the region lacked the sedentary Indian villages that were the base of its support on the central plateau." Mark Wasserman, *Capitalists, Caciques, and Revolution: The Native Elite and Foreign Enterprise in Chihuahua, Mexico, 1854–1911* (Chapel Hill: University of North Carolina Press, 1984), 10.

11. In addition to the north of Mexico, many Muslim Lebanese went to the center of the country, Mexico City, which had 24 percent of the Muslim immigrant population. Mexico City, as many capital cities, has served as a transitional location for immigrants to make contact with fellow countrymen. National Registry of Foreigners, Migration (1926–1950), Gallery 2. AGN, Mexico City, Mexico.

12. Justo Sierra, in his book *México social y político*, argues that the ethnic problem is the axis of national integration. Accordingly, the *mestizo* represented a way in which to create a liberal model of homogeneous integration of all ethnic groups. For a further discussion, see Liz Hamui-Halabe, "Re-creating Community: Christians from Lebanon and Jews from Syria in Mexico, 1900–1938," in *Arab and Jewish Immigrants in Latin America: Images and Realities*, ed. Ignacio Klich and Jeffrey Lesser (London: Frank Cass, 1998), 128.

13. Gladys Jozami, in writing about the Arabs in Argentina, notes that there is a pattern where the Arab immigrants in search of clients in which to sell their goods settled along railroad routes. Gladys Jozami, "Aspectos demográphicos y comportamiento espacial de los imigrantes árabes en el Noroeste Argentino," *Estudios Migratorios Latinoamericanos* 2, no. 5 (April 1987): 78.

14. Moisés González Navarro, *Los extranjeros en México y los Mexicanos en el extranjero 1821–1970*, vol. 3 (Mexico: El Colegio de México), 137.

15. Kermal H. Karpat, "The Ottoman Emigration to America, 1860–1914," *International Journal of Middle Eastern Studies* 17 (1985): 182.

16. Ibid., 182.

17. Susan Sanderson, Phil Sidel, and Harold Hims, "East Asians and Arabs in Mexico: A Study of Naturalized Citizens (1886–1931)," in *Asiatic Migrations in Latin America*, ed. Luz María Martinez Montiel (Mexico: El Colegio de Mexico, 1981), 175.

18. For a more detailed discussion of the revolutionary leaders, such as Emiliano Zapata, Pancho Villa, Venustiano Carranza and others, see Friedrich Katz, *The Life and Times of Pancho Villa* (Stanford: Stanford University Press, 1998); Alan Knight, *The Mexican Revolution*, vols. 1 and 2. (Cambridge: Cambridge University Press, 1986); and John Womack, Jr., *Zapata and the Mexican Revolution* (New York: Vintage, 1968).

19. William K. Meyers, *Forge of Progress, Crucible of Revolt* (Albuquerque: University of New Mexico Press, 1994), 239.

20. Alan Knight, "Racism, Revolution, and Indigenismo: Mexico 1910–1940," in *The Idea of Race in Latin America, 1870–1940*, ed. Richard Graham (Austin: University of Texas Press, 1990), 96–97.

21. During interviews with members of the Abusaid family in Torreón, Coahuila, I was told that Juan Abusaid apparently traded for Pancho Villa and helped obtain food and arms for the troops (February 1999).

22. Martinez Montiel, "Lebanese Immigration to Mexico," 158.

23. In 1921, the First Quota Law was passed in the United States, which limited immigration of each nationality to 3 percent of the number of foreign-born persons of that nationality living in United States in 1910. In 1924, Congress passed the National Origins Act, which limited immigration of each nationality to 2 percent of the number of persons of that nationality as determined in the 1890 census and set a minimum of 100 persons for each country. And, in 1929, the National Quota Law was passed, which set the annual quotas of 1924 for each country apportioned according to each nationality's percentage in the 1920 census.

24. John Wood, Veracruz, Mexico, to Secretary of State, U.S. National Archives, College Park, Md., U.S. State Department Records, Record Group 59 (1910–1929), 11 Oct. 1922.

25. Hamui-Halabe, "Re-creating Community," 129.

26. Guzman, "Los inmigrantes árabes en México," 130.

27. "Accord prohibiting the immigration of foreigners to enter the country to engage in manual labor for wages," *Diario Oficial*, 27 April 1929, first section; Hamui-Halabe, "Re-creating Community," 142, n. 11.

28. "Mexican Law of the Mexican United States," *Diario Oficial*, 30 Aug. 1930 (supplement to vol. 61, no. 52); Hamui-Halabe, "Re-creating Community," 142, n. 12.

29. Mishima, *Destino México*, 12, 13.

30. National Registry of Foreigners, Migration (1926–1950), Gallery 2. AGN, Mexico City, Mexico.

31. William Rogers Brubaker challenges the use of the term "sojourner" and asks, "Can the state insist on a sharp distinction between immigrants and sojourners, keeping the later in a strictly temporary status?" He continues his argument and adopts Tomas Hammar's use of "denizens" to describe "those whose prolonged sojourn, secure residence status, and extensive rights compel us to consider them members of state and society despite their lack of formal citizenship." William Rogers Brubaker, "Introduction" in *Immigration and the Politics of Citizenship in Europe and North America*, ed. William Rogers Brubaker (Lanham, Md.: University Press of America, 1989), pp. 18, 26. This discussion illustrates the complexity of employing such loaded terms as "sojourner" and "immigrant." For purposes of this chapter, I use the term "so-

journer" to refer to the immigrant's initial stage in the host country, during which he or she has the short-term goal of working and returning home.

32. González Navarro, *Los extranjeros en México*, 41, 42.

33. *El poblamiento de México: una vision histórico demgráfica. Tomo IV: Mexico en el Siglo* XX (Mexico: Angélica Reyna Bernal, Secretaría de Gobernación), 70.

34. National Registry of Foreigners, Migration (1926–1950), Gallery 2. AGN, Mexico City, Mexico.

35. Several Lebanese and Palestinian families, interviews by author, in Torreón, Coahuila, February 1999.

36. A plaque in the lobby of the mosque notes "Comunidad Islamica de la Laguna" on 15 June 1993.

37. Hassan Zain Chamut, interview in *El Puente* (May-June 1991), 50.

38. For a detailed architect's perspective, see Mohammad Alí Anzaldúa-Morales, *El siglo de Torreón* (24 July 1996), 7-C.

39. Sayyid Mujtaba Musavi Lari, *Los fundamentos de la doctrina islámica libro* I, trans. Haidar Taufiq Brusa (Qum: Foundation of Islamic Cultural Propagation in the World, n.d.); *El islam de un vistazo* (Plainfield, Ind.: no date); and *Que es islam* (Hialeah, Fla.: Bism Rabbik Foundation, no date).

40. Khurshid Ahmad, *El islam: prinicipios y características* (Islamabad, Pakistan: IFTA, 1986); and *Entiendo al islam y a los musulmanes* (Washington, D.C.: IFTA, 1998).

41. Mark (Omar) Weston, interview by author, Mexico City, Mexico, 25 Jan. 1999, and information from Dr. Mohammad Alí Anzaldúa-Morales, "La Primera Mezquita de México."

42. Islamic Cultural Center in Mexico, from information on the Internet.

43. Interview by author, Mexico City, Mexico, 27 April 1999.

44. Islamic Cultural Center, interview by author, Mexico City, Mexico, 19 Nov. 1998.

45. Ibid.

46. Islamic Cultural Center in Mexico (Centro Cultural Islamico de México, A.C.) website: http://www.planet.com.mx/islam/.

47. Ibid.

Bibliography

Abdal-Haqq, Irshad, and Qadir Abdal-Haqq. "Community-Based Arbitration as a Vehicle for Implementing Islamic Law in the United States." *Journal of Islamic Law* (Spring/Summer 1996): 61–88.

Abraham, Sameer Y., and Nabeel Abraham, eds. *Arabs in the New World: Studies on Arab-American Communities.* Detroit: Wayne State University Press, 1983.

Abu-Laban, Baha. "The Canadian Muslim Community: The Need for a New Survival Strategy." In *The Muslim Community in North America*, edited by Earle H. Waugh, Baha Abu-Laban, and Regula B. Qureshi, 75–92. Edmonton: University of Alberta Press, 1983.

Abu-Laban, Baha. "The Muslim Community of Canada." In *Muslim Minorities in the West*, edited by Syed Z. Abedin and Ziauddin Sardar, 134–49. London: Grey Seal, 1995.

Abu-Laban, Baha. "Muslims' Participation in Western Social and Political Structures: Problems and Prospects." Paper presented at the Symposium of the Organization of Islamic Conference, "Islam and the West—Toward Dialogue and Understanding," Toronto, October 1996.

Abu-Laban, Baha, and Sharon McIrvin Abu-Laban. "The Gulf War and Its Impact on Canadians of Arab and Muslim Descent." In *Beyond the Gulf War: Muslims, Arabs and the West*, edited by Baha Abu-Laban and M. Ibrahim Alladin, 119–42. Edmonton: Muslim Research Foundation, 1991.

Abu Shouk, Ahmed I., John O. Hunwick, and R. X. O'Fahey. "A Sudanese Missionary to the United States: Satti Majid, Shaykh al-Islam in North America and His Encounter with Noble Drew Ali, Prophet of the Moorish Science Temple Movement." *Sudanic Africa, a Journal of Historical Sources* 8 (1997–1998): 137–91.

Afzal, Omar. "An Overview of Asian-Indian Muslims in the United States." In *Indian Muslims in North America*, edited by Omar Khalidi, 1–16. Watertown, Mass.: South Asia Press, 1991.

Ahlberg, N. *New Challenges—Old Strategies, Themes of Variation and Conflict among Pakistani Muslims in Norway.* Helsinki: TAFAS 25, 1990.

Ahmad, Khurshid. *Etiendo al islam y a los musulmanes.* Washington, D.C.: IFTA, 1998.

Ahmed, Gutbi Mahdi. "Muslim Organizations in the United States," in *The Muslims of America*, edited by Yvonne Yazbeck Haddad, 11–24. New York: Oxford University Press, 1991.

Alla, Tawfik, Jean Paul Buffard, Michel Marie, and Tomaso Reggazola. *Situations migratoires.* Paris: Galilee, 1977.

Alleman-Ghionda, Christina. "Schule und Migration in der Schweiz: Zwischen dem Ideal der Integration und der Versuchung der Separation." *Schweizerische Zeitschrift für Soziologie*, 23, no. 3 (1997): 329–57.

Allen, James P., and Eugene Turner. *The Ethnic Quilt: Population Diversity in Southern California.* Northridge: California State University Press, 1997.

Allievi, Stefano. "L'Islam in Italia profili storici e sociologici." In *L'Islam in Europa: Lo statuto giuridico delle comunità musulmane*, edited by S. Ferrari. Bologna: Il Mulino, 1996.

Allievi, Stefano. *I nuovi musulmani: I convertiti all' Islam.* Roma: Edizioni Lavoro, 1999.

Allievi, Stefano, ed. *L'Occidente di fronte all'Islam.* Milano: Franco Angeli, 1996.

Allievi, Stefano, and Felice Dassetto. Il ritorno dell' Islam: I musulmani in Italia. Roma: Edizioni Lavoro, 1993.

Anigboh, Chike. "The African Neo-Diaspora: Dynamics and Prospects for Afro-Centrism and Counterpenetration—A Case Study of the Nigerian Community in the United States." Ph.D. diss., Howard University, 1994.

Anwar, Muhammad. Pakistanis in Britain: A Sociological Study. London: New Century, 1985.

Anwar, Muhammad. "Religious Identity in Plural Societies: The Case of Britain." Journal of the Institute of Muslim Minority Affairs 2, nos. 2–3, 1 (1987): 110–21.

Appignanesi, Lisa, and Sara Maitland. The Rushdie File. London: Fourth Estate, 1989.

Arjomand, Said. The Shadow of God and the Hidden Imam: Religion, Political Order and Societal Change in Iran from the Beginning to 1890. Chicago: University of Chicago Press, 1986.

Arkoun, Mohammed. Rethinking Islam: Common Questions, Uncommon Answers, trans. Robert D. Lee. Boulder, Colo.: Westview Press, 1994.

Arkoun, M., R. Leveau, and B. Jisr. L'islam et les musulmans dans le monde. Vol. 1. Beirut: Centre Culturel Hariri, Recherches et Documentation, 1993.

Arlettaz, Gérald. "Démographie et identité nationale (1850–1914): la Suisse et la 'question des étrangers.'" Etudes et Sources 11 (1985): 83–180.

Armstrong, David. Revolution and World Order. London: Clarendon, 1993.

Armstrong, Karen. Holy War: The Crusades and Their Impact on Today's World. New York: Doubleday, 1991.

Asad, Talal. "Multiculturalism and British Identity in the Wake of the Rushdie Affair." Politics and Society 18 (1990): 455–80.

Aswad, Barbara C., and Barbara Bilge. Family and Gender among American Muslims: Issues Facing Middle Eastern Immigrants and Their Descendants. Philadelphia: Temple University Press, 1996.

Athar, Shahid. Reflections of an American Muslim. Chicago: KAZI, 1994.

Austin, Allen D. African Muslims in Antebellum America: A Sourcebook. New York: Garland, 1984.

Azikiwe, Nnamdi. My Odyssey: An Autobiography. New York: Praeger, 1970.

Bamba, Adama. Introduction à la connaissance de l'islam et des musulmans dans le pays hélvétique: le cas de Genève. Genève: Institut Universitaire d'Études du Développement, 1992.

Barboza, Steven. American Jihad: Islam after Malcolm X. New York: Doubleday, 1994.

Batalla, Guillermo Bonfil. México Profundo: Reclaiming a Civilization, trans. Philip A. Dennis. Austin: University of Texas Press, 1996.

Battala, Guillermo Bonfil, comp. Simbiosis de culturas: los migrantes y su cultura en México. Mexico: Fondo de Cultura Economica, 1993.

Baumann, Christoph Peter, ed. Islam in Basel-Stadt und Basel-Land. Basel: Vorabdruck des Projekts Führer durch das religiöse Basel, 1999.

Baumann, Christoph Peter, and Christian Jäggi. Muslime unter uns—Islam in der Schweiz. Luzern: Rex-Verlag, 1991.

Baumann, Zygmunt. Globalization: The Human Consequences. New York: Columbia University Press, 1998.

Ba-Yunus, Ilyas, and M. Moin Siddiqui. A Report on the Muslim Population in the United States. New York: CAMRI, 1999.

Beckford, James, and Thomas Luckmann, eds. The Changing Face of Religion. London: Sage, 1989.

Bencheikh, Souhab. Marianne et le Prophète: l'islam dans la laïcité francaise. Paris: Grasset, 1998.

Bevelander, Pieter, Benny Carlson, and Mauricio Rojas. I Krusbärslandets Storstäder: Om Invandrare i Stockholm, Göteborg och Malmö. Kristianstad: SNS Förlag, 1997.

Bissoondath, Neil. Selling Illusions: The Cult of Multiculturalism in Canada. Toronto: Penguin, 1994.

Blach, Thorston. *Nach Mekka gewandt.* Kassel: Arbeitsgemeinschaft Friedhof und Denkmal, 1996.

Blom, S., and A. Ritland. "Levekår blant ikke-vestlige innvandrere." In *Innvandrere i Norge. Hvem er de, hva gjør de of hvordan lever de?*, edited by K. Vassenden. Oslo: Statistisk Sentralbyrå, 1997.

Blom, S., E. Gulløy, and A. Ritland. *Levekår blant innvandrere 1996.* Dokumentasjonsrapport med tabeller. Oslo: Statistisk Sentralbyrå 97/6.

Bloul, Rachel. "Engendering Muslim Identities: Deterritorialization and the Ethnicization Process in France." In *Making Muslim Space in North America and Europe*, edited by Barbara Metcalf, 234–50. Berkeley: University of California Press, 1996.

Blyden, Edward Wilmot. *Christianity, Islam and the Negro Race.* London: Whittingham, 1887.

Bokovska, Nada. "Feindbild Jugo." *Tages-Anzeiger Magazin* 19 (1999): 22–29.

Bolkenstein, Frits. *Address to the Liberal International Conference at Luzern.* Den Haag: VVD, 1991.

The Book of Secrets. Toronto: McClelland & Stewart, 1994.

Bowen, John. *Muslims through Discourse: Religion and Ritual in Gayo Society.* Princeton, N.J.: Princeton University Press, 1993.

Boyarin, Jonathan, and Daniel Boyarin, eds. *Jews and Other Differences: The New Jewish Cultural Studies.* Minneapolis: University of Minnesota Press, 1997.

Bozorgmehr, Mehdi. "Internal Ethnicity: Iranians in Los Angeles." *Sociological Perspectives* 40, no. 3 (1997): 387–408.

Bozorgmehr, Mehdi, and Alison Feldman, eds. *Middle Eastern Diaspora Communities in America.* New York: Hagop Kevorkian Center for Near Eastern Studies at New York University, 1996.

Brading, D. A. *The First America: The Spanish Monarchy, Creole Patriots, and the Liberal State, 1492–1867.* Cambridge: Cambridge University Press, 1991.

Brandt, Hans-Jürgen, and Claus-Peter Haase, eds. *Begegnung mit Türken, Begegnung mit dem Islam: Ein Arbeitsbuch.* Vol. 4. Hamburg: Rissen, 1984.

Brelvi, Farah Sultana. "'News of the Weird': Specious Normativity and the Problem of the Cultural Defense." *Columbia Human Rights Law Review* 28, no. 3 (1997): 657–83.

Brigham, John. *The Cult of the Court.* Philadelphia: Temple University Press, 1987.

Brubaker, Rogers. *Citizenship and Nationhood in France and Germany.* Cambridge, Mass.: Harvard University Press, 1992.

Burckhardt-Qureshi, Regula. *Sufi Music of India and Pakistan: Sound, Context, and Meaning in Qawwali.* Chicago: University of Chicago Press, 1995.

Burkhalter, Sarah. "La question du cimetière islamique en Suisse: quels enjeux pour la communauté musulmane?" *Revue Européenne des Migrations Internationales* 14, no. 3 (1998): 61–75.

Burkhalter, Sarah. *La question du cimetière musulman en Suisse.* Genève: CERA-Editions, 1999.

Bush, George. "Transcript of His Address to the Annual Convention of National Religious Broadcasters on January 28, 1991." In *Just War and the Gulf War*, edited by James Turner Johnson and George Weigel, 142–45. Washington: Ethics and Public Policy Center, 1991.

Campo, Juan E. "Islam in California: Views from *The Minaret.*" *Muslim World* 86, nos. 3–4 (1996): 294–312.

Carlbom, Aje. "Allahs tårar: Islam som integrerande kraft i stadsdelen Rosengård." Paper presented at the SAND conference, Lund University, Lund, 1998.

Carlen, Louis. "Das Verhältnis von Kirche und Staat in der Schweiz." In *Handbuch des katholischen Kirchenrechts: Herausgegeben von Joseph Listl und Heribert Schmitz*, edited by Joseph Listl et al., 1308–23. Regensburg: F. Pustet, 1999.

Castles, Stephen. "How Nation-States Respond to Immigration and Ethnic Diversity." *New Community* 21, no. 3 (1995): 293–308.

Centlivres, Pierre. *Devenir Suisse.* Genève: Georg Editeur, 1990.

Cesari, Jocelyne. *Etre musulman en France: associations, militants et mosquées*. Paris: Karthala, 1994.

Cesari, Jocelyne. "La guerre du Golfe et les arabes de France." *Revue du monde musulman et de la Méditerranée*. no hors série, Paris (1991): 125–29.

Cesari, Jocelyne. *Musulmans et républicains, les jeunes, l'islam et la France*. Brussels: Complexe, 1998.

Chang, Mitchell J. "Expansion and Its Discontents: The Formation of Asian American Studies Programs in the 1990s." *Journal of Asian American Studies* 2, no. 23 (1999): 181–206.

Chapin, Wesley D. *Germany for the Germans? The Political Effects of International Migration*. Westport, Conn.: Greenwood Press, 1997.

Charlton, Raymond, and Ronald Kaye. "The Politics of Religious Slaughter: An Ethno-Religious Case Study." *New Community* 12 (1985): 490–503.

Christensen, Connie Carøe, and Lene Kofoed Rasmussen. *Choosing the Headscarf: Young Women in Political Islam*. Copenhagen: Forlaget Sociologi, 1994.

Christoffersen, Lisbet, and Jørgen Bæk Simonsen, eds. *Visions of Freedom of Religion, Democracy and Ethnic Equality*. Copenhagen: Nævnet for Etnisk Ligestilling, 1999.

Clarke, Colin, Ceri Peach, and Steven Vertovec, eds. *South Asians Overseas: Migration and Ethnicity*. Cambridge: Cambridge University Press, 1990.

Clifford, James. "Notes on Theory and Travel." In *Traveling Theory Traveling Theorists*, edited by James Clifford and Vivek Dhareshwar, 185. Santa Cruz: Center for Cultural Studies, 1989.

Clifford, James. *The Predicament of Culture*. Cambridge, Mass.: Harvard University Press, 1988.

Coleman, David, and Eskil Wadensjö. *The Migration to Denmark: International and National Perspectives*. Copenhagen: af Spektrum, 1999.

Coleman, Doriane Lambelet. "Individualizing Justice through Multiculturalism: The Liberals' Dilemma." *Columbia Law Review* 96 (1996): 1093–167.

Comaroff, John. "The Discourse of Rights in Colonial South Africa: Subjectivity, Sovereignty, Modernity." In *Identities, Politics, and Rights*, edited by A. Sarat and T. R. Kearns, 193–236. Ann Arbor: University of Michigan Press, 1998.

Comaroff, John, and Jean Comaroff. *Of Revelation and Revolution*. Chicago: University of Chicago Press, 1991.

Commission for Racial Equality. *Britain: A Plural Society*. London: Commission for Racial Equality and the Runnymede Trust, 1990a.

Commission for Racial Equality. *Free Speech–Report of a Seminar*. London: Commission for Racial Equality and the Policy Studies Institute, 1990b.

Commission for Racial Equality. *Law, Blasphemy and the Multi-Faith Society–Report of a Seminar*. London: Commission for Racial Equality, 1989.

Commission for Racial Equality. *Second Review of the Race Relations Act of 1976*. London: Commission for Racial Equality, 1992.

Conway, Gordon. *Islamophobia: Fact not Fiction*. London: Runnymede Trust, 1997.

Council on American-Islamic Relations. *American Muslims and the 1996 Elections: A Poll of Political Attitudes on Selected Issues*. Washington, D.C.: Council on American-Islamic Relations, 1997.

Council on American-Islamic Relations. *A Rush to Judgment*. Washington, D.C.: Council on American-Islamic Relations, 1995.

Council on American-Islamic Relations. *The Status of Muslim Civil Rights in the United States: Unveiling Prejudice*. Washington, D.C.: Council on American-Islamic Relations, 1996, 1997, 1998, 1999.

Cueni, Andreas, and Stéphane Fleury. *Etrangers et droits politiques–l'exercise des droits politiques des étrangers dans les cantons de Neuchâtel et du Jura*. Bern: Commission nationale pour l'UNESCO, 1994.

Currie, Andreas, and George Kiefl. *Ethnocultural Groups and the Justice System in Canada: A Review of the Issues*. Ottawa: Department of Justice, 1994.

Dal, Güney, and Emine Sevgi Özdamar. *Europastrasse 5*, trans. Carl Koss. München: Piper, 1990.

Dambourges Jacques, Leo M. "The Chinese Massacre in Torreón (Coahuila) in 1911." *Arizona and the West* 16 (1974): 234–47.

Dassetto, Felice. *L'Islam in Europa*. Torino: Edizioni della Fondazione Agnelli, 1994.

Dassetto, Felice, and Albert Basternier. *Europa: Nuova frontiera dell'Islam*. Roma: Edizioni Lavoro, 1988.

Dassetto, Felice, and Albert Bastenier. *L'Islam transplanté*. Anvers: EPO, 1984.

Davidson, Basil. *Black Star: A View of the Life and Times of Kwame Nkrumah*. London: Allen Lane, 1973.

DeLorenzo, Yusuf Talal. "The Fiqh Councilor in North America." In *Muslims on the Americanization Path?* edited by Yvonne Haddad and John Esposito, 79–106. Atlanta: Scholars Press, 1998.

Dev Gupta, Satya. *The Political Economy of Globalization*. Boston: Kluwer Academic, 1997.

Díaz de Kuri, Martha, and Lourdes Maclut. *De Líbano a México: crónica de un pueblo emigrante*. México: Grafica, Creatividad y Diseño, S.A. de C.V., 1995.

Dobbelaere, K. *Secularization: A Multidimensionnal Concept*. London: Sage, 1981.

Dubet, François. *L'immigration: qu'en savons-nous? Un bilan des connaissances*. Paris : La Documentation Française, 1989.

Duffield, Ian. "Duse Mohamed Ali." Ph.D. diss., University of Edinburgh, 1981.

Dunn, D. Elwood, and S. Byron Tarr. *Liberia: A National Polity in Transition*. Metuchen, N.J.: Scarecrow, 1988.

Dunn, D. Elwood, and Svend E. Holsoe. *Historical Dictionary of Liberia*. Metuchen, N.J.: Scarecrow, 1985.

Eggenberger, Oswald. *Die Kirchen, Sondergruppen und religiösen Vereinigungen–Ein Handbuch*. Zürich: Theologischer Verlag Zürich, 1994.

Eickelman, Dale F., and Jon W. Anderson, eds. *New Media in the Muslim World: The Emerging Public Sphere*. Bloomington: Indiana University Press, 1999.

Elias, Norbert. *The Established and the Outsiders: A Sociological Enquiry into Community Problems*. London: Sage, 1994.

Ellis, Jean. *Meeting Community Needs: A Study of Muslim Communities in Coventry*. Coventry: Centre for Research in Ethnic Relations, University of Warwick, Monographs in Ethnic Relations, No. 2, 1991.

Esposito, John. *The Islamic Threat: Myth or Reality?* Oxford: Oxford University Press, 1992.

Esposito, John. *Islam: The Straight Path*. 3d ed. New York: Oxford University Press, 1998.

Etienne, Bruno. *La France et l'islam*. Paris: Hachette, 1989.

Ewick, Patricia, and Susan Silbey. "Subversive Stories and Hegemonic Tales: Toward a Sociology of Narrative." *Law and Society Review* 29, no. 10 (1995): 195–226.

Facchinetti, Thomas. "Musulmans à Neuchâtel ou musulmans neuchâtelois?" *Tangram–Bulletin de la Commission fédérale contre le racisme* 7 (1999): 62–66.

Fähndrich, Hartmut. "Glauben und glauben lassen, nicht glauben und nicht glauben lassen–c'est la vie, et la vie est dure." *Tangram–Bulletin der Eidgenössischen Kommission gegen Rassismus* 7 (1999): 9–11.

Fähndrich, Hartmut. "Unverträgliche Mentalitäten?–Muslime in der Schweiz" In *Blickwechsel–Die multikulturelle Schweiz an der Schwelle zum 21. Jahrhundert*, edited by Simone Prodolliet, 249–55. Luzern: Caritas-Verlag, 1998.

Faist, Thomas. *Social Citizenship for Whom? Young Turks in Germany and Mexican Americans in the United States*. Brookfield, N.H.: Ashgate, 1995.

Fandy, Mamoun. "Is Saddam a Threat to Middle East Security? Not a Military Threat." *The World & I* (September 1998): 70–71.

Fandy, Mamoun. *Saudi Arabia and the Politics of Dissent.* New York: St. Martin's, 1999.

Fandy, Mamoun, and Roy Mottahedeh. "The Islamic Movement: The Case for Democratic Inclusion." In *The Persian Gulf at the Millennium: Essays in Politics, Economy, Security, and Religion,* edited by Gary Sick and Lawrence Potter, 297–318. New York: St. Martin's, 1997.

Fariss, Nancy M. *Maya Society under Colonial Rule: The Collective Enterprise of Survival.* Princeton, N.J.: Princeton University Press, 1984.

Federation of Islamic Associations of Europe. *Sawt Uruba.* Milan: Federation of Islamic Associations of Europe, 1997.

Ferguson, James, and Akhil Gupta, eds. *Culture, Power, Place: Explorations in Critical Anthropology.* Durham, N.C.: Duke University Press, 1997.

Ferrari, Silvio, ed. *L'Islam in Europa: Lo statuto giuridico della comunità musulmane.* Bologna: Il Mulino, 1996.

Ferrari, Silvio, ed. *Musulmani in Italia: La condizione giuridica delle comunità islamiche.* Bologna: Il Mulino, 2000.

Fischer, Sabine, and Moray McGovern. "From *Pappkoffer* to Pluralism: On the Development of Migrant Writing in the German Federal Republic." In *Turkish Culture in German Society Today,* edited by David Horrocks and Eva Kolinsky, 1–22. Providence: Berghahn Books, 1996.

Fischli-Giesser, Liz. "Die öffentlich-rechtliche Stellung 'anderer' Religionsgemeinschaften." In *Kirche und Staat in Umbruch,* edited by Adrian Loretan, 161. Zurich: NZN-Buchverlag, 1995.

Foreman-Peck, James, ed. *Historical Foundations of Globalization.* Cheltenham: Edward Elgar, 1998.

Fornaro, Robert J. "Asian Indians in America: Acculturation and Minority Status." *Migration Today* 12 (1984): 28–32.

Fowler, Robert, and Allen Hertzke. *Religion and Politics in America: Faith, Culture, and Strategic Choices.* Boulder, Colo.: Westview Press, 1995.

Fraser, Nancy. "From Redistribution to Recognition? Dilemmas of Justice in a 'Post-Socialist' Age." *New Left Review* 212 (1995): 68–93.

Friederich, Ueli. "Einführung in das schweizerische Staatskirchenrecht." In *Kirche und Staat im Umbruch,* edited by Adrian Loretan, 19–32. Zürich: NZN-Buchverlag, 1995.

Gardell, Mattias. *In the Name of Elijah Muhammad: Louis Farrakhan and the Nation of Islam.* Durham, N.C.: Duke University Press, 1996.

Geist, Imanuel. *The Pan African Movement: A History of Pan-Africanism in America, Europe, and Africa.* New York: Africana, 1968.

Ghanea Bassiri, Kambiz. *Competing Visions of Islam in the United States: A Study of Los Angeles.* Westport, Conn.: Greenwood Press, 1997.

Gilmour, Glen A. *Hate-Motivated Violence.* Ottawa: Department of Justice, 1994.

Goldberg, Jonathan J. *Jewish Power: Inside the American Jewish Establishment.* Reading, Mass.: Addison-Wesley, 1996. 88, 197–226.

González Navarro, Moisés. *Los extranjeros en México y los mexicanos en el extranjero 1821–1970.* Vol. 3. Mexico: El Colegio de México, 1994.

González Navarro, Moisés. *Población y Sociedad en México (1900–1970).* Mexico: Universidad Nacional Autónoma de México, 1974.

Government of Canada. *Canadian Multiculturalism Act.* Ottawa: Supply and Services Canada, 1988.

Guzmán, Roberto Marín. "Los immigrantes árabes en México en los siglos XIX y XX: un estudio de historia social." In *El mundo árabe y américa latina,* edited by Francois-Guerra, 130. Madrid: Ediciones UNESCO, 1997.

Haddad, Yvonne Yazbeck. "At Home in the Hijra: South Asian Muslims in the United States." In *The South Asian Religious Diaspora in Britain, Canada, and the United States*, edited by Howard Coward, John R. Hinnells, and Raymond Brady Williams, 239-58. New York: State University of New York Press, 2000.

Haddad, Yvonne Yazbeck. "Towards the Carving of Islamic Space in 'the West.'" *ISIM Newsletter* 1 (1998): 5.

Haddad, Yvonne Yazbeck, ed. *The Muslims of America*. New York: Oxford University Press, 1991.

Haddad, Yvonne Yazbeck, and Adair Lummis. *Islamic Values in the United States: A Comparative Study*. New York: Oxford University Press, 1987.

Haddad, Yvonne Yazbeck, and Jane Smith. *Mission to America: Five Islamic Sectarian Communities in North America*. Gainesville: University Press of Florida, 1993.

Haddad, Yvonne Yazbeck, and Jane Smith, eds. *Muslim Communities in North America*. Albany: State University of New York Press, 1994.

Haddad, Yvonne Yazbeck, and John L. Esposito. *Muslims on the Americanization Path?* Atlanta: Scholars Press, 1998.

Hadden, Jeffrey K., and Anson D. Shupe, eds. *Secularization and Fundamentalism*. New York: Paragon House, 1989.

Haenni, Patrick. "Dynamiques sociales et rapport à l'Etat—l'institutionnalisation de l'islam en Suisse." *Revue Européene des Migrations Internationales* 10, no. 1 (1994): 183-98.

Haenni, Patrick. "L'islam pluriel des musulmans de Suisse: engagement et distanciation de 'l'autre intérieur.'" *Tangram—Bulletin der Eidgenössischen Kommission gegen Rassismus* 7 (1999): 12-15.

Haenni, Patrick. "Musulmans de Suisse et religion: d'un islam à l'autre." In *Minorités chrétiennes et musulmanes—aspects religieux*, edited by Jacques Waardenberg, *Cahiers de l'Université de Lausanne* 4 (1995): 8-48.

Haider, Gulzar. "'Brother in Islam, Please Draw Us a Mosque': Muslims in the West: A Personal Account." In *Expressions of Islam in Buildings*. Edited by Hayat Salam, 155-66. Geneva: Aga Khan Trust for Culture, 1990.

Haider, Gulzar. "Muslim Space and the Practice of Architecture." In *Making Muslim Space in North America and Europe*. Edited by Barbara Metcalf, 31-45. Berkeley: University of California Press, 1996.

Haley, Alex. *Roots*. Garden City, NY: Doubleday, 1976.

Hall, Stuart. "Cultural Identity and Cinematic Representation." *Framework* 36 (1989): 44-46.

Hall, Stuart. "Minimal Selves." In *Identity*, edited by Homi Bhabha, 45. London: Institute of Contemporary Arts, 1987.

Halliday, Fred. *Islam and the Myth of Confrontation: Religion and Politics in the Middle East*. London: Tauris, 1996.

Halstead, Michael. *Education, Justice and Cultural Diversity: An Examination of the Honeyford Affair, 1984-1985*. London: Falmer Press, 1988.

Hamberg, Eva. "Migration and Religious Change." In *Religion and Social Transition*, edited by Eila Helander. Helsinki: University of Helsinki, 1999.

Hamberg, Eva. "World-views and Value Systems among Immigrants: Long-term Stability or Change?" *Sociale Wetenschappen* 38, no. 4 (1995): 85-108.

Hamdani, Daood Hassan. "The Canadian Muslims on the Eve of the Twenty-first Century." *Journal of Muslim Minority Affairs* 19, no. 2 (October 1999): 197-210.

Hamdani, Daood Hassan. "Muslims in the Canadian Mosaic." *Journal of the Institute of Muslim Minority Affairs* 5, no. 1 (1984): 7-16.

Hamui-Halabe, Liz. "Re-creating Community: Christians from Lebanon and Jews from Syria in Mexico, 1900-1938." In *Arab and Jewish Immigrants in Latin America: Images and Realities*, edited by Ignacio Klich and Jeffrey Lesser, 125-145. London: Frank Cass, 1998.

Hassan, Hani. "Media and Ethnicity." Conference presentation, Mississauga, Ontario, April 1995.

Haug, Werner. Vom Einwanderungsland zur multikulturellen Gesellschaft. Bern: Bundesamt für Statistik, 1995.

Heine, Peter. Halbmond über deutschen Dächern–Muslimisches Leben in unserem Land. München: List-Verlag, 1997.

Heiniger, Marcel. "Daten zu Muslimen und Musliminnen in der Schweiz." Tangram–Bulletin der Eidgenössischen Kommission gegen Rassismus 7 (1999): 79–80.

Hermansen, Marcia K. "Hybrid Identity Formations in Muslim America: The Case of American Sufi Movements." Muslim World 90, nos. 1–2 (2000): 158–96.

Hifi, Belkacem. L'immigration algérienne en France: origines et perspectives de non retour. Paris: L'Harmattan, CIEM, 1985.

Hirst, Paul, and Grahame Thompson. Globalization in Question. Cambridge: Polity, 1999.

Hooglund, Eric J. Crossing the Waters: Arabic-Speaking Immigrants to the United States before 1940. Washington, D.C.: Smithsonian Institution Press, 1987.

Horrocks, David, and Eva Kolinsky, eds. Turkish Culture in German Society Today. Providence: Berghahn Books, 1996.

Howell, Sally. "Aesthetic Interventions: Arab (American) Artists between Ethnicity and Transnationalism." Diaspora 9, no. 1 (Spring 2001): 59–82.

Hu-De Hart, Evelyn. "Immigrants to a Developing Society: The Chinese in Northern Mexico, 1875–1932." Journal of Arizona History 21, no. 3 (1980): 275–312.

Huntington, Samuel P. The Clash of Civilizations and the Remaking of World Order. New York: Simon & Schuster, 1996.

Hunziker, Ernst. "Allah an der Limmat." Unizürich–Magazin der Universität Zürich 2 (1996): http://www.upd.unizh/magazin/2-96/muslime.htm.

Husain, Mir Zohair. Global Islamic Politics. New York: Harper/Collins, 1995.

Husaini, Zohra. Muslims in the Canadian Mosaic. Edmonton: Muslim Research Foundation, 1990.

Husband, Charles. "Differentiated Citizenship and the Multi-Ethnic Public Sphere." Journal of International Communication 5, no. 1 (1998): 134–48.

Hussain, Waseem. "Feindbild Islam: die Verantwortung der Redaktionen." Tangram–Bulletin der Eidgenössischen Kommission gegen Rassismus 2 (1997): 33–36.

Ingham, John. Mary, Michael, Lucifer: Folk Catholicism in Central Mexico. Austin, Texas: University of Texas Press, 1986.

Islam, Anwar. "Adoption of Guardianship." Manitoba Multicultural Resources Centre Magazine 1, no. 2 (Spring/Summer 1992): 8–9.

Issawi, Charles. The Economic History of the Middle East, 1800–1914. Chicago: University of Chicago Press, 1966.

Jawad, Haifaa, ed. The Middle East in the New World Order. 2d ed. London: Macmillan, 1997.

al-Jibouri, Yasin. "A Glance at Shi'a Communities in the U.S." In Islamic Insights, Virginia (October 1993): 1.

Jilberto, Alex E. Fernández, and André Mommen. Regionalization and Globalization in the Modern World Economy: Perspectives on the Third World and Transitional Economies. London: Routledge, 1998.

Johnson, Steve A. "Political Activity of Muslims in America." In Yvonne Yazbeck Haddad, The Muslims of America, 111. New York: Oxford University Press, 1991.

Jørgensen, T. "Utdanning." In Innvandrere i Norge. Hvem er de, hva gjør de of hvordan lever de? edited by K. Vassenden. Oslo: Statistisk Sentralbyrå, 1997.

Jozami, Gladys. "Aspectos demográficos y comportamiento espacial de los migrantes árabes en el Noroeste Argentino." Estudios Migratorios Latinamericanos 2, no. 5 (1987): 95–114.

Justo, Sierra. *México Social y Politico.* Mexico: Secretaría de Hacienda y Crédito Público, 1960.

Kaenel, Yvan. *La population musulmane du canton de Neuchâtel–pour un dialogue entre les associations musulmanes et le canton de Neuchâtel, 17.* Zurich: Rapport du Bureau du Délégué aux Étrangers, 1996.

Kalin, Walter, "Grundrechte in der Einwanderungsgesellschaft." In *Blickwechsel–Die multikulturelle Schweiz an der Schwelle zum 21. Jahrhundert.* Edited by Simone Prodolliet, 37–49. Luzern: Caritas-Verlag, 1998.

Kalka, Iris. "Striking a Bargain: Political Radicalism in a Middle-Class London Borough." In *Black and Ethnic Leaderships in Britain,* edited by Pnina Werbner and Muhammad Anwar, 203–25. London: Routledge, 1991.

Karakasoglu, Yasemin. "Turkish Cultural Orientations in Germany and the Role of Islam." In *Turkish Culture in German Society Today,* edited by David Horrocks and Eva Kolinsky, 157–80. Providence: Berghahn Books, 1996.

Karakasoglu, Yasemin, and Ursula Spuler-Stegemann. *Muslime in Deutschland: Nebeneinander oder Miteinander.* Freiburg: Herder Verlag, 1998.

Karim, Karim H. "The Historical Resilience of Primary Stereotypes: Core Images of the Muslim Other." In *The Language and Politics of Exclusion: Others in Discourse,* edited by Stephen Harold Riggins, 153–82. Thousand Oaks, Calif.: Sage, 1997.

Karim, Karim H. "Multiculturalism in Australia, US, and the UK." In *The Battle over Multiculturalism.* Edited by Andrew Cardozo and Louis Musto, 137–42. Ottawa: Pearson-Shoyama Institute, 1997.

Karim, Karim H. "Reconstructing the Multicultural Community: Discursive Strategies of Inclusion and Exclusion." *International Journal of Politics, Culture, and Society* 7, no. 2 (1993): 189–207.

Karlsson, Ingmar. *Islam and Europe.* Stockholm: Wahlström & Widstrand, 1994.

Karlsson, Pia, and Ingvar Svanberg. *Moskeer i Sverige en Religionsetnologisk studie i intolerans och administrativ vanmakt.* Serien Tro och Tanke 7/95. Uppsala: Svenska Kyrkans Forskningsråd, 1995.

Karlsson, Pia, and Ingvar Svanberg. *Religionsfrihet i Sverige.* Lund: Studentlitteratur, 1997.

Karpat, Kemal. "The Ottoman Emigration to the Americas, 1860-1914." *International Journal of Middle Eastern Studies* 7, no. 2 (1985): 175–209.

Kashmeri, Zuhair. *The Gulf Within: Canadian Arabs, Racism and the Gulf War.* Toronto: James Lorimer, 1991.

Katz, Friedrich. *The Life and Times of Pancho Villa.* Stanford, Calif.: Stanford University Press, 1998.

Kepel, Gilles. *Les banlieues de l'islam.* Paris : Seuil, 1987.

Kepel, Gilles. *Les banlieues de l'islam: naissance d'une religion en France.* Paris: Seuil, 1991.

Kettani, M. Ali. *Muslim Minorities in the World Today.* London: Mansell, 1986.

Khalidi, Omar. "Approaches to Mosque Design in North America." In *Muslims on the Americanization Path?* Edited by Yvonne Yazbeck Haddad and John Esposito, 399–424. Atlanta: Scholars Press, 1998.

Khan, Muhammed A. Muqtedar. "Muslims and American Politics: Refuting the Isolationist Arguments." *American Muslim Quarterly* 2, no. 1-2 (1998): 60–69.

Khanum, Saeeda. "War Talk." *New Statesman & Society* 1 (Feb. 1991): 12–13.

King, Kenneth. "James E. K. Aggrey: Collaborator, Nationalist, Pan African." *Canadian Journal of African Studies* 3, no. 4 (1970): 511–30.

King, Michael. "The Muslim Identity in a Secular World." In *God's Law versus State Law: The Construction of an Islamic Identity in Western Europe,* edited by Michael King, 91–114. London: Grey Seal, 1995.

Klich, Ignacio. "Introduction to the Sources for the History of the Middle Easterners in Latin America." *Temas de Africa y Asia* 2 (1993): 205–33.

Klich, Ignacio, and Jeffrey Lesser. "Introduction: 'Turco' Immigrants in Latin America." *The Americas* 53, no. 1 (1996): 1–14.

Klop, Kees J. "Religie of etniciteit als bindmiddel?" *Migrantenstudies* 4 (1999): 246–55.

Knight, Alan. *The Mexican Revolution.* Vols. 1 and 2. Cambridge: Cambridge University Press, 1986.

Knight, Alan. "Racism, Revolution, and Indigenismo, Mexico, 1910–1940." In *The Idea of Race in Latin America, 1870–1940*, edited by Richard Graham, 71–114. Austin: University of Texas Press, 1990.

Knippenberg, Hans. "The Ethnicity of National Integration: Religion, Education and Politics in the Netherlands." *Netherlands Journal of Social Sciences* 35, no. 1 (1999): 37–53.

Knott, Kim. "Bound to Change? The Religions of South Asians in Britain." In *Aspects of the South Asian Diaspora*, edited by Steven Vertovec, 86–111. Delhi: Oxford University Press, 1991.

Kolinsky, Eva. "Non-German Minorities in Contemporary German Society." In *Turkish Culture in German Society Today.* Edited by David Horrocks and Eva Kolinsky, 71–112. Providence: Berghahn Books, 1996.

Kreiger-Krynicki, Annie. *Les musulmans en France: religion et culture.* Paris: Maisonneuve-Larose, 1985.

Kürsat-Ahlers, Elçin. "The Turkish Minority in German Society." In *Turkish Culture in German Society Today*, edited by David Horrocks and Eva Kolinsky, 113–36. Providence: Berghahn Books, 1996.

Kymlica, Will. *Multicultural Citizenship: A Liberal Theory of Minority Rights.* Oxford: Clarendon Press, 1995.

Lal, Barbara. "Ethnic Identity Entrepreneurs: Their Role in Transracial and Intercountry Adoptions." *Asian and Pacific Migration Journal* 6, no. 3–4 (1997): 385–413.

Landman, Nico. *Van mat tot minaret. De institutionalisering van de islam in Nederland.* Amsterdam: VU Uitgeverij, 1992.

Langley, Jabez Ayodele. *Pan-Africanism and Nationalism in Africa 1900–45.* New York: Oxford University Press, 1973.

Leirvik, O. "State, Church and Muslim Minority in Norway." Paper presented at the conference *Dialogue of Cultures*, Berlin 21–23 April 1999.

Leonard, Karen Isaksen. "Hyderabadis in Pakistan: Changing Nations." In *Community, Empire, and Migration: South Asians in Diaspora*, edited by Crispin Bates, 224–244. New York: St. Martin's, 2000.

Leonard, Karen Isaksen. *Making Ethnic Choices: California Punjabi Mexican Americans.* Philadelphia: Temple University Press, 1992.

Leonard, Karen Isaksen. *The South Asian Americans.* Westport, Conn.: Greenwood Press, 1997.

Leonard, Karen Isaksen. "State, Culture, and Religion: Political Action and Representation among South Asians in North America." *Diaspora* 9, no. 1 (Spring 2000): 21–38.

Lewis, Philip. "The Bradford Council of Mosques and the Search for Muslim Unity." In *Islam in Europe: The Politics of Religion and Community*, edited by Steven Vertovec and Ceri Peach, 103–27. Basingstoke: Macmillan, 1997.

Lewis, Philip. *Islamic Britain: Religion, Politics and Identity among British Muslims.* London: Taurus, 1994.

Lindberg, Staffan, and Arni Sverrisson. *Social Movements in Development: The Challenge of Globalization and Democratization.* New York: St. Martin's, 1997.

Linder, Wolf. *Schweizerische Demokratie–Institutionen, Prozesse, Perspektiven.* Bern: Verlag Paul Haupt, 1999.

Luckmann, Thomas. *The Invisible Religion: The Problem of Religion in Modern Society.* New York: Macmillan, 1967.

Luthi, Angelika, and Leonhard Suter. *Musliminnen und Muslime in Zürich–Eine Dokumentation.* Zürich: Kirchlicher Informationsdienst, 1999.

Mahnig, Hans. *Contradictions of Inclusion in a Direct Democracy–The Struggle for Political and Cultural Rights of Migrants in Zurich,* 21-26. Paper for the UNESCO-MOST program "Multicultural Policies and Modes of Citizenship in European Cities." Neuchâtel: Swiss Forum for Migration Studies, 1999.

Mahnig Hans. "La question de l'intégration ou comment les immigrés deviennent un enjeu politique–une comparaison entre la France, l'Allemagne, les Pays-Bas et la Suisse." *Sociétés Contemporaines* 33, no. 34 (1999): 15-38.

Malewska-Peyre, Hélène. *Crise d'identité et déviance chez les jeunes immigrés.* Paris: La Documentation Française, 1982.

Marriott, McKim. "Alternative Social Sciences." In *General Education in the Social Sciences: Centennial Reflections,* edited by John MacAloon, 262-78. Chicago: University of Chicago Press, 1992.

Martin, David. *A General Theory of Secularization.* Oxford: Blackwell, 1978.

Martin, P. L. *The Unfinished Story: Turkish Labor Migration to Western Europe, with Special Reference to the Federal Republic of Germany.* Geneva: International Labour Office, 1991.

Martínez Montiel, Luz María. "Lebanese Immigration to Mexico." In *Asiatic Migrations in Latin America,* 147-61. Thirtieth International Congress of Human Sciences in Asia and Africa, 1976. Mexico: El Colegio de Mexico, 1981.

Mayer, Ann. *Islam and Human Rights.* Boulder, Colo.: Westview Press, 1991.

McCloud, Aminah Beverly. *African American Islam.* New York: Routledge, 1995.

Merry, Sally Engle. "Law, Culture, and Cultural Appropriation." *Yale Journal of Law and the Humanities* 10 (1998): 575-603.

Metaferria, Getachew, and Maiginet Shiffrew. *Ethiopian Immigrants in the United States.* Buffalo, N.Y.: Edwin Mellon, 1992.

Metcalf, Barbara. "New Medinas: The Tablighi Jama'at in America and Europe." In *Making Muslim Space in North America and Europe,* edited by Barbara Metcalf, 92-109. Berkeley: University of California Press, 1996.

Meyers, William K. *Forge of Progress, Crucible of Revolt: The Origins of the Mexican Revolution in La Comaraca, Lagunera, 1880-1911.* Albuquerque: University of New Mexico Press, 1994.

Minces, Juliette. *Les travailleurs étrangers en France.* Paris: Seuil, 1973.

Ministry of Internal Affairs. *Mindeerhedennota.* Den Haag: BiZa, 1983.

Mishima, Maria Elena Ota. *Destino México: un estudio de las migraciones asiáticas a México, siglos XIX y XX.* Mexico: El Colegio de Mexico, 1997.

Modood, Tariq. "British Asian Muslims and the Rushdie Affair." *Political Quarterly* 61 (1990): 143-60.

Mohammed, Warith Deen. "Our Duty and Pride as Muslims and American Citizens." *Journal of Islamic Law* 4, no. 1 (Spring/Summer 1999): 3-10.

Moore, Kathleen. *Al-Mughtaribun: American Law and the Transformation of Muslim Life in the United States.* Albany: State University of New York Press, 1995.

M'roueh, Youssef. "Shi'a Population in North America." In *Ahlul bayt Assembly of North America: Abstract of Proceedings of 1996,* 41-56. Beltsville, Md.: International Graphics, 1997.

Muhammad, Akbar. "Muslims in the United States: An Overview of Organizations, Doctrines, and Problems." In *The Islamic Impact,* edited by Yvonne Yazbeck Haddad, Byron Haines, and Ellison Findly, 195-218. Syracuse: Syracuse University Press, 1984.

Musalem Rahal, Doris. "La migración palestina a México, 1893-1949." In *Destino México: un estudio de las migraciones asiaticas a México, siglos XIX y XX,* edited by Maria Elena Ota Mishima, 305-64. Mexico: El Colegio de Mexico, 1997.

Mutlu, Hassan. *Le tissu associatif des communautés étrangères dans le canton de Neuchâtel–problèmes, besoins et demandes des associations*. Neuchâtel: Institut de Sociologie et de Science Politique, 1995.

Naber, Nadine. "Ambiguous Insiders: An Investigation of Arab American Invisibility." *Ethnic and Racial Studies* 23, no. 1 (2000): 37–61.

Nacif, Jorge Mina. *Crónicas de un inmigrante libanés en México*. Mexico: Edición de Jorge Nacif Mina en colaboración con el Instituto Cultural Mexicano Libanés, A.C., 1995.

Naff, Alixa. *Becoming American: The Early Arab Immigrant Experience*. Carbondale: Southern Illinois University Press, 1985.

Naipul, V.S. *Beyond Belief: Islamic Excursions among the Converted Peoples*. London: Vintage, 1999.

Nanji, Azim. "The Nizari Ismaili Muslim Community in North America." In *The Muslim Community in North America*, edited by Earle H. Waugh, Baha Abu-Laban, and Regula B. Qureshi, 93–110. Edmonton: University of Alberta Press, 1983.

Narayan, Uma. "Essence of Culture and a Sense of History: A Feminist Critique of Cultural Essentialism." *Hypatia* 13 (Spring 1998): 87–106.

Natvig, R. "Les musulmans en Norvège." In *L'islam et les musulmans dans le monde*, edited by M. Arkoun, R. Leveau, and B. Jisr, 421–51. Beirut: Centre Culturel Hariri, Recherches et Documentation, 1993.

Nielsen, Jørgen S. "Muslims in Britain and Local Authority Responses." In *The New Islamic Presence in Western Europe*, edited by Thomas Gerholm and Yngve G. Lithman, 53–77. London: Mansell, 1988.

Nielsen, Jørgen S. *Muslims in Western Europe*. Edinburgh: Edinburgh University Press, 1992.

Nimer, Mohamed. *The Usual Suspects: Media Coverage Following the Crash of TWA Flight 800*. Washington, D.C.: Council on American-Islamic Relations, 1996.

Nkrumah, Kwame. *The Autobiography of Kwame Nkrumah*. Edinburgh: Nelson, 1957.

Nonneman, Gerd, Tim Niblock, and Bogdan Szajkowksi, eds. *Muslim Communities in the New Europe*. Reading, U.K.: Ithaca Press, 1996.

Nu'man, Fareed H. *The Muslim Population in the United States*. Washington, D.C.: American Muslim Council, 1992.

Nussbaum, Martha. *Sex and Social Justice*. New York: Oxford University Press, 1999.

Nyang, Sulayman. "Islam in America: A Historical Perspective." *American Muslim Quarterly* 2, no. 1 (Spring 1998): 7–38.

Nyang, Sulayman. "African Muslims." In *American Immigrant Cultures: Builders of a Nation*, vol. 1, edited by David Lecincon and Melvin Ember, 20–31. New York: Macmillan, 1997.

Olson, Susan M., and Christina Batjer. "Competing Narratives in a Judicial Retention Election: Feminism versus Judicial Independence." *Law and Society Review* 33 (1999): 123–60.

Øsberg, S. *Pakistani Children in Oslo: Islamic Nurture in a Secular Context*. Ph.D. diss., University of Warwick, Institute of Education, 1998.

Osiel, Mark J. "Dialogue with Dictators: Judicial Resistance in Argentina and Brazil." *Law and Social Inquiry* 20, no. 2 (1995): 481–560.

Österberg, Eva. "Vardagens sträva samförstånd. Bondepolitik i den svenska modellen från vasatid till frihetstid." In *Tänka, Tycka, Tro*. Stockholm: Ordfronts Förlag, 1993.

Øya, T. *Generasjonskløfta som ble borte,Ungdom, Innvandrere og Kultur*. Oslo: Cappelens Akademiske Forlag, 1997.

Özdamar, Emine Sevgi. *Die Brücke vom Goldenen Horn*. Köln: Kiepenheuer & Witsch, 1998.

Özdamar, Emine Sevgi. *Das Leben ist eine Karawanserai*. Köln: Kiepenheuer & Witsch, 1992.

Özdamar, Emine Sevgi. *Mutterzunge: Erzählungen*. 2d ed. Köln: Kiepenheuer & Witsch, 1998.

Pacini, A. "I musulman in Italia." Dinamiche organizzative e processi d'interazione con la società e le instituzioni." In *Musulmani in Italia, la condizione giuridica delle communità islamiche*, edited by S. Ferrari. Bologna: Il Mulino, 1996.

Páez Oropeza, Carmen Mercedes. *Los Libaneses en México: asimilación de un grupo étnica.* Mexico: Instituto Nacional de Anthropología, 1984.

Parekh, Bhikhu. "British Citizenship and Cultural Difference." In *Citizenship*, edited by Geoff Andrews, 183–204. London: Lawrence & Wishart, 1991.

Parekh, Bhikhu. "Equality, Fairness and Limits of Diversity." *Innovation* 7, no. 3 (1994): 289–308.

Parekh, Bhikhu. "The Rushdie Affair and the British Press: Some Salutary Lessons." In *Free Speech–Report of a Seminar*, 59–78. London: Commission for Racial Equality and the Policy Studies Institute, Discussion Papers 2, 1990.

Parsons, Gerald, ed. *The Growth of Religious Diversity: Britain from 1945.* 2 vols. London: Routledge, 1993–1994.

Peach, C. "The Cultural Landscape of South Asian Religion in English Cities." Seminar paper given at School of Geography, University of Oxford, 2000.

Peach, C. "The Muslim Population of Great Britain." *Ethnic and Racial Studies* 13 (1990): 414–19.

Peach, Ceri, ed. *Ethnicity in the 1991 Census*, vol. 2: *The Ethnic Minority Populations of Great Britain.* London: Office for National Statistics/HMSO, 1996.

Pearl, David. "South Asian Communities and English Family Law, 1971–1987." *New Community* 14 (1987): 161–69.

Pederesen, Lars. *Newer Islamic Movements in Western Europe.* Aldershot: Ashgate, 1999.

Pelletreau, Robert Jr., Daniel Pipes, and John Esposito. "Symposium: Resurgent Islam in the Middle East." *Middle East Policy* 3, no. 2 (1994): 1–21.

Peters, Rudolph. *Islam and Colonialism: The Doctrine of Jihad in Modern History.* The Hague: Mouton, 1979.

Pfaff-Czarnecka, Joanna. "Collective Minority Rights in Switzerland?" *Tsantsa* 4 (1999): 199–203.

Pfaff-Czarnecka, Joanna. "Let Sleeping Dogs Lie! Non-Christian Religious Minorities in Switzerland Today." *Journal of the Anthropological Society of Oxford* 29, no. 1 (1998): 29–51.

Philips, James. "Islamic Terrorists Pose a Threat." In *Urban Terrorism*, edited by A. E. Sadler and Paul Winters, 62–65. San Diego: Greenhaven Press, 1996.

Porter, Dennis. "Orientalism and Its Problems." In *Colonial Discourse and Post-Colonia Theory: A Reader*, edited by Patrick Williams and Laura Chrisman, 150–61. New York: Harvester Wheatsheaf, 1994.

Poston, Larry. *Islamic Da'wah in the West.* New York: Oxford University Press, 1992.

Poulter, Sebastian. *Asian Tradition and the English Law.* London: Trentham Books, 1990.

Ramadan, Tariq. *Etre musulman en Europe.* Lyons: Editions Tawhid, 1999.

Ramadan, Tariq. "L'islam d'Europe sort de l'isolement." *Le Monde Diplomatique* (avril 1998): 13.

Ramadan, Tariq. "Islam en Suisse: etats des lieux et perspectives." *Tangram–Bulletin der Eidgenössischen Kommission gegen Rassismus* 1 (1999): 24–28.

Ramadan, Tariq. *Les musulmans dans la laïcité: responsabilités et droits des musulmans dans les sociétés occidentales.* Lyon: Tawhid, 1994.

Ramadan, Tariq. *Peut-on vivre avec l'islam? Le choc de la religion musulmane et des sociétés laïques et chrétiennes. Entretiens avec Jacques Neirynck.* Lausanne: Favre, 1999.

Ramadan, Tariq. *To Be a European Muslim.* Leicester: Islamic Foundation, 1999.

Ramírez Carrillo, Luis Alfonso. *Secretos de familia: Libaneses y élites empresariales en Yucatán.* Mexico: Consejo Nacional para la Cultura y las Artes, 1994.

Raselli, Niccolò. "Schickliche Beerdigung für 'Andersgläubige.'" *Aktuelle Juristische Praxis* 9 (1996): 1103–10.

Rath, Jan, and Thijl Sunier. "Angst voor de islam in Nederland?" In *Kritiek. Jaarboek voor socialistische discussie en analyse 1993–1994*, edited by W. Bot, M. van der Linden, and R. Went, 53–62. Utrecht: Stichting Toestanden, 1994.

Rath, Jan, Kees Groenendijk, and Rinus Penninx. "The Recognition and Institutionalization of Islam in Belgium, Great Britain and the Netherlands." *New Community* 18 (1991): 101–14.

Rath, Jan, Rinus Penninx, Kees Groenendijk, and Astrid Meyer. *Nederland en zijn islam.* Amsterdam: Het Spinhuis, 1996.

Reid, Angus. *Multiculturalism and Canadians: Attitude Study 1991–National Survey Report.* Ottawa: Multiculturalism and Citizenship, 1991.

Riggins, Stephen Harold. "The Rhetoric of Othering." In *The Language and Politics of Exclusion: Others in Discourse,* edited by Stephen Harold Riggins, 1–30. Thousand Oaks, Calif.: Sage, 1997.

Rist, Ray C. *Guestworkers in Germany.* New York: Praeger, 1978.

Robinson, Francis. "Varieties of South Asian Islam." Coventry: Centre for Research in Ethnic Relations, University of Warwick, Research Paper No. 8, 1988.

Rojas, Mauricio. *The Rise and Fall of the Swedish Model.* London: Social Market Foundation, 1998.

Roy, O. "Naissance d'un islam européen." *Esprit* 1 (1998): 10–35.

Rückert, Günter. *Untersuchungen zum Sprachverhalten türkischer Jugendlicher in der BDR.* Pfaffenweiler: Centaurus Verlagsgesellschaft, 1985.

Runnymede Trust Commission on British Muslims and Islamophobia. *Islamophobia: A Challenge for Us All.* London: Runnymede Trust, 1997.

Ruthven, Malise. *A Satanic Affair: Salman Rushdie and the Wrath of Islam.* London: Hogarth Press, 1990.

Rutz-Imhoof, Ernst. "Zum Verhältnis von Kirche und Staat im Kanton Zürich." In *Kirche und Staat im Umbruch,* edited by Adrian Loretan, 50–61. Zürich: NZN-Buchverlag, 1995.

Sachedina, Abdulaziz. "Activist Shi'ism in Iran, Iraq and Lebanon." In *Fundamentalisms Observed,* edited by M. Marty and R. Appleby, 403–56. Chicago: University of Chicago Press, 1991.

Sachedina, Abdulaziz. "A Minority within a Minority: The Case of the Shi'a in North America." In *Muslim Communities in North America,* edited by Yvonne Yazbeck-Haddad and Jane Smith, 3–14. New York: State University of New York, 1991.

Safran, William. "Diasporas in Modern Societies: Myths of Homeland and Return." *Diaspora* 1 (1991): 83–99.

Said, Edward. *Covering Islam.* New York: Pantheon, 1981; 2d ed. New York: Vintage, 1997.

Said, Edward. *Orientalism.* Harmondsworth: Penguin, 1978.

Saint-Blancat, Chantal. *L'Islam della diaspora.* Roma: Edizioni Lavoro, 1995.

Saint-Blancat, Chantal, ed. *L'Islam in Italia: Una presenza plurale.* Roma: Edizioni Lavoro, 1999.

Sander, Åke. "The Road from Musalla to Mosque." In *The Integration of Islam and Hinduism in Western Europe,* edited by W. A. R. Shadid and P. S. van Koningsveld, 63–69. United Kingdom: Kok Pharos, 1994.

Sander, Åke. "The Status of Muslim Communities in Sweden." In *Muslim Communities in the New Europe,* edited by Gerd Nonneman, Tim Niblock, and Bogdan Szajkowski, 272–88. London: Ithaca, 1996.

Sander, Åke. *I vilken utsträckning är den svenska muslimen religiös.* Gothenburg: KIM, 1993.

Sanderson, Susan, Phil Sidel, and Harold Hims. "East Asians and Arabs in Mexico: A Study of Naturalized Citizens (1886–1931)." In *Asiatic Migrations in Latin America,* edited by Luz Maria Martinez Montiel, 175. Mexico: El Colegio de Mexico, 1981.

Sayad, Abdelmalek. "Les trois âges de l'émigration algérienne en France," *Actes de la recherche en sciences sociales* 15 (June 1977): 59–76.

Schmidt, Garbi. *American Medina: A Study of the Sunni Muslim Immigrant Communities in Chicago.* Lund, Sweden: University of Lund, 1998.

Schmidt di Friedberg, Ottavia. *Islam, solidarietà e lavoro: I muridi senegalesi in Italia*. Torino: Edizioni Fondazione Agnelli, 1994.

Schubel, Vernon. "Karbala as Sacred Space among North American Shi'a: 'Every Day Is Ashura, Everywhere Is Karbala.'" In *Making Muslim Space in North America and Europe*, edited by Barbara Metcalf, 186–203. Berkeley: University of California Press, 1996.

Schubel, Vernon. "The Muharram Majlis: The Role of a Ritual in the Preservation of Shi'a Identity." In *Muslim Families in North America*, edited by E. Waugh, S. M. Abu-Laban, and R. Qureshi, 118–31. Edmonton: University of Alberta Press, 1991.

Schubel, Vernon. *Religious Performance in Contemporary Islam: Shi'i Devotional Rituals in South Asia*. Columbia: University of South Carolina Press, 1993.

Schwencke, Hendrik Jan. "Schoolstrijd in Den Haag. Veranderingen in de religieuze cultuur van Surinaamse Hindoes in Nederland." *Migrantenstudies* 10, no. 2 (1994): 97–111.

al-Seestani, Ayatollah al-Sayyid 'Ali al-Husayni. *Contemporary Legal Rulings in Shi'i Law*. Translated by Hamid Mavani. Montreal: Organization for the Advancement of Islamic Knowledge and Humanitarian Services, 1996.

Service de documentation du Centre Maghrebin de Recherche et d'Information. *The Impact of the Gulf War on Muslim Communities: Press Clippings*. Montreal: Le Centre Maghrebin de Recherche et d'Information, 1991.

Siddiqui, Haroon. "Perceptions and Misrepresentations of Islam and Muslims by the Media." *Islam in America* 3, no. 3 (Fall 1996): 41–42.

Sigillino, Innocenzo, ed. *I bambini dell'Islam*. Milano: Franco Angeli, 2000.

Sigillino, Innocenzo, ed. *I luoghi del dialogo, Cristiani e Musulmani in Italia*. Melzo: Editrice Cens, 1997.

Simonsen, Jørgen Bæk. "A Means to Change or Transform Images of the Other–Private Arab Schools in Denmark." In *The Arabs and the West: Mutual Images*, edited by Jørgen S. Nielsen and Sami A. Khasawnih, 115–27. Amman: University of Amman Press, 1998.

Simonsen, Jørgen Bæk. *From Defensive Silence to Creative Participation–Muslim Discourses in Denmark* (forthcoming).

Simonsen, Jørgen Bæk. *Islam in Denmark: Muslim Institutions in Denmark, 1970–1989*. Århus: Århus Universitetsforlag, 1990.

Smith, Jane. *Islam in America*. New York: Columbia University Press, 1999.

Soysal, Yasemin. *Limits of Citizenship: Migrants and Post-national Membership in Europe*. Chicago: University of Chicago Press, 1994.

Spuler-Stegemann, Ursula. *Muslime in Deutschland: Nebeneinander oder Miteinander*. Freiburg: Herder Verlag, 1998.

State's Official Reports. *Investigation of Immigrants 3*. Stockholm: Regeringskansliet, 1974.

Statistiska Centralbyrån. *Utbildning för utrikes födda*. Örebro: SCB, 1995.

Strawson, John. "Interpreting Oriental Cases: The Law of Alterity in the Colonial Courtroom." *Harvard Law Review* 107 (1994): 1711–30.

Strawson, John. "Islamic Law and English Texts." *Law and Critique* 7 (1995): 21–38.

Streiff-Fenart, Jocelyne. *Les couples franco-maghébins en France*. Paris: Le Centurion, 1990.

Stuurman, Siep. *Verzuiling, Kapitalisme en Patriarchaat*. Nijmegen: SUN, 1983.

Sunier, Thijl. *Islam in beweging. Turkse jongeren en islamitische organisaties*. Amsterdam: Het Spinhuis, 1996.

Svanberg, Ingvar, and David Westerlund, eds. *Blågul Islam? Muslimer i Sverige*. (Blue-yellow Islam? Muslims in Sweden.) Nora: Nya Doxa, 1999.

Svanberg, Ingvar, and Pia Karlsson. *Religionsfrihet i Sverige (Freedom of religion in Sweden)*. Lund: Studentlitteratur, 1997.

Takougang, Joseph. "Recent African Immigrants in the United States: An Historical Perspective." *Western Journal of Black Studies* 19, no. 2 (Spring 1995): 50–57.

Talha, Larbi. *Le salariat immigré dans la crise.* Paris: CNRS, 1989.

Tan, Dursun, and Hans-Peter Waldhoff. "Turkish Everyday Culture in Germany and its Prospects." In *Turkish Culture in German Society Today*, edited by David Horrocks and Eva Kolinsky, 143–44. Providence: Berghahn Books, 1996.

Taylor, Charles. *Multiculturalism and "The Politics of Recognition."* Princeton: Princeton University Press, 1992.

Tololyan, Khachig. "Rethinking Diaspora(s): Stateless Power in the Transnational Moment." *Diaspora* 5, no. 1 (1996): 3–36.

Turner, Bryan S. *Orientalism, Postmodernism and Globalism.* London: Routledge, 1994.

Turner, Richard B. *Islam in the African-American Experience.* Indianapolis: Indiana University Press, 1997.

Tutino, John. "The Revolution in Mexican Independence: Insurgency and the Renegotiation of Property, Production, and Patriarchy in the Bajio, 1800–1855." *Hispanic American Historical Review* 78, no. 3 (1998): 367–418.

University of Derby, Religious Resource and Research Centre. *Research Project on Religious Discrimination: An Interim Report.* London: Home Office, 2000.

Vanderwood, Paul. *The Power of God against the Guns of Government.* Stanford: Stanford University Press, 1998.

Vasconcelos, José. *The Cosmic Race: La raza cósmica, misión de la raza iberoamericana.* Translated by Didier T. Jaen. Baltimore: John Hopkins University Press, 1979.

Vassanji, M. G. *The Gunny Sack.* Portsmouth, N.H.: Heinemann, 1989.

Vassanji, M. G. *Uhuru Street: Short Stories.* Toronto: McClelland and Stewart, 1993.

Vassenden, K., ed. *Innvandrere i Norge. Hvem er de, hva gjør de og hvordan lever de?* Oslo: Statistisk Sentralbyrå, 1997.

Vertovec, Steven. "Introduction." In *Migration and Social Cohesion*, edited by S. Vertovec, 1–44. Cheltenham: Edward Elgar, 1999a.

Vertovec, Steven. "Minority Associations, Networks and Public Policies: Re-assessing Relationships." *Journal for Ethnic and Migration Studies* 25, no. 1 (1999b): 21–42.

Vertovec, Steven. "Multiculturalism, Culturalism and Public Incorporation." *Ethnic and Racial Studies* 19, no. 1 (January 1996): 49–70.

Vertovec, Steven. "Multicultural, Multi-Asian, Multi-Muslim Leicester: Dimensions of Social Complexity, Ethnic Organisation and Local Government Interface." *Innovation* 7, no. 3 (1994): 259–76.

Vertovec, Steven. "Muslims, the State and the Public Sphere in Britain." In *Muslim Communities in the New Europe*, edited by Gerd Nonneman, Tim Niblock, and Bogdan Sjazkowski, 167–86. London: Ithaca Press, 1996.

Vertovec, Steven. "Three Meanings of 'Diaspora,' Exemplified among South Asian Religions." *Diaspora* 6, no. 3 (1997): 277–99.

Vertovec, Steven, and Ceri Peach. "Introduction: Islam in Europe and the Politics of Religion and Community." In *Islam in Europe: The Politics of Religion and Community*, edited by Steven Vertovec and Ceri Peach, 1–29. Basingstoke: Macmillan, 1997.

Voll, John Obert. *Islam: Continuity and Change in the Modern World.* Boulder, Colo.: Westview Press, 1982.

Volpp, Leti. "(Mis)Identifying Culture: Asian Women and the 'Cultural Defense.'" *Harvard Women's Law Journal* 17, no. 57 (1994): 57–101.

Walbridge, Linda. *Without Forgetting the Imam: Lebanese Shi'ism in an American Community.* Detroit: Wayne State University Press, 1997.

Walbridge, Linda, and Fatimah Haneef. "Inter-Ethnic Relations within the Ahmadiyya Muslim Community in the United States." In *The Expanding Landscape: South Asians and the Diaspora*, edited by Carla Petievich, 144–68. Delhi: Manohar, 1999.

Wallraff, Günter. *Ganz Unten*. Köln: Kiepenheuer & Witsch, 1985.

Wasserman, Mark. *Capitalists, Caciques, and Revolution: The Native Elite and Foreign Enterprise in Chihuahua, Mexico, 1854–1911*. Chapel Hill: University of North Carolina Press, 1984.

Waugh, Earle H., Sharon McIrvin, Baha Abu-Laban, and Regula Burckhardt-Qureshi, eds. *Muslim Families in North America*. Edmonton: University of Alberta Press, 1991.

Weller, Paul, ed. *Religions in the UK: A Multi-Faith Directory*. Derby: University of Derby, 1997.

Wells, Allen, and Gilbert M. Joseph. *Summer of Discontent, Seasons of Upheaval*. Stanford: Stanford University Press, 1996.

Werbner, Pnina. "Essentialising Essentialism, Essentialising Silence: Ambivalence and Multiplicity in the Construction of Racism and Ethnicity." In *Debating Cultural Hybridity: Multi-Cultural Identities and the Politics of Anti-Racism*, edited by Pnina Werbner and Tariq Modood, 226–54. New Jersey: Zed Books, 1997.

Williams, Raymond. "Asian-Indian Muslims in the United States." In *Indian Muslims in North America*, edited by Omar Khalidi, 17–26. Watertown, Mass.: South Asia Press, 1991.

Wittwer, Peter. "Muslime in Zürich: Unruhe um Ruhestätte." *IRAS-Panorama* 1 (July 1996): 7–8.

Womack, John, Jr. *Zapata and the Mexican Revolution*. New York: Knopf, 1968.

Wong, Sau Ling. "Denationalization Reconsidered: Asian American Cultural Criticism at a Theoretical Crossroads." *Amerasia Journal* 21, no. 1–2 (1995): 1–27.

Yuksel, Nuri M. *Konzeptstudie für islamische Friedhöfe in Zürich*. Zürich: Islamisches Zentrum, 1995.

Zaimoglu, Feridun. *Kanak Sprak, 24 Misstöne from Rande der Gesellschaft* Hamburg: Rotbuch Verlag, 1995.

Zeraoui, Zidane. "Los árabes en México: el perfil de la migración." In *Destino México: un estudio de las migraciones asiáticas a México, siglos XIX a XX*, edited by María Elena Ota Mishima, 257–304. Mexico: El Colegio de México, 1997.

Index

NATIONAL
POLICE
LIBRARY